TENTH EDITION

D0817753

ASSIGNMENTS IN EXPOSITION

Georgia Dunbar
Hofstra University

Clement Dunbar
Lehman College,
The City University
of New York

Louise E. Rorabacher

HarperCollins*Publishers*

Sponsoring Editor: Patricia Rossi
Project Editor: Brigitte Pelner
Art Direction/Cover Coordination: Mary Archondes
Text Design: Brand X Studios/Robin Hoffmann
Cover Design: Edward Smith Design, Inc.
Production Administrator: Paula Keller
Compositor: ComCom Division of Haddon Craftsmen, Inc.
Printer and Binder: R. R. Donnelley & Sons Company
Cover Printer: The Lehigh Press, Inc.

Assignments in Exposition, Tenth Edition
Copyright © 1991 by HarperCollins Publishers, Inc.

Library of Congress Cataloging-in-Publication Data

Dunbar, Georgia Dolfield Sherwood, 1919-
     Assignments in exposition / Georgia Dunbar, Clement Dunbar, Louise
E. Rorabacher.—10th ed.
          p.   cm.
     Rev. ed. of: Assignments in exposition / Louise E. Rorabacher,
Georgia Dunbar, Clement Dunbar. 9th ed. c1988.
     Includes bibliographical references and index.
          1. English language—Rhetoric.   2. Exposition (Rhetoric)
3. College readers.   I. Dunbar, Clement.   II. Rorabacher, Louise
Elizabeth, 1906-   .   III. Rorabacher, Louise Elizabeth, 1906-
Assignments in exposition.   IV. Title.
     PE1429.R5   1991   90-4960
     808'.042—dc20   CIP
Student Edition: ISBN 0-06-041808-7
Teacher Edition: ISBN 0-06-041809-5

90   91   92   93   9   8   7   6   5   4   3   2   1

CONTENTS

   *indicates selection with marginal gloss

PART II
Developing the Thesis: Basic Methods

UNIT·:·4

Description   85

PART III
Supporting the Thesis: Logical Methods

UNIT·:·11

Classification   226

UNIT·:·14

Definition

UNIT∴15

Induction and Deduction   306

PART IV
Writing for a Larger Purpose

PART V
Writing for Special Purposes

PART VI
Essays for Further Reading

PREFACE

An effective essay, like a well-built house, must have a firm structural foundation and sound materials. This tenth edition of *Assignments in Exposition,* like the preceding editions, emphasizes the basic structural patterns of organization and the materials—the substance—fundamental to effective writing and logical thinking. These do not limit our creative ability. Instead, like the foundations and framework of a house, they act as a support, liberating our imaginations to discover new approaches and fresh insights.

Assignments in Exposition, Tenth Edition, offers these major features:

a substantial unit on composing, with two essays that show a student writer's development in one term

a unit on revising, with three drafts of a student's essay, his log entries tracing its development, and two drafts of the opening paragraphs of another student's research paper

131 selections of writing exemplifying one or more structural patterns

22 new in this edition, each a complete essay or self-contained excerpt, short enough to be seen as a structural whole and analyzed in a single class session or less, most with headnotes and cross-references to make comparisons among the selections easy

47 by good student writers—a special feature of this as of earlier editions

77 by a wide variety of contemporary published writers on a wide variety of topics, including 22 on word choice and on writing processes

7 "classic" essays exemplifying various combinations of structural patterns and including 4 that, having been composed as speeches, provide a clear basis for comparisons of structures and rhetorical methods of persuasion and argument; rough drafts of President Kennedy's Inaugural Address, giving valuable insights into the composing process

detailed information on both the MLA and APA systems for documenting research, covering 34 types of sources, several with multiple examples, and including basic legal references and the more common nonprint sources to stimulate student curiosity and encourage original research

a table of contents grouping selections according to academic disciplines

Each unit offers these features:

a definition of the structural pattern discussed in the unit

step-by-step directions on how—and how not—to use the pattern

examples of the pattern in published writing and in good student writing

an introduction to the examples giving cross-references to selections elsewhere in the book in which the pattern appears in combination with one or more other patterns

questions to direct attention to specific points in the examples and to encourage close reading and class discussion

writing assignments for which the particular pattern would be appropriate, designed to encourage peer evaluation, collaborative criticism, and awareness of audience

Assignments in Exposition, Tenth Edition, like previous editions, also offers these features to make the book easy to use:

a descriptive rhetorical table of contents

an alternate thematic table of contents

an author and subject index with special marking to indicate rhetorical
terms

an identifying letter as well as number for each example to make
reference easy

numbered lines in all examples for precise reference

a flexible sequence of units adaptable to the needs and interests of
different classes

an instructor's manual with further background information on the
selections and with suggestions for using the book

A note to instructors

Process? Product? Good writing demands both.

At the beginning of a recent term, students in a typical composition
section wrote an impromptu diagnostic essay on an argumentative topic. In
the 40 minutes available, they produced papers varying in length from 71
words in a single paragraph to 214 words in six paragraphs. The average was
160 words in two or three paragraphs. At the end of the term, without
warning, the assignment was repeated. The students had not seen their
diagnostic essays since their first conference eleven weeks before, but without exception they now wrote longer, more effective essays, averaging 316
words in four paragraphs.

The key difference was not mere length, however, and we mention it
only as an objective measure of fluency. Nor was it the improvement in
sentence and paragraph structure, although this was an important gain. The
key difference was *substance.*

Students in comparable sections who had practiced primarily expressive
and imaginative writing also made gains in fluency, but they repeatedly
asserted opinions without support—their essays lacked substance. For them,
the writing process had improved, but not the product.

In contrast, the students first mentioned produced evidence to support
their opinions in their final essays—description, comparison, examples, analysis, logical deduction—all the methods for exploring material and discovering ideas that they had studied in this book and practiced during the term.
For them, both the writing process and the writing product had demonstrably
improved.

∴   ∴   ∴

Dr. Rorabacher ended her preface to the fifth edition by thanking her
former students at the University of Illinois, Purdue University, and Western

Carolina University; the *Green Cauldron,* a magazine of freshman writing at the University of Illinois; Professor Janet McNary, South Carolina State College at Orangeburg; Dr. Mildred Martin, Bucknell University; Mrs. John Karling, West Lafayette, Indiana; and Carol Lawrence, Cullowhee, North Carolina. The 6th, 7th, 8th, 9th, and now the 10th edition are all direct descendants of the 5th, and so we, too, thank those named, for we have been their beneficiaries.

We also again thank the many faculty members whose thoughtful advice helped to guide us in preparing earlier editions: Professors Evan Antone, the University of Texas at El Paso; D. A. Bartlett, the University of Alaska; Elizabeth S. Byers, Virginia Polytechnic Institute; Kathy A. de Ste Croix, Angelo State University; Herbert S. Donow, Southern Illinois University at Carbondale; Sister Mary Ely, Rosary College; Mary Ann Emery, the University of Wisconsin; Sylvia H. Gamboa, the College of Charleston; Alan J. Glossner, Monroe Community College; L. D. Groski, La Roche College; Ken Hammes, Cisco Junior College; James Hines, Saddleback College; Joseph Keller, Iowa Central Community College; Russell Long, Tarleton State University; Helen Maloney, Tidewater Community College; Debra Munn, Northwest Community College; Patsy B. Perry, North Carolina Central University; Monty Pitner, Montgomery College; Martin Ranft, Harcum Junior College; Manuel Schonhorn, Southern Illinois University at Carbondale; R. Baird Shuman, the University of Illinois at Urbana; Carolina Smith, Independence Community College; William R. Thurman, Jr., Georgia Southwestern College; James Tichenor, Emory University; Edward L. Tucker, Virginia Polytechnic Institute; Arthur Wagner, Macomb College; and Terry S. Wallace, Harrisburg Area Community College.

In preparing the tenth edition, we are indebted to all those listed above and also to David Anderson, Butler County Community College; Delores Bird, Cape Cod Community College; Mary Cullinan, California State University, Hayward; William Gilbert, California State University, Long Beach; Steve Glassman, Embry-Riddle Aeronautical University; Stephen Hathaway, Wichita State University; Charles Johnson, Iowa Central Community College; Peggy Jolly, University of Alabama at Birmingham; Beth Richards, University of Nebraska; Elaine Sheridan, Manchester Community College; Donald Milton Smith, University of New Haven.

In addition, we thank all our own students, present and past, at Lehman College (CUNY), Hofstra University, Borough of Manhattan Community College (CUNY), and the Hofstra-District 65 Institute of Labor Studies; Carol Demitz, attorney, who advised us on correct legal citations; and the many colleagues and friends who gave invaluable help in finding appropriate student papers, particularly Professors Donald Wolf and Gloria Beckerman of Adelphi University; Robert Sargent, Gayle Teller, and Robert Keane of Hofstra University; William Wallis of the University of California at Santa Barbara; Monty Pitner of Montgomery College; Edwina Jordan of Illinois

Central College; Arlette Lurie; Keith Pugliese; and especially Sandra Enzer of Nassau Community College.

We also thank the members of the HarperCollins staff, who have been unfailingly helpful and encouraging throughout the work of producing this edition, most notably Patricia Rossi, our editor; Phillip Leininger, our former editor, now retired; and Brigitte Pelner, our project editor. Last, but most important, we thank Dr. Rorabacher, who so generously gave us a free hand with a fine book.

Georgia Dunbar
Clement Dunbar

PART I

The Fundamentals
of Writing

UNIT 1

Composing a Rough Draft and Finding a Thesis

The two essays that follow were written by the same student as in-class exercises in a course in expository writing, one in the first week of the term and the other in the last week. Neither exercise was announced in advance, and the first essay was not returned so that the two exercises give an accurate picture of the student's writing ability before and after the work of the course. The same general topic was assigned for both exercises (at the end of the term the students were asked to write again on the same celebrity):

> Write an essay on a well-known person whom you admire—someone in science, the arts, sports, or politics—explaining why you admire him or her. Assume that your readers are other college students, some of whom may not agree with you. Try to convince these readers that your opinions are correct or at least deserve serious consideration.

Note: To help you concentrate on the content and organization of each essay, errors in grammar, spelling, and punctuation have been corrected.

First version

Billy Joel

Dawn Gorlitsky

Many people feel that Billy Joel is overpraised and overcredited. Some say his songs are extremely repetitive in the words and the music. Unlike his critics, I feel Billy Joel is one of the best musicians around today.

To begin with, Billy Joel's music has been around for at least   5
a decade. He understands that as time changes, so must his music. Joel easily can and has the ability to vary his writings from slow love songs to fast rock-and-roll songs. This marks a high degree of skill.

Secondly, for everyone around, including teenagers, pre-teens,   10
and middle-aged people, Billy Joel's music is easily related to. Joel's words to his well-sung songs consist of much reality. His songs, such as "I Love You Just the Way You Are," are expressed in a sense where it can be the listener's experience as well as the writer's.   15

In conclusion, I would like to express to those that are constantly condemning him that they should give his music a chance. Personally, I don't know one particular person who has really put his music down after seriously listening to it. All in all, Billy Joel is still and will always be number one in my book!!!!!!.   20

Second version

Billy Joel

Dawn Gorlitsky

Many people believe that the admirers of Billy Joel, a pianist and singer, are wrong. They claim that he is overpraised, but they ignore these facts: Billy Joel's music varies with the times, all age groups can appreciate it, and he has struggled to reach his summit. Unlike his critics, I think Billy Joel is the number one musician   5
today.

To begin with, Billy Joel's music changes with the times. When new styles are introduced and new problems appear, his songs reflect them. Unlike most musicians, who follow one familiar mode for all their performances, Billy Joel is open to what is new. For example, during the "punk" fad, he produced a song, "It's Still Rock and Roll to Me." During the energy crisis in the early 1970s he wrote "Close to the Borderline." He sings, writes, and performs with vehement emotions, reflecting the times in which he is writing.

As an average eighteen-year-old, I really can't relate to Frank Sinatra or Bing Crosby. I understand people older than I may react in a similar fashion to Billy Joel. But, in actuality, the people who have such feelings have never given Billy Joel's music a chance. I asked my mother, who is fifty-four, "Mom, do you like Billy Joel?" "Who's that?" she replied. When I played a few of his records for her, she exclaimed, "This guy is great!" When my six-year-old cousin, Tony, visited us for Thanksgiving, I found that he was familiar with all Joel's songs and liked them. Obviously, all age groups can appreciate Joel.

Billy Joel has struggled a lot to reach his peak. Born in the Bronx, raised in the Hell's Kitchen slum of Manhattan, he has had a tough life. At birth, he had a malfunction of his left eye, and in school he suffered from dyslexia. After several operations and some special training, he has overcome these problems. His success was not handed to him on a silver platter.

I feel sorry for the people who don't enjoy Billy Joel's music. It's not the music itself they dislike, I think, but the lyrics. He writes songs related to his personal struggles, for example, "Uptown Girl," "Summer—Highland Falls," and "Piano Man," and perhaps people who have experienced similar difficulties would rather not be reminded of their own hard times. They should learn to face their problems and appreciate someone who has made it to the top the hard way.

In conclusion, I praise Billy Joel for three reasons: his music and lyrics change with the times, all age groups can appreciate them, and the road to success has not been easy. Billy Joel is an inspiration to us all.

The major difference between the two essays is obvious. The first essay is merely a series of exclamations and unsupported claims; the second is a **reasoned argument**—a major step forward for the writer in only twelve weeks of work.

The second version is twice as long as the first because it has **much more evidence to support the main point,** more ideas and more factual information. In her first essay Dawn began by simply asserting her admiration, and in the body of the essay she gave only two reasons: Billy Joel varies his style to suit the occasion, and listeners of any age can relate to his songs. She cited only one example to support her claim and did not discuss it at all. The ending was especially weak. She merely repeated that she admired Joel, a fact her readers had known from the first, and the multiple exclamation marks only show that she recognized the weakness of the ending and could not strengthen it.

In her second essay she began by listing **three specific** reasons for her admiration, and then in the main body she gave a **full paragraph to analyzing and developing each.** Her concluding paragraph is in part a summary of what she has already said, but the compactness makes it forceful, and her final sentence is **a brief, strong statement of her position** to impress her point on her readers' minds.

To sum up, the big difference between the two essays is in **content,** in what the writer has to say. In the first, the claims are not supported, so the argument is unlikely to make many readers change their minds. In the second essay, the writer explores the basis for her opinions and tries to answer the objections of others.

Dawn learned that asking herself questions about each topic helped her to gather material, to develop her opinions, and to understand the opinions of others. Through practice in **using various strategies for exploring and handling material,** such as description, narration, analysis, and logical deduction, she learned to present her material and opinions more convincingly. She also learned to **make notes before writing** and to **plan the organization** so that her readers would follow her line of thought easily. By reading her essays aloud and by hearing other students read theirs, she learned to **omit unnecessary words** and **revise the structure** to emphasize important points.

∴   ∴   ∴

Four elements are essential for effective writing:

1. **content** (something to say)
2. **logical organization**
3. **appropriate word choice and sentence and paragraph structure**
4. **mechanical correctness** (standard grammar, spelling, punctuation)

In this book we analyze and discuss the strategies that will help you **to discover** subject matter; **to develop, analyze, and define** ideas; to organize those ideas; and **to choose** words to present them clearly.

∴   ∴   ∴

For most writers, the process of writing does not move along a straight path from point A to point Z. Instead, writers often backtrack, start off in a new direction, then change again, stumble a little, move sideways, and, in general, proceed by stopping and starting. Do not be surprised if you do the same. The more thought you put into a piece of writing, the more you, too, are likely to proceed by stops and starts.

The best way to begin writing a paper is by *not* **writing it.** First, review the precise nature of the assignment—any specifications as to your choice of topic and the readers to whom you should direct the essay.

Unless the assignment states otherwise, assume that your readers will be "general readers"—people with as much general knowledge as the average college student but without specialized knowledge of the subject. How can you show them that **your information is accurate,** that **your opinions have a firm basis,** and that **your main point deserves their attention?** You can sharpen your thinking and compose a much stronger paper if you **assume that your readers disagree with you** and that you must convince them that your opinions deserve their serious consideration. Dawn's second essay is much stronger than her first because she considers objections to her argument and answers them.

Do not think of your instructors as your only readers and therefore omit everything they know about your topic. Remember that when they read your essay, they act as your editors. They will judge it on the basis of how interesting and worthwhile it would seem to the **general reader**—in other words, on the essentials listed at the end of Unit 1: the general interest of your topic, the accuracy and strength of the supporting content, and the effectiveness of your organization and expression.

Preparing to write on an assigned topic

In courses that concentrate on a particular body of knowledge, such as "The Philosophy of Plato," your assignment will probably include the topic or a choice of topics and may also include a minimum reading list. Make sure that you know exactly what each topic covers and any special requirements for handling it. When you have gathered general information as a background for your topic, use the strategies of brainstorming or of focused free writing or both to help you define the topic more precisely, clarify your opinions, and discover specific support for them in the information you have gathered.

Brainstorming is a way of finding out everything you know about a topic. Think over the assignment, and, at the same time, jot down notes on every thought that comes to mind. Do not omit any because they seem unrelated or trivial; later, they may be a source of inspiration. Make your notes brief—a word or two for each, if possible—just enough to jog your memory later. The briefer they are, the more inspiration they are likely to give you when you glance back over them. If at all possible, brainstorm in more than one session. The pause and change of pace will stimulate your imagination and memory and help you to think of more material and of new ways to view material you collected earlier. When you feel that you have exhausted all the possibilities, look over your notes. The sight of them together may suggest new connections and give you more ideas.

Throughout the process, give yourself ample opportunity for two very different kinds of thinking—logical analysis and free-wheeling association. Our minds are wonderfully complex, and we can switch back and forth between the two many times in only a few moments. In the first we concentrate on the subject and systematically examine all its parts and purposes. In the second we let our minds range freely over and around the subject, even off it, and ideas seem to pop up of their own accord. Never be in such a hurry to write a paper that you limit yourself to the logic of the first kind of thinking; always take advantage of the imaginative insights of the second. If your mind goes blank, as it sometimes will, try to see your subject from your readers' point of view. Jog your imagination with questions:

What will be most valuable or interesting for my readers to learn about my general subject?
What should I assume that my readers already know about my subject?
What should I assume that my readers do not know about it?
What opinions on it are they likely to have?
What opinions do I want them to form?

In the first week of the term, when Dawn received the in-class assignment for which she chose Billy Joel as her general subject, she made no notes to help her compose an essay. Instead, like most of the other students, she spent much of the class time staring into space or at the blank page before her and was left with little time to write. In the last week of the term, however, when she received the same in-class assignment, she began by jotting down these notes on material she might use:

personal struggles
good looking
appeals to all age groups
changes with the times
why do some dislike him?

Uptown Girl
Summer —
Captain Jack
Allentown
Billy the Kid
It's Still R + R
Borderline

Next, she looked over the lists and decided on the order in which to take up her material, numbering the items accordingly. She decided not to mention Joel's looks because some readers would certainly argue that appearances are not important, and she added the examples of her mother and Tony to support her claim that Joel appeals to all age groups. She drew arrows to connect the song titles with her material, and while writing the essay she added one song and decided to omit two others. She revised her notes as she progressed, so that eventually they looked like this:

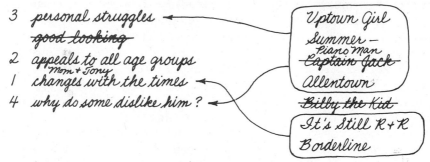

3 *personal struggles*

~~*good looking*~~

2 *appeals to all age groups*
  Mom + Tony
1 *changes with the times*

4 *why do some dislike him?*

Uptown Girl
Summer —
Piano Man
~~*Captain Jack*~~
Allentown
~~*Billy the Kid*~~
It's Still R + R
Borderline

Making the notes took several minutes of the time allowed for writing the essay, but they were time well spent. Although the resulting essay is not a brilliant literary work—few in-class essays are—it is logically organized, and the claims are adequately supported and clearly expressed.

Focused Free Writing

Focused free writing is a strategy that can be very helpful when you have more time than is usually allowed for an in-class writing assignment. It gives you practice in finding ideas and expressing yourself quickly. Using a clock or timer, allow yourself a specific short period of time—five or ten minutes—and write whatever comes into your mind on the general topic of your paper. Do not stop, even for a split second, and do not cross out or correct what you are writing even when you know you have made a mistake. Keep your pen or the keys of your typewriter or word processor moving. Remember that no one else will read what you are writing. Grammar, spelling, and punctuation do not matter. What does matter is that you are writing, and your words will suggest ideas. When you cannot think of the next word, repeat the topic or the words you just wrote or even describe something in the room, but do not stop writing until the time is up. In several sessions of free writing, with time to rest in between and do other things, you will produce a lot of words. When you read them over, you will find that many of them suggest ideas for your paper. Free writing is particularly helpful if you have not had many writing assignments before. It can do for your writing skill what stretching exercises do for your body—loosen your mental muscles and warm you up for the start.

Preparing to write when no topic is assigned

If you are free to find your own topic in a subject matter course, such as "Child Psychology" or "The History of China," think over your work for the course, glance through the pages that you have already read in your textbook (many textbooks include suggestions for writing assignments), look over your lecture and reading notes, and glance through recent magazines and newspapers to find an article, editorial, or letter to the editor that interests you and that you can relate to the subject matter of the course. Any of these may give you the spark to start forming an opinion of your own that you can present in your paper. Brainstorming and free writing on the general subject of the course can also help you to focus your thinking, form opinions, and discover a topic. When you have found something that seems suitable, use one or both of these strategies to help you generate more ideas on it.

In a course that concentrates on developing a skill, as do most writing courses, rather than on acquiring a body of information, your instructor may suggest a general subject, such as describing a room in a way that will reveal the personality of the occupant or analyzing an experience that influenced your thinking, and you will be expected to find a specific topic. Sometimes, you may be left entirely free, with no restrictions or suggestions whatever. In either case, the primary source for your material will be your own experiences and your observations of other people. For such courses, keep a journal, and every day jot down notes on your thoughts, experiences, memories, and observations of others and of the world around you. Then, when you wish to choose a subject for an essay, you will have a storehouse of material on which to draw. The material does not have to be dramatic or unusual. The most ordinary experience may give you the basis for an excellent essay—the behavior of drivers in a traffic jam, the regular customers at the diner or coffee shop you know best, an early morning walk, a birthday party for your grandmother, and so on. Brainstorming and free writing can also help you to generate ideas for developing such topics into effective essays. With the methods discussed in the later chapters of this book, you will be able to develop material on these topics and bring them to life for your readers.

To make the process of composing clearer, let us imagine that you have two days to write an essay of about 500 words describing the activities of a typical freshman on a typical day at your college. Imagine, also, that your instructor plans to give copies of the essays from your class to the guidance counselor of a nearby high school where all the juniors and seniors will read them for up-to-date, firsthand information on what to expect if they go to college. Your general purpose, therefore, is to give a particular group of readers the information that you think they will need and to make it as interesting for them as you can.

Gathering material

First, think back over your experiences and those of your friends, using several sessions of brainstorming or free writing or both to generate ideas. Stimulate and guide your thinking by asking yourself the general questions listed and jot down your answers:

What can I tell my readers that will be valuable or interesting for them to know about college?

What can I assume that my readers already know about college?

What can I assume that my readers do not know about it?

What opinions on it are they likely to have?

Then, using your answers to these questions, ask yourself more questions. As later chapters of this book show in detail, these additional questions will help you to discover more ideas and develop content to strengthen your essay:

How can I **describe** my material so that my readers will be able to imagine it vividly?

What **examples** would best illustrate my main points?

What **processes** are involved in my material and how do they operate?

What **comparisons and contrasts** can I make with material that is already familiar to my readers?

Into what smaller parts can I break down my material by **analyzing** it, and how would I **classify** the parts?

What are the **causes** and **effects** in what I have observed?

What **logical deductions** about my material can I draw from studying it?

How do I **define** each of the main parts of my material?

Do not stop gathering material when you think you have enough. The more you have to choose from, the more you can make your paper a selection of the very best. Continue until you think that you have exhausted the possibilities.

When you are sure that you have noted all the more important material that could be useful, stimulate your thinking further by considering these additional questions:

To which other items, if any, is each item related?

Under what headings can I group the items? (For this imagined assignment, some headings might indicate the nature of the activities, such as "recreation" and "classes"; others might indicate the time of day when the activities occur, or the location, or the number of people involved, and so on.)

What subdivisions and sub-subdivisions can I make in each group of items? (For example, under "morning classes" you might group the classes according to subject matter, class size, academic level, location on the campus, and type, such as discussion, lecture, or laboratory.)

What combinations of headings can I make? (For this assignment, "morning classes," "afternoon classes," "outdoor recreation," and "indoor recreation" might be appropriate.)

Choosing and defining your main point

To hold your readers' attention, your essay must have a main point, a controlling idea—the fact, opinion, or emotion that you most want your readers to recognize in your material and to understand and remember. When you have thought of as many groupings as you can, begin to narrow your subject by considering these questions in relation to your purpose. In this imaginary assignment, your purpose is to inform your readers. These questions will help you find the information that should be most useful for them:

What general parts of the material do I want my readers to notice most? what specific parts?

What opinions do I want them to form?

What interests me most in my material? (You are more likely to be able to interest your readers in what you find interesting.)

Whatever you most want your readers to see in your material will be your **main point**. For example, in this imaginary assignment, you may want them to see that a college program for a typical freshman is more demanding than is suggested by the number of hours spent in class.

When you have chosen a main point, sharpen your thinking by assuming that your readers will be difficult to convince. You must therefore present your main point very clearly and support it with solid evidence. To make it definite in your own mind, try on scratch paper to express it in as few words as you can, preferably in a single sentence. This will be the rough draft of the **thesis statement** for your paper. A thesis is a proposition, the main point that a writer not only presents and explains but defends throughout a piece of writing. In the thesis statement, the writer is, in effect, saying, "I believe this is true and hope to make my readers agree or at least give it serious consideration."

In most expository writing you will find the thesis directly stated, but sometimes it is only implied. You will find examples of both methods in this book. Whichever way you present it, your thesis will determine what material you use in your essay and how you organize it. Do not, however, close your mind to making changes in your thesis. At every stage in composing your essay test the validity of your thesis in relation to the particular part of your material that you are considering. You may decide to modify it or even to reject it entirely and start again. Keep your mind open to new ideas and new interpretations.

Composing: Patterns for organizing the body

With your readers and thesis in mind, consider three more questions:

What general background information will my readers need to understand my thesis?
What specific information will they need to understand it?
What information, general or specific, will they need to convince them that my thesis is valid or at least deserves serious consideration?

For our sample assignment, you would need to explain little or nothing about high school programs to show that a college program is more demanding because your readers are already familiar with high school, but you would need to explain such things as the length and difficulty of the reading lists some of your instructors have given you and the frequency and nature of your writing assignments. Mark in your notes all the items that directly explain and support your thesis. If you find many, make a separate list of the marked items so that you can see them more easily. They will form the basis for the body of your essay.

When you believe that you have found every usable item, ask yourself how you can best organize them to make your thesis clear, interesting, and convincing for your readers. On more scratch paper, **try out as many patterns of organization as you can.** If you see any items that duplicate others or seem weak or not very relevant, eliminate them. You may find it helpful at this stage, if time permits, to express your thoughts in rough sentences, as well as in notes. Constructing sentences may sharpen your thinking, but do not let them freeze your ideas into a permanent form. Keep your mind open to new insights and interpretations. These are all part of the two kinds of thinking required for writing, **logical analysis and free-wheeling association.** Nothing is final until you hand in your paper.

Important: If at this stage you fear that you will not have enough material for a paper of the required length, go over all your notes in close detail, rethink them from every angle, discuss your thesis with friends, and ask for their suggestions. You may think of material you overlooked before or have new insights into what you have already gathered. Whatever you find, add it to your notes. Achieve the required length by going more deeply into material that contributes to your thesis, not merely by adding words.

Chronological Pattern

Use a chronological pattern when you wish to emphasize the time sequence of events. This is the simplest pattern for organization because it leaves you no choice on the order in which to present your material. Your choices will be limited to what information to include, what details to give, and how much emphasis to place on each. Using a chronological pattern to describe a typical freshman's activities on a typical day, you might cover the following list of items:

Getting up	Soda with friends
Washing and dressing	Part-time campus job
Straightening up room	Dinner
Collecting books and notes	Studying in room
Breakfast	Relaxing with friends in lounge
English 101	and watching TV
Studying in library	Snack in coffee shop
Economics 103	Reviewing Chem notes
Lunch in cafeteria	Undressing and washing
Chemistry lab	Going to bed

This covers your account of a typical day, but grouping the small details may make your point clearer. With general headings, you can group the details under them and show their relative importance:

1. Early morning activities
   a. Getting up
   b. Washing and dressing
   c. Straightening up room
   d. Breakfast
   e. Collecting books and notes
2. Late morning activities
   a. English 101
   b. Studying in library
   c. Economics 103
3. Afternoon activities
   a. Lunch in cafeteria
   b. Chemistry lab
   c. Soda with friends
   d. Part-time campus job
4. Early evening activities
   a. Dinner
   b. Studying in room
5. Late evening activities
   a. Relaxing with friends in lounge and watching TV
   b. Snack in coffee shop
   c. Reviewing Chem notes
   d. Undressing and washing
   e. Going to bed

Notice that the items and their order have not changed, but now, instead of giving equal attention to nineteen small items, you are planning five large groups made up of varying numbers of subpoints. With this new perspective, you can easily ask yourself what is really of first importance, what is second, and so on. It can also help you to see where you should develop your material further with more subpoints and perhaps with sub-subpoints and even sub-sub-subpoints, and where you should perhaps condense it by eliminating subpoints or even points. For our imagined thesis—that a college program for a typical freshman is more demanding than attending two classes and a lab on a typical day might suggest—you would probably want to emphasize the time spent studying outside of class and the extent to which your conversations with friends are about your studies, mentioning other activities only briefly, perhaps omitting altogether such completely routine ones as washing and dressing.

An assignment to describe a typical day makes the choice of a chronological pattern for the essay obvious, but most assignments give you more freedom. Imagine, for example, that you have been asked to discuss a new freshman's first impressions of college life and that you want to show your readers that the program is demanding. You could choose among the other chief patterns: spatial, familiar-to-unfamiliar, or the reverse, and general-to-specific, or the reverse.

Spatial Pattern

Use a spatial pattern if you want your readers to have a picture of the campus in their minds as a background for a typical freshman's activities. Imagine that you are taking your readers on a walking tour. Depending on the geography of the campus, some of the headings in your rough outline might be these:

Location and approximate size of campus
  Location, size, and general appearance of buildings
Library
  Long reading assignments in most courses
Classroom buildings
  Lecture rooms—Economics 103
  Seminar rooms—English 101
  Laboratories—Chemistry 105
  Other special facilities

Other possibilities with a spatial pattern are to begin with the most noticeable feature and move by degrees to the least noticeable features or to view the scene from a single position, looking from left to right, or from near to far, and so on. For a more detailed discussion and for examples, see Unit 4, "Description."

General-to-Specific Pattern

Use a general-to-specific pattern if your readers are likely to know little about your subject. For example, if the high school to which your instructor will send your essay in our imagined assignment emphasizes the laboratory sciences rather than other fields, you might begin with an overview of the freshman program at your college and then by stages focus on more and more specific material to fill in the whole picture. Some of the headings for your rough outline might be these:

> Chief characteristics of the freshman program
> > Wide choice of courses in almost every subject
> > > Specific examples

Specific-to-General Pattern

A **specific-to-general pattern** can be useful if you want to catch the attention of readers who are likely to be familiar with your subject or find it easy to understand. You might begin with a specific example, such as a description of a few typical minutes in a particular class, then fit this into the larger picture of the course as a whole, and then show how that course is typical of the experience of being a freshman. Some of the headings in a rough outline might then be these:

> 9:30 to 9:45 on Sept. 12th—English 101
> course work for week of Sept. 12th
> > Chapter 5 in textbook
> > > discussion of chapter
> > > writing exercises in class
> > > outside writing assignment—relating Chapters 4 and 5
> course work for term—overview

Familiar/Unfamiliar Patterns

Two other sequences are from the **familiar to the unfamiliar** and the reverse—from the **unfamiliar to the familiar.** The first may be appropriate if you think your readers are likely to find parts of your material difficult to understand. Begin by building a foundation on what they already know before you go on to the rest of your material. For our imagined assignment directed to readers who are high school students, you could begin by briefly describing such routine activities as meals, then the athletic and extracurricular activities, and lead up to the academic work, which you would describe in detail to emphasize the greater demands of college work.

The unfamiliar-to-familiar pattern may be appropriate if your readers are likely to know a good deal about your subject. Catch their attention and stimulate their curiosity by beginning with details of what they are least likely to know and then treat briefly what they know well. You might, for example, begin by explaining how much more freedom of choice a student has in college than in high school or how, in some courses, you are expected to keep up with reading assignments and produce papers on time without any reminders.

Combining Patterns

In most books and longer essays writers **combine these methods of organization,** moving back and forth between the general and the specific or between the familiar and the unfamiliar, first orienting their readers to a section of their subject, then examining a part of it in detail, next drawing general conclusions about that part based on the examination, and then applying those conclusions to another part which they proceed to examine in detail, and so on.

With these methods of organization you have a further choice: (1) You may make your main point—your thesis—clear to your readers from the beginning of your essay and present all your material as supporting evidence; **or** (2) you may reverse that procedure and present the evidence first, saving your main point to be the climax at or near the end of your essay. The second arrangement is more dramatic and can help you to produce a memorable essay, but at the risk of confusing some readers. The first arrangement is safer—your readers will know from the start what you want them to see in your material and will therefore follow your line of thought easily. Most scholarly writing, especially in the sciences and social sciences, uses this arrangement, and it will be appropriate for most of your writing assignments in college.

To choose the organization for an essay, always **consider carefully the nature of your material and what you want your readers to see in it.** On scratch paper, try out every possibility before choosing one for your rough draft. List each sequence and imagine how an essay developed from it would seem to your readers. You will not need a formal outline to plan most papers, but a list like the ones just given that shows the relative importance of the parts of your material can be a great help. With it, you can keep a sense of proportion and not give too much attention to a minor point or too little to a major one.

When you have chosen what appears to be the best arrangement for your material, you are ready to write a rough draft of the whole essay. With all the notes on your material handy to refresh your memory, and with your thesis statement and notes on organization in an eye-catching position as reminders, forge ahead and write as rapidly as you can. **Concentrate on the content,** on what you have to say. Remember that everything you choose to include should lead your readers to one conclusion: that your thesis is valid or at least deserves serious consideration.

As you start your first draft, do not spend time and energy trying to think of the perfect beginning, and as you finish the draft, do not struggle to think of the perfect ending. You can compose them more effectively when you have finished the draft and can see your work as a whole. If inspiration does not strike quickly, use a statement of your topic or your thesis as a temporary beginning and repeat it as a temporary ending. **Do *not* worry now about mechanics** (spelling, punctuation, and grammar). Important though these will be in your final copy, you can repair them more easily and effectively when the rough draft is complete and you can see your essay as a whole. Also postpone trying to solve problems of precise word choice and forceful sentence and paragraph structure. **Remember that this is a *rough* draft** and that you may write several more before you are satisfied. You can polish it more effectively when you can see it as a whole.

Important: As you write and see your thoughts take shape in sentences, new ideas may occur to you, new interpretations of your material, even new material that you have overlooked. Make notes on each so that you can use it later if you wish and so that you will not find yourself wondering what that forgotten flash of inspiration was. If you think of a better way to arrange your material and decide to start a new draft for any section, be sure to keep the old version—later you may want to salvage part of it. The more thoroughly you have planned before starting the rough draft, the less likely you will be to make big revisions as you go along, but when you can see the rough draft as a whole, you may want to perform major surgery. **Such changes are all part of the composing process.**

Revising as Reseeing

When you have finished your rough draft, set it aside for a while, at least an hour or two, preferably overnight, while you do something else quite different. Then, refreshed mentally, read it through quickly. Remember that a revision, as the root of the word shows, is a *reseeing,* not a mere hunt for mistakes. In planning and writing the rough draft you probably had many moments of reseeing what you wrote and made changes accordingly. Now you can resee everything as parts of a whole. Imagine as strongly as you can that you are seeing your paper through your readers' eyes. How would your readers answer these questions?

Does the main line of thought develop clearly?
Does each point support the thesis?
Is each point supported by examples and details?
Are any parts not necessary?
Do any parts need strengthening?
Would any part be more effective in another position?

To gain perspective on what you have written, read your paper aloud. Saying it and hearing it will help you to notice awkward repetitions, long-winded spots, and illogical thinking.

Then, using your own fresh view of what you wrote and what you imagine your readers' answers would be to your questions, **compose the beginning and ending and revise your rough draft thoroughly**—perhaps reorganizing sections, adding or deleting details or examples, rewriting sections, even rewriting the entire essay from a different point of view.

Composing the beginning

The beginning of your essay is essential. It gives your readers their first impression of your subject, purpose, and general thesis, and their understanding of them will depend on it. But your beginning must do more than help them to understand your essay. It must also catch their interest.

For the topic used earlier in this chapter as an example of a writing assignment—the activities of a typical college freshman—any of the following forms could be appropriate, depending on your precise purpose in writing and what you know about your readers.

1. An explicit statement of your topic and purpose:

> A typical day in the life of a college freshman is likely to be long and full of varied activities—course work, a part-time job, extracurricular affairs, social gatherings, and the routine duties of daily living.

This kind of beginning is preferred for technical types of writing, such as reports, for essays in the sciences and social sciences, and for writing on any topic that the readers may find difficult or unfamiliar. When using an explicit statement, avoid obvious, flatfooted beginnings, such as "In this paper I intend to show that a typical day in the life of a college freshman is long and varied."

2. The history or background of the subject, giving the context and suggesting why it is important:

> The number of high school graduates who go on to college has steadily increased over recent years, but many of these students have no idea beforehand what a typical day in the life of a college student is like.

3. A definition of the subject or of the key terms used in discussing it:

> A "typical" day is probably one that never occurs in reality because no two days are ever exactly the same. A typical day for me as a college freshman is a composite picture, an average, formed from several quite different days.

Do not, however, begin with a definition quoted from a dictionary. It will make a boring beginning because it will be very general. Quote a dictionary only when you must define something both complicated and unknown to your readers. Even then, you should reword the definition, at least in part, to make it fit smoothly into your own writing. For further discussion of writing definitions, see Unit 14.

4. An indication of your qualifications to discuss the subject, especially if it is unusual or technical, so that readers will have confidence in your accuracy:

> As an entering freshman in college, I have been on campus only a short time, but I know many other freshmen and think that my activities are fairly typical.

5. A quoted remark that draws the reader into the situation:

> "Read at least the first forty pages by Thursday," the instructor announced at the end of our first class meeting. "Take full, careful notes. It's a vital section of the book." In all my other classes the instructors made much the same announcement. The work load for the typical freshman is demanding.

6. An appropriate quotation from a well-known source:

> "Of making many books there is no end, and much study is a weariness of the flesh"—the Book of Ecclesiastes in the Bible was written many centuries ago, but the message is truer than ever, especially for the typical college freshman.

7. A description of something familiar that is comparable to your subject in important ways:

> Ants seem to lead frantically busy lives. Around an anthill we can watch lines of creatures rush in different directions, intent on reaching their destinations as quickly as possible, but sometimes pausing to greet each other with a waving antenna. Between classes the campus resembles a busy anthill.

8. A direct appeal to your readers' concerns or a reminder of a current problem or issue that will make your readers identify with your subject:

> If you are like most high school students who plan to go to college, you are concentrating now on your grades, thinking that once you are accepted by the college of your choice your worries will be over and you will relax.

9. A rhetorical question to arouse curiosity:

> With only a few hours a week spent in class, how can a typical freshman claim to be busy?

10. A startling statement or exclamation to catch the reader's eye:

(a) On most days, the typical college freshman has had about four hours sleep, missed breakfast, slept through several classes, and thought about nothing but drugs and sex—or so some magazine writers suggest.

(b) Work! Work! Work! Nobody warned me that I'd have my nose in a book fifteen hours a day.

11. A brief narrative, especially if humorous or dramatic, to stimulate the reader's curiosity:

My alarm rings—7:00 A.M. I leap from my bed in the dorm and dash to the bathroom in hopes of a vacant shower stall. No luck. Back to my own room and a quick wash in the basin. I pull on underwear, tee shirt, and jeans, and by 7:35 I'm in the cafeteria line for breakfast. At 7:59 I slide into my seat in Psych class, ten seconds before the professor arrives. Another typical day has begun.

Composing the ending

The ending, like the beginning, should be relatively brief, preferably not more than one-seventh of the whole paper. Most devices suggested for beginnings are appropriate for endings. The shorter you make your ending, the more forceful it will seem to your readers and the more easily they will remember it.

We cannot fully judge the function and effectiveness of an ending until we have read the whole essay. The following list of suggestions, therefore, refers you to essays in the book for examples instead of attempting to quote them here out of context.

Writers in the sciences and social sciences use the first three types for almost all their writing, and editorial writers are likely to use the fourth type, but you will find examples of all of the types in every field.

1. **A brief restatement of the thesis** to impress it on your readers' memories. The brevity will give it force, and it may be the best type of ending if your readers are unfamiliar with your subject or likely to be hard to convince. See "Do You Inherit Your Personality?" by Maron Tysoe (6-E).

2. **Suggesting a result or finding a significance that goes beyond the immediate scope of the paper** to show your readers the wider importance of your thesis and material. See "Sex and the Split Brain" by Carol Johmann (7-B).

3. **A redefinition of the topic or of a key term in the light of what you have said in the main body of your paper** to pinpoint your meaning for your readers in a memorable statement. See "A Plea for Free Speech in Boston" by Frederick Douglass ("Essays for Further Reading"-D).

4. **A rhetorical question, an exclamation, a challenging statement, or a direct appeal to your readers for action** to make them rethink your thesis and your whole essay. See "Clutter" by William Zinsser (8-D).

5. **A specific reference to the beginning of the essay or to the title** to round off the whole essay by creating a kind of frame. See "Is Anyone Listening?" by Isaac Asimov (13-H).

6. **An appropriate bit of narrative, a brief example, or a quotation from a well-known source that sums up or illustrates your main point** to help your readers remember it. See "The Flight of Refugees" by Ernest Hemingway (3-B).

7. **The only complete statement of your thesis,** saved for the end to give it dramatic force. This inductive pattern of organization may be difficult to handle but is worth trying if your readers are likely to be familiar with your material and able to follow your development of it easily. See "Three Incidents" from *The New Yorker* (15-A).

Composing a title

The title will, of course, appear at the beginning of your paper. Nevertheless, it will often be the last part that you write. You have known your general topic from the start, of course, and it has determined your choice of plan and development, but only now, with the last rough draft before you, can you decide definitely on what to call it.

A title should be brief—a word or phrase, not a complete sentence. It should indicate both the specific topic of the paper and its purpose. For matter-of-fact, informative writing, such as reports, a descriptive title stating the actual content of the paper as clearly and briefly as possible is best, as in "Alcohol, Marijuana, and Memory," the title of a recent magazine article. For less utilitarian writing, when you wish to catch the attention of readers who might otherwise skip past your essay, try to find a more imaginative title, such as *Life for Death,* a book on how the life-sentence verdict for a convicted murderer affected the victim's family. Often, writers add a subtitle to explain an imaginative title, as in "Matter over Mind: The Big Issues Raised by Newly Discovered Chemicals."

∴　　∴　　∴

You now have a complete rough draft and can begin to revise and polish it. Rethink your sentence and paragraph structures and your word choice to make sure that they present your meaning effectively.

In Unit 2 there are detailed suggestions for revising sentences and paragraphs. Unit 3 concentrates on word choice. When you are satisfied that your rough draft is as good as you can make it, write your final copy.

Format for the final copy

The final copy of your paper should follow the conventional format unless your instructor has given you specific instructions to do otherwise.

1. Use white, standard-size paper ($8\frac{1}{2}'' \times 11''$). Do *not* use pages torn from a spiral binder.

2. Write or type on only one side of each page.

3-a. If you are writing, choose wide-lined paper (about $\frac{3}{8}''$ between lines) or skip a line after each line of writing. Leave a left-hand margin at least $1\frac{1}{2}''$ wide. Use ink, either blue or black, not any other color. Never use pencil.

3-b. If you are typing, double-space (skip a line after each typed line). Leave margins at least $1\frac{1}{2}''$ wide at the left side and the top and bottom of the page; leave at least a 1-inch margin on the right. Skip one space after each comma and semicolon and two after all other forms of punctuation except dashes. Indicate a dash by typing two hyphens with *no* space before, after, or between them. Add in ink any symbols that are not on the typewriter.

3-c. If you are using a word processor, follow the instructions in 3-b. If your printer is capable of proportional spacing, this option will make your finished text easier to read. Do not, however, use the option of a justified or "flush" *right* margin, unless you can combine it with proportional spacing; used alone, a justified right margin makes text more difficult to read, even though it gives an overall appearance of greater neatness at first glance.

4. Avoid splitting a word to fill up the end of a line. Instead, leave the extra space blank and put the whole word on the next line—your readers will be grateful.

5. Indent the beginning of each paragraph the equivalent of a five-letter word.

6. Spell out all numbers below ten unless you are using several in a small space (many authorities recommend spelling out all numbers below one hundred). Spell out any number, large or small, that begins a sentence.

If the result seems awkward, as it will in a sentence with other numbers that are not spelled out, try to revise the sentence so that you can begin it with a word instead.

Proofreading

Proofread your final copy with great care, paying close attention to mechanics—spelling, punctuation, grammar, and usage. Accuracy in mechanics will not guarantee you a good grade, but it is essential. The best subjects and plans will not impress readers who are constantly distracted or confused by mechanical errors. Solve difficulties with mechanics by studying a good handbook. (Ask your instructor which to buy.)

In proofreading, watch especially for careless mistakes. You may know the difference between *to* and *too,* but just "didn't think." You must try to develop the eagle eye of the professional proofreader, who is responsible for the almost flawless pages of the better books and magazines. Careful correction is an essential last step for anything you write outside of class, but remember that it is equally important in letters, in-class themes, and examinations written under pressure. Write less, if necessary, to save time for proofreading. It is a good rule never to give anything you have written to a reader until you have checked it carefully, *letter by letter,* for possible slips.

If you are using a word processor or a typewriter with a memory, making corrections is easy. If you are using an ordinary typewriter or writing by hand, correct any slips by firmly crossing out the error and writing the correct version neatly above it. If you find several errors on a page or a large one involving a whole line, recopy the page.

EXAMPLE

Sunday Morning in Haiti

Anaica Lodescar (student)

The writer uses the chronological pattern to organize her material. Since her subject is not difficult, she can safely imply her general thesis—that in her childhood a typical Sunday morning was enjoyable. She came to the United States when she was twelve years old and has been unable to return to Haiti because of the political problems there, but she cherishes her memories of it at a time when she was too young to recognize those problems.

Outline
I. First time
division
  A. Sounds
    of
    activity
  B. Purpose
    of
    activity
  C. Imagin-
    ed com-
    ment by
    out-
    sider

Three o'clock on Sunday morning. I have been sound asleep. I hear only the end of the carillon for the first call to go to mass. Three-thirty. The sound of steps breaks the silence of the dark street outside my window and tells me that I am already almost late. Dogs are barking everywhere. Alarm clocks are ringing in other houses. People from a distance are arriving, rushing toward the cathedral. Even people in the neighborhood are hurrying because the seats will soon be filled with churchgoers. 5

At a time like this, so early in a Sunday morning, a stranger would not believe that there are so many people going to mass. He would think that there must be some very unusual event—a fire or some other disaster, perhaps, to bring so many people out into the streets when it is still dark. 15

II. Second
time
division
  A. Sounds
  B. Sights
  C. Other
    Sounds

By the time I reach the stairs of the big cathedral, the carillon wakes me up. My ears ring with the ringing bells. The churchyard is full of cars and of early vendors of fruit, vegetables, milk, patés, candles. Inside, the cathedral is crowded. There are no more seats. Some people would rather stand up so that they won't fall asleep during the service, and others have brought their own chairs. The priest is wide awake in his white robe. He moves quickly to and fro as he conducts the mass. The attend- 25

ance of the choir is excellent, and all through the service
the singing is loud, clear, very alive. Outside, the streets
are calm again and the latecomers move quietly, trying
to slip in unobserved.

III. Third   The service is long, but at last it reaches the end. It's   30
time   five-thirty, still dark, and almost time to go back home.
division   I must choose what to do: go back to bed, or study my
A. Sights   many lessons for Monday, or go to the market or to the
B. Sounds   baker. The streets are full of people now, and there are
C. Smells   many more food vendors. From each corner they're call-   35
ing "Paté, paté." Oh, how I love those patés! Other
vendors are selling candles to people coming for the next
service.

About five or six blocks away from the cathedral are
the vendors of "café" and bread. They are not calling   40
anybody. They don't have to. The smell of their merchandise is call enough. They're sitting calmly in front of
their big pots, an oil lamp standing behind each vendor
on a small table. For some grown-ups a good cup of black
coffee is a delight, but the "café au lait" I'll have at home   45
will be even better.

IV. Fourth   A new carillon in the air is announcing the next ser-
time   vice. The roosters everywhere are calling "co-co-ri-co."
division   The dogs sound louder—they are competing with each
A. Sounds   other. From the radios in the houses comes soft music or   50
B. Color   hymns. A new group of churchgoers streams toward the
cathedral. I hear many greetings—"Bonjour," "Bonjour!"

The sky in the east has turned a golden pink. Soon a
beautiful sun will show its round face in a beautiful blue   55
sky. In Haiti it seems that the weather is always lovely on
Sunday.

1. The writer indicates the passing of time in a variety of ways. What are
they?

2. The overall pattern of the essay is chronological, but where does the writer
also use a spatial pattern?

3. Why does the writer tell us so much about sounds?

4. Which details seem most vivid? What makes them vivid?

ASSIGNMENTS

1. For each of the following general subjects, make a list of five or six specific topics drawn from your own experiences on which you think you can write 250-to-500-word papers of interest to the general reader: laboratory science, religion, education, cars, music, agriculture, sports, literature, television programs, nature, social change, art.

   Example: General subject—Education

           Specific topics—My First Day of College Classes

                           Taking Examinations

                           My Interview for Admission to College

                           My Most Memorable Teacher

                           My Favorite Extracurricular Activity

                           Graduation Day

2. For any one of the topics you listed in answer to the preceding question, write five different openings, a sentence to a paragraph in length, each suitable for a different purpose or directed to a different type of reader. In an accompanying note, explain what you hope the effects of each will be and why.

3. Prepare a plan for a paper on several hours spent at a shopping mall, on a job, at a beach, at a family picnic, or in some other specific environment.

   a. List in chronological order the dozen or so items you wish to discuss.

   b. Group them under appropriate headings into a few manageable units.

   c. Regroup them according to some order other than chronological.

   d. Arrange your groupings in item c into what you consider the most effective order and explain why you chose it.

4. Look over the photographs on pages 29 and 55. In what groups can you arrange them according to subject matter, the number of people involved, the types of people, and so on? List them in as many combinations as you can imagine.

5. a. For six of the theme subjects you listed in assignment 1, compose titles to stimulate interest as well as to inform, for example, "Graduation Day—Start or Finish?"

   b. Choose one of the groups in which you arranged the photographs for assignment 4; compose a title for the group and a separate title for each photograph in it. Compose titles that will catch your readers' attention.

   c. For class discussion, bring in a list of five titles of nonfiction books or magazine articles that have especially caught your attention, stating after each the subject with which it deals.

6. On one of the following topics write an essay in which you present your experiences in chronological order; you may choose either a specific or a typical experience:

   a. A day or night at a job you have held recently

   b. A day at a summer camp you attended or at which you worked

   c. A family celebration, such as a birthday party or a wedding

   d. A sports event

   e. A car accident

Observing Details—An Experiment

Close observation of the details of your subject is essential. If you are inaccurate or omit something that your readers want to know, they will lose confidence in you and your thesis.

How good an observer are you? Test yourself by examining these photographs and then answering the questions on the next page. Be honest with yourself and do not turn back to look at the photographs until you have finished the experiment.

Photograph A   Wide World Photos

Photograph B   Val Gerry

QUESTIONS ON THE PHOTOGRAPHS

Photograph A

1. How many people are pushing the car?
2. How many other people are in the picture?
3. What are the other people doing?
4. How many people are wearing belted coats?
5. What is the dog doing?
6. One other car is visible—where is it?

Photograph B

1. How many doors did the car originally have?
2. How many does it have now?
3. Which way is the car facing, to your right or your left?
4. Which windows, if any, are not broken?

WRITING ASSIGNMENTS BASED ON THE PHOTOGRAPHS

1. Assume that photograph A is to be published in a newspaper in a northern city in the winter and compose a title and a statement about 50 words long to attract the reader's attention.
2. Assume that photograph A is to be published in a city in the Sunbelt and compose a title and a statement of about 50 words to attract the reader's attention. In what ways would your approach differ from the one you used for the first question?
3. Assume that photograph B is to be published in a newspaper to illustrate an article on abandoned cars. Compose a title and a statement of about 50 words to attract the reader's attention.

UNIT 2

Revising
and Editing

The following drafts of an essay, with the student's descriptions of his experiences, provide a fairly typical example of the processes involved in composing and revising.

David Parker composed the rough draft as an impromptu in-class assignment. Later, he described his procedures and thinking in the log that he was required to keep on all his writing assignments. At the next class meeting the students formed groups of three or four, read their rough drafts aloud, and offered each other suggestions and criticisms. As homework, they revised the drafts thoroughly, made final copies, and described their procedures in their logs.

Rough draft as written in class

To make the drafts easier to read so that you can concentrate on the important elements in the process of composing and revising, they are presented as if typewritten and errors in spelling, punctuation, and grammar have been corrected. The revisions David made while composing the first draft are handwritten.

The assigned topic required no special information or controversial argument, and the students were asked to concentrate on close observation of the material and on their word choice and sentence and paragraph structure:

Describe what you observed in this room before class began this morning. Assume that your readers are other students who have not had a class in this room at this hour. To allow space for revisions, skip a line after each line of writing and leave a wide margin on each side of the page. Time allowed: 40 minutes.

Monday Paralysis

When I walked into the classroom and sat down,
~~What is this classroom like at nine o'clock on~~

I saw
~~Monday morning? Today, it was~~ the usual Monday morning

scene of general paralysis. Two people seemed to be

sleeping ~~at least, they had~~ their heads down on their

arms on top of their books, ~~which were~~ piled on the desk

arms of their chairs. Almost everybody was silent. They

were staring at the floor or just out into space. Only a

few people were having conversations with their neighbors.

I could see only the backs of most people's heads in

front of me and the profiles of the ones sitting in my

row. Legs sprawled in the aisles and the rows between

the chairs ~~everybody was wearing~~ *all in* blue jeans, but they

were in many shades of blue and in different styles.

Someone had written this message on the blackboard:

"You have only 5 more minutes." That was a gloomy

thought. ~~to start off with on Monday morning~~. What would

I do if I had only five minutes left to live? ~~Better not~~

~~think about that~~.

There was a lot of noise going on in the hall. The

next door classroom's door was opening and shutting, and

people coming out ~~of~~ (a Psych quiz) were groaning over ~~it~~

and welcoming each new escapee.

All the windows were open, and a warm breeze

brought in the pleasant smell of burning leaves. ~~I could~~

~~see~~ Outside, ~~that~~ the tree branches were almost all bare

against the blue sky.

The sounds in the hall died down as people moved

off
~~away~~ toward the stairway ~~at the other end of the hall~~,

and our room seemed very quiet. I noticed the soft buzz

of the fluorescent lights overhead, and I began to feel

drowsy. ~~As I said, there was~~ *A* typical Monday morning

filled
feeling ~~about the scene in~~ the room.

David's log entry on the rough draft

After receiving the assignment, I thought back over the few minutes I was in the classroom before the instructor arrived. I tried to remember in detail what I had seen, heard, and felt. At the same time, I jotted down these notes so that I would not forget anything important while writing the paper. The list shows the order in which I noticed things. I noticed the open windows first of all because they were unusual so late in the fall. The two sleeping students caught my eye because they were the only people who didn't have their heads up:

open windows
people sleeping
blackboard message
noise in the hall
people talking in the room
legs—all in blue jeans
most people just sitting and staring

Next, I wondered what to make my main point. I decided that the material added up to a picture of a typical class at the beginning of Monday morning. Next, I tried to work out the best order for taking up the items on my list so that the overall effect would emphasize the picture of a bunch of sleepy students in class on Monday morning. Since the list was short and I had so little time, I numbered things. If I'd had the time to recopy it, the list would have looked like this:

1. people sleeping
2. most people just sitting and staring
3. some people talking
4. legs, all in blue jeans
5. blackboard message
6. noise in the hall
7. open windows

I decided to begin with my main point—that it was a typical Monday morning scene—and then to describe the students because they're what make a room a classroom, after all. I used the assignment question for a temporary beginning to get started and then went on to the two sleepers because they were eye-catching and then the blue jeans. I thought the blackboard message would add a little humor, and then I could go on to things outside the room—the noise in the hall and the blue sky—to fill in the whole picture.

As I was writing the last paragraph and remembering the noise that had been in the hall earlier, I noticed how quiet the room had become, so quiet that the buzz of the lights was the loudest sound, and I added that as a final detail to help readers imagine exactly how quiet it was. Also, I thought it would help to emphasize the general effect of a typical Monday morning paralysis.

I had saved a couple of minutes to reread my rough draft, and so I fixed up some spots where I saw I'd wasted words, but I didn't have time to think about any big repairs.

Rough draft—revisions

The rough draft shows the main stages in David's process of revision. Gray highlighting marks the changes he made in class while writing and after hearing his classmates' suggestions. The other changes are those he made later after rereading the paper yet again, as he explains in his log.

From ~~Room~~ 305 → *Jefferson Hall*
~~Monday Paralysis~~
~~I took~~ *my usual seat in the last row*x,
~~When I walked into the classroom and sat down,~~
~~What is this classroom like at nine o'clock on~~
I see only the backs of most people's heads in the
~~I saw~~ *other three rows and a few profiles.*
~~Monday morning? Today~~ It ~~was~~ the usual Monday morning
is
students,
scene of general paralysis. Two ~~people seemed to be~~
~~sleeping—at least, they had~~ their heads down on their
chair arms, are catching a last minute nap. A few
~~arms on top of their books,~~ which were ~~piled on the desk~~
^
others are talking, but most are
~~arms of their chairs. Almost everybody was~~ silent, ~~They~~

There is not much in the room to catch attention. The walls are painted a neutral color, between gray and green. Around the light switch, near the door, somebody's fingers have left gray smudges, and on several spots on the baseboard are the scuff marks of passing shoes.

~~were~~ staring at the floor, the ceiling or ~~just out~~ into space. ~~Only~~

~~a few people were having conversations with their~~

~~neighbors.~~ I could see only the backs of most people's

heads in front of me and the profiles of the ones [move earlier]

sitting in my row. ~~Legs sprawled in the aisles and the~~

~~rows between the chairs~~ all in ~~everybody was wearing blue~~

~~jeans, but they were in many shades of blue and in~~

~~different styles.~~

Someone ~~had~~ has written ~~this message~~ on the ~~blackboard:~~ blackboard, ~~green~~ really a greenboard, that covers most of the wall at the front of the room, "You have only 5 more minutes." Words of doom. ~~That was a gloomy~~

~~thought~~ to start off with on Monday morning. ~~What would~~

~~I do~~ If I had only five minutes left to live, how would ~~Better not~~

I spend them?
~~think about that.~~

A few sounds of life outside enter the room. From the hall come the click and slam of
~~There was a lot of noise going on in the hall. The~~

the door of the next classroom and shouts and exclamations
~~next door classroom's door was opening and shutting, and~~

as students   of
~~people~~ coming out ~~of~~ (a Psych quiz) ~~were groaning over it~~

exchange reactions and welcome each escaping classmate.
~~and welcoming each new escapee.~~

↳ From the open windows comes
~~All the windows were open, and~~ a warm breeze
that ruffles the hair of the girl   and the sound
in front of me and brings   of distant traffic.
~~brought~~ ∧in the ~~pleasant~~ smell of burning leaves∧ ~~I could~~

                                    are   and glitter
~~see~~ Outside, ~~that~~ the tree branches ~~were~~ almost all bare∧

            late-autumn
against the blue∧ sky.

      As the
~~The~~ sounds in the hall ~~died down as people~~ moved
away
~~off~~   case, I start to drift off to sleep,
~~away~~ toward the stair~~way, at the other end of the hall,~~

soothed by the steady,
                                        hum
~~and our room seemed very quiet. I noticed the~~ soft ~~buzz~~

                        ....Monday.
of the fluorescent lights overhead ~~and I began to feel~~

~~drowsy. As I said, there was~~ A ~~typical Monday morning~~

            filled
~~feeling about the scene in the room.~~

Log entry on revising the rough draft

After Carol and Jim heard my paper, they made several suggestions: (1) locate myself in the room so that my readers will know what angle I was seeing things from; (2) leave out the reference to blue jeans—they're not a special feature of this class because anybody would see the same thing in just about any classroom at any hour of the day or night; (3) it's a green board, not a blackboard; (4) mention the wall color because in some buildings on campus the classrooms are other colors; (5) "next-door classroom's door" is awkward with all those "doors"; (6) why the sudden jump to the windows and breeze in between descriptions of noises in the hall? how are they connected? That night, reread essay and made changes and additions according to the suggestions. Then read it all again, trying to imagine what Carol's and Jim's opinions would be and how readers who hadn't seen the room would react.

Decided that the first paragraph is much too long. Also, it's weak. If I tell my readers right off that I'm writing about a boring scene, they won't want to go on. I need something to catch their attention. Moved the thesis sentence to the end of the paragraph. At least the beginning has a little interest now because readers will have to wonder for a few moments what my subject is, and the details about the various student activities may seem amusing. Also moved the information about seeing only backs of heads and profiles to the first sentence because it belongs with establishing my location in the room.

Rearranged the sequence in which I described what other students were doing and shortened it a little by taking out words I didn't need. Now it starts with the two students who are doing something different from everybody else (sleeping), then tells what several others are doing, and then what most are doing (staring blankly in silence), and this gets emphasized by being last. Added information on where I was sitting, as Carol and Jim had suggested, and also indicated how many rows of chairs there were so that readers would have a rough idea of the size of the classroom right from the beginning. That would help them to fit together the rest of the details. Decided not to try to be more precise and guess the room measurements or count up how many students were present because that might be more details than readers would want.

Carol's reminder to mention the wall color made me look at the walls more closely, and I noticed the fingerprints around the light switch and the marks on the baseboard. Moved the blackboard (greenboard) message with my comment on it to the end of that paragraph as a kind of climax. Hope it will strike readers as funny and also remind them of the pressures of college work.

Changed "escapee" to "escaping classmates"—"escapee" sounds too cutesy.

Put the mention of the hall noises in the same paragraph with the description of the open windows and breeze and connected them by adding a mention at the beginning that they are both outside the classroom and make a kind of background for it. Tried to make the scene more vivid for readers by adding details about the breeze ruffling a girl's hair and by using "glitter" to describe the tree branches. Also added mention of the sound of traffic—I'd overlooked it before because the noises in the hall were so much louder, but as I thought back I remembered hearing it. In the last paragraph, changed "off" back to "away" because I need "off" with "drift off" and changed "stairway" to "staircase" to avoid repeating the "way" sound so close together, and changed "buzz" to "hum"—a buzz can be angry, but I think of a hum as peaceful. Cut the final sentence down to the one key word, "Monday," to make readers notice it more. Besides, the word really sums up the main point of the paper.

Reread it and decided to switch the whole thing to the present tense to make readers feel that they're really there. Also changed the title to plain information so that the thesis at the end of the first paragraph will seem stronger. Also, since I'm meant to be thinking of readers who haven't seen this particular classroom, I should let them know right away exactly which room it is.

Final draft

This is the draft that David made after revising the paper thoroughly, as described in his log entry. Notice that he made several small, last-minute revisions and additions on this draft so that his description would be more precise and therefore more vivid.

305 Jefferson Hall

From my usual seat in the last row, I see only the

backs of heads in the other three rows and a few

profiles. Two students, their heads down on their chair

arms, are catching a last-minute nap. A few others are

talking, but most are silent, staring at the floor, the

ceiling, or into space. It is a typical Monday morning

paralysis.

There is not much in the room to catch

attention. The walls are painted a neutral color,

between gray and green. Around the light switch, near

the door, ~~somebody's~~ *fumbling* fingers have left gray smudges, and

on several spots on the baseboards are the scuff marks

of passing shoes. On the blackboard—really a

greenboard—that covers most of the wall at the front of

the room, someone has written∧ *in yellow chalk,* "You have only 5 more

minutes." Words of doom. If I had only five minutes left

to live, how would I spend them?

A few signs of life outside enter the room. From

the hall come the click and slam of the door of the next

classroom and shouts and ~~exclamations~~ *groans* as students coming

out of a Psych quiz exchange reactions and welcome each

escaping classmate. From the open windows comes a warm

breeze that ruffles the hair of the girl in front of me

and brings a smell of burning leaves and the sound of

distant traffic. The∧ *bare* tree branches ~~are almost all~~

~~bare now and~~ glitter against the blue late-autumn sky.

```
     As the sounds in the hall move away toward the


staircase, I start to drift off to sleep, soothed by the
```
                            two rows of
```
steady, soft hum from the ˄fluorescent lights overhead.


. . . Monday.
```

⋰ ⋰ ⋰

Revision is reseeing through fresh eyes—reseeing your work as a whole and reseeing the parts and how they contribute to the whole. As David resaw what he had written and tried to imagine his readers' reactions, he made changes, both large and small. He strengthened the essay as a whole by rearranging his material and by omitting some details and adding others to make his main points clearer for his readers. He strengthened his word choice by making it more precise, and he strengthened his sentences and paragraphs by cutting out long-winded expressions and by changing their structure to emphasize important words, particularly in the paragraphs forming the beginning and ending of his essay. The result is a competent piece of work that fulfilled the assignment. By applying similar methods, you will compose effective essays.

For a famous example of the composing process, examine the final draft of John F. Kennedy's inaugural address and his plans and rough drafts ("Essays for Further Reading"-F).

Shaping effective paragraphs

In everything you write, your paragraph structure should guide your readers through your material. A paragraph develops one main thought. To help readers see paragraphs as units within the essay, we indent the beginning of each paragraph, and after the last word, we leave the rest of the line blank.

A paragraph may be any length, from one sentence to hundreds, just as a sentence may have from one word to hundreds, or a book from a few pages to thousands. Newspaper paragraphs are usually brief, often only one sentence each, because the narrow columns cause most sentences to occupy several lines and therefore look longer than they are. In most other forms of writing, however, paragraphs are longer, and the one-sentence paragraph is rare, reserved to emphasize a dramatic or especially significant remark. A series of short paragraphs will make your writing look choppy. Conversely, a series of paragraphs each a page or more long will discourage your readers from even starting. In most writing, paragraphs average between 75 and 175 words, or roughly one-third to two-thirds of a double-spaced, typed page.

All the patterns for organizing essays described in Unit 1 apply to organizing paragraphs as well. Indeed, many paragraphs can be read alone as if they were miniature essays. Choose the structure for each paragraph as you choose the organization for the whole paper, according to your thesis, your content, and your readers' needs.

Topic Sentences

However long or short a paragraph is and however the content is organized, it should concentrate on one main thought. It may, however, contain related thoughts to help readers understand the main one easily. The main thought is often presented in a single sentence, which is therefore called a **topic sentence.** A topic sentence is to a paragraph what a thesis sentence is to an essay.

In most paragraphs, particularly those by writers on subjects in the sciences and social sciences, the topic sentence is at or very near the beginning, but writers may place a topic sentence in the middle or at the end of a paragraph, and sometimes, particularly when narrating an event or describing a person or object, writers may imply the topic of a paragraph instead of stating it directly.

Where to place the topic sentence depends on how much help you think your readers will need in following your line of thought, on how the paragraph is related both to what precedes and to what follows it, and on how much emphasis you wish to give the thought that the sentence expresses.

In the following examples the topic sentences are italicized so that you can see the position of each at a glance.

1. **Paragraph beginning with the topic sentence**

The human skin is not merely "skin deep." On the average adult it measures about 21 square feet. Under the outside layer, or epidermis, is the dermis, and under that is the subdermis. A single square inch of skin has 20 blood vessels, 65 hairs, 65 muscles, 78 nerves, 78 sensors for heat, 13 sensors for cold, from 160 to 165 sensors for pressure, 100 sebaceous glands, 650 sweat glands, and 1300 nerve ends. Altogether, a square inch of skin contains 19,500,000 cells.

Here, the writer is assuming that readers need the topic sentence to help them follow the information in the main body, which provides the supporting details. Also, the topic sentence will catch the attention of most readers by making them wonder how the writer can support what it claims. The paragraph ends with a specific statement that emphasizes the information in the main body by summing it up. This structure would make the paragraph useful after a paragraph on how little most people know about the complexity of the skin and leading to a paragraph on another complex part of the body or to one going into further detail on the skin.

Other examples of paragraphs in which the topic sentence is at the beginning: "More Power to You" (4-C), second and third paragraphs; "Yamacraw" (4-F), both paragraphs; "Yumbo" (5-A), third paragraph; "A Loaf of Bread and the Stars" (5-B), fifth paragraph; *Le Contrat Social* (6-B), all four paragraphs.

2. Paragraph with the topic sentence in the middle

Twenty blood vessels, 65 hairs, 65 muscles, 78 nerves, 78 sensors for heat, 13 sensors for cold, from 160 to 165 sensors for pressure, 100 sebaceous glands, 650 sweat glands, 1300 nerve ends, and 19,500,000 cells are in a single square inch of human skin. *With so many parts, the skin is not merely "skin deep."* These parts are located in the epidermis, or outer layer of skin, under the epidermis in the dermis, and under that in the subdermis. On the average adult, the skin measures about 21 square feet.

This version gives exactly the same information, but the writer is assuming that the intended readers will be interested in the details and able to follow them. The structure would be appropriate for a paragraph following a discussion of the general complexity of the human body and leading to a discussion of the general importance of the skin.

Other examples of paragraphs in which the topic sentence is near the middle: "Yumbo" (5-A), first paragraph; "On Societies as Organisms" (3-C), eighth paragraph; "The House" (4-E), lines 6–8.

3. Paragraph ending with the topic sentence

On the average adult, the skin measures about 21 square feet. Under the outer layer of skin, or epidermis, is the dermis, and under that is the subdermis. A single square inch contains 20 blood vessels, 65 hairs, 65 muscles, 78 nerves, 78 sensors for heat, 13 sensors for cold, and from 160 to 165 sensors for pressure, along with 100 sebaceous glands, 650 sweat glands, 1300 nerve ends, and 19,500,000 cells. *The skin is not merely "skin deep."*

In this version the writer assumes that the intended readers will be interested in the details and will follow them easily. The writer saves the topic sentence until the end so that it can act as a climax, summing up everything that precedes it in a short statement that readers can remember easily. This structure would be appropriate following a paragraph or another major part of the body and leading to a detailed discussion of the skin and its importance.

For other examples of paragraphs in which the topic sentence is at the end, see "The Great Blue" (4-B), first paragraph; "A Hanging" ("Essays for

Further Reading"-B), tenth paragraph; "A Plea for Free Speech in Boston" ("Essays for Further Reading"-D), third paragraph.

4. Paragraph with an implied topic

> On the average adult, the skin measures about 21 square feet. The outer layer is the epidermis, under which is the dermis, and under that the subdermis. In a single square inch are 20 blood vessels, 65 hairs, 65 muscles, 78 nerves, 78 sensors for heat, 13 sensors for cold, from 160 to 165 sensors for pressure, 100 sebaceous glands, 65 sweat glands, 1300 nerve ends, and 19,500,000 cells.

In this version the writer assumes that the intended readers will find details interesting in themselves and will need no reminder to see that they add up to a picture of the complexity of the human skin. This version would be appropriate following a paragraph that pointed out the skin's complexity and could lead to a discussion of one or more of the details or to a paragraph comparing the structure of the skin with that of another complex part of the body or contrasting it with a simply structured part.

This version could also serve as the beginning of an essay on the complexity of the human skin, in which case the next paragraph would begin with "The human skin is not merely 'skin deep' " as the thesis sentence and could continue with a discussion of the general importance of the skin to lead to further information on the human body in the rest of the essay.

Other examples of paragraphs in which the topic is implied, not stated, are "How Dictionaries Are Made" (9-E), "Vietnam Memories: The War Within" (13-C), and "Indian Bones" (16-A). Of course, it is common in narrative paragraphs for the topic to be implied rather than stated; for clear examples, see Hemingway's "The Flight of Refugees" (3-B) and Orwell's "A Hanging" ("Essays for Further Reading"-B).

Transitions

Help your readers to see the connections between your paragraphs and among the sentences within the paragraphs by using transitional devices. A transition, from the Latin word meaning a crossing over from one place to another, is a link of some kind. In writing, a transitional device connects what has just been said and what is about to be said. It may be a single word, such as "therefore," or a group of words, such as "on the contrary," or "to sum up the problem," and it usually appears at or near the beginning of a sentence or paragraph so that readers can make the connection easily with what went before and with what is to follow.

Although the versions of the paragraph on the human skin are short, they use transitional devices to guide readers. In version 1 "Altogether" signals that the last sentence will sum up the others. Similarly, in version 2 "With so many parts" signals that the second sentence will interpret or comment on what preceded it. In version 3, "along with" near the end of the third sentence signals that still more information of the same kind is forthcoming. *This, that, these,* and *those,* the demonstrative adjectives and pronouns, can also help to connect sentences and paragraphs. In version 2 "These" connects "These parts" to "parts" in the preceding sentence, and in all four versions "that" in "under that" refers to "the dermis" mentioned in the phrase before.

You will find transitional devices in almost every example of writing in this book. In "More Power to You" (4-C) are "Yet," line 4; "Next moment," line 19; "Then," line 22; and "Now," line 28. In "How Dictionaries Are Made" (9-E) are "That is to say," line 22; "then," line 30; "Finally," line 35; "therefore," lines 41 and 51. In "Dashers and Dawdlers" (6-D) are "for instance" lines 12–13, 24, and 66; "however," line 20; "Indeed," line 21; "At one point," line 34 ; "a different form," lines 53–54; "In the case of," line 60; "this fear . . . this inability," line 64; "For some . . . For others," lines 65–68; and so on, throughout the book.

Shaping effective sentences

1. **Revise your sentences to make every word work for you.**

Unnecessary words will weaken the force of your sentences, just as too much water will weaken the flavor of a cup of coffee. These strategies will help you to get rid of them:

a. Use **meaningful verbs** instead of nouns. For example, compare the effectiveness of these versions of a sentence from Truscott's "The Great Blue" (4-B):

> **weak version** Maybe three feet tall, he was like a great tower over the beaver pond.
> **Truscott's version** Maybe three feet tall, he towered greatly over the beaver pond. (lines 18–19)

b. Use the **active voice** for verbs instead of the passive. For example, compare the effectiveness of these versions of a sentence from Lewis Thomas's "On Societies as Organisms" (3-C):

> **weak version** Science is violated when human meanings are attempted to be read in their arrangements.
> **Thomas's version** We violate science when we try to read human meanings in their arrangements. (lines 5–6)

c. Use **pronouns** instead of repeating a word or phrase. For example, compare the effectiveness of these versions of a sentence from William Zinsser's "Clutter" (8-D):

> **weak version** Clutter is a laborious phrase. The phrase has pushed out a short word. The short word means the same thing.
> **Zinsser's version** Clutter is the laborious phrase which has pushed out the short word that means the same thing. (lines 37–38).

Note: Deliberate repetition, however, can be an effective method for making your readers notice an important word. In the following sentence from "Lagniappe" (14-D), Mark Twain emphasizes his delight in a particular word:

> We picked up one excellent word—a word worth travelling to New Orleans to get; a nice, limber, expressive, handy word—"Lagniappe." (lines 1–3)

To see how repetition helps to emphasize Mark Twain's point, compare his sentence with this version, in which "word" appears only once:

> We picked up one excellent word, worth travelling to New Orleans to get, nice, limber, expressive, handy—"lagniappe."

2. **Revise your sentence structures to make your meaning clear.**

Take advantage of these structures:

a. **Coordination** When two or more related points are of roughly equal importance, present them in coordinate structures so that your readers will see the relationship quickly. We usually join such structures with coordinating conjunctions: *and, but, or,* or *so,* and sometimes *for,* in the sense of "because." These examples are from "Yamacraw" by Pat Conroy (4-F):

> There is something eternal and indestructible about the tide-eroded shores and the dark threatening silences of the swamps in the heart of the island. (lines 7–9)
> Thus far, no bridge connects Yamacraw with the mainland, and anyone who sets foot on the island comes by water. (lines 14–16)

You may use a semicolon instead of a coordinating conjunction when the relationship between the parts of the sentence is clear and when the second part is equal in importance to the first or when it develops the point made in the first, as in this sentence from *"Le Contrat Social"* by Mencken (6-B):

> Political revolutions, in truth, do not often accomplish anything of genuine value; their one undoubted effect is simply to throw out one gang of thieves and put in another. (lines 43–46)

You may use a colon instead of a comma and coordinating conjunction when the first part could stand alone as a sentence but you wish to show that it leads up to the second, usually more important, part, which serves as an explanation or illustration, as in this sentence, also by Mencken:

> All government, in its essence, is a conspiracy against the superior man: its one permanent object is to police him and cripple him. (lines 1–3)

b. **Subordination** When you have one or more points that are less important than another point to which they are related, use subordinate structures to help your readers see the relationship. We may indicate the connection between the subordinate structure and the rest of the sentence with a subordinating conjunction, such as *when, because, as,* or *if;* or by a pronoun, such as *who* or *which;* or by a preposition, such as *with, to,* or *from;* or by the grammatical structure itself, as with a participial phrase or an appositive. Consult a handbook for a full discussion of subordinate structures of all kinds.

> I had just fished the pool and was rounding a gradual bend upstream, wading slowly so as not to disturb the slow-moving clear water, when up ahead I noticed a gigantic bird atop a tiny, demure beaver dam, a creature almost too large to be real. (lines 1–4)

In this sentence from "The Great Blue" (4-B), "I had just fished the pool and was rounding a gradual bend upstream" is the main clause, the part that is essential to form a complete sentence. The rest is composed of various subordinate structures that tell us what happened when the writer rounded the bend in the stream. To give the same information without using subordination, Truscott would have had to write something awkward and long-winded like this, in which everything seems equally important—or equally unimportant:

> I had just fished the pool and was rounding a gradual bend upstream. I was wading slowly. I had a purpose. I did not disturb the slow-moving clear water. Up ahead I noticed a gigantic bird. It was on a tiny, demure beaver dam. It was a large creature. It was almost not real.

3. **Revise your sentences to emphasize your important ideas.**

Take advantage of these strategies:

a. **Parallelism** Parallelism is a form of repetition. It is the use of similar grammatical structures to present similar pieces of information, making a kind of list. It catches the attention of readers and helps them to see the similarities in the material. Also, the last parallel part will stand out simply because it is the last. A famous example is the concluding sentence in Lincoln's Second Inaugural Address ("Essays for Further Reading"-E):

With malice towards none, with charity for all, with firmness in the
right, as God gives us to see the right, let us strive on to finish the work
we are in, to bind up the nation's wounds, to care for him who shall have
borne the battle, and for his widow and orphans; to do all which may
achieve and cherish a just and lasting peace among ourselves and with
all nations.

Printed to make the parallel structures easier to see, the sentence looks like
this:

> With malice towards none,
> with charity for all,
> with firmness in the right
>   as God gives us to see the right,
> let us strive on
>   to finish the work we are in,
>   to bind up the nation's wounds,
>   to care for him who shall have borne the battle,
>   and
>   for his widow and orphans;
>   to do all which may achieve a just and lasting peace
>   among ourselves
>   and
>   with all nations.

b. **Climactic order** The structure of a climactic sentence is rather like
that of a mystery story. Readers must wait to find out the meaning because
the main subject and verb do not appear until the end or very near the end.
The following sentence by Lewis Thomas is from "On Societies as Organisms" (3-C):

> Although we are by all odds the most social of all animals—more
> interdependent, more attached to each other, more inseparable in our
> behavior than bees—we do not often feel our conjoined intelligence.
> (lines 70–74)

To see how Thomas's sentence structure helps to emphasize his main point,
compare his sentence with a rewritten version that is not climactic:

> We do not often feel our conjoined intelligence, although we are by
> all odds the most social of all animals, more interdependent, more at-
> tached to each other, more inseparable in our behavior than bees.

c. **Cumulative order** A cumulative sentence is the reverse of a climactic sentence. In it, the main subject and verb occur at or near the beginning
so that readers know the general point of the sentence from the start, but
additional information follows to develop the point, making it more precise
and therefore more memorable. Cumulative sentences are relatively long,
usually more than twenty words. This example is in "Yamacraw" (4-F):

There is something unquestionably moving about the line of utility poles coming across the marsh, moving perhaps because electricity is a bringer of miracles and the journey of the faceless utility poles is such a long one—and such a humane one. (lines 23–26)

To see how the structure helps to emphasize Conroy's point, compare his sentence with a rewritten version that is not cumulative:

There is something unquestionably moving about the line of utility poles coming across the marsh. Perhaps this is because electricity is a bringer of miracles, and the journey of the faceless utility poles is such a long one. Also, it is such a humane one.

4. **Reversals** A reversal of normal word order can catch the readers' attention and make the sentence build up to the most important words. The following sentence is from John F. Kennedy's "Inaugural Address" ("Essays for Further Reading"-F):

In your hands, my fellow citizens, more than mine, will rest the final success or failure of our course. (lines 98–99)

To see how Kennedy's sentence structure helps to emphasize his point, compare his sentence with a rewritten version in which the main subject and verb are in normal order:

The final success or failure of our course will rest in your hands more than mine, my fellow citizens.

5. **Variety** Revise your sentences to avoid monotony. Use varied structures and lengths to hold the interest of your readers. A series of short sentences will seem choppy, and a series of long sentences will discourage readers from continuing or even from starting to read your essay. Notice the varied sentence structures and lengths in this paragraph by Lewis Thomas (3-C), which is typical of his style:

[1]Still, there it is. [2a]A solitary ant, afield, cannot be considered to have much of anything on his mind; [2b]indeed, with only a few neurons strung together by fibers, he can't be imagined to have a mind at all, much less a thought. [3]He is more like a ganglion on legs. [4]Four ants together, or ten, encircling a dead moth on a path, begin to look more like an idea. [5]They fumble and shove, gradually moving the food toward the hill, but as though by blind chance. [6a]It is only when you watch the dense mass of thousands of ants, crowded together around the Hill, blackening the ground, that you begin to see the whole beast, [6b]and now you observe it thinking, planning, calculating. [7]It is an intelligence, a kind of live computer, with crawling bits for its wits. (lines 25–36)

The first sentence, which is much shorter than the others, is a transition, linking this paragraph to the one before it. Sentence 2 has two parts, each of which could stand as a separate sentence, and the semicolon indicates that the second part develops the thought of the first. Notice that in the second part, a ten-word introduction leads to the main subject and verb, "he can't be imagined," making us wait to find out what that part of the sentence is about, and in sentence 4 ten words of description come between the subject, "ants," and the verb, "begin," making us wait for the completion of the thought. In all the other sentences, however, the main subject and verb are at or very close to the beginning. In sentence 6, Thomas uses an "It is . . . that . . ." construction to lead to the main thought of the first part of the sentence—"you begin to see the whole beast"—so that it receives emphasis. Notice also his use of parallel structures in sentence 6 to emphasize the relationships among some of his points.

In the seven sentences in this paragraph Thomas has nine independent grammatical structures, ranging in length from only four words in sentence 1 to twenty-nine in sentence 6b. A string of sentences all about the same length creates a steady rhythm that puts readers to sleep, but a varied pattern will help to keep them alert. Presented graphically, the sentences in this paragraph have these relative lengths:

1	2a	2b	3	4	5	6a	6b	7

Revising sentences: An example

The following paragraphs formed the beginning of a research paper on the reactions of children to comic-book superheroes. They are typical of the student's writing throughout the paper. Although the student used conventional grammar and punctuation, his writing was not effective. Notice the many unnecessary words and the weak sentence and paragraph structures, which the student mistakenly thought would sound sophisticated.

"Up, up and away!" or "Holy frosty freezes, Batman!" are just some of the familiar phrases that are jamming our airways and infesting the pages of comic books. These phrases and many others like them are associated with a concept dating back a little over fifty years ago. This concept was the creation of a race of fictitious characters who were greater than the traditional heroic figures that children had admired. This new breed would be referred to as Super-heroes. They are unlike any mortal men or women. Incredible strength, speed and agility are just some of the many attributes that these Super-heroes possess.

Children love to observe many different individuals on television and in comic books. Among these individuals are the various super-heroic characters. Most parents see no harm in their children's interest in these characters and therefore do not hinder their children's watching or reading about them. However, contrary to this belief, watching and reading about Super-heroes are detrimental to the mental growth and health of young children. These characters give children a false sense of reality about how people really behave in our society. Other bad effects emanating from the fictitious heroes are laziness in the child's attitude towards solving difficult problems, misconceptions about the physical consequences of violent acts, and the alienation of the children from their parents.

It is interesting to examine the development of the Super-heroes to see what made them so popular with the American public.

In 1938, Jerry Siegel and Joe Schuster created Superman. He was the very first Super-hero to appear before the public's eye, and, based on Philip Wylie's novel, *Gladiator,* Superman formed the mold from which all the other Super-heroes would eventually be cast. Superman possesses most of the attributes that can be desired in a Super-hero: he is fantastically strong, able to reach incredible speeds (both on the ground and in the air), and, most important of all, he is impervious to anything man or nature on earth can unleash against him. All Super-heroes to follow would be endowed with some, but not all, of Superman's capabilities.

On the advice of his instructor, the student revised the paper thoroughly, reading it through again and again, eliminating unnecessary words and emphasizing important points by reconstructing the sentences and paragraphs. As a result, the final draft of the opening paragraphs is clearly stronger and more compact. **Notice where the student has taken advantage of pronouns and the active voice for verbs to eliminate unnecessary words, and of subordination, parallelism, and climactic structures to emphasize important points.** After you have examined it thoroughly, answer the questions following it on the student's changes.

"Up, up and away!" or "Holy frosty freezes, Bat-

man!" are just some of the familiar phrases ~~that are~~

filling

jamming our airways and ~~infesting~~ the pages of comic

They

books. ~~These phrases and many others like them~~ are associated with a concept ~~dating back a little~~ over fifty

years ~~ago. This concept was~~ *old:* the creation of a race of

fictitious characters ~~who were~~ greater than ~~the tradi-~~
~~tional heroic figures~~ *those* that children had *traditionally* admired. ~~This~~
~~new breed would be referred to as~~ *Called* Super-heroes, ~~They are~~
~~unlike any mortal men or women.~~ *have* Incredible strength,

speed and agility. ~~are just some of the many attributes~~

~~that these Super-heroes possess.~~

Children love to observe many different individuals

on television and in comic books, Among *them* ~~these individu-~~
~~als are~~ the various super-heroic characters. Most par-

ents see no harm in ~~their children's interest in these~~ *this.*

~~characters and therefore do not hinder their children's~~

~~watching or reading about them.~~ However, ~~contrary to~~

~~this belief,~~ watching and reading about Super-heroes, *can be* ~~are~~

detrimental to ~~the mental growth and health of~~ young

children. A false sense of reality, ~~is given to children~~

~~by~~ These characters *create* ~~about the real behavior of people in~~

~~our society,~~ ~~Other bad effects emanating from the ficti-~~

encourage

~~tious heroes are~~ laziness ~~in the child's attitude~~ to-

                                           create

wards solving difficult problems,ʌ misconceptions about

the physical consequences of violent acts, and ~~the~~

alienate

~~alienation of the~~ children from their parents.

~~It is interesting to examine the development of the~~

~~Super-heroes to see what made them so popular with the~~

~~American public.~~

In 1938, Jerry Siegel and Joe Schuster created

Superman, ~~He was~~ the ~~very~~ first Super-hero. ~~to appear~~

~~before the public's eye, and,~~ Based on Philip Wylie's

novel, *Gladiator,* Superman formed the ~~mold from which~~ all

model for

the other Super-heroes ~~would eventually be cast. Superman~~

~~possesses most of the attributes that can be desired in a~~

Superman

~~Super-hero: he~~ʌ is fantastically strong, able to reach in-

credible speeds (both on the ground and in the air), and,

most important, ~~of all, he~~ is impervious to anything man or

nature ~~on earth~~ can unleash against him. ~~All Super-heroes~~ to follow, ~~would be endowed with some, but not all, of Super-~~

~~man's capabilities.~~

1. Where has the student used these strategies in revising sentences: a. subordination? b. parallelism? c. climactic structure? d. variety in sentence structure and length? e. a verb instead of a noun? f. the active voice for a verb instead of the passive? g. a pronoun instead of repeating a noun?

2. What reasons did the student probably have for the many cuts made in the first paragraph? in the second paragraph? in the fourth paragraph? Why is the third paragraph unnecessary?

ASSIGNMENTS

1. Revise an essay that you wrote for Unit 1, giving particular attention to your sentence and paragraph structure and your selection of supporting details.
2. Revise an essay that you wrote in another course.
3. Read an essay that you have written into a tape recorder. Then make a second recording in which you talk through your topic without looking back at your essay. Compare the two recordings. What changes, if any, did you make in your organization? in your emphasis? What fresh ideas and word choices occurred to you? Revise your essay accordingly.
4. Read aloud to a friend or classmate an essay that you have written recently. Ask your listener to jot down whatever seem to be the main point and the main supporting points of your essay. Review your listener's list. Are these the points you intended to emphasize? If not, how can you revise your essay to achieve your purpose?

Observing Details—An Experiment

Close observation of the details of your subject is essential. If you are inaccurate or omit something that your readers want to know, they will lose confidence in you and your thesis.

How good an observer are you? Test yourself by examining these photographs and then answering the questions on the next page. Be honest with yourself and do not turn back to look at the photographs until you have finished the experiment.

Photograph A   Hoops, de Wys

Photograph B   Hoops, de Wys

QUESTIONS ON THE PHOTOGRAPHS

Photograph A

1. Which of the woman's hands is the man holding?
2. How far across his body does her other hand reach?
3. How many of her fingers can you see?
4. In which of his hands is the man holding the woman's hand?
5. What clothing can you see on the man?
6. What jewelry of any kind can you see?

Photograph B

1. On which child can you see part of a shirt?
2. Do the children's jackets seem to be the same style?
3. What kind of shirt can you see on one child?
4. Is there a knife or a fork in the picture?
5. How many plates can you see in the picture?
6. What is the design of the plates?

WRITING ASSIGNMENTS BASED ON THE PHOTOGRAPHS

1. Assume that these photographs are to be published together in a small-town newspaper as examples of "human interest" photography. For each one, compose a title and a statement of about 50 words to attract the readers' attention.
2. Choose one of the two photographs and compose a short narrative for which it could be an illustration.

UNIT 3

Choosing Words

"Open sesame!" commanded Ali Baba, and the door of the robbers' cave obeyed. Folk tales throughout the world give similar examples of the power of words. "Spell," meaning to say the letters of a word, comes from "spell," a magic formula. The *accurate* use of words will not give you magical powers, but it is essential for your primary purpose—communicating your meaning. A *forceful* use of words is essential for your secondary purpose—catching and holding your reader's attention.

The earlier units on composing in general included recommendations to choose appropriate words. This unit will concentrate on how to choose them.

The level of the language in any piece of writing determines how formal—or informal—it will seem to readers. English has a large number of words that are **synonyms** or near-synonyms of each other. But synonyms are

hardly ever truly interchangeable. The **denotations**—the dictionary definitions—of two words may be exactly the same; but their **connotations**—the
associated meanings they have acquired through use—are rarely the same.
For example, *female* is one of the dictionary definitions for *woman* and *woman*
for *female,* but someone who says "Two females sat in the car" probably has
a very different opinion of them from someone who says "Two women sat
in the car." Similarly, both *noted* and *notorious* can be defined as *well-known,*
and they even come from the same Latin root, but they connote two very
different kinds of reputation.

Colloquial, Scholarly and Standard English

Our many synonyms and varying connotations give us a choice of levels
on which to write, from the very formal to the very informal. **Colloquial
English** is informal—the level most of us use when writing and speaking to
friends. The vocabulary and the sentence structure are relatively simple and
may include many contractions, some slang, and some regional and dialect
words. A college or unabridged dictionary will tell you if a word is colloquial,
dialectal, or slang—and, therefore, perhaps not appropriate in a formal
paper.

Scholarly and technical English includes whatever specialized words
and phrases are appropriate to the particular subject. The sentences have
standard English structures but are often relatively long with many subdivisions.

Standard English (or "standard edited English") is somewhere between colloquial and scholarly English. It has the kinds of words and sentence
structures used by writers for the more serious publications meant for the
general reader—big city newspapers, national circulation magazines, and
textbooks like this one.

Consider these versions of a single request:

Leave us go (dialectical/nonstandard)
Let's split (slang)
Let's go (informal)
Let us go (formal)

Each will be appropriate at some time, including the ungrammatical version
if you are quoting a speaker who used it. Whatever level you choose, be
consistent. A sudden shift will startle your readers and make them wonder
if you have changed your purpose. Good English is appropriate English—
appropriate to the occasion, to the subject, and especially to the intended
reader.

Dictionaries

A good dictionary is as essential for a writer as ink and paper. The more words you know well, the more you will choose those that precisely fit your needs. Keep a dictionary beside you when you write. A pocket-sized edition can help with spellings when you write in class, and an unabridged edition—every library has at least one—will help you with complicated problems. But the college edition is the one you should have on your desk—small enough to be picked up with one hand but detailed enough to answer most of your questions about words.

There are four widely respected American dictionaries. In alphabetical order they are:

American Heritage, published by Houghton Mifflin
The Random House College Dictionary, published by Random House
Webster's New Collegiate, published by G. & C. Merriam
Webster's New World, published by New World Dictionaries/Simon & Schuster

Each has over 150,000 entries, gives much the same kind of information on each word, and has much the same kind of additional material on punctuation, the history of the language, and so on. Also, they are nearly the same in size, weight, and price. Examine all four carefully before you choose. Decide which seems to have the most readable type, the most understandable abbreviations, and the clearest diagrams and illustrations. A comparison of their entries for "infer" and "irregardless" will give you a good indication of their differences in presentation and degree of conservatism.

Ask for them by the names of their publishers as well as by their titles, particularly the two "Webster's." There are many dictionaries, some relatively worthless, that use Noah Webster's name, so that "Webster's" in the title guarantees nothing. Remember also to check the copyright date on the back of the title page so that you can be sure of getting the latest edition.

Whichever dictionary you buy, study its opening pages carefully for directions on using it. Each has its own system for presenting information and its own methods of abbreviation. For a sample, see the entry for *pleasure* from *Webster's New World Dictionary* on the next page.

To find more synonyms for a word than your dictionary includes, consult a *thesaurus,* or "treasury" of synonyms. The best known, *Roget's Thesaurus,* is published in a variety of editions. When you choose a word from a thesaurus, always check your dictionary as well to be sure that the word has the connotations you want. For example, you may find *fluent, voluble, glib,* and *flippant* listed together, but although speakers will thank you

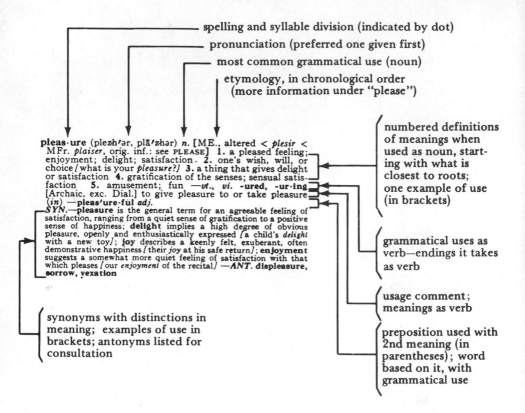

spelling and syllable division (indicated by dot)

pronunciation (preferred one given first)

most common grammatical use (noun)

etymology, in chronological order
(more information under "please")

numbered definitions
of meanings when
used as noun, start-
ing with what is
closest to roots;
one example of use
(in brackets)

pleas·ure (plezh′ər, plā′zhər) *n.* [ME., altered < *plesir* < MFr. *plaiser*, orig. inf.: see PLEASE] **1.** a pleased feeling; enjoyment; delight; satisfaction. **2.** one's wish, will, or choice [what is your *pleasure?*] **3.** a thing that gives delight or satisfaction **4.** gratification of the senses; sensual satisfaction **5.** amusement; fun —*vt., vi.* -**ured,** -**ur·ing** [Archaic, exc. Dial.] to give pleasure to or take pleasure (*in*) —**pleas′ure·ful** *adj.*
SYN.—**pleasure** is the general term for an agreeable feeling of satisfaction, ranging from a quiet sense of gratification to a positive sense of happiness; **delight** implies a high degree of obvious pleasure, openly and enthusiastically expressed [a child's *delight* with a new toy]; **joy** describes a keenly felt, exuberant, often demonstrative happiness [their *joy* at his safe return]; **enjoyment** suggests a somewhat more quiet feeling of satisfaction with that which pleases [our *enjoyment* of the recital] —**ANT. displeasure, sorrow, vexation**

grammatical uses as
verb—endings it takes
as verb

usage comment;
meanings as verb

synonyms with distinctions in
meaning; examples of use in
brackets; antonyms listed for
consultation

preposition used with
2nd meaning (in
parentheses); word
based on it, with
grammatical use

for calling them fluent, they will not be much pleased to be called voluble and will certainly take offense at being called glib or flippant.

Choose specific, concrete words

In most of your nonspecialized writing, in college and later, "standard English" will be appropriate. But this does not mean that you must limit yourself to "safe," dull words. The more precise and economical your word choice is, the more your writing is likely to be clear and forceful. As mentioned in the section on shaping effective sentences in Unit 2, a specific word like *shuffle* or *trudge* or *saunter* is not only briefer than *walk slowly* but is also more precise and therefore more effective. Notice how Shana Alexander piles up specific words for a dramatic and humorous effect in this paragraph:

> Instead of harrying, chivying, threatening with travel taxes and otherwise cramping the tourist's style, I think we ought to coddle, cosset, encourage, advise, underwrite and indemnify him in every possible way. Huge herds of vigorous, curious, open-eyed Americans freely roaming the world are, it seems to me, quite possibly a vital national resource today as at no other time in our history. . . . I am for tourists of any and

all kinds: sneakered and sport-shirted and funny-hatted, pants-suited and pajamaed and jetsetted, knapsacked and bearded, festooned with Instamatics and phrase books and goofy sunglasses, traveling scientists and schoolteachers and schoolchildren and trade missions, Peace Corpsmen, ballet corps, opera companies and symphony players, tennis players, footballers, junketeering congressmen and highballers—all of them to be set wandering and peering and snooping and migrating and exploring and studying and just mooching all over the face of the globe. (Shana Alexander, "The Real Tourist Trap," *Life.*)

Short, simple words in standard English are usually best

Choose longer, more complicated, or technical ones only when they are absolutely necessary to make your meaning clear. More and more often, critics are complaining of the pompousness of much modern writing and of the confusions that result. Some branches of the federal government and some businesses are trying to simplify the language of their reports and contracts, but we still have a long way to go. Theodore Bernstein, a former editor of the *New York Times* and author of several books on writing, calls such pompousness "windyfoggery" and illustrates it with this anecdote:

> Dr. William B. Bean, who in the *Archives of Internal Medicine* often tilted a lancet at the writing operations of his fellow healers, has passed on the story of a New York plumber who had cleaned out some drains with hydrochloric acid and then wrote to a chemical research bureau, inquiring, "Was there any possibility of harm?" As told by Dr. Bean, the story continues:
>
> "The first answer was. 'The efficacy of hydrochloric acid is indisputably established but the corrosive residue is incompatible with metallic permanence.' The plumber was proud to get this and thanked the people for approving of his method. The dismayed research bureau rushed another letter to him saying, 'We cannot assume responsibility for the production of a toxic and noxious residue with hydrochloric acid. We beg leave to suggest to you the employment of an alternative procedure.' The plumber was more delighted than ever and wrote to thank them for reiterating their approval. By this time the bureau got worried about what might be happening to New York's sewers and called in a third man, an older scientist, who wrote simply, 'Don't use hydrochloric acid. It eats hell out of pipes.' " (Theodore M. Bernstein, *The Careful Writer,* 1973.)

Bernstein goes on to say that specialized terminology is, of course, appropriate in technical writing, but "windyfoggery, which often is technical jargon gone wrong and blanketed in blurriness, is not useful to any purpose."

Be concise. Use only as many words as you need to convey your meaning effectively. Omit any that are not necessary, even simple ones. Why, for example, write "It is my opinion that the team won the game due to the fact that they tried really hard" when you can write "I think that the team won because they tried hard"? When you are afraid that your essay is not long enough, do not stretch it with extra words. Find more material—more examples, more details. These will strengthen what you say; extra words will only dilute it.

Be sure to read James Michaels' "Out, Out Foul Phrases," example G in this unit, and William Zinsser's "Clutter" (8-D), which gives more advice on how to strengthen your writing by leaving out words you don't need; look again at the students' revisions in Unit 2; and examine President Kennedy's rough drafts of his Inaugural Address ("Essays for Further Reading"-F).

∴   ∴   ∴

Figures of speech are a special use of words, most of them involving a comparison of some kind. Comparisons can help to make the unfamiliar seem familiar to your readers. They bring the abstract and general to life by relating it to the concrete and specific. To show a reader how hot a room was, you could simply state the fact, "The room was 98° Fahrenheit," but a straightforward comparison would help the reader to see that you wanted to emphasize the heat: "The room was almost as hot as an oven."

A figure of speech might be more memorable, because instead of making a logical, literal comparison, it is imaginative. There are several kinds; among the most common and useful are the following:

1. **Simile** "The room was like an oven." The room and the oven are compared, but the writer takes for granted that the reader thinks of an oven as hot, whereas in "The room was as hot as an oven" this point is included.

2. **Metaphor** "The room was an oven." The room and the oven are presented as one thing, but the writer assumes that the reader knows they are not.

3. **Implied metaphor** "The room baked us." Ovens are enclosed spaces used for baking, but they are not mentioned. The writer assumes that the reader will make the connection.

4. **Extended metaphor** "The room was an oven that baked our conversation dry, and the soufflé of fantastic ideas on which we had hoped to feast was now only a burnt crust." The association of heat and an oven is carried through several related applications to describe the psychological effect of heat.

5. **Personification** "Like a fevered invalid, the room enclosed us in a smothering embrace." The room is described as though it had the characteristics of a human being.

∴ ∴ ∴

Two other figures of speech use comparison less directly:

6. **Hyperbole** "The temperature of the room felt like 1000°." The extreme exaggeration emphasizes the point.

7. **Understatement** "With the thermometer at 98°, we can safely describe the room as warm." Understatement is the opposite of hyperbole, but the reader is expected in both cases to realize that the statement should not be taken literally. A variation on understatement, called *litotes,* uses a negative for the same effect, as in "With the thermometer at 98°, the room was not underheated."

Use figurative language cautiously. It can stimulate your reader's imagination and make your writing more memorable, but, to borrow an old simile, it is like seasoning on food—a little goes a long way.

Avoid the mixed metaphor, a combination of comparisons that do not fit together. A political speaker recently claimed, "My ace in the hole is that I'm not a bull in a china shop swinging a meat axe." *Avoid comparisons that may call up inappropriate associations,* as in "With a good manager, the business sprouted like potatoes in a damp cellar." This is partly appropriate because potatoes do indeed sprout quickly in a damp cellar, but most readers will think of damp cellars as unpleasant and will probably go on to imagine the potatoes as rotting. *Avoid clichés,* comparisons that have grown stale through overuse, such as "green as grass," "busy as a bee," or "old as the hills," unless you can breathe new life into them as in "He seemed as busy as a bee, but we never saw any honey."

Euphemisms are related to figurative language. They are words or phrases that let us soften a harsh or unpleasant or embarrassing fact. We have a variety of expressions to describe physical acts we would rather not name directly. For example, rather than say we are going to the toilet, we may say we are going to the bathroom or the john or the rest room, but "toilet" itself is an old euphemism—check its etymology. Many people are reluctant to say that someone has died and prefer saying that he has passed away. Old people are now called senior citizens, and garbage collectors are sanitary engineers. Use such expressions when you think your readers would be offended by more accurate words, but also be on guard against words that conceal the truth. Someone who steals information from our government for a foreign one is a spy, but we call someone who steals information for us an intelligence agent. Is being terminated from your job really easier than being fired? Is an experienced car in better condition than a used car? Don't be afraid to call a spade a spade, or even, sometimes, a shovel.

EXAMPLES

In the following selections the writers use precise, concrete words and economical phrases, but they nevertheless differ sharply from each other in style. Notice the discussion of word choice in selections in other units, notably in Mencken's "Le Contrat Social" (6-B), McBee's "Gobbledygook" (6-H), Zinsser's "Clutter" (8-D), Twain's "Lagniappe" (14-D), Greer's "In the 'Lite' Decade, Less Has Become More" (14-H), Cohen's "The Language of Uncertainty" (15-C), Shulman's "Love Is a Fallacy" (15-K), Hankins's "Clues to Meaning" (17-B), and Mahood's "Puns and Other Wordplay" (17-C).

3-A   Listening to Words

Eudora Welty

The author is one of the most admired fiction writers in the United States. In 1972 she received a gold medal from the American Academy and Institute of Arts and Letters; in 1973 her novel, *The Optimist's Daughter,* won the Pulitzer Prize for fiction; and in 1980 she received the National Medal for Literature. In 1989 PBS presented a television documentary, *American Experience,* based on her autobiography, *One Writer's Beginnings,* in which the following selection appears as part of Welty's description of her early childhood. Notice in it her use of sensory detail and her pleasure in the sounds as well as the meanings of words. Throughout, she emphasizes that the *enjoyment* of words is essential for effective writing and makes the difference between mere information-giving and writing as an art.

metaphor

Learning stamps you with its moments. Childhood's learning is made up of moments. It isn't steady. It's a pulse.

In a children's art class, we sat in a ring on kindergarten chairs and drew three daffodils that had just been picked out of the yard; and while I was drawing, my sharpened yellow pencil and the cup of the yellow daffodil gave off whiffs just alike. That the pencil doing the drawing should give off the same smell as the flower it

precise
words

5

comparison

drew seemed part of the art lesson—as shouldn't it be? 10
Children, like animals, use all their senses to discover the
world. Then artists come along and discover it the same
way, all over again. Here and there, it's the same world.
Or now and then we'll hear from an artist who's never
lost it. 15

In my sensory education I include my physical awareness of the *word.* Of a certain word, that is; the connection it has with what it stands for. At around age six,
perhaps, I was standing by myself in our front yard waiting for supper, just at that hour in a late summer day 20
when the sun is already below the horizon and the risen

precise word · full moon in the visible sky stops being chalky and begins
to take on light. There comes the moment, and I saw it
then, when the moon goes from flat to round. For the
first time it met my eyes as a globe. The word "moon" 25

simile · came into my mouth as though fed to me out of a silver
metaphor · spoon. Held in my mouth the moon became a word. It
metaphor · had the roundness of a Concord grape Grandpa took off
precise verbs · his vine and gave me to suck out of its skin and swallow
whole, in Ohio. 30

This love did not prevent me from living for years in
foolish error about the moon. The new moon just appearing in the west was the rising moon to me. The new
should be rising. And in early childhood the sun and

metaphor · moon, those opposite reigning powers, I just as easily 35
assumed rose in east and west respectively in their oppo-

simile · site sides of the sky, and like partners in a reel they
advanced, sun from the east, moon from the west,
crossed over (when I wasn't looking) and went down on
the other side. My father couldn't have known I believed 40
that when, bending behind me and guiding my shoulder,
he positioned me at our telescope in the front yard and,

hyperbole · with careful adjustment of the focus, brought the moon
close to me.

metaphor · The night sky over my childhood Jackson was velvety 45
black. I could see the full constellations in it and call their
names; when I could read, I knew their myths. Though
I was always waked for eclipses, and indeed carried to the
window as an infant in arms and shown Halley's Comet

paradox · in my sleep, and though I'd been taught at our dining- 50
room table about the solar system and knew the earth
revolved around the sun, and our moon around us, I
never found out the moon didn't come up in the west

until I was a writer and Herschel Brickell, the literary critic, told me after I misplaced it in a story. He said 55 valuable words to me about my new profession: "Always

colloquial   be sure you get your moon in the right part of the sky."

precise words

My mother always sang to her children. Her voice came out just a little bit in the minor key. "Wee Willie 60 Winkie's" song was wonderfully sad when she sang the lullabies.

colloquial

"Oh, but now there's a record. She could have her own record to listen to," my father would have said. For there came a Victrola record of "Bobby Shafftoe" and 65 "Rock-a-Bye Baby," all of Mother's lullabies, which could be played to take her palce. Soon I was able to play my own lullabies all day long.

Our Victrola stood in the diningroom. I was allowed to climb onto the seat of a diningroom chair to wind it, 70 start the record turning, and set the needle playing. In a

precise verbs   second I'd jumped to the floor, to spin or march around the table as the music called for—now there were all the other records I could play too. I skinned back onto the

colloquial   chair just in time to lift the needle at the end, stop the 75 record and turn it over, then change the needle. That brass receptacle with a hole in the lid gave off a metallic

simile   smell like human sweat, from all the hot needles that
precise verbs   were fed it. Winding up, dancing, being cocked to start and stop the record, was of course all in one the act of 80 *listening*—to "Overture to *Daughter of the Regiment*," "Se-

precise details   lections from *The Fortune Teller*," "Kiss Me Again," "Gypsy Dance from *Carmen*," "Stars and Stripes For-ever." "When the Midnight Choo-Choo Leaves for Ala-bam," or whatever came next. Movement must be at the 85 very heart of listening.

Ever since I was first read to, then started reading to myself, there has never been a line read that I didn't *hear*. As my eyes followed the sentence, a voice was saying it silently to me. It isn't my mother's voice, or the voice of 90 any person I can identify, certainly not my own. It is human, but inward, and it is inwardly that I listen to it. It is to me the voice of the story or the poem itself. The

personifica-   cadence, whatever it is that asks you to believe, the feel-
tion   ing that resides in the printed word, reaches me through 95 the reader-voice. I have supposed, but never found out,

that this is the case with all readers—to read as listeners—
and with all writers, to write as listeners. It may be part

metaphor

of the desire to write. The sound of what falls on the page
begins the process of testing it for truth, for me. Whether   100
I am right to trust so far I don't know. By now I don't
know whether I could do either one, reading or writing,
without the other.

My own words, when I am at work on a story, I hear
too as they go, in the same voice that I hear when I read   105
in books. When I write and the sound of it comes back

metaphor

to my ears, then I act to make my changes. I have always
trusted this voice.

1. In this selection Welty uses several words and phrases metaphorically, for
example, "stamps" and "pulse." What words could we choose to replace her similes
and metaphors if we wished to make her statements literal?

2. What may have been Welty's reasons for saying in her eighth paragraph "I
skinned back onto the chair" instead of "I hurried back"?

3. What advice does Welty give all writers about listening to the *sound* of what
they write?

3-B

The Flight of Refugees

Ernest Hemingway

Hemingway has had more influence on contemporary prose than any other
modern writer. Sometimes he went to extremes in simplifying word choice and
sentence structure and in using understatements, but his news reporting provides
excellent examples of forceful simplicity. In the following, a complete news dispatch
headed "Barcelona: 3 April 1938," he describes several hours in the Spanish Civil
War. Notice his concentration on facts, his choice of details, and the rare indications
of his emotions.

It was a lovely false spring day when we started for the front
this morning. Last night, coming into Barcelona, it had been grey,
foggy, dirty and sad, but today it was bright and warm, and pink
almond blossoms coloured the grey hills and brightened the dusty
green rows of olive trees.   5
Then, outside of Reus, on a straight smooth highway with olive

orchards on each side, the chauffeur from the rumble seat
shouted, "Planes, planes!" and, rubber screeching, we stopped
the car under a tree.

"They're right over us," the chauffeur said, and, as this corre-   10
spondent dived head-forward into a ditch, he looked up sideways,
watching a monoplane come down and wing over and then evidently decide a single car was not worth turning his eight ma-
chine-guns loose on.

But, as we watched, came a sudden egg-dropping explosion of   15
bombs, and, ahead, Reus, silhouetted against hills a half mile
away, disappeared in a brick-dust-coloured cloud of smoke. We
made our way through the town, the main street blocked by
broken houses and a smashed water main, and, stopping, tried to
get a policeman to shoot a wounded horse, but the owner thought   20
it was still possibly worth saving and we went on up toward the
mountain pass that leads to the little Catalan city of Falset.

That was how the day started, but no one yet alive can say how
it will end. For soon we began passing carts loaded with refugees.
An old woman was driving one, crying and sobbing while she   25
swung a whip. She was the only woman I saw crying all day. There
were eight children following another cart and one little boy
pushed on a wheel as they came up a difficult grade. Bedding,
sewing-machines, blankets, cooking utensils and mattresses
wrapped in mats, sacks of grain for the horses and mules were   30
piled in the carts and goats and sheep were tethered to the tail-
boards. There was no panic, they were just plodding along.

On a mule piled high with bedding rode a woman holding a
still freshly red-faced baby that could not have been two days old.
The mother's head swung steadily up and down with the motion   35
of the beast she rode, and the baby's jet-black hair was drifted
grey with the dust. A man led the mule forward, looking back
over his shoulder and then looking forward at the road.

"When was the baby born?" I asked him, as our car swung
alongside. "Yesterday," he said proudly, and the car was past.   40
But all these people, no matter where else they looked as they
walked or rode, all looked up to watch the sky.

Then we began to see soldiers straggling along. Some carried
their rifles by the muzzles, some had no arms. At first there were
only a few troops, then finally there was a steady stream, with   45
whole units intact. Then there were troops in trucks, troops
marching, trucks with guns, with tanks, with anti-tank guns and
anti-aircraft guns, and always a line of people walking.

As we went on, the road choked and swelled with this migra-
tion, until, finally, it was not just the road, but streaming alongside   50

the road by all the old paths for driving cattle came the civilian
population and the troops. There was no panic at all, only a steady
movement, and many of the people seemed cheerful. But perhaps
it was the day. The day was so lovely that it seemed ridiculous that
anyone should ever die.   55

Then we began seeing people that we knew, officers we had
met before, soldiers from New York and Chicago who told how
the enemy had broken through and taken Gandesa, that the
Americans were fighting and holding the bridge at Mora across
the Ebro River and that they were covering this retreat and   60
holding the bridgehead across the river and still holding the
town.

Suddenly, the stream of troops thinned and then there was a big
influx again, and the road was so choked that the car could not
move ahead. You could see them shelling Mora on the river and   65
hear the pounding thud of the guns. Then there came a flock of
sheep to clog the roads, with shepherds trying to drive them out
of the way of the trucks and tanks. Still the planes did not come.

Somewhere ahead, the bridge was still being held, but it was
impossible to go any farther with the car against that moving   70
dust-swamped tide. So we turned the car back toward Tarragona
and Barcelona and rode through it all again. The woman with the
newborn baby had it wrapped in a shawl and held tight against
her now. You could not see the dusty head because she held it
tight under the shawl as she swung with the walking gait of the   75
mule. Her husband led the mule, but he looked up at the road
now and did not answer when we waved. People still looked up
at the sky as they retreated. But they were very weary now. The
planes had not yet come, but there was still time for them and they
were overdue.   80

1. What words describe how crowded the road was? How specific are they?
What words describe other actions of any kind? colors? sounds?

2. What reaction from the reader does the writer seem to want?

3. In lines 28–32, why list the kinds of things piled on the carts instead of saving
space by calling them "household effects" or "portable possessions"? What distinction may be drawn between "crying" and "sobbing"?

4. Are there any words that you could remove without changing the meaning
and effect of the description?

3-C   On Societies as Organisms

Lewis Thomas

This essay, here almost complete, was first published in the *New England Journal of Medicine* and then in *The Lives of a Cell* (1974), a collection of Dr. Thomas's essays. The writer, a noted research scientist, is fascinated by the behavior of living things of all kinds, from the parts of a single cell to human beings. He begins the essay by pointing out that although we often compare the behavior of humans to that of insects, scientists object to any interpretation of insect behavior in human terms.

The writers of books on insect behavior generally take pains, in their prefaces, to caution that insects are like creatures from another planet, that their behavior is absolutely foreign, totally unhuman, unearthly, almost unbiological. They are more like perfectly tooled but crazy little machines, and we violate science   5
when we try to read human meanings in their arrangements.

It is hard for a bystander not to do so. Ants are so much like human beings as to be an embarrassment. They farm fungi, raise aphids as livestock, launch armies into wars, use chemical sprays to alarm and confuse enemies, capture slaves. The families of   10
weaver ants engage in child labor, holding their larvae like shuttles to spin out the thread that sews the leaves together for their fungus gardens. They exchange information ceaselessly. They do everything but watch television.

What makes us most uncomfortable is that they, and the bees   15
and termites and social wasps, seem to live two kinds of lives; they are individuals, going about the day's business without much evidence of thought for tomorrow, and they are at the same time component parts, cellular elements, in the huge, writhing, ruminating organism of the Hill, the nest, the hive. It is because of this   20
aspect, I think, that we most wish for them to be something foreign. We do not like the notion that there can be collective societies with the capacity to behave like organisms. If such things exist, they can have nothing to do with us.

Still, there it is. A solitary ant, afield, cannot be considered to   25
have much of anything on his mind; indeed, with only a few neurons strung together by fibers, he can't be imagined to have a mind at all, much less a thought. He is more like a ganglion on legs. Four ants together, or ten, encircling a dead moth on a path, begin to look more like an idea. They fumble and shove, gradu-   30

ally moving the food toward the Hill, but as though by blind chance. It is only when you watch the dense mass of thousands of ants, crowded together around the Hill, blackening the ground, that you begin to see the whole beast, and now you observe it thinking, planning, calculating. It is an intelligence, a   35
kind of live computer, with crawling bits for its wits.

At a stage in the construction, twigs of a certain size are needed, and all the members forage obsessively for twigs of just this size. Later, when outer walls are to be finished, thatched, the size must change, and as though given new orders by telephone, all the   40
workers shift the search to the new twigs. If you disturb the arrangement of a part of the Hill, hundreds of ants will set it vibrating, shifting, until it is put right again. Distant sources of food are somehow sensed, and long lines, like tentacles, reach out over the ground, up over walls, behind boulders, to fetch it in.   45

Termites are even more extraordinary in the way they seem to accumulate intelligence as they gather together. Two or three termites in a chamber will begin to pick up pellets and move from place to place, but nothing comes of it; nothing is built. As more join in, they seem to reach a critical mass, a quorum, and the   50
thinking begins. They place pellets atop pellets, then throw up columns and beautiful, curving, symmetrical arches, and the crystalline architecture of vaulted chambers is created. It is not known how they communicate with each other, how the chains of termites building one column know when to turn toward the crew   55
on the adjacent column, or how, when the time comes, they manage the flawless joining of the arches. The stimuli that set them off at the outset, building collectively instead of shifting things about, may be pheromones [odors] released when they reach committee size. They react as if alarmed. They become   60
agitated, excited, and then they begin working, like artists. . . .

The phenomenon of separate animals joining up to form an organism is not unique in insects. Slime-mold cells do it all the time, of course, in each life cycle. . . . Herring and other fish in schools are at times so closely integrated, their actions so coor-   65
dinated, that they seem to be functionally a great multi-fish organism. Flocking birds, especially the seabirds nesting on the slopes of offshore islands in Newfoundland, are similarly attached, connected, synchronized.

Although we are by all odds the most social of all social animals—more interdependent, more attached to each other, more   70
inseparable in our behavior than bees—we do not often feel our conjoined intelligence. Perhaps, however, we are linked in circuits for the storage, processing, and retrieval of information,

since this appears to be the most basic and universal of all human   75
enterprises. It may be our biological function to build a certain
kind of Hill. We have access to all the information of the biosphere, arriving as elementary units in the stream of solar pho-
tons. When we have learned how these are rearranged against
randomness, to make, say, springtails, quantum mechanics, and   80
the late quartets, we may have a clearer notion how to proceed.
The circuitry seems to be there, even if the current is not always
on.

The system of communications used in science should provide
a neat, workable model for studying mechanisms of information-   85
building in human society. Ziman, in a recent *Nature* essay, points
out, "the invention of a mechanism for the systematic publication
of *fragments* of scientific work may well have been the key event
in the history of modern science." He continues:

> A regular journal carries from one research worker to another   90
> the various . . . observations which are of common interest. . . .
> A typical scientific paper has never pretended to be more than
> another little piece in a larger jigsaw—not significant in itself but
> as an element in a grander scheme. *This technique, of soliciting many
> modest contributions to the store of human knowledge, has been the secret*   95
> *of Western science since the seventeenth century, for it achieves a corporate,*
> *collective power that is far greater than one individual can exert* [italics
> mine].

With some alteration of terms, some toning down, the passage
could describe the building of a termite nest.   100

It is fascinating that the word "explore" does not apply to the
searching aspect of the activity, but has its origins in the sounds
we make while engaged in it. We like to think of exploring in
science as a lonely, meditative business, and so it is in the first
stages, but always, sooner or later, before the enterprise reaches   105
completion, as we explore, we call to each other, communicate,
publish, send letters to the editor, present papers, cry out on
finding.

1. What specific, concrete words describe actions? living things?

2. Where does Thomas use figurative language? What seems to be the purpose?

3. What distinctions does Thomas make among words in a kind of list at the
end of his first sentence, in the sentence beginning in line 8, and in the sentence
beginning in line 67?

4. Can you shorten any of Thomas's sentences by changing or omitting words
without at the same time changing the meaning and effect?

5. The sentences vary in length from short (under 10 words) to long (over 30 words). Where and how does this variation emphasize Thomas's main points?

6. Check the etymology, denotation, and connotation of these words: *launch, ruminating, neuron, ganglion, forage, tentacle, termites, pellets, quorum, explore.*

3-D   A Pop Fly to Short

Gary Bucello *(student)*

The writer's pleasure in the special terminology of baseball is similar to Cumming's pleasure in the precise terminology of many subjects (3-F).

Baseball is a sport, and like most sports it requires many skills. But baseball is not just any sport; it is our national passion and pastime. Throughout the long season, it entertains millions and millions of Americans daily. Baseball fans and players have a special vocabulary to describe the skills required for the game. It   5
is composed of colorful words and phrases that pack a lot of meaning into a few syllables.

Many words describe the special skills in batting. The "swing" of a bat may be called a "cut" because in swinging the bat the batter "cuts" the air. It may also be called a "stroke," as in "The   10
next hitter, Brooks, stroked a hot line drive to short left field." When a batter hits a home run with three men on base, he is said to make a "grand slam." In the card game of bridge, making a grand slam is winning every "trick" in the game. "Grand" suggests something magnificent and unusual, and "slam" suggests an   15
extremely forceful action; in both games a grand slam is an extraordinary success for the player. A "cleanup man" is not the janitor, but the fourth batter in the batting order. If three men get on, he is the person on the team most likely to clear the bases with a home run, thus "cleaning up" the field.   20
Another group of terms describes different kinds of pitchers. A "junk pitcher" is one who does not throw fastballs and who is therefore not very good. The "ace pitcher" is the best on the team. The word "ace" comes from the Latin *as,* a "unit" or "unity," and is therefore the name of playing cards with only one   25
pip. In most card games, aces are the top-ranking cards. "Ace" is also a tennis and golf term. A "relief pitcher" is one who is sent into the game to take the place of, or "relieve," the original pitcher when the original pitcher is not performing adequately.

A relief pitcher is sometimes dubbed a "fireman" because he   30
comes to the rescue of his team by putting out the "fire" of the
opposing team.

The skill needed for pitching has become so highly specialized
that the words describing pitching form a group in themselves.
The three major types of pitches are the "fastball," mentioned   35
already, the "curveball," and the "offspeed pitch." Someone
throwing a fastball may be said to be "throwing smoke" or
"throwing heaters," implying that the ball moves so fast it will
burn what it hits. A curveball is also called "breaking pitch" or
"deuce" because the catcher puts down two fingers as the curve-   40
ball sign. The word "deuce" is also used for playing cards with
two pips and in tennis scoring. It comes originally from the Latin
word *duos,* a form of *duo,* meaning "two." An offspeed pitch is
called a "change of pace" or "change" because it is a change in
speed from an ordinary pitch. Among many other special types   45
of pitches is a "screwball," which is one that reverses the normal
curve and goes to the right, if the pitcher is right-handed, or to
the left, if he is left-handed. A screwball used to be called a
"fadeaway," and so we now have both "screwball" and "fadeaway fastball."   50

Among special terms for catching are "shoestring catch" and
"backhand stab." In the first, a player catches a ball just before
it hits the ground—close to his shoes. In the second, a player must
reach across his body and turn his glove backwards to catch the
ball. In this phrase "stab" suggests that the player makes a quick,   55
hard, thrusting movement.

The parts of the playing field and the positions on it that the
players occupy have special terms too. The third base position
may be called the "hot corner" because more hard-hit balls are
sent toward third base than anywhere else. A "gap" or "alley"   60
is the area between a center-fielder and the left- or right-fielder.
"The ball's hit in the left-center gap!" is a quick but precise way
of saying "The ball is hit in the area between the left-fielder and
the center-fielder!"

Besides being colorful, most baseball terms contain a lot of   65
information in a small number of syllables, as in "gap," just
mentioned. Baseball can be an explosive game. Although it may
seem to drag on and on at times, much can happen all at once.
Terms that say a lot in a short space can be very important,
especially to a broadcaster. Anyone trying to describe a game in   70
standard English phrases would not be able to keep up with the
action. For example, a "ribbie" is a "run batted in," and a "triple
crown" means leading the league in three things—home runs,

runs batted in, and batting average. Triple crown is borrowed
from American horse racing, where it is the name for the three   75
biggest races of the year for three-year-olds. Together, the pitcher
and catcher are called the "battery." A "spray hitter" is a player
who has the ability to pull the ball if it is an inside pitch or hit it
up the middle if the pitch is thrown over the middle of the plate
or even push the ball in the opposite way if the pitch is thrown   80
outside. A "looper" is a softly hit ball that brings the batter to first
base and forces the outfielders to play the diamond instead of
playing the field. A "pop fly to short" means that the ball was hit
in the air, did not go very far or very high, and was directed
toward the shortstop, and a "slider" from a right-handed pitcher   85
to a right-handed batter will generally come in fast and straight
until it is a couple of feet in front of the batter, and then it will
suddenly dip down and tail away.

　　Baseball is so popular and its vocabulary is so useful that many
baseball terms are listed in standard dictionaries. In the latest   90
edition of *Webster's New World Dictionary* I found all of the following listed specifically as baseball terms: cut, grand slam, cleanup
man, fireman, screwball, curve, backhand, battery, pop, fly, and
slider. The dictionary lists as tennis terms the following words
that are also baseball terms: stroke, deuce, ace, and alley. In   95
looking up the words I have discussed, my eye was caught by two
other baseball terms: "double-header," which describes two
games played one after the other on the same day, and "twi-
nighter," which describes a special kind of double-header, one
that begins in the late afternoon so that the second game will be   100
played at night.

　　Baseball is a great American tradition. In 1976 the American
League celebrated its seventy-fifth anniversary and the National
League celebrated its one hundredth anniversary. Over the years,
more than a billion fans have attended major league games. No   105
wonder more and more baseball terms are being included in
standard dictionaries.

　　A piece of advice often given to tourists going to a foreign
country is "You'll have more fun if you know a little of the
language." The same advice applies to baseball. Learn the lan-   110
guage—you'll have more fun the next time you watch a
game.

1. How has the writer grouped the baseball terms he discusses?

2. What transitional devices connect the groups of terms?

Jesse Jackson

These paragraphs come from the Reverend Jesse Jackson's speech to an audience composed primarily of black high school students at the 1979 convention of
Operation PUSH. Note his use of colloquial language.

The reason I have so much faith in this generation of young
people is because down through the years student involvement
has made a difference in social change. During the McCarthy Era,
students fought the threat of free speech being taken away from
us. When Rosa Parks found herself in anguish she went to Dr.   5
King who was a student who led that great struggle somewhere
between Selma and Montgomery. Students met a struggle and
made a difference. The reason some of us can't make sound
decisions is that we've been sidetracked. Some by violence, some
by sex, some by lack of opportunity. I tell the story over and over   10
again, how do you measure a man. You can't look at some cowboy definition of a man. You're not a man because you got
notches on your belt; you're not a man because you can violate
somebody; you're not a man because you can push somebody else
down; you're not a man because you can kill somebody.   15
     You're a man because you can heal somebody. You're not a
man because you can make a baby; you're a man because you can
raise a baby and provide for a baby and produce for a baby. That
makes you a man. Young sisters, there's another side to that story.
You can't measure yourself by your bosom—you've got to do it   20
by your books. You've got to have something in your mind.
There's nothing that's more perverted than to see somebody with
a fully developed bottom and a half developed brain. You've got
to check out your mind. I got a little message that says—the buses
are not leaving now; so just sit down and be cool. We have this   25
situation for many of us do not want to face the reality and the
options of our lives. So when we begin to remind you about sex,
we're not being unreal. Someone said "Rev., you don't understand about sex—there's a thrill in sex." I understand there's a
thrill. I've got five children; I understand thrill, I'm not unaware   30
of that. Except, I also know this, that when people all around you
tell you that you can't do something and you can do it, and you

do it—that's a thrill. When you graduate from high school, that's
a thrill. When you come across that stage and have a Medical
Degree or a Law Degree, that's a thrill. When you make a touch-   35
down, that's a thrill. When you do your best against the odds and
make it when everybody around you says you couldn't make it,
that's a thrill. When you end up going to college instead of to jail,
that's also a thrill. And all I'm saying is that we should not have
a one-thrill syndrome; all of life can be thrilling if you develop   40
your mind, develop your body, and develop your soul. Say amen.

1. What specific, concrete words are used?

2. Where is repetition used for emphasis?

3. Can you condense any of the sentences by changing or omitting words or
phrases without at the same time changing the meaning and effect?

3-F Dottle and the Bottle with a Punt

Doug Cumming

The writer of this essay, here complete, is a reporter for the *Providence Journal-
Bulletin* in Rhode Island. His pleasure in precise word meanings is similar to Mark
Twain's in "Lagniappe" (14-D) and complements the attacks on sloppy word use
made by James Michaels (3-G) and William Zinsser (8-D).

Not many people know the word for the dent in the bottom
of a wine bottle. For that matter, not many people even know
there *is* a word for it. There is. It's called a punt, and when I
learned it I felt a delicious surge of power. A word like that plugs
you right in. There's nothing abstract about it like those wispy   5
words used to describe the wine inside: smoky, velvety, pert. You
can argue till the candles gutter out about a wine's subtlety, but
not about the bottle's punt.

The world is full of things whose names escape us. "The thing
in our electric oven broke," I complain to Sears in a snit. I can't   10
think of what it's called, which frustrates me even more. When
"heating element" comes to mind, I regain some control, almost
as if I'd fixed the thing myself.

More often, we have never been formally introduced. We say

we respect them, admit our dependence on them, still we re-   15
gard the objects that surround us with the subtlest sort of contempt. We have gradually lost all feeling for the stuff that tex-
tures our life—for the things that swing on hinges and the
gizmos that zip and coil and creak. The poet Gerard Manley
Hopkins once praised the "gear and tackle and trim" of all   20
trades, but to help us restore our senses these days, we need to
be more specific than that. We need to learn a thing's name.
Like the gunk that gets left in the bowl of a pipe after it's been
smoked. It's called dottle.

They don't teach us words like that in school. They teach us a   25
required "vocabulary"—a word, by the way, that one of my
elementary-school teachers deliberately used to embarrass one of
the slower students in class. "Clint," I clearly remember her
asking, "do you have a vocabulary?" And after a moment of
consideration he answered, "I think I have one at home."   30

As we all do in the beginning, Clint still dwelled in the sensual
land of things, but the function of school is to fog over everyday
objects with words that are pompous, and sometimes quite useless. If we learn words like inchoate, tendentious and recondite,
we score high on verbal SAT's and go to Princeton. If we're slow 35
to catch on, we go into voke ed, where we might learn a few
things—words like brake caliper and floor joist.

I have just discovered a book that is full of thing words, the
kind of words we mean when, thanks to our education, we say
whatchamacallit, thingamajig and thingamabob. It's called *What's* 40
What: A Visual Glossary of the Physical World. And it's a treasure.
Ordinary doohickeys like clothespins and paper clips, when you
are introduced to their six or seven named parts, suddenly radiate
with significance. A key is just a key to most of us, but when you
learn that it's the serrations and warding that do the trick, you've   45
really unlocked something.

Having opened the door (with its stiles, panels and mail drop)
to this mansion of doodads, I couldn't stop exploring. I looked
for things I knew—the lovely words of magazine layout like slug,
gutter and bleed—and things I had no business knowing, like the   50
parts of planes, ships, guns and nuclear power plants. I studied the
guide lugs, breeches, chocks and wing-fixed gloves like the places
on a map. For without such words we are like the ape-men in
2001: A Space Odyssey, shaking our knuckles at a monolith that
sings back in the eerie polytones of technology. The words bring 55
us to our senses and give us authority.

Who would've thought that the squiggles in a cartoon that
indicate various actions all have names? The coil showing drunk-

enness is a spurl, running feet are blurgits, sweat drops are
plewds, an odor line is a waftarom and the dust cloud left by   60
someone running is a briffit. The @, #, * and ! of a "maledicta
balloon" carry names like grawlix, nittles, jarns and quimp, which
have even more zip than the words they replace.

Knowing what the experts call the dojiggers of their occupa-
tions in some mysterious way lets us share in their expertise. Talk   65
wall flange and packing nut to your plumber and see if it doesn't
improve the relationship. Talk crampon and chocks to a mountain
climber and the air will grow thin around you.

But thing words are more than the mumbo jumbo of a spe-
cialty. Whether technical or trivial, they anchor us in a world that 70
is rich and specific; they hook into reality like crampons and
chocks into the mountain face. They are not subject to the
manipulations and fudges of the rest of our language.

Helen Keller knew how to ask for several things by name
before that April morning in Tuscumbia, Ala., when her teacher   75
placed her hand under a spout and, as cool water gushed over one
hand, spelled W-A-T-E-R in the other. This time a deeper connection was made between a word and a thing, and suddenly, as if
a light had come on, Helen Keller wanted to know the name for
everything in her life.   80

I can catch a glimpse of that light now when I learn that the part
of a recliner chair that knocks your feet up is a hassock, that the
connection between the handle and blade of a dinner knife is a
tang. Even if I don't often eat chicken with those little frilly paper
things capping the bone ends, I know they are called papillotes.   85
And having learned the incantations used by the gem cutter—
pavilion, crown and fire—the glitter of a diamond seems more
brilliant.

"Things are in the saddle," wrote Ralph Waldo Emerson. He
was lamenting the materialism of American life, but if he were   90
still around he might find a few pages from "What's What" as
bracing as his loftiest ideals. We're in the saddle still. But know
a pommel from a cantle and, at the very least, you'll be facing in
the right direction.

1. How has the writer organized his material?

2. What examples of figurative language can you find? of colloquial language?

3. Where does the writer use narrative?

4. Check the etymology and various meanings of *wispy, gutter, tackle, monolith,
expertise, incantations.*

3-G   Out, Out Foul Phrases

James W. Michaels

The author of this editorial, here complete, is the editor of *Forbes,* a biweekly business magazine. Compare his choice of examples of sloppy word use with Zinsser's choice in "Clutter" (8-D).

In another business journal the other day I read that "investor attitudes have undergone a sea change since the big rise in the stock market over the past few months." Sea change? What do 'sea changes' have to do with stock markets? Webster's dictionary sent me to Shakespeare's *The Tempest:*   5

Full fathom five thy father lies;
Of his bones are coral made;
Those are pearls that were his eyes:
Nothing of him that doth fade
But doth suffer a sea change. . . .   10

Sea change? Investor attitudes had changed fairly importantly, but Shakespeare was talking about transformation, about life and death. We see and hear this all the time: Phrases once beautiful or witty or mind-stretching are ignorantly misused and repeated until, degraded into meaninglessness, they become clichés.   15
(Twenty percent on the Dow compared to human destiny?) Such clichés make for tiresome reading and, worse, imprecise writing.

Does *Forbes* never commit clichés? Alas, like all journalists, we do, and that brings me to our New Year's resolution, which we share with you: To give our excellent Copy Desk additional au-   20
thority to delete tired phrases and jargon that too often creep into our copy. Below a few of the terms henceforth to be avoided:
Big Blue (for IBM); Ma Bell (for AT&T); game plan; ongoing; revolution (as in "an auditing revolution"); soaring (or plummet-ing) stock prices on a 1% move in the Dow; upscale (for affluent);   25
superstar (what's a mere star?); baby boomers; pricey (for expen-sive); whopping; bottom line (when no numbers are involved); track record (what does "track" add?); Young Turks; Big Apple; downside risk (what's an upside risk?); bells and whistles; free fall; world class; hands-on management; guru, for any vaguely   30
venerated authority. . . .

Slated for strict rationing but not complete elimination: sexy, applied to things like packaging and stocks; red ink (need it always come in seas, pools, baths, rivers?). Loose use of ready-made ideas or words: Rust Belt, Third World, fast track. 35

Our linguistic hit list is longer than the above, but this gives an idea of some of the atrocities we business journalists often inflict on the English language. Out, out, foul phrases.

1. Which words and phrases mentioned by Michaels can you find in use? Look over the editorials, letters to the editor, and financial news in a recent newspaper and listen to a news commentator and a financial analyst on radio or TV; list the words and phrases you find.

2. Check the etymology and meanings of *degraded, jargon, affluent, whopping, venerated, slated, atrocities.*

ASSIGNMENTS

1. Write a paper of about 300 words on the word choice and figurative language in the description of the jet engine (4-C).
2. Revise one of your earlier essays by replacing vague words with precise, concrete ones and by omitting words that you do not need.
3. Read a column by a sports writer or listen to a radio sports announcer who you think makes events exciting; then write an essay discussing how particular words and phrases made the action seem vivid.
4. Compose a three-minute radio commercial for something you like very much, such as a particular product, a performer, a movie, a political leader. Assume that your commercial will be broadcast only on your campus.
5. Rewrite the commercial you composed for assignment 4, but this time assume that it will be broadcast on a regular station. What changes must you make for the different audience?
6. Choose something inanimate, such as a pair of shoes, a bicycle, a stone, or a river, and in 200 to 300 words describe it as if it were a specific kind of animate creature, anything from a single-cell animal to a human being.

PART II

Developing the Thesis: Basic Methods

UNIT 4

Description

Which way of expressing a thought are you more likely to notice and remember—"There was a dishonest financial transaction" or "George Henderson's check for fifty dollars bounced, and it's stamped 'Account closed' "? "Natural scenes are beautiful" or "In the sunlight, the trumpets of the honeysuckle sparkled with dew"? "Humanity is interesting" or "Her brown eyes shining, the little girl puffed her cheeks and leaned forward to blow out the four candles on her birthday cake"?

We must often deal with abstract concepts such as dishonesty, nature, or humanity, but the concrete catches our attention more easily—a bad check, a flower, a child. Yet even these are general, and our imaginations respond most to details like those in the examples above. With specific, concrete details you can make a vivid and memorable point of something that your readers might otherwise forget or never notice.

For this unit you will write short pieces of almost unmixed description to practice accurate observation and word choice. But remember to use description only to help in informing or persuading your readers and to make your main point clear and memorable.

·:· ·:· ·:·

Description may be informative or evocative, depending on your purpose. You may wish simply to give your readers facts, or you may wish to give them pleasure as well. Both types aid exposition—the first is a necessity, the second an enjoyable luxury.

1. **Use informative description** to explain a mechanism or a process. Be practical, not poetic. Give the essential facts in the briefest and clearest terms you can find. If these are not sufficient, use comparisons with more familiar objects: "The shovel handle is D-shaped"; "Sand the wood until smooth as glass"; "The mixture gave off the odor of rotten eggs." Drawings may supplement or replace words in such descriptions. Be as brief as you can without losing clarity and completeness. Your goal is information, only information. Such description is required in technical reports and all writings calling only for facts.

2. **Use evocative description** to appeal to your readers' senses and emotions and to add vividness to facts. In "Your dollar will help to feed this haggard mother and her crippled child," what might have been bare fact becomes a plea because of the emotional power of specific details that *suggest* as well as *mean.* A general idea—your money is needed—comes alive in the particulars. *Money* is your tangible dollar; *need* is the hunger of a definitely pictured woman and child.

·:· ·:· ·:·

Your **selection of descriptive details** must fit your purpose. From a mass of sense impressions, take the few that are relevant, the ones your readers must have to understand your point, and omit the rest. In describing a machine in terms of its function, you need not mention its odor; in creating a mood of gloom, you should omit any details that might suggest cheerfulness. Moreover, your physical point of view will limit you to the sensations you would actually have at the time and place you describe. You cannot see the back jeans pocket of your host as he opens the door or smell the flowers on a distant hillside. If you are walking around a building or across a field, your description must take into consideration the changes in your viewpoint.

⁘ ⁘ ⁘

The **organization of descriptive details** is usually easy because in most expository essays you will need only one or two details to illuminate any one point, but when you must describe something at greater length, the arrangement of the details becomes an important choice.

1. **The chronological pattern** is the simplest—the arrangement of details according to the time sequence in which they were observed. The examples in Unit 1 are organized chronologically, as are the first three in this unit.

2. **The spatial pattern** is next in simplicity—the arrangement of details according to physical shape and position. In describing a room, you might start at one side and walk around it, naming the objects you see as you move. Similarly, you might describe a person from head to foot or from foot to head, or a landscape from near to far or far to near.

3. **The most noticeable feature** can be the basis for a more selective arrangement. In describing the room, you might first mention a piano or a fireplace, for the person perhaps a big nose, and for the landscape a large tree; then you would give the rest of the details in relation to the outstanding feature.

4. **Relative importance** can be the basis for a still more selective arrangement. This pattern centers on the detail you want your readers to notice most—an unmade bed, a shy smile, the honeysuckle on a fence— including other details only to reinforce the impression of the important one.

⁘ ⁘ ⁘

Word choice is by far the most important element in creating an effective description. Our awareness of the physical world comes to us primarily through our senses, and well-chosen words can stimulate readers' imaginations to recreate physical sensations.

1. **Use concrete, specific words.** Avoid the abstract and general whenever you can. Saying that a room is clean or a girl is beautiful gives your opinion but creates no picture for the reader. A mention of a freshly waxed floor, however, or of large brown eyes with long lashes will stimulate your readers' imaginations.

2. **Appeal to all the senses.** Most often, we think of description in terms of what we see. But the sensations of sound and scent, touch and flavor, can be essential in description. Imagine trying to tell foreigners about the fun of an American country fair. If you described only what you saw, they would miss much of the experience—the shouts of the barkers at the amusement concessions and the clatter of the machinery for the various rides; the odor from the food stands, the barns, and the crowd, the spicy flavor of the hot dogs and the intense sweetness of the cotton candy; and everywhere the grittiness of the dust stirred up by hundreds of feet.

3. **Use a comparison or contrast** with something familiar. English has many words describing size, shape, and color but few for sound, flavor, odor, or texture. After classifying a taste sensation as sweet or sour, bitter or salty, you have used almost all our appropriate adjectives, but you have not re-created that sensation for the reader. A description such as "Venison tastes like beef but has a more intense flavor," however, will help your reader imagine the taste of the less familiar meat. The comparison does not have to be literal; it may only suggest a point of similarity as in "The bad news was like a slap in the face," or, more forcefully, "The bad news was a slap in the face."

4. **Consider using personification**—describing animals, inanimate objects, or abstractions as if they have human characteristics can also help the reader to imagine them more vividly, as in "The engine coughed and sneezed before it died," or "The neighborhood dogs held a committee meeting behind the garage."

5. **Consider using onomatopoetic words**—these are words whose sounds imitate the sounds they name, for example, *crash, murmur, buzz, whir, sigh,* or *shuffle.*

See Unit 3 for a more detailed discussion of word choice and of figures of speech.

EXAMPLES

In each of the following selections, the writer's main point is to make a description, but all the other writers in this book also use description to some degree, for example, in Lodescar's "Sunday Morning in Haiti" in Unit 1, Ward's "Yumbo"

(5-A), Lowe's "The Twelfth Day of Christmas" (5-F), Krulish's "The Start of a Long Day" (6-F), all the selections in Unit 10, Lanning's "The Ones Left Behind" (11-B), Berendt's "The Button" (11-E), Nemy's "Business Status" (11-G), Peeples' "Branch Libraries" (12-B), Conza's "Christmas Eve" (12-I), Satriale's "Dix Hills" (13-E), Twain's "Lagniappe" (14-D), Keremes's "The Passing of Little Gibbs Road" (15-J), and Shulman's "Love Is a Fallacy" (15-K).

4-A   Cold Orange Juice

Wayne Smith *(student)*

This description was written as a fifteen-minute exercise in class. The assignment was to describe in detail the sensations of drinking something very cold.

I was so thirsty that I could already taste the orange and feel the cold go down my throat. My mouth started to water when I picked up the glass. As the cold numbed my fingers I felt the frost melt under them. I took my first gulp. It was so cold that I had to squint my eyes. My teeth tingled. The tiny fruit cells popped   5
against my tongue and filled my mouth with acid sweetness. A piece of ice slid down, leaving my mouth numb and my throat aching. I sucked in air to make my throat warm again and licked my teeth to warm them, too.

How does each of these words chosen by the writer differ from the near synonym paired with it: *gulp* and *swallow; squint* and *narrow; tingled* and *felt cold; popped* and *broke open; sucked* and *breathed in?*

4-B   The Great Blue

Lucian K. Truscott IV

This is the second half of an informal essay published in the *Saturday Review.*
In the first half, the writer described an uneventful afternoon fishing alone in
Maine as background to emphasize the drama of his sudden view of the rare bird.

I had just fished the pool and was rounding a gradual bend
upstream, wading slowly so as not to disturb the slow-moving
clear water, when up ahead I noticed a gigantic bird atop a tiny,
demure beaver dam, a creature almost too large to be real. He
had his back to me and seemed to be peering intently into the   5
pool on the other side of the dam. I froze, stood perfectly still as
I watched him preside magnificently over the pond. I was only
about fifteen or twenty feet away, and he was an elegant sight—a
great blue heron.

The beaver pool was twenty or thirty yards in length and pear-   10
shaped; it was shallow at the near end, deep at the far. Over to
one side I could see a beaver lodge—still lived in, it appeared; in
good repair at any rate—and at the far end a brief falls, where
water rushed into the pond with a white giggle, audible even
from where I stood. The woods were that quiet.   15

The heron had the hue of a blue-point Siamese cat, a dusky
grayness, bluish only on the edges, the high points in the fading,
late-afternoon sun. Maybe three feet tall, he towered greatly over
the beaver pond. I wondered: Do the beavers know he is here,
and if so, does his great size cause them to slap the water and   20
crash-dive, heading for the womb of their upside-down coffee-cup
lodge?

Then, suddenly, he whooossshhhed his wings upward once,
then down, stretched to their full four or five feet—it seemed
like six—and took off from the dam, glided over the beaver   25
pond for a few yards, and rose slowly, his wings beating the air
slowly like a rug strung over a clothes line in the backyard, his
great neck doubled back arrogantly against his chest, then thrust
forward almost wantonly as he passed above the trees, heading
north.   30

I watched his low and easy disappearance against the sky until
he was as blue as it was.

1. Which words and groups of words give you the most precise impressions of what the writer saw and heard?

2. Why does he describe the bird's color twice in one sentence: "the hue of a blue-point Siamese cat" and "a dusky grayness, bluish only on the edges"?

3. What is gained by the spelling "whooossshhhed"?

4. What may have been his reason for comparing the bird's wings to a rug on a clothesline instead of to something graceful?

5. Check all the definitions for these words in a large dictionary: *demure, wantonly.*

4-C   More Power to You

Time

This description was written in 1948, when jet engines were new, but the thrill for an observer can be much the same today. Vivid description is as possible with a mechanical subject as with a natural one.

DESCRIPTIVE DEVICES Negatives Contrast	Bolted motionless on a test stand, the little monster is not impressive. It has no coolly symmetrical propeller, no phalanx of cylinderheads, none of the hard geometrical grace of the conventional aircraft engine. Yet the unprepossessing turbo jet engine has thrown the air designers into ecstatic confusion: nobody yet knows how fast the jet will enable man to fly, but the old speed ceilings are off. In their less guarded moments, sober designers
Comparison Animation	talk of speeds so high that aircraft will glow like meteors. To watch a jet engine spring into life is to feel that power. (Only when the engine is set up with a pipe to catch its gases is it safe to watch the fires kindle.) Dimly
Comparison Sound Smell	visible inside is the turbine, like a small windmill with close-set vanes. When the starting motor whines, the turbine spins. A tainted breeze blows through the exhaust vent in the tail, followed by a thin grey fog of
Onomatopoeia; Sight Onomatopoeia	atomized kerosene. Deep in the engine a single spark plug buzzes. A spot of fire dances in a circle behind the turbine. Next moment, with a hollow *whoom,* a great yellow flame leaps out. It cuts back to a faint blue cone,
Comparison	a cone that roars like a giant blowtorch. The roar increases to thunder as the turbine gathers speed. Then it

Line numbers: 5, 10, 15, 20

diminishes slightly, masked by a strange, high snarl that
is felt rather than heard. This is "ultrasonic" sound (a
frequency too high for the ear to hear). It tickles the deep   25
Feeling   brain, punches the heart, makes the viscera tremble. Few
men like to stay in a test room when a jet is up to speed.

The engine now has the fierce beauty of power. Its
massive rotor, the principal moving part, is spinning
some 13,000 times per minute (though with only the   30
Informative   faintest vibration). The fire raging in its heart would heat
comparisons   1,000 five-room houses in zero weather (though much of
the engine's exterior is cool). From the air intake in its
Animation   snout, invisible hooks reach out: their suction will clasp
a man who comes too close and break his body. The blast   35
Informative   roaring out the tail will knock a man down at 150 feet.
comparisons   The reaction of the speeding jet of gas pushes against the
test stand with a two-ton thrust. If the engine were point-
ing upward and left unshackled, it would take off like a
rocket, each pound of its weight overbalanced by more   40
than two pounds of thrust.

1. Point out in this section any effective choices of concrete, specific words.

2. What is the cumulative effect of the words *life, tail, snarl* (¶2), *heart, snout* (¶3)?

3. Check all the definitions for these words in a large dictionary: *unprepossessing, ecstatic, meteor, turbine, tainted, cone, viscera, snout, unshackled.*

4-D   The Hellbender

The *Encyclopedia Americana*

This paragraph from an encyclopedia is intended to give facts and is a typically informative description. Essential details are listed in such an objective manner that only one word, "repulsive," expresses an opinion. Scientists in all fields use objective description as an aid in explaining all kinds of natural phenomena.

Hellbender, *Cryptobranchus alleganiensis,* most robust and second largest of North American salamanders. It attains a length of
slightly more than two feet. Despite a somewhat repulsive appearance, and the presence of teeth in both upper and lower jaws, the
hellbender is quite harmless. The small eyes are set in a massive   5

head. Both head and body are much depressed, and the outlines
of the body are disguised by a fleshy fold of wrinkled skin along
either side and the posterior aspects of each limb. Though relatively short, the limbs are functional, the front pair being provided with four toes, the hind limbs with five. A crest is present   10
along the upper side of the strongly compressed tail. Hellbenders
are entirely aquatic, yet the adults are without gills and have only
a single pair of inconspicuous gill slits, which are more or less
concealed by skin folds. Their coloration varies considerably,
ranging from yellowish brown through dull brick red to near   15
black.

The organization of Examples A, B, and C was determined by the chronology
of the experiences. What principle of organization is used here? What reason may the
writer have had to use it?

4-E   The House

Anne Moody

This is the first paragraph of a book, *Coming of Age in Mississippi.* It is the
autobiography, starting with her childhood, of a young black woman who was active in the Civil Rights movement of the 1960s when she was a college student.

I'm still haunted by dreams of the time we lived on Mr. Carter's
plantation. Lots of Negroes lived on his place. Like Mama and
Daddy they were all farmers. We all lived in rotten wood two-
room shacks. But ours stood out from the others because it was
up on the hill with Mr. Carter's big white house, overlooking the   5
farms and the other shacks below. It looked just like the Carters'
barn with a chimney and a porch, but Mama and Daddy did what
they could to make it livable. Since we had only one big room and
a kitchen, we all slept in the same room. It was like three rooms
in one. Mama [and the rest of] them slept in one corner and I had   10
my little bed in another corner next to one of the big wooden
windows. Around the fireplace a rocking chair and a couple of
straight chairs formed a sitting area. This big room had a plain,
dull-colored wallpaper tacked loosely to the walls with large
thumbtacks. Under each tack was a piece of cardboard which had   15
been taken from shoeboxes and cut into little squares to hold the
paper and keep the tacks from tearing through. Because there

were not enough tacks, the paper bulged in places. The kitchen
didn't have any wallpaper and the only furniture in it was a wood
stove, an old table and a safe.   20

1. How has the writer used a spatial order to organize details?

2. What details support her point that her parents tried to make the shack
livable?

3. Why does she devote one-fifth of the paragraph to the wallpaper?

4-F   Yamacraw

Pat Conroy

This excerpt comes from *The Water Is Wide* (1972), in which the writer describes a year he spent as a teacher on Yamacraw. The book has been made into a
movie, *Conrack.* His most recent book is *The Prince of Tides* (1986).

Yamacraw is an island off the South Carolina mainland not far
from Savannah, Georgia. The island is fringed with the green,
undulating marshes of the southern coast; shrimp boats ply the
waters around her and fishermen cast their lines along her bountiful shores. Deer cut through her forests in small silent herds. The   5
great southern oaks stand broodingly on her banks. The island
and the waters around her teem with life. There is something
eternal and indestructible about the tide-eroded shores and the
dark, threatening silences of the swamps in the heart of the island.
Yamacraw is beautiful because man has not yet had time to de-   10
stroy this beauty.
     The twentieth century has basically ignored the presence of
Yamacraw. The island is populated with black people who depend on the sea and their small farms for a living. . . . Thus far,
no bridge connects Yamacraw with the mainland, and anyone   15
who sets foot on the island comes by water. The roads of the
island are unpaved and rutted by the passage of ox carts, still a
major form of transportation. The hand pump serves up questionable water to the black residents who live in their small familiar
houses. Sears, Roebuck catalogues perform their classic function   20
in the crudely built privies, which sit, half-hidden, in the tall
grasses behind the shacks. Electricity came to the island several
years ago. There is something unquestionably moving about the

line of utility poles coming across the marsh, moving perhaps
because electricity is a bringer of miracles and the journey of the   25
faceless utility poles is such a long one—and such a humane one.
But there are no telephones (electricity is enough of a miracle for
one century). To call the island you must go to the Beaufort
Sheriff's Office and talk to the man who works the radio. Otherwise, Yamacraw remains aloof and apart from the world beyond   30
the river.

1. What characteristics of the island does Conroy emphasize?

2. What pattern of arrangement does he use for the details?

4-G   ## Remembering the Child

Zayra Raiano *(student)*

A mere stripling, almost but not quite a man, in country boots
and dungarees—he's cautious and anxious and sometimes full of
range. Still, when I look into his eyes, I see a boy of five.

He frolics by the ocean's edge, chasing waves and ducking sun
rays. Distractions are few and fleeting—a shiny object or a stran-   5
ger's dog—and, impatient at approaching nightfall, he resumes
playing with the frothy surf, oblivious of the scorching sun. And
I, from behind my sunglassed facade, watch intently as he prances.

He plucks seashells from their watery graves and flowers from
their obscured beds, then darts to his secret cove to hide their   10
fragile beauty. And I, pretending not to look, make mental note
of his secret places.

He delights in tasting raindrops, cussing, storms, and taking
long and tiring drives up winding roads. He can shinny up almost
any tree and romp all day out in the meadow, oblivious of the   15
singeing heat. And I feign sleep . . . and watch intently.

1. How has the writer organized her description of her son?

2. What concrete, specific words does the writer use to help us to picture her
son?

3. What similarities and differences can you find between this example and the
one that follows?

My Son Jonah

Cecilia Cardeli *(student)*

Green eyes, speckled with gold, rush colored baby-fine hair bluntly cut in a Buster Brown, jeans worn out at the knees, unlaced pro-Keds on feet forever moving—that is my son Jonah.

From Jonah's lips laughter flows uncensored by propriety. He sees humor in the bra advertisements of the *Ladies Home Journal,*   5 stout people bending over, and the gait of intoxicated gentlemen. He idolizes Robin Williams, and Orkian is his favorite language. But nothing is funnier than his mom trying to do the steps of the latest dance craze.

A male chauvinist with nine years of experience in male/female   10 relationships, Jonah has deduced that boys are smarter than girls and mothers shouldn't work. He is a firm believer in girls with long hair down to the waist and boys with hair going no further than the neck. Against all current psychological theories, Jonah is convinced that dolls, washing dishes, anything pink, and pants   15 without flies are sissy. In fact, he won't wear the hand-knit Aran sweater I bought on sale for him because the label reads "Mimi, Ltd."

My son—what a curious mixture of humanity he is. Jonah can spell "Khomeini," collects Billy Joel records, is an avid Yankee   20 fan, and beats me at chess. On the other hand, he still makes knots of his shoelaces, forgets to brush his teeth, does not believe in undershirts, loses one mitten a week, and needs a nightlight to sleep.

1. How has the writer organized her description?

2. Why does she emphasize the information on Jonah's childishness by giving it last? How does this information affect our understanding of everything preceding it?

3. What similarities and differences can you find between this example and the one that precedes it?

4-I   Small Town Summer

Jerry Klein

This essay, by a writer for the *Peoria Journal Star* in Illinois, is here complete
and describes a distinctively American experience. Compare his selection of details
and organization with those used by Anaica Lodescar in Unit 1.

Now, in that slow, sweet time between the Fourth of July and
Labor Day, summer makes its deepest, most profound impression
upon the human psyche with an old-fashioned cadence and
rhythm. To those who live in cities, it may be nothing more than
a succession of oppressive days of baked brick and steaming as-   5
phalt, hot nights when violence seethes below the surface, when
the humid blanket dampens the spirit and the heat is an awesome,
almost malevolent force. And yet summer in small-town America
remains a magic, treasured time.

Here there are the houses set far back on their spacious front   10
yards, cool and shady streets where ancient elms, sycamores and
oaks muffle the sounds of children and traffic passing—sun-dap-
pled by day, soft and beguiling at dusk, beckoning and mysterious
tunnels by night.

One has the feeling that things have not changed here, that the   15
cars might well be square-nosed with wire wheels and softly
blipping engines and that within these houses people might be
listening to Fibber McGee and Molly or playing cards around
their pedestal oak tables. An illusion, obviously, but things
change slowly here and life is circumscribed by the grain elevator,   20
the church, the park and the thin strip of downtown with its
1890's Victorian building fronts. And summer flows past as lazily
as the creek wandering between its tree-shaded banks at the edge
of town.

Already the afternoons drone with the cicadas, rising and fall-   25
ing in their peculiar intensity as if cued by some unseen director. It is a drowsy, somnolent sound, an invitation to such
timepassing activities as throwing a tennis ball against the front
porch steps and fielding the grounders, or sitting out in front of
the tavern watching the flow of life at the little supermarket   30
across the street.

Out beyond the cool oasis of town, the corn is a green-black
sea, rising steadily toward high tide, and farther on, almost like

mirages, the distant farmhouses and barns have the appearance of
ships at anchor on the placid surface.   35

Noon whistles and church bells mark the passing of the day. A
breeze flaps through the cottonwoods and then dies away. Clothes
hang from the backyard lines as still and unmoving as if they are
part of a painting. Porch swings stand empty. Later, when the
night wind comes, they might creak softly, a welcome retreat for   40
people sated with television and wanting a breath of fresh air.
Real country air.

In the heat of the afternoon, the swimming pool in the park is
churned into foam by scores of thrashing bodies. Hardly room to
stand, much less to swim. Nearby, the little bandstand with its 50   45
or so seats stands empty.

At dusk, a three-piece countrywestern group will appear and
play old songs. There will be a girls' league night softball game,
too, with half a hundred people or more crowding the bleachers
or sitting along the first base line in their colorful lawn chairs. The   50
town policeman will stop and watch and the young men will
cruise past in their cars. And there will be activity down at the
tavern on the main street, where men in seed hats grip frosty
glasses of beer and talk about the corn and beans and the need
for some rain—and quick.   55

Night comes slowly and the fireflies wink along the darkening
streets and trimmed lawns like a sky full of stars brought down
to earth for the season. The wind that springs up has the rich
earthy smell of fertile cornfields and maybe distant pigs as well.
In the park, the concert has ended. The softball game ends with   60
a shout of triumph from one team and the lines of players passing
one another, touching hands and repeating that sporting litany,
"Good game, good game, good game. . . ."

Then the lights go out. The tavern down the street empties and
an almost surreal silence falls across the town. Only the crickets   65
and the night insects now, and the winking fireflies. In the distance, there is the low rumble of thunder. The farmers listen and
hope for rain. The younger people hope for another sunny day
tomorrow. For them, summer stretches on almost forever. For the
older folks, this small-town summer is too short and fall comes too   70
soon.

1. How has the writer organized his details?

2. Most of the details appeal to our senses of sight and hearing, but some appeal
to our senses of touch and taste—where are they?

3. Check the etymology, denotation, and connotation of *psyche, cadence, malevolent, beguiling, circumscribed, cicadas, mirages.*

ASSIGNMENTS

1. Make basic statements vivid by adding descriptive details. For example:
   Basic statement: A child was looking out of a window.
   Version 1: A chubby girl of six with a tangle of brown curls wriggled on her stomach across the window ledge as she stared in boredom at the empty street below.
   Version 2: A skinny, undersized girl of six, her matted brown hair hanging to her shoulders and her smudged cheeks streaked by tears, shivered fearfully in a corner of the window as she peered between the curtains at the angry, shouting mob in the street below.
   Write two very different versions of each statement, using concrete, specific words to evoke a particular situation and mood for your readers.
   a. A car went by.
   b. The rain fell.
   c. The music began.
   d. A man started to speak.
   e. A woman stood still.
   f. The crowd began to move.
2. Replace the following trite descriptions with fresher ones, as in this example:
   Trite description: My feet felt as cold as ice.
   Revised version: My feet felt like gravestones in a lonely cemetery.
   a. You look as fresh as a daisy.
   b. He turned as white as a sheet.
   c. The price of steak has gone sky-high.
   d. We laughed our heads off.
   e. The flowers danced in the breeze.
3. a. Imagine yourself alone in a completely dark room, obliged to rely on senses other than sight, and write a paragraph describing your physical sensations as you try to find your way across the room.
   b. Imagine yourself in the same place in daylight with a blind person and write another paragraph describing the room to that person.
4. a. Using strictly informative words, describe your room at home or at college so factually and accurately that the reader could easily draw a floor plan, complete with furnishings.
   b. Then write an evocative description of the same place, determining before you start exactly how you wish your reader to react and choosing your details carefully to evoke that reaction.
5. Write an exposition of some personal experience, enlivening it by whatever descriptive devices you find suitable, particularly those that will evoke for the reader the sensations you yourself experienced. Look through the examples of descriptive writing in this unit for suggestions. Other possible subjects (which may remind you of still better ones) are getting up on a cold morning, attending a football game,

participating in a swimming meet, riding on a roller coaster or an iceboat or in a racing car or a small plane, eating at a quick-lunch counter, visiting a fair or a stockyard, attending a religious service or a wedding reception.

6. Study the use of description as an aid to exposition in other selections, particularly those mentioned in the introductory note for the examples in this unit.

Observing Details—An Experiment

Close observation of the details of your subject is essential. If you are inaccurate or omit something that your readers want to know, they will lose confidence in you and your thesis.

How good an observer are you? Test yourself by examining these photographs and then answering the questions on the next page. Be honest with yourself and do not turn back to look at the photographs until you have finished the experiment.

Photograph A Val Gerry

Photograph B Courtesy Ken
Tiemeyer, *Hutchinson News,* Kansas

Newspaper Snapshot Awards—1983
Kodak International

QUESTIONS ON THE PHOTOGRAPHS

Photograph A

1. What is the physical position of the child in the lower section of the photograph?

2. What large object is fastened on the freight car behind the locomotive?

3. How many people can be seen?

Photograph B

1. How many figures are painted on the wall?

2. How many of the painted figures have hats? rolled-up sleeves?

3. Which of the two seated people is looking up?

4. What are the positions of the arms and hands of the seated figure on your left? of the seated figure on your right?

5. How many steps down would someone leaving the building have to take to reach the ground?

6. What words are painted above the entrance to the building?

WRITING ASSIGNMENTS BASED ON THE PHOTOGRAPHS

1. Assume that these photographs are to be published together in a newspaper or magazine as examples of contrasting moods and activities. Compose a title and a statement of about 50 words for each, emphasizing how they can be seen as examples.

2. In an essay of about 300 words describe the behavior of the people on a sunny afternoon in an outdoor recreation area. Use the people in the two photographs as examples and add whatever other examples you wish from your own observations.

3. What may the child in Photograph A be thinking of what he sees? Compose an essay of about 250 words describing the child's reaction, as you imagine it, and the basis for it.

4. What do you think is the mood and the relationship of the two people in Photograph B? Compose an essay of about 300 words describing that mood and using the people in the photograph as an extended example. Imagine personalities and a situation appropriate to what can be seen in the photograph.

UNIT 5

Narration

What happened when Mary told her boss she wanted a raise? Did you hear about Dr. Brown and the rattlesnake in Arizona last summer? When Jim Drake was mayor, what were the main events in the city's history? What's the story behind your company's merger? Have you heard the one about the guy who bought a kayak to impress his girl friend, but. . . .

Our curiosity about other people, real or imaginary, seems endless. We all enjoy a good story, not only in a novel, a play, or a movie, but in almost anything we read. Narration, like description, particularizes rather than generalizes; it deals with the concrete rather than the abstract. An appropriate narrative, whether short or long, can strengthen and enliven almost anything you write. With it, you not only inform your readers but stimulate their imaginations so that they feel as if they themselves are experiencing the events you present, not merely hearing about them.

⋰   ⋰   ⋰

A narrative may be any length, from an anecdote to a long, complex story. You may use it to make your expository point explicit or only to imply it.

1. **The brief narrative** An anecdote can catch your readers' attention *at the beginning* of a serious discussion. You may wish to make it humorous or provocative, but it should be related to your main idea and lead your readers into the main body of your essay. For example, the story of the three blind men who each formed a different idea of what an elephant was like could begin a discussion of a serious problem that you think is the result of misunderstanding. *Throughout the main body* of your essay, you may use brief narratives to make difficult points clear and vivid.

2. **A long narrative as the main body** Over half your essay may be narrative, ending with an expository discussion of the point made. For example, in the parables of Jesus, a story is told and then interpreted as a moral lesson. *Aesop's Fables* are almost entirely narrative, with only the final line stating the expository purpose, the "moral."

3. **A long narrative as the entire essay** Any account that lists consecutive actions or events is essentially a narrative; yet it is intended, of course, to explain, and is therefore basically informative rather than entertaining. An allegory, such as Bunyan's *Pilgrim's Progress,* and a satire, such as Swift's *Gulliver's Travels,* may at first seem to be only story-telling, but they are really narrative presentations of deeper moral meanings and social criticism. The "social purpose" novel concentrates on some problem that the story illustrates. In Steinbeck's *Grapes of Wrath,* for instance, the experiences of the Joad family are particular examples of the general problems farmers faced in the severe drought of the 1930s. These works are completely narrative in presentation but completely expository in purpose.

⋰   ⋰   ⋰

Catching and holding your readers' interest is essential to the success of any narrative. You do not have to write of dramatic adventures to make a good story. Indeed, some of the best stories tell of everyday experiences. Whether you describe a plane crash or a sandlot baseball game, a trip into space or a backyard picnic, the purpose of your essay will determine your choice of narrative material. What matters is how you handle it.

1. **Subject matter** Choose an event that has *significance* for you—an emotional force or an intellectual meaning that you can pass on to your readers. If your only point about a trip is that "We went to Key West" or about a ball game that "Our side won," your narrative will not interest your readers. The more strongly you care about an event, whether real or imaginary, the more likely you are to make it interesting for your readers, and your point of view, whether humorous, whimsical, or serious, will give it unity.

2. **Suspense** All narratives should have suspense. They should make readers want to know what happened next, who won, what was the final outcome. Suspense is based primarily on conflict—whether mild or intense—between characters, between a character and circumstances, between conflicting desires in a single character's mind. Two students struggling for the same prize, a woman battling against alcoholism, a teenager torn between duty to parents and the desire to leave home—all these conflicts and similar ones create suspense.

3. **Climax** Narrative incidents should build up progressively to the climax, the highest point of interest. Some narratives stop short when they reach that point, as O. Henry did with his "surprise endings," and others unwind more slowly after it, but the ending should always be brief. Any material after the climax may seem anticlimactic and dull.

4. **Time** Description deals primarily with spatial patterns, but narrative deals primarily with chronological patterns.

a. **Sequence** For a short incident, the normal sequence of start-to-finish may work well; for a longer one, it is often more effective to begin at an exciting point anywhere in the action to catch your readers' interest, returning to it later to fill in briefly any necessary background. Compare these two ways of handling the same material:

(1) One fine April afternoon three of us sixth-grade boys decided to skip school. We wandered for an hour or two through the outskirts of the town and finally landed at the ball park, where we began a game of old cat, doubly delightful because illicitly enjoyed. Bill finally hit the ball over the fence, where it went through the window of the caretaker's cottage.

(2) "Home run!" yelled Bill triumphantly, leaning on his bat while he watched the ball he had just struck sail over the park fence. But his triumph was short—a shattering of glass from the caretaker's cottage struck us all numb. A broken window on top of our earlier sin! For we three sixth-grade boys had skipped school that fine April afternoon, and after an hour or so of indecisive wandering through the outskirts of town had wound up at the ball park for a game of old cat—doubly delightful because illicitly enjoyed.

b. **Compression and expansion** In narration, you may compress or expand the time element to suit your purpose, summarizing ten unimportant years in less than a sentence but spending pages to recount the events of ten shattering seconds. Such variations in time can help you to emphasize important incidents and to ignore unimportant ones.

·:·   ·:·   ·:·

Creating the illusion of reality is the special strength of narrative, and your effectiveness will depend on it. Consider these devices to help you.

1. **Present tense verbs** can make past events come to life, as in "Then I start to run, and he throws to first, but Mac fumbles the ball." Remember, however, not to change tenses within a single part of your narrative unless you wish to indicate a change in time.

2. **Concrete and specific diction** is as important to narrative as it is to description. Help your readers to see and hear the events you narrate (and to smell, taste, and feel them if they involve other sensations). In dialogue, for instance, if the speakers reveal their emotions by their tone of voice, choose verbs that suggest the tone, such as *mutter, sigh,* or *yell.*

Caution: Do not overdo this. Vigorous words call attention to themselves. If what is said is important but not the manner of speaking, a simple *said* will be better.

3. **Dialogue,** directly quoted, is more lifelike and often more compact than indirect reporting of what was said. For example, compare the directly reported dialogue in "Yumbo" (page 108) with this indirectly reported version:

> The eruptive girl at the counter asked what the man wanted. He repeated that he wished to order a ham and cheese sandwich. The girl said that she was sorry but that they did not carry ham and cheese sandwiches. All that they had was what was on the menu board above her.

If you must make up the dialogue, take care that the content and the manner of speaking are appropriate to the speakers. For the conventional methods of punctuating dialogue, consult a handbook and note the examples in this unit.

4. **Characters, setting, and details** should be as real and vivid as the events of the narrative. Action does not occur in a vacuum. Give specific, concrete descriptions to show your readers when, where, and how it takes

place. Also show briefly the kinds of people involved by giving speech, actions, and specific details of appearance, not by making long explanations. Readers cannot have much interest in "us" or "them" if they are never told who "we" and "they" are. Compare these two versions of the same incident:

(a) We had been working for an hour to get our old truck jacked up so that my companion could change a tire that had gone flat on our way to town. Once more the jack slipped, and he started to try yet again.

(b) The slab of wood on which the jack was resting tilted gently into the roadside ooze and let the rear of the heavy truck down for the third time in that hour of mud and sweat.

"Dang it! Er—pardon me, miss" was the only reaction of the patient, elderly "hired hand" who was helping me to deliver my load of sheep. Without another word he gave his suspenders a hitch and crawled doggedly under the truck to try again.

5. **Personal experience** is always the best source of narrative material. A student once tried to write dramatically of a parachute jump; but factual errors revealed what she later confessed—that she had never even been in an airplane. Some professional writers of fiction can produce the illusion of reality without having known the people, visited the scenes, or experienced the events they describe. As a beginning writer, however, you will be wise to base your narratives entirely on your own experiences. Then you will have a large fund of accurate, specific details and can select the best to give your narrative reality.

EXAMPLES

In the following selections, the writers support their main points primarily by narration; you will find that nearly half the writers of the other selections in this book also use narratives, sometimes only a few sentences, sometimes several paragraphs long. Look again at Dawn Gorlitsky's second essay in Unit 1, at the final version of David Parker's essay in Unit 2, and at Zayra Raiano's essay, Unit 4-G. Also look at Santiago's "Super Bowl Champions" (6-A), Krulish's "The Start of a Long Day" (6-F), Davenport's " 'Trees' " (7-A), Richardson's "In Praise of the Archenemy" (9-D), Hoffman's "How to Have Free Entertainment with Your Meal" (9-G), Nemy's "Business Status—How Do You Rate?" (11-G), Peeples' "Branch Libraries" (12-B), Teitler's "Vietnam Memories: The War Within" (13-C), Claus's "Passing on the Legacy of Nature" (13-F), Hall's "Bring Back the Out-Loud Culture" (13-G), Twain's "Lagniappe" (14-D), Zinsser's "Letter from Home" (15-E), Shulman's "Love Is a Fallacy" (15-K), and all the essays in Unit 17.

5-A　　　　　　　　Yumbo

Andrew Ward

This short essay appeared in the *Atlantic Monthly* (1977). The writer narrates two experiences to explain his dislike of the way some restaurants treat their customers.

NARRATIVE
DEVICES
Setting,
character

Generaliza-
tion

Details

Generaliza-
tion
Details

Generaliza-
tion

Details

Generaliza-
tion

I was sitting at an inn with Kelly Susan, my ten-year-old niece, when she was handed the children's menu. It was printed in gay pastels on construction paper and gave her a choice of a Ferdinand Burger, a Freddie the Fish Stick, or a Porky Pig Sandwich. Like most children's 5 menus, it first anthropomorphized the ingredients and then killed them off. As Kelly read it her eyes grew large, and in them I could see gentle Ferdinand being led away to the stockyard, Freddie gasping at the end of a hook, Porky stuttering his entreaties as the ax descended. Kelly 10 Susan, alone in her family, is a resolute vegetarian and has already faced up to the dread that whispers to us as we slice our steaks. She wound up ordering a cheese sandwich, but the children's menu had ruined her appetite, and she spent the meal picking at her food. 15

Restaurants have always treated children badly. When I was small, my family used to travel a lot, and waitresses were forever calling me "Butch" and pinching my cheeks and making me wear paper bibs with slogans on them. Restaurants still treat children badly; the differ- 20 ence is that restaurants have lately taken to treating us all as if we were children. We are obliged to order an Egg McMuffin when we want breakfast, a Fishamajig when we want a fish sandwich, a Fribble when we want a milkshake, a Whopper when we want a hamburger with all 25 the fixings. Some of these names serve a certain purpose. By calling a milkshake a Fribble, for instance, the management need make no promise that it contains milk, or even that it was shaken.

But the primary purpose is to convert an essentially 30 bleak industry, mass-marketed fast foods, into something festive. The burger used to be a culinary last resort; now resorts are being built around it. The patrons

Details · in the commercials for burger franchises are all bug-
eyed and goofy, be they priests or grandmothers or   35
crane operators, and behave as if it were their patriotic
duty, their God-given right, to consume waxy buns,
translucent patties, chewy fries, and industrial strength
Coca-Cola.

Setting, · Happily, the patrons who actually slump into these   40
character · places are an entirely different matter. I remember with
fond admiration a tidy little man at the local Burger
King whom I overheard order a ham and cheese sandwich.

"A wha'?" the eruptive girl at the counter asked, pen-   45
cil poised over her computer card.

"I wish to order a ham and cheese sandwich," the man
repeated.

Dialogue · "I'm sorry, sir," the girl said, "but we don't carry ham
and cheese. All we got is what's on the board up there."   50

"Yes, I know," the man politely persisted, "but I believe it is up there. See? The ham and cheese?"

The girl gaped at the menu board behind her. "Oh,"
she finally exclaimed. "You mean a *Yumbo.* You want a
Yumbo. "   55

"The ham and cheese. Yes."

Conflict · "It's called a *Yumbo,* sir," the girl said. "Now, do you
want a Yumbo or not?"

Suspense · The man stiffened, "Yes, thank you," he said through
his teeth, "the *ham* and *cheese.* "   60

"Look," the girl shouted, "I've got to have an order
here. You're holding up the line. You want a *Yumbo,*
don't you? You want a *Yumbo?* "

But the tidy man was not going to say it, and thus
were they locked for a few more moments, until at last   65
he stood very straight, put on his hat, and departed intact.

1. Where does the writer first state his thesis?

2. How are the generalizations placed in relation to the specific details?

3. In the second illustration how does the writer indicate the stages of increasing tension between the counter girl and the man?

4. The first illustration contains no dialogue. Why is it unnecessary here?

5. Check all the definitions for these words in a large dictionary: *anthropomorphized, resolute.*

5-B   A Loaf of Bread and the Stars

Richard Wright

Wright narrates this experience in his autobiography, *Black Boy* (1937), in
which a major point is his struggle growing up black in a white-dominated society.

One day I went to the optical counter of a department store to
deliver a pair of eyeglasses. The counter was empty of customers
and a tall, florid-faced white man looked at me curiously. He was
unmistakably a Yankee, for his physical build differed sharply
from that of the lanky Southerner.   5
    "Will you please sign for this, sir?" I asked, presenting the
account book and the eyeglasses.
    He picked up the book and the glasses, but his eyes were still
upon me.
    "Say, boy, I'm from the North," he said quietly.   10
    I held very still. Was this a trap? He had mentioned a tabooed
subject and I wanted to wait until I knew what he meant. Among
the topics that southern white men do not like to discuss with
Negroes were the following: American white women; the Ku
Klux Klan; France, and how Negro soldiers fared while there;   15
Frenchwomen; Jack Johnson; the entire northern part of the
United States; the Civil War; Abraham Lincoln; U. S. Grant;
General Sherman; Catholics; the Pope; Jews; the Republican
party; slavery; social equality; Communism; Socialism; the 13th,
14th, and 15th Amendments to the Constitution or any topic   20
calling for positive knowledge or manly self-assertion on the part
of the Negro. The most accepted topics were sex and religion. I
did not look at the man or answer. With one sentence he had
lifted out of the silent dark the race question and I stood on the
edge of a precipice.   25
    "Don't be afraid of me," he went on. "I just want to ask you
one question."
    "Yes, sir," I said in a waiting, neutral tone.
    "Tell me, boy, are you hungry?" he asked seriously.
    I stared at him. He had spoken one word that touched the very   30
soul of me, but I could not talk to him, could not let him know
that I was starving myself to save money to go north. I did not
trust him. But my face did not change its expression.

"Oh, no, sir," I said, managing a smile.

I was hungry and he knew it: but he was a white man and I felt   35
that if I told him I was hungry I would have been revealing
something shameful.

"Boy, I can see hunger in your face and eyes," he said.

"I get enough to eat," I lied.

"Then why do you keep so thin?" he asked me.   40

"Well, I suppose I'm just that way, naturally," I lied.

"You're just scared, boy," he said.

"Oh, no, sir," I lied again.

I could not look at him. I wanted to leave the counter, yet he
was a white man and I had learned not to walk abruptly away from   45
a white man when he was talking to me. I stood, my eyes looking
away. He ran his hand into his pocket and pulled out a dollar bill.

"Here, take this dollar and buy yourself some food," he said.

"No, sir," I said.

"Don't be a fool," he said. "You're ashamed to take it. God,   50
boy, don't let a thing like that stop you from taking a dollar and
eating."

The more he talked the more it became impossible for me to
take the dollar. I wanted it, but I could not look at it. I wanted
to speak, but I could not move my tongue. I wanted him to leave   55
me alone. He frightened me.

"Say something," he said.

All about us in the store were piles of goods; white men and
women went from counter to counter. It was summer and from
a high ceiling was suspended a huge electric fan that whirred. I   60
stood waiting for the white man to give me the signal that would
let me go.

"I don't understand it," he said through his teeth. "How far
did you go in school?"

"Through the ninth grade, but it was really the eighth," I told   65
him. "You see, our studies in the ninth grade were more or less
a review of what we had in the eighth grade."

Silence. He had not asked me for this long explanation, but I
had spoken at length to fill up the yawning, shameful gap that
loomed between us; I had spoken to try to drag the unreal nature   70
of the conversation back to safe and sound southern ground. Of
course, the conversation was real; it dealt with my welfare, but it
had brought to the surface of day all the dark fears I had known
all my life. The Yankee white man did not know how dangerous
his words were.   75

(There are some elusive, profound, recondite things that men
find hard to say to other men; but with the Negro it is the little

things of life that become hard to say, for these tiny items shape
his destiny. A man will seek to express his relation to the stars;
but when a man's consciousness has been riveted upon obtaining   80
a loaf of bread, that loaf of bread is as important as the stars.)

Another white man walked up to the counter and I sighed with
relief.

"Do you want the dollar?" the man asked.

"No, sir," I whispered.   85

"All right," he said. "Just forget it."

He signed the account book and took the eyeglasses. I stuffed
the book into my bag and turned from the counter and walked
down the aisle, feeling a physical tingling along my spine, knowing that the white man knew I was really hungry. I avoided him   90
after that. Whenever I saw him I felt in a queer way that he was
my enemy, for he knew how I felt and the safety of my life in the
South depended upon how well I concealed from all whites what
I felt.

1. Where does Wright place his chief expository remarks?

2. How is this placement different from that in the first example of narrative
used for an expository purpose?

3. What would have been the effect if Wright had placed all of them at the very
end? at the beginning?

4. Check all the definitions for these words in a large dictionary: *elusive, profound, recondite.*

5-C   A New Life

Carl Granville *(student)*

It was 9:26 P.M. on December 11th, 1974. I had awaited
this moment nine months. I had left work early to be by her
side. She was always adamant that I should be there when it
happened.

She had been in the labor room for almost ten hours. The
endless screams from the woman in the next room made my wife
become more and more frightened. As gently as possible, I tried
to calm her, but I myself had been having doubts. What if something went wrong? What if their lives were in danger? My fears

were forgotten as the baby's head began to emerge. I felt a sparkling tingle throughout my body. What a moment! The birth of my child!

"Mr. Granville, you'll have to leave now." Pause.

"Sir, you'll have to leave now." The voice was firm, official.

It was like being rudely interrupted in the middle of a wonderful dream, and a full minute elapsed before I realized what was happening. I started to speak, but seeing the futility of a protest, I dejectedly left the room. At 9:35 P.M. they whisked her off to the delivery room.

Here I am in the waiting room. There are three more expectant fathers present. One is anxiously wearing out the carpet, pacing up and down. Another seems nervously impatient. The third one, seated in a corner away from the rest, seems to be in a daze. I sit and try to read a book.

"This is your first?" asks the impatient one.

"Uhh?"

"This your first?"

"Oh, yes . . . yes."

"This is my third. I got two girls already. Man, girls cost too much, but with my old lady always wrapped around me, what else can I do?"

My sudden laughter disrupts the pacer and breaks the trance of the man in the corner.

"Oh, man," the talkative one goes on, "she's been in there for about a half-hour already. What the hell's keeping them this long?"

My analysis was right. He is impatient. Five minutes later the nurse announces that he has girl number three. He shakes my hand gloomily and wishes me luck as he leaves. Immediately after, a very broad smile runs across the face of the man in the corner. He has just heard that his wife has given birth to an eight-pound boy.

I put down the book. "I hope I get a boy, too," I think. I start to imagine all the fun we will have together. Why, when he's six, I'll only be twenty-six myself. He will be "wicked" but obedient. He will be just like his daddy. We will have such fun. Please, please, let it be a boy.

The pacer leaves to purchase a soda. We have exchanged only a few words so far. In his absence the nurse appears to announce that his wife gave birth to a ten-pound boy. I find that his wife is the woman who was screaming. I greet him with the news as he returns, and his face lights up like a Christmas tree. He startles me with a tremendous shout of glee. I cannot help feeling happy

for him. The joy in his face is overwhelming. Now more than
ever I want a boy.

The nurse appears again. "Mr. Granville, your wife gave birth
to a girl. She weighs six pounds, eleven ounces."

The time is 10:11 P.M. For the second time tonight I feel throbs   55
of depression. My wife is aware of this as I stand by her bed. She
reminds me that I should be thankful that she and the baby came
through in good health. I feel ashamed at my show of depression.
Oh, but I so wanted a boy. How can I have much fun with a girl?
Try as I do, it's hard to shake off the depression that engulfs me.   60
After half-heartedly joking with my wife for a while, I leave for
home.

I buy myself a tall can of beer to celebrate my parenthood and
I telephone my best friend to let him know the news. While I am
chatting with him, a new thought dawns. What important differ-   65
ence, other than sexual, is there between a boy and a girl? I mean,
why can't I have as much fun with a girl as I think I will have with
a boy? Why try to put people into pigeonholes? Why don't I give
her a chance to prove herself?

The next day at 8:40 A.M. I present myself at the Kings County   70
Hospital, maternity section. I am joyful with a vibrant new perspective, evident in my bounce and spirit. I kiss my baby and look
upon her not as a girl or boy, but as a living, capable, human
being. I ask my wife's forgiveness for my behavior last night and
tell her how much I love her for bringing us closer together   75
through our baby.

Now, two years later, I could not be happier as a father. I have
kept my resolution to treat my daughter as a human being, which
in turn has made me more appreciative of my wife. The fun that
I have with my daughter goes way beyond my expectations; the   80
joy she has brought into my life can never be described in mere
words. She surely has had a positive effect in changing my attitude
towards others, sex notwithstanding. As a matter of fact, I could
not care less whether my next baby is a boy or a girl.

I'll always treasure my daughter for this change in me, but right   85
now all I can do is reflect on the beauty, the mystery, the sweetness, the power of life and love. Thank you, Chère, and you, too,
Pauline.

1. Why does the author begin with verbs in the past tense and then shift to verbs
in the present tense?

2. What do the references to the specific times and the descriptions of the other
expectant fathers contribute? Why is the nurse only a voice?

5-D   Your Parents Must Be Proud

Richard Rodriguez

The author, the son of Mexican immigrants, was born and raised in California. Although he entered the first grade speaking almost no English, he progressed rapidly, eventually earning a Ph.D. in English literature at the University of California at Berkeley and teaching there. In the following selection from his autobiography, *The Hunger of Memory* (1982), he describes some of the difficulties and successes of his early struggles to adjust to life in the United States.

"Your parents must be very proud of you." People began to say that to me about the time I was in sixth grade. To answer affirmatively, I'd smile. Shyly I'd smile, never betraying my sense of irony: I was not proud of my mother and father. I was embarrassed by their lack of education. It was not that I ever thought   5 they were stupid, though stupidly I took for granted their enormous native intelligence. Simply, what mattered to me was that they were not like my teachers.

But, "Why didn't you tell us about the award?" my mother demanded, her frown weakened by pride. At the grammar school   10 ceremony several weeks after, her eyes were brighter than the trophy I'd won. Pushing back the hair from my forehead, she whispered that I had "shown" the *gringos.* A few minutes later, I heard my father speak to my teacher and felt ashamed of his labored, accented words. Then guilty for the shame. I felt such   15 contrary feelings. (There is no simple roadmap through the heart of the scholarship boy.) My teacher was so soft-spoken and her words were edged sharp and clean. I admired her until it seemed to me that she spoke too carefully. Sensing that she was condescending to them, I became nervous. Resentful. Protective. I tried   20 to move my parents away. "You both must be very proud of Richard," the nun said. They responded quickly. (They were proud.) "We are proud of all our children!" Then this afterthought: "They sure didn't get their brains from us." They all laughed. I smiled.   25

Tightening the irony into a knot was the knowledge that my parents were always behind me. They made success possible. They evened the path. They sent their children to parochial schools because the nuns "teach better." They paid a tuition they couldn't afford. They spoke English to us.   30

For their children my parents wanted chances they never had—
an easier way. It saddened my mother to learn that some relatives
forced their children to start working right after high school. To
her children she would say, "Get all the education you can." In
schooling she recognized the key to job advancement. And with   35
the remark she remembered her past.

As a girl new to America my mother had been awarded a high
school diploma by teachers too careless or busy to notice that she
hardly spoke English. On her own, she determined to learn how
to type. That skill got her jobs typing envelopes in letter shops,   40
and it encouraged in her an optimism about the possibility of
advancement. (Each morning when her sisters put on uniforms,
she chose a bright-colored dress.) The years of young woman-
hood passed, and her typing speed increased. She also became an
excellent speller of words she mispronounced. "And I've never   45
been to college," she'd say, smiling, when her children asked her
to spell words they were too lazy to look up in a dictionary.

In contrast to my mother, my father never verbally encouraged
his children's academic success. Nor did he often praise us. My
mother had to remind him to "say something" to one of his   50
children who scored some academic success. But whereas my
mother saw in education the opportunity for job advancement,
my father recognized that education provided an even more startling possibility: It could enable a person to escape from a life of
mere labor.   55

In Mexico, orphaned when he was eight, my father left school
to work as an "apprentice" for an uncle. Twelve years later, he
left Mexico in frustration and arrived in America. He had great
expectations then of becoming an engineer. ("Work for my hands
and my head.") He knew a Catholic priest who promised to get   60
him money enough to study full time for a high school diploma.
But the promises came to nothing. Instead there was a dark
succession of warehouse, cannery, and factory jobs. After work he
went to night school along with my mother. A year, two passed.
Nothing much changed, except that fatigue worked its way into   65
the bone; then everything changed. He didn't talk anymore of
becoming an engineer. He stayed outside on the steps of the
school while my mother went inside to learn typing and shorthand.

By the time I was born, my father worked at "clean" jobs. For   70
a time he was a janitor at a fancy department store. ("Easy work;
the machines do it all.") Later he became a dental technician.
("Simple.") But by then he was pessimistic about the ultimate

meaning of work and the possibility of ever escaping its claims. In some of my earliest memories of him, my father already seems aged by fatigue. (He has never really grown old like my mother.) From boyhood to manhood, I have remembered him in a single image: seated, asleep on the sofa, his head thrown back in a hideous corpselike grin, the evening newspaper spread out before him. "But look at all you've accomplished," his best friend said to him once. My father said nothing. Only smiled.

It was my father who laughed when I claimed to be tired by reading and writing. It was he who teased me for having soft hands. (He seemed to sense that some great achievement of leisure was implied by my papers and books.) It was my father who became angry while watching on television some woman at the Miss America contest tell the announcer that she was going to college. ("Majoring in fine arts.") "College!" he snarled. He despised the trivialization of higher education, the inflated grades and cheapened diplomas, the half education that so often passed as mass education in my generation.

It was my father again who wondered why I didn't display my awards on the wall of my bedroom. He said he liked to go to doctors' offices and see their certificates and degrees on the wall. ("Nice.") My citations from school got left in closets at home. The gleaming figure astride one of my trophies was broken, wingless, after hitting the ground. My medals were placed in a jar of loose change. And when I lost my high school diploma, my father found it as it was about to be thrown out with the trash. Without telling me, he put it away with his own things for safe-keeping.

These memories slammed together at the instant of hearing that refrain familiar to all scholarship students: "Your parents must be very proud. . . ." Yes, my parents were proud. I knew it. But my parents regarded my progress with more than mere pride. They endured my early precocious behavior—but with what private anger and humiliation? As their children got older and would come home to challenge ideas both of them held, they argued before submitting to the force of logic or superior factual evidence with the disclaimer, "It's what we were taught in our time to believe." These discussions ended abruptly, though my mother remembered them on other occasions when she complained that our "big ideas" were going to our heads. More acute was her complaint that the family wasn't close anymore, like some others she knew. Why weren't we close, "more in the Mexican

style"? Everyone is so private, she added. And she mimicked the
yes and no answers she got in reply to her questions. Why didn't
we talk more? (My father never asked.) I never said.

I was the first in my family who asked to leave home when it
came time to go to college. I had been admitted to Stanford, one   120
hundred miles away. My departure would only make physically
apparent the separation that had occurred long before. But it was
going too far. In the months preceding my leaving, I heard the
question my mother never asked except indirectly. In the hot
kitchen, tired at the end of her workday, she demanded to know,   125
"Why aren't the colleges here in Sacramento good enough for
you? They are for your brother and sister." In the middle of a car
ride, not turning to face me, she wondered, "Why do you need
to go so far away?" Late at night, ironing, she said with disgust,
"Why do you have to put us through this big expense? You know   130
your scholarship will never cover it all." But when September
came there was a rush to get everything ready. In a bedroom that
last night I packed the big brown valise, and my mother sat nearby
sewing initials onto the clothes I would take. And she said no
more about my leaving.   135

Months later, two weeks of Christmas vacation: The first hours
home were the hardest. ("What's new?") My parents and I sat in
the kitchen for a conversation. (But, lacking the same words to
develop our sentences and to shape our interests, what was there
to say? What could I tell them of the term paper I had just finished   140
on the "universality of Shakespeare's appeal"?) I mentioned only
small, obvious things: my dormitory life; weekend trips I had
taken; random events. They responded with news of their own.
(One was almost grateful for a family crisis about which there was
much to discuss.) We tried to make our conversation seem like   145
more than an interview.

1. Where and how does Rodriguez use direct quotation to support and illustrate his narrative?

2. What specific concrete details does the writer use to help us visualize the
scenes?

3. What details show the differences in the personalities of the writer's parents?

5-E A Cultural Divorce

Elizabeth Wong

The conflict between generations in a family is more intense when there is a cultural gap between parents and children as well as the inevitable age gap. In most of her essay Wong seems still to have her childhood desire to ignore her Chinese heritage and become thoroughly "American," but her last four words set the whole essay in a new light.

Compare Wong's experiences with those described by Richard Rodriguez in 5-D.

It's still there, the Chinese school on Yale Street where my brother and I used to go. Despite the new coat of paint and the high wire fence, the school I knew 10 years ago remains remarkably, stoically the same.

Every day at 5 P.M., instead of playing with our fourth- and 5
fifth-grade friends or sneaking out to the empty lot to hunt ghosts and animal bones, my brother and I had to go to Chinese school. No amount of kicking, screaming, or pleading could dissuade my mother, who was solidly determined to have us learn the language of our heritage. 10

Forcibly, she walked us the seven long, hilly blocks from our home to school, depositing our defiant tearful faces before the stern principal. My only memory of him is that he swayed on his heels like a palm tree, and he always clasped his impatient twitching hands behind his back. I recognized him as a repressed mania- 15
cal child killer, and knew that if we ever saw his hands we'd be in big trouble.

We all sat in little chairs in an empty auditorium. The room smelled like Chinese medicine, an imported faraway mustiness. Like ancient mothballs or dirty closets. I hated that smell. I fa- 20
vored crisp new scents. Like the soft French perfume that my American teacher wore in public school.

There was a stage far to the right, flanked by an American flag and the flag of the Nationalist Republic of China, which was also red, white and blue but not as pretty. 25

Although the emphasis at the school was mainly language—speaking, reading, writing—the lessons always began with an exercise in politeness. With the entrance of the teacher, the best student would tap a bell and everyone would get up, kowtow,

and chant, "Sing san ho," the phonetic for "How are you,   30
teacher?"

Being ten years old, I had better things to learn than ideographs copied painstakingly in lines that ran right to left from the
tip of a *moc but,* a real ink pen that had to be held in an awkward
way if blotches were to be avoided. After all, I could do the   35
multiplication tables, name the satellites of Mars, and write reports on "Little Women" and "Black Beauty." Nancy Drew, my
favorite book heroine, never spoke Chinese.

The language was a source of embarrassment. More times than
not, I had tried to disassociate myself from the nagging loud voice   40
that followed me wherever I wandered in the nearby American
supermarket outside Chinatown. The voice belonged to my
grandmother, a fragile woman in her seventies who could out-
shout the best of the street vendors. Her humor was raunchy, her
Chinese rhythmless, patternless. It was quick, it was loud, it was   45
unbeautiful. It was not like the quiet, lilting romance of French
or the gentle refinement of the American South. Chinese sounded
pedestrian. Public.

In Chinatown, the comings and goings of hundreds of Chinese
on their daily tasks sounded chaotic and frenzied. I did not want   50
to be thought of as mad, as talking gibberish. When I spoke
English, people nodded at me, smiled sweetly, said encouraging
words. Even the people in my culture would cluck and say that
I'd do well in life. "My, doesn't she move her lips fast," they
would say, meaning that I'd be able to keep up with the world   55
outside Chinatown.

My brother was even more fanatical than I about speaking
English. He was especially hard on my mother, criticizing her,
often cruelly, for her pidgin speech—smatterings of Chinese scattered like chop suey in her conversation. "It's not 'What it is,'   60
Mom," he'd say in exasperation. "It's 'What *is* it, what *is* it, what
is it!'" Sometimes Mom might leave out an occasional "the" or
"a," or perhaps a verb of being. He would stop her in mid-
sentence: "Say it again, Mom. Say it right." When he tripped over
his own tongue, he'd blame it on her: "See, Mom, it's all your   65
fault. You set a bad example."

What infuriated my mother most was when my brother cor-
nered her on her consonants, especially "r." My father had played
a cruel joke on Mom by assigning her an American name that her
tongue wouldn't allow her to say. No matter how hard she tried,   70
"Ruth" always ended up "Luth" or "Roof."

After two years of writing with a *moc but* and reciting words
with multiples of meanings, I finally was granted a cultural divorce. I was permitted to stop Chinese school.

I thought of myself as multicultural. I preferred tacos to egg   75
rolls; I enjoyed Cinco de Mayo more than Chinese New Year.
At last, I was one of you; I wasn't one of them.
Sadly, I still am.

1. What is the Cinco de Mayo?

2. Until her final sentence, the writer records her early childhood dislike of
Chinese culture without criticizing herself. What hints does she give that she now
thinks she was mistaken?

3. Check the etymology, denotation, and connotation of *kowtow, ideographs,
pidgin.*

5-F   The Twelfth Day of Christmas

Denise Lowe *(student)*

Compare this writer's reaction to death with George Orwell's reaction to a
death in which he is less personally involved in "A Hanging" ("Essays for Further
Reading"-B).

On Monday night, I climbed into bed completely exhausted.
The frantic activity of Christmas and New Year celebrations was
finally over, and I could look forward to re-establishing a routine.
My husband would be back at work, my three-year-old daughter
back at play school, and I could at last get to know and enjoy my   5
new infant daughter. Victoria was now fifteen days old; she had
a mass of black hair, and eyes so dark they seemed as endless as
the night sky. Already her sweetness and beauty had won our
hearts. However, the events of the next thirty-six hours destroyed
my orderly plans.   10
Ivan woke me on Tuesday morning to say he was leaving for
work and that the baby was making grunting noises as if she
would soon be awake. I leapt out of bed and went over to the
basinette because my body was making me painfully aware that
it was well past feeding time. I picked her up, but when she   15
showed no interest in nursing, panic surged through me. Something was wrong. The grunting noises continued as I hurriedly
dressed and called the pediatrician. He calmly told me to meet
him at his office immediately, where he conducted a swift, expert
examination of Victoria. He gently said, "I want to admit her to   20

the hospital. She has a lung infection." I felt another surge of panic, but he smiled, adding, "I don't think it's anything really serious." So I relaxed a little, confident in his healing ability.

At the hospital, a nurse took Victoria from me and numerous consent forms were presented for my signature. Meanwhile, the   25
doctor scrubbed up and performed a spinal tap. To my horror, the fluid drawn was cloudy, almost like milk, and I began to scream hysterically, "She has meningitis!"

A nurse took me gently but firmly by the arm and led me to the admitting office where, in a daze, I signed still more papers.   30
In my panic I could not recall Ivan's work phone number so I called my mother and asked her to contact him.

When I returned to the pediatric unit, I was told that my baby was no longer there; she had been transferred to the Intensive Care Nursery. By now I felt a sense of unreality—this was surely   35
a bad dream.

By the time my husband and parents arrived, our baby was in a sterile incubator, fighting for her life. She was connected by a maze of tubes and wires to numerous electronic devices that clicked and slurped as they mechanically recorded her vital signs.   40
The priest came to baptise Victoria, but even his eyes avoided ours and he spoke not a word to us.

In the fifteen hours that followed, our infant underwent a battery of procedures, including X-rays, blood tests, antibiotic administrations, EKG's, EEG's, all performed by backstage, faceless   45
people—experts in white coats.

At 2:00 A.M. the doctor told us to go home; there was nothing we could do but pray. His words were clear and simple enough, but their real meaning failed to penetrate our fogged minds. Ivan and I spent a tortured night filled with restless dreams, and at 7:00   50
A.M. we returned to the hospital.

In dismay and disbelief, we heard the doctor say she was unconscious, she'd had several seizures during the night, and she was hemorrhaging internally. Why wouldn't someone pinch me hard to wake me from this nightmare?   55

Without speaking, we scrubbed up and entered the sterile room to see for ourselves. Ivan soon walked out in tears, but I stayed to stroke her head. Her eyes briefly fluttered open in response to my touch, but they were clouded and unseeing. For two hours I stood, holding her tiny hand in mine, praying that   60
somehow my strength could be transferred into her body so that she could win the fight.

I fell crying into my husband's arms as I was at last asked to leave. A sense of helplessness enveloped us as we sat together in

numb silence. After what seemed an eternity, the pediatrician 65
emerged. Head bowed, he took our hands and whispered, "It's
all over. I'm sorry."

Holding my dead baby, I could not accept the finality of her
death. She was still warm; why couldn't God breathe life back into
her as he had into the Centurion's daughter? "Why not? Where 70
are you, God?" cried my tormented soul! My tears soaked her
hair as I rocked her in my arms. This was the Twelfth Day of
Christmas, the Feast of the Epiphany, celebrating the visit of the
Magi to the Christ Child, but no one came bearing gifts for my
baby. The day she was born I had nicknamed her "my cherub"; 75
now she was indeed a cherub.

This experience changed me and changed my life. It made me
realize the harsh truth that I too am vulnerable; bad things do not
happen only to other people. Not all tragedies make the headlines; they occur insidiously to someone, somewhere, every day. 80
Life is as fragile as a crystal rose, a precious gift from God to be
cherished and never taken for granted.

1. The writer uses many specific details to help her readers imagine her experience. Which do you find particularly vivid?

2. The writer presents her thesis statement in her final paragraph. In your
opinion, would the essay be easier to understand if she had placed it at the beginning?

5-G   If in Doubt, Clout It

Sue Birchmore

The author of this humorous account, first published in the *New Scientist* in
1989, is a design engineer working in England. She gives several brief narratives to
illustrate her implied thesis: A simple physical action can often solve a complex
mechanical problem.

A computer terminal with which I am acquainted whistles. It's
a nice, new, modern terminal, anti-glare technicolor screen and
all that, but every so often it emits an annoying whistling noise,
just at the upper threshold of the audible frequency range. I told
a more experienced user about this irritating habit. 5

"Ah, easily cured," he said, delivering a nonchalant thump to
the side of the offending machine.

The noise stopped immediately.

I derived a vague sense of comfort from the incident. Computers have always seemed to me to be sophisticated contraptions   10
from the world of electrickery, a little beyond the understanding
of mere mechanicals. Finding them amenable to the good, old-
fashioned engineering technique of a hefty clout makes them
seem somehow friendlier.

Shortly after the whistling terminal, I encountered another   15
piece of advanced technology, in the shape of the checkout computer at the book counter in W.H. Smith. The girl behind the
counter vainly tried to persuade it to register my purchase and spit
out a receipt. With a weary sigh which indicated that this was no
new phenomenon, she belted the machine on the head a few   20
times until it bleeped complainingly and condescended to cooperate.

Then there are those handy, high-tech central locking systems
obligatory in all self-respecting cars with pretensions to sophistica-
tion. Once I had occasion to use a company car with such a lock   25
for a business trip: I got as far as Watford Gap, locked the machine
while I went for a cup of tea, and returned to find it sulking and
refusing to let me back in. I eventually made an undignified entry
head first through the hatchback.

I was subsequently informed—I am in no position to test the   30
truth of the statement, as my finances don't run to that sort of
car—that a sharp blow to the correct spot close to the lock will
trip the mechanism and allow a distressed driver (or a thief)
entry rather more easily than the old-fashioned sort of lock used
to.   35

All of this leads me to suspect that the old adage "If all else fails,
hit it" still holds good, despite the advance of technology. Of
course, I really can't approve of it. Here is a machine which
armies of engineers have laboured to design and manufacture;
they have written handbooks to instruct the user in its correct   40
care, operation and maintenance; they provide back-up in the
form of advice and servicing; and here is a user subjecting the
delicate, complex mechanism which is the result of their en-
deavours to crude swipes with a blunt instrument.

And yet, sometimes, it works. Presumably, a sharp shock has   45
the effect of overcoming friction and allowing the relevant bits to
drop into their proper places.

There's an old story which periodically circulates among engineers. Once upon a time, a large, expensive and sophisticated
production line jerked to an unscheduled halt. A senior consult-   50
ing engineer was summoned post-haste. He surveyed the line,

thought carefully, and then took out a watchmaker's hammer and gave the mechanism a sharp tap.

Instantly, it sprang to life again.

The owners of the line were delighted—until they received a bill for £200. A bit steep for 10 minutes' work, surely? Without a word, the engineer withdrew his bill and wrote out a new one:

"Fee for one tap with hammer: 1p

Fee for knowing exactly where to tap: £199.99"

If in doubt, clout. So goes the cynical saying. In truth, an ignorant thwack usually does more for the user's temper than for the machine, but I suspect there is something inherent in human nature which will go on making us resort to violence against our own creations. Perhaps we should start designing machines with built-in protection against user abuse. Better still, take inspiration from those American alarm clocks, shaped like baseballs, which you switch off by hurling them against a wall. Perhaps, too, we should incorporate into designs some mechanism which responds to beating by making grovelling apologies for the machine's poor performance. I can just see it:

User: You scrambled my files again, you useless heap of junk. *Thump!*

Computer: I'm sorry. It was all my fault.

User: I've got a good mind to wipe your hard disc for good. *Thud!*

Computer: Don't hit me! I'll get it right next time, I promise.

It wouldn't get the work done any quicker, but it might do something for reducing the incidence of high blood pressure in people working in industry.

Note: In British currency a penny (1 p) is roughly equal to one and half cents in American currency, and £200 to $300.

1. What narrative devices does the writer use to make her account more lively?

2. How many short narratives does she use to illustrate her points? Which are drawn from her own experience? Which are based on hearsay or are imaginary?

3. Where has the writer used especially concrete, specific words and phrases to make her narratives more vivid?

4. Check the etymology, denotation, and connotation of *amenable, obligatory, adage, grovelling.*

5-H   Conflict

Roger A. Painter *(student)*

The writer begins by narrating three incidents to illustrate his point and lead to his expository discussion. Note how the ending unifies the essay and emphasizes the conflict.

He came into the house quietly and made sure the door was locked. He walked silently to his bedroom and turned the lamp on low-beam.

"Where have you been?"

"Mother, I've been out."   5

"What were you doing?"

"Mother, I was out."

"Who were you with?"

"Mother, please go to sleep. I was out."

"But what were you doing this late?"   10

"Mother, if you didn't live here and I went to school here you wouldn't know I was out and it wouldn't bother you."

"But I'm worried."

"I know, Mother. It is late. Good night."

∴   ∴   ∴

"Where were you?"   15

"Hello."

His bicycle had jangled as he put the kickstand down and the sound brought her to the door.

"I was studying."

"Have you had supper?"   20

"Yes."

"Where?"

"At the Union."

"I had supper for you."

"I'm sorry. I tried to call."   25

∴   ∴   ∴

"You can't go to class in that outfit."

"Why not?"

"You have better shoes than that. Those things look like your parents don't give you any money."

"This is what I feel like wearing today."   30
"You had better not leave with those shoes on."
"I'm almost late now—good-bye."
"Change them."
"Good-bye."

⋰ ⋰ ⋰

With these sketches I hope to illustrate the sometimes trivial,   35
but nevertheless real conflict from which I draw certain conclusions. Residing under the wings of the hen in the postadolescent
years may cause problems that, while seemingly only trivial at the
time, collectively produce an amount of friction that makes
smoke.   40
   Living at home has advantages for the college student: automobile, cheap room and board, and a vast number of other benefits
easily enumerated by most parents. These things tend to build
dependence on parents that is hard to break later on. At school,
attendance is not taken in most classes, daily assignments are not   45
collected, and students are, to a large extent, on their own. The
campus students, in most cases, must keep a watch on their money
supply, their time, and their actions, and in general must learn to
get along without their parents. This is part of education that I
miss.   50
   I am rebellious, as is natural at my age, and, whereas the campus students take this feeling out in actions and bull-sessions with
their friends, I take it out on my parents. This isolation and lack
of communication with campus life is one of the greatest problems the "townies" have to cope with. The effort to fit in socially   55
is hampered by the fact that many campus organizations and
activities are organized on the housing-unit basis: intramurals,
dances, programs, and a large number of lesser things. But it is
hard to justify a separate residence and its expense for these
activities alone.   60
   The questions and conflicts are many, and I think that the
conflict of interest will inevitably cause a break. If the break is
hastened by prolonged and forced confrontation, it is less likely
to be friendly. The on-campus student does not have the burden
of forcing such a break, and I think this is much better. It is a real   65
problem that I face, and it is not an easy one.

⋰ ⋰ ⋰

"What are you writing?"
"A rhetoric theme, Mother."

ASSIGNMENTS

1. Think back to your earliest memories of school. What incident stands out most? Why? Compose a narrative about it in which you give your readers the details they need to be able to picture the experience and relive it with you.

2. Choose a personal experience for which an old proverb such as "He who hesitates is lost," "A stitch in time saves nine," "A friend in need is a friend indeed," "Man proposes, God disposes," or "Penny-wise but pound-foolish" would make an appropriate title. Then narrate the experience briefly in such a way that your readers will see your point with little or no direct explanation from you.

3. Imagine that the editor of a magazine that tries to appeal to the "general reader" plans to use one of the photographs on page 55 or 101 and has asked you to write a narrative of about 300 to 500 words for which the photograph would be an appropriate illustration. You may draw on your own experience, actual events, your imagination, or any combination of these.

4. Most well-known children's stories have strong moral points. Choose a familiar one such as "Little Red Ridinghood," "Cinderella," or "Jack and the Beanstalk" and retell it with specific descriptive detail and as much suspense as you can create, building up to the moral point. Imagine that you will read your version to an intelligent, appreciative child about seven or eight years old.

5. Use the plot of the same story or a similar one, but this time give it a modern setting and logical explanations for any fantastic elements. Imagine that your readers will be people of your age and general interests.

6. Choose any fairly short television drama or comedy that you have enjoyed and that made a strong point. Retell it as a story, with full background detail.

7. Choose an editorial with which you agree and compose a short anecdote that illustrates its point in some way and that could therefore be used to introduce it.

8. Study the contribution that narrative makes to exposition in examples in other units, particularly those mentioned in the introductory note for the examples in this unit.

Observing Details—An Experiment

Close observation of the details of your subject is essential. If you are inaccurate or omit something that your readers want to know, they will lose confidence in you and your thesis.

How good an observer are you? Test yourself by examining these photographs and then answering the questions on the next page. Be honest with yourself and do not turn back to look at the photographs until you have finished the experiment.

Photograph A   Teresa Sabala/NYT Pictures (Census Bureau-computer disk file)

Photograph B   Edward Hausner/NYT Pictures

QUESTIONS ON THE PHOTOGRAPHS

Photograph A

1. What is the man wearing?

2. Can you see both of his hands or only one?

3. How many rows of disks are on each side of the aisle?

4. How many empty places show where discs have been removed?

Photograph B

1. What bird is near the ceiling in the corner of the room?

2. How many pictures of Mickey and/or Minnie Mouse can be seen?

3. How many Coca Cola signs can be seen?

4. In what position are the left arm and leg of the man seated near the center of the picture?

5. What time does the clock say?

6. Where is the telephone?

WRITING ASSIGNMENTS BASED ON THE PHOTOGRAPHS

1. Assume that these photographs are to be published in your college newspaper and compose a title and a statement of about 50 words for each to attract the readers' attention.

2. Assume that these photographs are to be published together as a contrast in ways to organize things. Compose an essay of about 250 words in which you discuss the methods of classification suggested by the two pictures.

UNIT 6

Exemplification

"A picture is worth a thousand words," the familiar saying tells us. A single example—a picture in words—can help to explain, support, and bring to life a theory or opinion more effectively than a thousand generalizations can. Of all the ways to make theories and opinions understandable, examples are by far the most widely used and helpful.

The writer of "More Power to You" (4-C) does not merely claim that "To watch a jet engine spring to life is to feel that power." He goes on to give us the sight, sound, smell, and throbbing feeling of the engine. Andrew Ward does not merely claim that "Restaurants have always treated children badly" (5-A). He immediately tells us that when he was small "waitresses were forever calling me 'Butch' and pinching my cheek and making me wear paper bibs with slogans on them." You may have noticed that all the pieces of writing in this book are presented as "examples" of exposition and are further labeled as examples of description, narration, and so on, because they are chosen to help explain what those generalized terms mean.

Choosing what examples to use and deciding where and how to use them in any piece of writing will depend on your answers to these closely related questions:

1. **What is your precise subject?**

2. **Who are your intended readers**—what are they likely to know of your subject, what are they likely *not* to know of it, and what opinions on it are they likely to have formed?

3. **What is your main purpose** in writing on this particular subject for these particular readers?

4. **What should you most emphasize** to achieve your purpose?

The less your readers know about the subject, the more they will need examples to help them understand it and the more detailed and basic those examples must be. Even knowledgeable readers need examples when the subject is complex or controversial. If your main purpose is to do more than simply inform them, choose examples that are lively and colorful as well as understandable.

This advice will be clearer if we take it ourselves and illustrate it with examples. Imagine that two recent graduates of your college who now live far away and who are ardent soccer fans have asked you to write them about a recent game. You know that they will be happy to learn that the home team played well. In your narrative of who did what and when during the game, you will therefore choose examples of the players' skill to support your claim that the team played well. Since your intended readers are soccer fans and familiar with the team and the college, you can freely use technical terms and local references. To give your readers the feeling that they are actually watching the game, you will include as many examples of the play in as much detail as you have the time and strength to write, arranging them in chronological order.

Now, imagine instead that your intended readers are recent graduates who have little interest in soccer but who love the college and will be pleased to learn that the team has won a major victory. For them you will select the most dramatic moment of the game as your main example of the team's skill and describe it in some detail but with few technical terms. To increase the dramatic effect, you will lead up to it with short descriptions of three or four exciting moments as examples of the team's skill, starting with the least dramatic so that your sequence will build up to the most important moment.

Next, imagine that your intended readers are friends who live too far away for you to see them often and who have never visited your college. You suspect that they have asked you to describe a soccer game only out of politeness because they know of your interest in the sport. For them you will choose examples—two or three at the most—with a general appeal, those primarily of human interest and, if possible, with humorous overtones. You will present these briefly with just enough specific detail to make them colorful, saving the best for last to serve as a climax and using technical terms only when you also define them.

You may draw examples from your subject matter, as in the case of the soccer game, or from any source that you think will help your readers to understand your point. For instance, in a discussion of political leaders you might use George Washington as an example of a generally admired president, thus drawing on your historical knowledge and reminding your readers of their own study of history. You might use Romeo and Juliet as examples of young lovers, drawing on your own and your readers memories of a well-known literary work. Using your imagination, you might describe a child who shares his favorite toy with a playmate and who does not complain when the playmate accidentally breaks it to illustrate the meaning of unselfishness.

EXAMPLES

The writers of the following selections rely primarily on exemplification to support their main points; you will find exemplification in some degree in almost every selection in this book. Look again at Thomas's "On Societies as Organisms" (3-C), Bucello's "A Pop Fly to Short" (3-D), Cumming's "Dottle and the Bottle with a Punt" (3-F), Raiano's "Remembering the Child" (4-G), Cardeli's "My Son Jonah" (4-H), Jerry Klein's "Small Town Summer" (4-I), Ward's "Yumbo" (5-A), and Wright's "A Loaf of Bread and the Stars" (5-B), Rodriguez's "Your Parents Must Be Proud" (5-D), and Wong's "A Cultural Divorce" (5-E). In later units you will find exemplification used extensively in Zinsser's "Clutter" (8-D), Sybul's "Taking Care of Contacts" (9-C), Hoffman's "How to Have Free Entertainment with Your Meal" (9-G), all the selections in Units 10, 11, and 12, Satriale's "Dix Hills: The Grown-Ups' Toy" (13-E), Claus's "Passing on the Legacy of Nature" (13-F), Asimov's "Is Anyone Listening?" (13-H), all the examples in Units 14, 15, 16, 17, and 18, and Woolf's "The Patron and the Crocus" ("Essays for Further Reading"-C).

6-A   Super Bowl Champions

Hilda Santiago *(student)*

This essay was written on an assigned topic: Describe a person or group you admire and explain the basis for your admiration. The writer combines detailed description and narration to present the example supporting her claims.

The San Francisco Forty-Niners played the most exciting game of their season against the Cincinnati Bengals on January 22, 1989. In a surprising ending that day, the Forty-Niners won Super Bowl XXIII, the world championship of professional football. This is the third time in the '80s that the Forty-Niners have   5 won the championship. From beginning to end, they played a sensational game, one that was dramatically decided within the last 34 seconds.

January 22 was a beautiful day in Miami. About 80,000 fans were on hand in Joe Robbie Stadium, and as the players reached   10 the field, the crowd yelled and cheered. The Forty-Niners were the favorite and stronger team. When the game started, they had possession of the ball and scored the first three points with a field goal. Then the Bengals began to play a good defensive game and kept the Forty-Niners from scoring any more points during that   15 quarter.

During the second quarter, both teams used many complicated defensive strategies. The Forty-Niners missed several opportunities to score, but the Bengals did not, and they were able to tie the game with a field goal. For the first time in Super Bowl   20 history, a game was tied at halftime. When the third quarter started, the Bengals scored another field goal, momentarily taking the advantage. Three minutes later, the Forty-Niners made a field goal, tying the game for the second time. Obviously, the Bengals were not happy with this. In the kickoff return, they made a   25 93-yard touchdown; by the finish of the third quarter the game was 10 to 6 in favor of the Bengals.

As the last quarter began, the Forty-Niners made a touchdown, tying the game for the third time. Within minutes, however, the Bengals regained the advantage with a field goal. Although the   30 Bengals were the underdog team, they played like champions, repeatedly ruining the Forty-Niner's best plays. It seemed that it was going to be a Bengal's victory and that the Forty-Niners had

lost all hope of scoring. Then, in an unforgettable ending, with
only thirty-four seconds left to play, the Forty-Niners made a   35
touchdown. The final score was 20 to 16, a dramatic victory for
the Forty-Niners.

The Bengals, despite their loss, demonstrated that they are a
very good team; but, for the San Francisco Forty-Niners and their
fans, this game was a dream come true. Their quarterback, Joe   40
Montana, has become one of the best quarterbacks of all time.
Their wide receiver, Jerry Rice, has won the title of most valuable
player. The team itself has become the best in the National Football League in the 1980s.

6-B   *Le Contrat Social*

H. L. Mencken

Henry Louis Mencken (1880–1956), an American journalist, editor, and critic,
was respected for his intelligence and feared for his satiric wit. His book *The American
Language,* first published in 1918 and revised several times, remains a classic on the
subject. Mencken delighted in taking an adversary position on most issues and attacking widely held beliefs of all kinds. This essay, here complete, appears in his *Prejudices:
Third Series* (1922).

ANALYSIS   All government, in its essence, is a conspiracy against
General   the superior man: its one permanent object is to police
assumption   him and cripple him. If it be aristocratic in organization,
Conclusions   then it seeks to protect the man who is superior only in
#1 and #2   law against the man who is superior in fact; if it be demo-   5
based on   cratic, then it seeks to protect the man who is inferior in
assumption   every way against both. Thus one of its primary functions

Conclusion   is to regiment men by force, to make them as much alike
#3, based on as possible and as dependent upon one another as possi-
#1 and #2   ble, to search out and combat originality among them.   10
All it can see in an original idea is potential change, and
hence an invasion of its prerogatives.

Conclusion   The most dangerous man, to any government, is the
#4   man who is able to think things out for himself, without
regard to the prevailing superstitions and taboos. Almost   15
inevitably he comes to the conclusion that the govern-
Conclusion   ment he lives under is dishonest, insane and intolerable,
#5   and so, if he is romantic, he tries to change it. And even
if he is not romantic personally he is very apt to spread

discontent among those who are. Ludwig van Beethoven   20
was certainly no politician. Nor was he a patriot. Nor had
he any democratic illusions in him: he held the Viennese
in even more contempt than he held the Hapsburgs.
Nevertheless, I am convinced that the sharp criticism of
the Hapsburg government that he used to loose in the   25
cafés of Vienna had its effects—that some of his ideas of
1818, after a century of germination, got themselves
translated into acts in 1918. Beethoven, like all other
first-rate men, greatly disliked the government he lived
under. I add the names of Goethe, Heine, Wagner and   30
Nietzsche, to keep among Germans. That of Bismarck
might follow: he admired the Hohenzollern idea, as Carlyle did, not the German people or the German administration. In his "Errinerungen," whenever he discusses
the government that he was a part of, he has difficulty   35
keeping his contempt within the bounds of decorum.

Nine times out of ten, it seems to me, the man who
proposes a change in the government he lives under, no
matter how defective it may be, is romantic to the verge
of sentimentality. There is seldom, if ever, any evidence   40
that the kind of government he is unlawfully inclined to
would be any better than the government he proposes to
supplant. Political revolutions, in truth, do not often accomplish anything of genuine value; their one un-
doubted effect is simply to throw out one gang of thieves   45
and put in another. After a revolution, of course, the
successful revolutionists always try to convince doubters
that they have achieved great things, and usually they
hang any man who denies it. But that surely doesn't
prove their case. In Russia, for many years, the plain   50
people were taught that getting rid of the Czar would
make them all rich and happy, but now that they have got
rid of him they are poorer and unhappier than ever
before. The Germans, with the Kaiser in exile, have
discovered that a shoemaker turned statesman is ten   55
times as bad as a Hohenzollern. The Alsatians, having
become Frenchmen again after forty-eight years anxious
wait, have responded to the boon by becoming extrava-
gant Germanomaniacs. The Tyrolese, though they hated
the Austrians, now hate the Italians enormously more.   60
The Irish, having rid themselves of the English after 700
years of struggle, instantly discovered that government
by Englishmen, compared to government by Irishmen,

Example #1
of conclusion
#4

Five more
examples

Assumption
#2

Example of
assumption
#2

Example #2

Example #3

Example #4

Example #5

Example #6
extended

was almost paradisiacal. Even the American colonies
gained little by their revolt in 1776. For twenty-five years   65
after the Revolution they were in far worse condition as
free states than they would have been as colonies. Their
government was more expensive, more inefficient, more
dishonest, and more tyrannical. It was only the gradual
material progress of the country that saved them from   70
starvation and collapse, and that material progress was
due, not to the virtues of their new government, but to
the lavishness of nature. Under the British hoof they
would have got on just as well, and probably a great deal
better.   75

Summing up

The ideal government of all reflective men, from Aris-
totle to Herbert Spencer, is one which lets the individual
alone—one which barely escapes being no government
at all. This ideal, I believe, will be realized in the world
twenty or thirty centuries after I have passed from these   80
scenes and taken up my home in Hell.

1. To what extent is the last paragraph a repetition of the first three sentences?
What is the effect of the repetition?

2. Why has Mencken placed America as the last of the examples?

3. Check all the definitions of these words in a large dictionary: *prerogative,
supplant.*

6-C   Lillybrook

Vera Sanford *(student)*

Compare the writer's picture of the gradual decay of a mining town with Pat
Conroy's description of the decay of an island in 13-B.

From the new highway, I see gouged out patches of red earth,
scattered like scabs over the mountains; fallen plank houses, concealed by a new growth of evergreens; the old general store,
standing alone amid the rubble. It's tragic that Lillybrook was
among the communities of West Virginia worked out by coal   5
mining companies. A world in a world, it was once my home
town.

The narrow valley was guarded on all sides by the beautiful
Blue Ridge mountains, untouched mountains except for the
neatly squared off gardens at their feet. A bubbling creek of hard   10
mountain water flowed before the gardens; rhododendrons, huge
and heavily blossomed, stooped to touch the cool traveler.
Wooden foot bridges straddled the creek behind each little com-
pany-owned house, behind each little shanty out back. Weathered
plank houses trimmed the dirt road to Aunt Lilly's boarding   15
house.

The aroma from Aunt Lilly's kitchen lured passers-by. Luscious
pastries lined the gingham covered table: blackberry dumplings,
lemon pies, peach cobblers. Everyone said she was the best cook
in Lillybrook. She was as firmly rooted as the Blue Ridge spruces.   20
Wise and strong, she was the backbone of the First Baptist Church
congregation. Sunday evenings, I'd hear her mellifluous voice
leading the choir in "Down at the Cross." Like a rock, the stee-
pled white structure endured the shouting and the singing, and
was as conspicuous as a full moon in the night sky. The people   25
drew their strength and perseverance from the church. They cried
in the church. They aired their differences in the church. It was
the core of the community. Sheriff O'Neal was as close as the one
telephone in the general store, but few occasions called him to
Lillybrook.   30

Lillybrook Coal Company owned and operated the general
store which housed the post office, the pool room, the gas pump,
and the office of old Doc Hedson, the company doctor. Lillybrook Coal Company built the two room school, the church, and
the houses. With a prosperous coal company and a powerful   35
union, the miners thought they had security—Utopia! Even that
December when they were laid off and Christmas didn't come
because John L. Lewis, the union president, had "killed Santa
Claus," they waited for the whistle to call them back to work. The
whistle didn't blow that winter, and it hasn't blown since.   40

Desperate, most miners followed Tom Durgan's example
when he moved his family to Ohio. Some were financially unable
to move elsewhere, but moved from house to house in Lillybrook
when it rained boulders on their homes. A few diehards, known
as strip miners, dredged the mountains for coal. They chopped   45
down the blue and green that dressed the mountains. They loosened boulders and gouged out chunks of earth. This desperate
attempt soon failed, and no one stayed behind.

The slate dumps are still there; heat rising from them in waves.
Yet, no clanging comes from the tipple where coal was separated   50
from slate; no bucket lines groan under the weight of slate hauled

up the mountain; and most noticeable of all, no whistle calls the
miners out of their pits. I will always remember waking to the
sounds of Lillybrook. The two-room schoolhouse, Aunt Lilly's
boarding house, the general store: the memories belong to me.   55

1. What examples of daily life does the writer describe to show the differences
between Lillybrook as it once was and as it is now?

2. Where does the writer use spatial organization? chronological organization?

3. Where does the sentence structure emphasize important words?

6-D   Dashers and Dawdlers

Michiko Kakutani

In this essay, here complete, a book critic for the *New York Times* quotes famous
writers who found writing a painful, long, drawn-out task. Compare their descriptions
of their struggles with those in the student's log in Unit 2.

Samuel Johnson used to contend that "a man may write at any
time if he will set himself doggedly to it," and he made a point
of living up to those words. It is estimated that he wrote the
Parliamentary Debates at the astonishing rate of 1,800 words an
hour, and he claimed to have completed his life of the poet   5
Richard Savage in thirty-six hours. Urging a young friend to try
to write as quickly as possible, he argued that "if a man is accus-
tomed to compose slowly and with difficulty upon all occasions,
there is danger that he may not compose at all, as we do not like
to do that which is not done easily."   10
In reading about and talking with authors, one occasionally
comes across similar examples of fluency. Ann Beattie, for instance, finished *Chilly Scenes of Winter* in several weeks, and John
Updike recalls writing short stories with "that sense of just being
like a piece of ice on a stove." In *Soldiers' Pay* and *Mosquitoes,* said   15
Faulkner, he discovered that writing was actually "fun," and
Hemingway maintained that writing was not only his "major
vice" but also his "greatest pleasure." It is the wait until the next
day," he said, "that is hard to get through."
Most writers, however, are complainers, and even those who   20
are passionate about their work tend to procrastinate. Indeed,

biographies, interviews and collections of authors' letters all attest
to the difficulty and pain involved in writing.

In a letter to a friend, for instance, Joseph Conrad wearily
recounted his efforts to finish *The Rescue:* "I sit down for eight   25
hours every day and the sitting down is all. In the course of that
working day of eight hours I write three sentences which I erase
before leaving the table in despair." Though he finished that
novel twenty-five years later—many other works of fiction inter-
vened—he felt such frustration at the time that he considered   30
giving up writing altogether and going back to sea. Collaboration
with Ford Madox Ford helped him through that bout of paralysis,
but Conrad suffered recurrent attacks the rest of his life.

At one point, he fell so behind schedule on *Under Western Eyes*
that his agent offered him a wage of £6 a week in return for   35
"regular supplies of manuscript." The offer infuriated him. "It is
outrageous," he wrote to John Galsworthy. "Does he think I am
the sort of man who wouldn't finish the story in a week if he
could? Do you? Why? For what reason? Is it my habit to lie about
drunk for days instead of working? I reckon he knows well   40
enough I don't. It's a contemptuous playing with my worry."

Charles Dickens, too, worried about meeting deadlines, and in
his case, serial publication meant that the deadlines were both
frequent and strict. Having found *Dombey and Son* especially hard,
he moved from Lausanne to Paris, hoping the change would oil   45
his imagination. It didn't. "I took a violent dislike to my study,"
he recalled, "and came down into the drawing room, couldn't
find a corner that would answer my purpose; fell into a black
contemplation of the waning month, sat six hours at a stretch" and
wrote only six lines. He then tried rearranging the furniture, sat   50
down again and started "dodging at it, like a bird with a lump of
sugar."

John Steinbeck's "dawdling," as he called it, took a different
form. When his prose failed to "coagulate"—"it is as unmanage-
able as a raw egg on the kitchen floor," he complained once—he   55
would begin fussing about his desk, debating the merits of a plain
wood surface versus those of a green blotter. After sandpapering
the callus on his writing finger, he would sharpen a couple of
pencils and then set about cleaning the pencil sharpener itself.

In the case of Katherine Anne Porter, distractions—which in-   60
cluded music lessons, love affairs and frequent moves from one
country to another—were so effective they kept her from writing
anything for years.

What causes this fear of putting pen to paper, this inability to
work? For some, it is simply a technical problem. E. M. Forster,   65
for instance, who usually found writing pleasant, said he couldn't

figure out the plot of a work entitled "Arctic Summer" and so, after much agonizing, abandoned the project. For others, it may stem from almost superstitious meditations on the vocation of writing itself or from the solitude of sitting alone in a room. 70

Perhaps the most common cause of paralysis is expectation—not so much the expectation of others, but the writer's own. Will the finished product confirm one's talent? Will the propositions of the imagination be expressed artfully and faithfully? "When I think of what it can be, I am dazzled," wrote Flaubert of *Madame* 75 *Bovary*. "But then, when I reflect that so much beauty has been entrusted to me—to me—I am so terrified that I am seized with cramps and long to rush off and hide, no matter where. I have been working like a mule for fifteen long years. . . . Oh, if I ever produce a good book I'll have earned it." 80

1. Which of the writers described are "dashers"? Which are "dawdlers"?

2. Why does Kakutani give more attention to the dawdlers?

3. Check the etymology, connotation, and denotation of *contend, doggedly, fluency, procrastinate, attest, recurrent, contemptuous, waning, coagulate, vocation.*

6-E   Do You Inherit Your Personality?

Maryon Tysoe

The following essay, here complete, first appeared in *New Society,* a British publication in the social sciences. Notice how the writer uses a variety of examples of opinions and interpretations by experts to arrive at her conclusion.

How often have you heard parents say things like "Our little Florence is *so* unlike her brother. She's good-tempered and easygoing, but he *frets* all the time. And they were like that," they add darkly, "from the very beginning."

For those of us who are predisposed to believe that our genes 5 have only a small part to play in the development of our personalities, this looks like bad news. But parents' expectations—wherever they come from—do, of course, influence their offspring. Psychologists have, for example, shown that parents treat boy and girl, ugly and attractive babies, differently from birth. 10

The idea that genes have much to do with anything but our

physical condition has, for obvious reasons, been very unpopular
since the second world war. It smacks of evil massacres and breeding programs. And the work on intelligence and heredity became
linked with racism in the furore over Arthur Jensen's and Hans   15
Eysenck's writings over a decade ago.

But there are signs that "behavior genetics"—the study of the
genetic influences on individual differences in behavior—is beginning to come out of the closet. Last week, London saw the
thirteenth annual meeting of the Behavior Genetics Association,   20
held for the first time outside the United States. There were 172
delegates (including 29 from Britain) from a total of 14 countries.
The majority were Americans, who the previous week had been
attending the Fourth International Congress on Twin Studies.
They say that interest in their research *is* growing. (When asked   25
about its ethical implications, they reply that their endeavors are
scientific and do not have any inherent ideological connotations.)

The study of twins has been the most popular method of investigating the role of genes in behavior. This is because identical
twins ("monozygotics") come from the same egg and so they   30
share exactly the same genes. But fraternal twins ("dizygotics")
come from two eggs, and therefore they have only 50 per cent
of their genes in common. So if you assume that both types of
twins share their environments to the same extent (are treated
equally alike and so on) then, they argue, you can calculate the   35
influence of genes on any particular behavior you want to measure. If there *is* any influence, identical twins should be more
similar than fraternal twins.

It has been estimated that there are about 100 million twins in
the world. The Institute of Psychiatry at London University has   40
a register of British twins, some 2,500 pairs of adults and 2,000
pairs of children. The results produced by research on twins seem,
on the face of it, quite remarkable.

To take one example, Phil Rushton, associate professor of psychology at the University of Western Ontario, on sabbatical at the   45
Institute, presented a paper at the twins conference, outlining his
recent findings on "altruism and genetics." He sent questionnaires measuring kindness, empathy and concern for others to all
the adult twins. Analyzing the responses from 297 identical and
179 fraternal twins, he found that "virtually half the individual   50
difference variance in altruism is inherited."

He says this is in line with other studies: "Variations between
people on all kinds of personality and cognitive scales—like aggression, anxiety, criminality, dominance, intelligence, locus of
control, neuroticism, political attitudes like conservatism, sexual- 55
ity, sociability, shyness—all seem to be about the same, which is

50 per cent due to genetic differences and 50 per cent attributable to environmental factors."

These percentages are, of course, averages only and so could *not* be taken to apply to any particular individual. Behaviour geneticists also say the proportions are likely to vary between times and cultures.

But—hold everything. The main criticism of twins studies has probably already occurred to you. The assumption that identical and fraternal twins share their environments to the same extent seems unlikely. After all, most identical twins *do* look like two peas in a pod, hence the favorite literary ploy of having them mistaken for each other in all sorts of embarrassing circumstances. They do seem likely to be treated as more similar—and to see themselves as more similar—than fraternal twins, who are no more "close" genetically or physically than normal siblings. And certainly identical twins have been found to spend more time together, to be more likely to share the same bedroom, friends, teacher, and so on. So this could account for their greater similarity.

What do behavior geneticists have to say to this? David Fulker has just been elected the first British president of the Behavior Genetics Association, is senior lecturer in psychology at the Institute of Psychiatry and director of their twins register. He says, "The counter to this argument is, first, are the ways they are treated more alike relevant to the trait in question? It seems to me very unlikely that their great similarity in, say, intelligence is all due to, for example, dressing alike or sharing the same room. Second, there are some studies where people asked parents if they treated their twins alike. Testing if this influences the trait in question, the evidence is that being treated more alike makes no difference to their similarity." But one wonders how accurate parents are when they're asked how similarly they treat their children—and being treated alike is more than likely to affect how you think and behave.

And perhaps identical twins *see* themselves as more alike, as well as being treated more alike? But Phil Rushton says, "One of the most compelling arguments is the case where the parents misclassify their twins, and think that identicals are fraternal when in fact they are identical, and vice-versa. And the twins themselves go through life believing they are identical or fraternal when they are the opposite. If you then establish their true zygosity by, for example, bloodtyping and fingerprint analysis, you have a lovely test of the environmentalists' argument. What will predict the degree of similarity the most, the social labeling or the true biological zygosity? And the answer appears to be, true zygosity."

To this the critics reply that there have only been a few of these kinds of studies, and that the number of twin pairs examined has been too small to warrant confidence in the results.

But the behavior geneticists then say, "Well, what about identi-   105
cal twins reared apart?" Three major studies have been done. But when psychologists such as Leon Kamin, professor of psychology at Princeton University, started rooting around in the detailed case studies, it emerged that "apart" was a bit of a misnomer. It turned out that they were, as someone said to me, "mainly reared   110
in auntie's house." Many of the twins had been raised by different branches of the same family, or at least in the same neighbor-hood—and some even attended the same school.

There is a study that is still going on, called the Minnesota Study of Twins Reared Apart. It was publicised in Britain in Peter   115
Watson's book, *Twins* (Hutchinson, 1981). The researchers, headed by Thomas Bouchard, professor of psychology at Min-nesota University, have now tested thirty-four pairs of identical twins, many of them British. Most were separated within the first year of life (usually by six months) and never saw each other again   120
until Bouchard brought them together when they were in their late teens at the earliest, some being in their forties.

In his book, Watson chose to concentrate on what seemed to be incredible coincidences in the twins' lives. Probably the most famous pair are the "Jim twins," James Lewis and James Springer.   125
Watson lists a large number of coincidences, including: both had married a woman called Linda, divorced her, then married some-one called Betty; one twin named his first son James Alan, the other called his James Allan; both had had a dog they named Toy; both spent their holidays at the same small beach in Florida; both   130
drove a Chevrolet; both bit their fingernails to the quick; both built white benches round the trunk of a tree in their gardens; both have had vasectomies.

But some of these activities, at least, are not so unusual and, as Watson points out, what are the chances that any two people—   135
particularly if asked the thousands of questions that these twins were—would come up with large numbers of coincidences and similarities? This research just hasn't yet been done, and Bouch-ard himself is cautious about drawing any conclusions until some base rates for these kinds of coincidences can be estimated.   140

But Bouchard has also administered to the twins a number of personality questionnaires and measures of intelligence and "vo-cational interests" (such as: preferring to be an accountant rather than an engineer; liking to make things or not). Very few of the results have been published yet; only presented at conferences.   145
But the twins are apparently turning out to be very similar—more

similar (according to the standard twin studies) than fraternal twins reared together.

Bouchard says, "It appears there is a greater influence by heredity than we thought in the past. Our findings on personality and intelligence continue to be true as new cases are added. The general picture is very consistent. But our data are barely scratched." And, no doubt, as his findings find their way into print the attention of critics will soon beam in upon them. Bouchard himself points out that many of the twins *were* raised in similar households.

When pressed on the quality of twin studies, behavior geneticists tend to say, "But we don't need to rely on twin studies. We have adoption studies, and studies of family members with different degrees of relatedness, and these are consistent with the findings of the twin studies." Critics tend to say the family studies can be criticised on the same sorts of grounds as the twin studies, it being more likely that very close relatives share a similar (or even the same) environment than less close relatives. So you'd expect people to be more alike the more they were genetically similar.

But what about the adoption studies? Professor Steven Rose of the Open University, who is a neuro-biologist and the staunchest British critic of behavior genetics, says, "The adoption studies look quite convincing. When children are taken from their parents at or near birth to an adoptive family, you can compare their behavior with that of the biological parents and of the adoptive parents. The trouble is, when you look at the studies in detail— the best study was Danish, of schizophrenia—you find there is selective placement for adoption. Adoption agencies go to considerable lengths to find families similar in social class and environment."

David Fulker says, "This has happened in some studies, not all, and not to a sufficient extent to explain the findings [that around 50 per cent of the variance in measured traits is due to heredity]. In the most recent one, the Colorado Adoption Study, there is no evidence of selective placements for social class, abilities, or any measures of personality." But this study undoubtedly won't go unscathed either.

The argument about genes and environment does look like it's hotting up. As behavior genetics pokes its head round the door, Leon Kamin and Steven Rose are waiting with a club. With a colleague, Richard Lewontin, they have written a book called *Not in Our Genes,* to be published by Penguin, probably later this year.

Rose is vehement that behavior genetics is totally misconceived, and that it is impossible to separate out the effects of genes and the environment. "Genes and environment interact during development to produce something that is not reducible to x per cent genes and y per cent environment. To make a cake, you mix sugar, flour, butter, spices and so on. You bake the cake, and when you taste it you can't say 5 per cent of the taste is due to the butter, 10 per cent is due to the flour, and so on. It is qualitatively different from the ingredients you started with." 195

Social psychologists would probably agree. It's been argued that genes may set some general limits on the way that, say, our personality is likely to develop. For example, extroversion is thought to have something to do with our chronic levels of physiological arousal. But if you're extroverted, they point out, that says *nothing* about how that extroversion will be expressed—whether you'll spend all your time at noisy parties, take up politics, or jump your motorbike over a row of London buses. 200 205

We have plenty of scope to become the person we want. Whatever the role of genetics finally turns out to be, no one is suggesting that we are the puppets of our genes.

1. Tysoe alternates between two opposing views on the extent to which personality may be inherited. What transitional devices indicate the shifts from one view to the other? Look particularly at the first and last sentences of each paragraph.

2. In presenting the views of the behavior geneticists, how and where does Tysoe suggest the possibility of flaws in their logic?

3. Check the etymology, connotation, and denotation of *predisposed, sabbatical, altruism, cognitive, locus, ploy, staunchest, extroversion.*

6-F   The Start of a Long Day

William Krulish *(student)*

In this essay, here complete, the writer gives a colorful extended example of the extra work at round-up time on a ranch. Notice his use of concrete, specific detail to make clear an experience that few of his readers are likely to know firsthand.

A new day dawned bright and early, greeting the earth beneath it with life-giving light and warmth. It was round-up time again and the normal workday of sunup to sundown was extended to cover the extra work that had to be done, a schedule designed to sap the strength of even the strongest ranch hands. 5

The man, having worked late the night before, had fallen asleep on his bunk fully clothed and now faced the consequences of his act. His feet, confined in shoes all night long, were the first to complain as they were swung over the side of the bunk and slammed onto the floor. He winced at this action, his nose recoil- 10 ing as the grimace freed the stale odors that had been trapped in his mouth all night long. His head ached, as with leaden arms he went through the motions of the morning wash-up.

Clothes were another matter. After little consideration, a rea-sonably clean shirt was pressed into service to replace the malo- 15 dorous one he now wore. Blue jeans that had seen better days would do, and the stickiness of his undergarments was over-looked as he heeded the grumblings of a chronically complaining stomach.

Stumbling half-asleep towards the cook house, he exchanged 20 greetings of a sort with others—cowboys, farriers [blacksmiths who shoe horses] and the like—who shared his life and who at this time felt and smelt the same as he did, moving woodenly through a brand new sunshiny morning. A thrush was stunned into silence by the many dark looks sent its way. 25

The man finished his breakfast and pushed himself away from the table, his stomach quiet for the moment. Stretching, stomping and scratching, he made his way to the tool shed where the tools he had dropped unceremoniously the night before awaited him.

A cowboy by choice, he had been pressed into service as a 30 farrier for the round-up and, while shoeing horses might seem romantic on television, he had his druthers. That is to say, if he had a choice he would rather be doing something else.

The corral that he and another farrier had been assigned to was simply a hard-packed, sun-baked square of dirt surrounded by old 35 plumbing pipe loosely laid between posts, with a snubbing post set in the middle of it. Two horses were already in command of this space and as they had spent a quiet, restful night looked forward to the coming activity with more spirit than did the men.

Sometimes a man can walk up to a horse, put a rope on him and 40 settle down to work. This was not about to be one of those times.

The first horse approached by the man was a misnamed, lop-eared, slot-sided son of a bitch who was prone to acrobatics that would have made a gymnast proud. Even when he managed to get one front leg through the railing, a hind leg somehow lashed 45 out and got caught in the farrier's shirt sleeve, ventilating it for all time. The man grunted as the force of the action pushed him to one side. A halter was quickly slipped on and the horse made fast to a length of pipe.

The man turned to help the other farrier.   50

The second horse must have served an apprenticeship on a merry-go-round, judging by the way he ran around and around the corral. A corral is built square so that you can trap a horse in a corner, but a smart horse will get round this by hugging the snubbing post. The dust raised was enough to choke a horse, but the   55
one in question simply held his head above it, letting the men have it all. To show his dexterity a hoof would slice through the dust, just missing the men, although the harsh words permeating the atmosphere seemed to indicate otherwise. Not to be outdone, the other horse at the rail sent a hoof into the foray from time to time.   60

Finally tiring of the game, the horse slowed down. As a last show of camaraderie he squeezed the men against the rails, causing them to inhale more dust.

But the farriers quickly recovered and bent to their tasks. Their curses resounded as the horses kicked over tool boxes and yanked   65
their hooves capriciously through work-worn hands. Sweat and flies were troubling men and horses alike, causing the men to swear even more. The horses helped to fend off the flies by flicking their tails across the men and themselves.

Suddenly it was game time again as both horses realized that   70
they were tied to the same length of pipe and it was lying loose in the posts. They shifted and took off at a run, leaving the men gaping at each other. But the horses, still joined by their tethers at each end of the length of pipe, couldn't really run because of their shackles. They simply swept the pipe around the corral,   75
circling the snubbing post, forcing the farriers into an unexpected game of jump-rope in which they leapt higher than they ever had as children.

Some spoil sport from a crowd that had gathered to see this brief return to childhood stepped in and stopped the horses   80
before they exhausted themselves, and things slowly eased back to normal.

The horses settled down, the men settled back to their work, and the dust settled over everything as the first hour of the workday passed without further incident.   85

It was about this time, when the flies had cut their way through all the dust and heat and homed in on the freshly warmed, live meat at the railing, that the man's stomach started again to rumble.

1. Although most of his word choices are formal, Krulish occasionally uses slang and colloquial expressions, such as "stomping" (line 27) and "druthers" (line 32) for local color. What other examples can you find?

2. Krulish concentrates almost exclusively on the man's physical sensations instead of describing his thoughts and opinions. Also, he refers to him only as "the man." What is the effect of this lack of information about the man's personality and background?

6-G   Gobbledygook

Susanna McBee

The writer of this essay, which first appeared in *U. S. News & World Report,* never explicitly states that she is opposed to "gobbledygook." Instead, she *implies* her opinion throughout by her choice of words, such as "language disorder."

College officials used to talk to one another. No longer. Today, they *articulate* with one another.

Gym classes once were in the physical-education department. No longer. At Rutgers University, they are in the department of *human kinetics.* In many schools, what was the library is now a   5
learning-resource center.

Those are just a few examples of a language disorder known as "educationese," variants of which afflict business, science and medicine. Its governmental form is gobbledygook, a term coined in the late 1930s by a Texas congressman after he spent months   10
reading official reports larded with bloated, empty words.

A more serious ailment is newspeak, euphemism gone bonkers to the point of standing truth on its head—such as the Ministry of Truth, which in the George Orwell novel *1984* propagated lies.   15

Plain-English advocates despair over such linguistic maladies. "They debase the language and obscure thought," charges Lt. Col. Robert Murawski, associate professor of English at the Air Force Academy.

Murawski, who advises the White House on clear writing,   20
contends that "the real danger is not grammatical flubs but clotted expression that makes ideas needlessly complex."

Signs of improvement pop up from time to time. Last year, Navy Secretary John Lehman ordered the service to stop using certain terms that took root in the 1970s. A *Navy correctional*   25
facility is once more a brig. *Unaccompanied officer personnel housing* is back to BOQ—bachelor-officer quarters. *Human resources* once again are people.

Commerce Secretary Malcolm Baldrige heartened purists
when he ordered word processors in his agency programed to   30
reject such terms as *task out* and *liaison with.*

"Gem" collectors. The bright spots, however, do not out-
weigh the assaults on clear communication, according to W.T.
Rabe, head of the Unicorn Hunters, a plain-English group at Lake
Superior State College in Michigan, and William Lutz, head of   35
the English department at Rutgers University and editor of the
Quarterly Review of Doublespeak. Rabe and Lutz offer these examples:

> *Predawn vertical insertion,* a White House coinage for the inva-
>
> sion of Grenada by parachutists.   40
> *Wood interdental stimulator,* Pentagonese for toothpick.
> *Experienced cars,* latest automotive euphemism to displace previ-
> ously owned or used cars.
> *Normally occurring abnormal occurrence,* the nuclear industry's
> description of something that goes wrong all the time.   45
> A *therapeutic misadventure,* medical jargon for an operation that
> kills the patient.

Why do such linguistic atrocities persist? Sometimes, people
want to make the common things they do seem more important.
Thus, an elevator operator becomes a *vertical-transportation-corps*   50
member.

Officials in government and industry use foggy phrases to hide
harsh truths. An airline's report to stockholders referred to the
"involuntary conversion of a 727." It was, in fact, a plane crash
that killed three passengers. Medical experts and social scientists   55
often create a jargon so abstruse that it discourages outsiders from
second-guessing them.

"Pollution of the language keeps getting worse," complains
Professor Lutz of Rutgers. "No one wants to talk directly any
more."

1. Where does the writer first indicate her main point?

2. What examples can you find besides "language disorder," of words or
phrases that suggest that what McBee calls gobbledygook is a physical or mental
disorder?

3. Check the etymology, denotation, and connotation of *articulate* (when used
as a verb), *kinetics, euphemism, bonkers* (*Hint:* It's British slang.), *propagated, flubs, brig,*
liaison, therapeutic, atrocities, abstruse, pollution.

ASSIGNMENTS

1. Choose a public figure you particularly admire, such as a TV or movie performer, an athlete, or a singer, and write an essay explaining the basis for your admiration. Assume your readers know little about the person. Support your claims with several examples.
2. What place do you particularly like to visit on a vacation? Write an essay explaining your choice by giving examples of whatever makes the place attractive. Assume your readers are friends who have asked your advice on where to go.
3. What kinds of drivers do you find most annoying and/or dangerous? Assume that your readers come from another part of the country where driving practices are very different from the ones familiar to you and that they have asked your advice. Support your claims with several examples.
4. Choose a familiar saying such as "Absence makes the heart grow fonder" or "Haste makes waste" and write an essay with examples to show that it is *not* always true.

UNIT 7

Quotation,
Paraphase,
Summary

"According to Webster's. . . ." "In the words of Shakespeare. . . ."
"Mary knows the company president, and she says the stock is sure to go up."
"Einstein wrote. . . ." "I saw it on the six o'clock news." "I heard it on the
radio." "This tip comes straight from the horse's mouth."

In all sorts of situations we use the opinions and often the words of
others to illustrate a point, support an opinion, or show our factual accuracy
and firsthand knowledge of a book or speaker. A glance through the examples in this book will show that many of the writers quote, paraphrase, or
summarize the writings or sayings of others, often extensively. You can
strengthen your own writings by using their methods.

Quote when the original is particularly forceful or colorful in expression or when you think your readers may doubt your accuracy. A quotation
is like a *photographic copy* of the original.

Paraphrase when the original may be difficult for your readers to understand because of the word choice, sentence structure, or content of the original. A paraphrase is a *translation* of the original into simpler language.

Summarize when the original is long and your readers will need only the main thought, not all the details. A summary is a *condensed version* of the original.

Important: In writing a formal critical essay or a research paper, you must document the source of each quotation, paraphrase, and summary. See Unit 18 for information on the two styles of documentation most widely used.

Quotations

Several conventions apply when quoting. They help readers to see precisely where each quotation begins and ends. Enclose short quotations—ones of not more than four typed lines or one full line of poetry—with a pair of double quotation marks, as in this use of a sentence quoted from an essay in Unit 7:

> In his essay "Clutter," William Zinsser gives this advice to his readers: "Re-examine each sentence that you put on paper."

Often, you will not need to quote a complete sentence. Fit the important part into your own sentence:

> In "Clutter," William Zinsser advises us to "re-examine each sentence" in everything we write.

For an indirect quotation—one in which you give the writer's thought but do not use precisely the same words in precisely the same sequence—do *not* use quotation marks:

> In "Clutter," William Zinsser advices us to re-examine every sentence we write.

If the writer you are quoting uses a quotation, enclose it with a pair of single quotation marks to set it off within the quotation containing it:

> "Even before John Dean gave us 'at this point in time,' people had stopped saying 'now,'" Zinsser writes in "Clutter."

Usually, the writer being quoted is named before or after the quotation, as in the preceding examples, but this method can grow monotonous when you make several quotations. Occasionally, insert the name of the speaker or writer within the quotation:

> "Even before John Dean gave us 'at this point in time,' " Zinsser writes in "Clutter," "people had stopped saying 'now.' "

Note: A period or comma at the end of a quotation goes *inside* the closing quotation mark, whether or not it is part of the original—these two punctuation marks are so small that readers may overlook them if they are not close to a word. Place any other punctuation *inside* the concluding quotation marks if it is part of the original and outside if it is an *addition:*

> Chris wrote, "The bill was ten dollars!" (Chris was exclaiming.)
> Chris wrote, "The bill was ten dollars"! (The person recording Chris's
>   remark is exclaiming.)

Set off long prose quotations—ones of more than four typed lines—by placing them as a block, conspicuously indented from the left margin. Otherwise, your readers may forget that you are quoting and think that they are reading your words. Since this method sets the quotation off visibly, do not also use quotation marks around it. If it contains any quotations, set them off in double quotation marks:

> In the third chapter of his book, *On Writing Well,* William Zinsser discusses clutter, which he had earlier called "the disease of American writing":
>> Clutter is the laborious phrase which has pushed out the short word that means the same thing. These locutions are a drag on energy and momentum. Even before John Dean gave us "at this point in time," people had stopped saying "now." They were saying "at the present time," or "currently," or "presently" (which means "soon"). Yet the idea can always be expressed by "now" to mean the immediate moment ("Now I can see him"), or by "today" to mean the historical present ("Today prices are high"), or simply by the verb "to be" ("It is raining"). There is no need to say, "At the present time we are experiencing precipitation."

A long quotation of poetry should also be set off in a block, but you may, if you wish, run two or three lines of poetry into the text of your paper, enclosing them in double quotation marks and indicating the end of each line by a slash mark with a space before and after it:

> One of Shakespeare's sonnets begins: "Let me not to the marriage of true minds / Admit impediments. Love is not love / Which alters when it alteration finds."

When quoting, always reproduce the original exactly. You must give not only the original words but also the punctuation and spelling. You may, however, *omit* part of what you are quoting if it is not relevant to your point, provided, of course, that the omission will not change the meaning of the original. Substitute three dots, called *ellipsis points,* for the omitted words. If the omission runs to the end of a sentence, add a fourth dot to indicate the period:

> Zinsser writes that "Clutter is the ponderous euphemism that turns . . . a salesman into a marketing representative, a dumb kid into an underachiever. . . ."

You may also *add* an explanation or comment to a quotation. To show that it is not part of the original, enclose it in a pair of brackets (if you are using a typewriter that has none, add them in ink):

> Zinsser writes that "before John Dean [a special adviser to former President Nixon] gave us 'at this point in time,' people had stopped saying 'now.' "

If the original contains an error of any kind—in spelling, word use, grammar, or fact—write "sic" enclosed in brackets immediately after it. This Latin word means "thus" or "in this manner" and indicates to your reader that you are aware of the error but that it appears in the original and the author wrote thus, in this manner:

> A Connecticut newspaper recently gave this household hint: "Sprinkle on the shelves a mixture of half borax and half sugar. This will poison every aunt [sic] that finds it."

Note: "Sic" is used so often that, even though it is a word in a foreign language, underlining it is no longer required.

Use quotations to add authority and color to your writing, but do *not* overload your pages with them, and do *not* use them to avoid finding ideas and words of your own.

Paraphrases

There are no formal conventions to follow when paraphrasing. You must rely on whatever knowledge you have of your readers to guide you in deciding how much to simplify the original writer's word choice and sentence structure. Remember that your purpose is only simplification, with the complete meaning, emphasis, and point of view of the original kept intact.

If the original is fairly short, quote it in full and then paraphrase it so that your readers can see it for themselves. If it is long, incorporate a few quotations of key phrases and sentences in your paraphrase; they will add authenticity.

Follow the original sentence by sentence. If it contains long, complicated sentences that your readers will find difficult to follow, break the sentences into shorter ones. Be sure to remind your readers where the paraphrase begins and ends. If it is long, remind them in the middle as well. Remember that they will have no quotation marks to show them that these are not your thoughts. If you omit any words or phrases that are not relevant to your point, indicate the omission with dots, as in quoting, or give a short explanation such as, "Later in this paragraph, the author says. . . ."

For example, a sentence for which many readers would need a paraphrase appeared in a recent announcement by the state of South Carolina that it was issuing bonds for sale to the public in order to raise $65,000,000 for state capital improvements. As with most bond issues, these bonds mature at various dates, some each year, starting in 1988 and ending with the last $5,000,000 in 2000. The sentence mentioned gives special information on some of the bonds:

> Bonds maturing 1994–2000 will be callable in whole or in part but if in part in inverse chronological order of maturity and if less than all the bonds of a single maturity are to be redeemed, the bonds to be redeemed shall be determined by lot within such maturity by the Registrar on March 1, 1993 and all subsequent Bond payment dates at par and accrued interest plus a premium of 2%.

To make this clear to the general reader, the paraphrase uses four sentences:

> The state may call in—insist on buying back early—some or all of the bonds due to mature between 1994 and 2000. If it does not call in the whole $5,000,000 for one of those years, it will choose the bonds to call in by having a lottery on the date when the interest is due, starting in 1993. It will buy the bonds at par—the value printed on them—which may be less than the price of the bonds on the open market. It will pay whatever interest is due up to that date along with an additional 2% interest as a premium.

Summaries

The purpose of a summary—also known as an abstract, digest, or précis—is to condense the essential thoughts of a piece of writing into a short readable statement, not more than one fourth the length of the original and often much less than that. These steps will help you to compose an accurate summary, one that is faithful to the intention of the original.

1. **Read through the entire work to see it as a whole,** jotting down notes on the main points to help you later.

2. **Determine the length of your summary by your needs.** You may reduce a 500-page book to a tenth of its length, to a few paragraphs, or to a single sentence, depending on how much detail you require.

3. **Apportion your space according to the material.** The summary should be the essay in miniature, a condensation of the whole, not a selection of bits and pieces. A more or less literal reproduction of one or more important paragraphs in an essay is not a summary (unless, of course, the author has included summarizing paragraphs that you can use).

4. **Select the main points.** Pick your way through rhetorical devices such as figures of speech, deliberate repetitions, and narrative examples, and concentrate on the essentials.

5. **Omit all extraneous comments.** Do not include your own opinion of the material. The summary should be a condensation of the facts and opinions presented by the author—nothing more.

6. **Paragraph according to your material,** not the author's. The number of paragraphs in the summary should be determined only by the rules of good paragraph development (see Unit 1 for a discussion of paragraphing).

7. **Write your summary from the author's point of view.** Try to keep the flavor, the tone, of the original. Avoid such expressions as "the author says," and concentrate instead on *what* he or she says. Compare the informativeness of these two sentences summarizing Example D in Unit 14:

> a. Mark Twain discusses the meaning of the word lagniappe.
> [This adds little to what the title and the author's name tell us.]
> b. Lagniappe, a Spanish word we picked up in New Orleans, means something extra thrown in for good measure.
> [This tells us not merely that Twain said something but what he said, from the first-person point of view used in the essay.]

8. **Be faithful to the author's emphasis and interpretation.** A good summary is not your own interpretation of the author's material.

9. **Avoid, in general, the author's phrasing and sentence structure.** A summary involves no question of plagiarism, but if you depend heavily on the author's phrasing and sentence structure, you will produce a copy, not a summary. Putting an idea into your own words is the best way to prove that you understand it.

10. **Do not, however, write a paraphrase.** A paraphrase, like any careful translation, includes every thought, and the process of simplifying will almost certainly make the paraphrase longer than the original.

Note: Composing a summary of something you have read is an excellent way to impress it on your memory. Putting it into your own words forces you to come to a much closer understanding than if you merely read it. While you are a student, summarize important lectures and reading assignments: At the end of the term your summaries will make reviewing for examinations easy. Summary writing also gives excellent practice in composing clear, compact sentences and in choosing words accurately.

∴   ∴   ∴

The following three summaries are all of "The Fifth Freedom," which appears in the next unit (pages 174–176), where it is also outlined. Compare these summaries with each other and with the sentence and topic outlines to determine the advantages and disadvantages of each as a way to reduce material to its essential elements.

1. **This summary reduces the essay to one-fourth its original length.**

More than three centuries ago a few pioneers came to America in search of the freedoms we still cherish: freedom from want, freedom from fear, freedom of speech, and freedom of religion. Today their descendants and others are fighting to protect those freedoms everywhere. But there is a fifth freedom, basic to these four, that we are in danger of losing—the freedom to be one's best through the opportunity of developing to one's highest power. (¶¶ 1–2)

This freedom is in danger because of three misunderstandings. The first is about the meaning of democracy. This misunderstanding has defeated attempts to give special opportunities to superior students. The second is about what makes for happiness. Our culture's stress on material well-being has been reflected in the schools by too little discipline and too easy subjects. The third is about the importance of values. The recent denial of such ultimates as eternal truth, absolute moral law, and the existence of God is already reflected in increasing mass selfishness. (¶¶ 3–6)

To preserve the fifth freedom, we must do three things. First, we must give our children the most challenging curriculum of which they are capable, for only a disciplined training produces great people. Second, we must give them the right to fail, for only through standards that make for success or failure can they learn what real life is like. Third, we must give them the best values that history has given us; these will assure them of freedom. (¶¶ 7–9)

1. What supporting details are omitted in the summary?

2. Why is the first paragraph of the summary as long as the last although the original material that it condenses is only half the length of that condensed in the last paragraph?

2. **This summary reduces the essay to a single paragraph and is slightly more than one-tenth the original length.**

We are still fighting today to protect what the pioneers sought in America three centuries ago: freedom from want and fear, and of speech and religion. Basic to these, a fifth freedom—to be one's best by developing to one's highest power—is now endangered by three misunderstandings: of the meaning of democracy, the nature of happiness, and the importance of moral values. As a result, all our standards have deteriorated alarmingly. To preserve this freedom, we must give our children the most challenging curriculum possible, the right to fail, and exposure to the highest moral values.

3. **This summary reduces the essay to a single sentence and is less than one-tenth the original length.**

To preserve the traditional four freedoms for our children, we must also preserve a fifth, freedom to be one's best through full development, which we must safeguard by intellectual challenges, realistic testing, and high moral standards.

EXAMPLES

Writers rely on quotation, paraphrase, and summary so often to illustrate, develop, and support their ideas that you will find examples in almost every essay in this book. We therefore give only three essays in this unit. The first is an example of literary research and criticism, the second and third of research in the social sciences. For more examples of the extensive use of quotation, paraphrase, and summary in essays on literary topics, see Unit 17-A, B, C, D, and E. For more examples of their use in essays in the social sciences, see particularly Unit 6-D, E, and G; Unit 11-C; Unit 17-G; and the research paper in Unit 18.

7-A   "Trees"

Guy Davenport

This essay, here complete, appears in *The Geography of the Imagination* (1981), a collection of the author's essays. Notice how he uses direct and indirect quotations, paraphrase, and summary to make his main point, that "Trees," like many poems, draws on a variety of sources and combines them in surprising ways.

In June, 1918, the Cincinnati poet Eloise Robinson was in the wasteland of Picardy handing out chocolate and reciting poetry to the American Expeditionary Forces. Reciting poetry! It is all but unimaginable that in that hell of terror, gangrene, mustard gas, sleeplessness, 5 lice, and fatigue, there were moments when bone-weary soldiers, for the most part mere boys, would sit in a circle around a lady poet in an ankle-length khaki skirt and Boy Scout hat, to hear poems. In the middle of one poem the poet's memory flagged. She apologized profusely, for the 10 poem, as she explained, was immensely popular back home. Whereupon a sergeant held up his hand, as if in school, and volunteered to recite it. And did.

So that in the hideously ravaged orchards and strafed woods of the valley of the Ourcq, where the fields were 15 cratered and strewn with coils of barbed wire, fields that reeked of cordite and carrion, a voice recited "Trees."

Indirect
quotation
Direct
quotation How wonderful, said Eloise Robinson, that he should know it. "Well, ma'am," said the sergeant, "I guess I wrote it. I'm Joyce Kilmer." 20

He wrote it five years before, and sent it off to the newly founded magazine *Poetry,* and Harriet Monroe, the editor, paid him six dollars for it. Almost immediately it became one of the most famous poems in English, the staple of school teachers and the one poem known by 25 practically everybody.

Sergeant Alfred Joyce Kilmer was killed by German gunfire on the heights above Seringes, the 30th of July, 1918. The French gave him the *Croix de Guerre* for his gallantry. He was thirty-two. 30

"Trees" is a poem that has various reputations. It is all right for tots and Middle Western clubwomen, but you

Summary

are supposed to outgrow it. It symbolizes the sentimentality and weak-mindedness that characterizes middle-
class muddle. It is Rotarian. Once, at a gathering of poets	35
at the Library of Congress, Babette Deutsch was using it
as an example of the taradiddle Congressmen recite at
prayer breakfasts and other orgies, until Professor Gor-

Indirect
quotation

don Wayne coughed and reminded her that the poet's
son, Kenton, was among those present. No one, how-	40
ever, rose to defend Kipling and Whittier, at whom La
Deutsch was also having.

It is, Lord knows, a vulnerable poem. For one thing,
it is a poem about poetry, and is thus turned in on itself,
and smacks of propaganda for the art (but is therefore	45
useful to teachers who find justifying poetry to barbarian
students uphill work). For another, the opening statement is all too close to Gelett Burgess's "I never saw a
Purple Cow," lines that had been flipping from the
tongues of wits since 1895.	50

Partial
quotation

And if the tree is pressing its hungry mouth against the
earth's sweet flowing breast, how can it then lift its leafy
arms to pray? This is a position worthy of Picasso but not
of the *Cosmopolitan* Cover Art Nouveau aesthetic from
which the poem derives. Ask any hard-nosed classicist,	55

Indirect
quotation

and she will tell you that the poem is a monster of mixed
metaphors.

And yet there is a silvery, spare beauty about it that has
not dated. Its six couplets have an inexplicable integrity,
and a pleasant, old-fashioned music. It soothes, and it	60
seems to speak of verities.

The handbooks will tell you that Yeats and Housman
are behind the poem, though one cannot suspect from it
that Kilmer was one of the earliest admirers of Gerard
Manley Hopkins. Poems of great energy are usually dis-	65
tillations of words and sentiments outside themselves.
Poems are by nature a compression. Another chestnut,
Longfellow's "A Psalm of Life," was generated by the
Scotch geologist Hugh Miller's *Footprints of the Creator*
and *The Old Red Sandstone,* books made popular in Amer-	70
ica by Longfellow's colleague at Harvard, Louis Agassiz.
It is an example of the miraculous (and of the transcen-
dentally vague) how Longfellow, reading about fossils in

Quotation of
poetry
incorporated
in sentence

Miller, latched onto the sandstone and the vestiges there-
upon, to intone "Lives of great men all remind us / We	75
can make our lives sublime / And in passing leave behind
us / Footprints on the sands of time."

Poets work that way, condensing, rendering down to essence. Another poem, as popular in its day as "Trees," Edwin Markham's "The Man with the Hoe" lived in   80
Ezra Pound's mind until it became the opening line of

Quotation *The Pisan Cantos*—"The enormous tragedy of the dream in the peasant's bent shoulders."

"Trees" is, if you look, very much of its time. Trees were favorite symbols for Yeats, Frost, and even the   85
young Pound. The nature of chlorophyll had just been discovered, and *Tarzan of the Apes*—set in a tree world— had just been published. Trees were everywhere in art of the period, and it was understood that they belonged to the region of ideas, to Santayana's Realm of Beauty.   90

But Kilmer had been reading about trees in another context that we have forgotten, one that accounts for the

Quotation self-effacing closing lines ("Poems are made by fools like me, / But only God can make a tree"), lines that have elevated the poem into double duty as a religious homily.   95
Kilmer's young manhood was in step with the idealism of the century. One of the inventions in idealism that attracted much attention was the movement to stop child labor and to set up nursery schools in slums. One of the most diligent pioneers in this movement was the English-   100
woman Margaret McMillan, who had the happy idea that a breath of fresh air and an intimate acquaintance with grass and trees were worth all the pencils and desks in the whole school system. There was something about trees

Summary that she wanted her slum children to feel. She had them   105
take naps under trees, roll on grass, dance around trees. The English word for gymnasium equipment is "appara- tus." And in her book *Labour and Childhood* (1907) you

Quotation will find this sentence: "Apparatus can be made by fools, but only God can make a tree."   110

1. In the second paragraph, Davenport quotes Kilmer directly but Robinson indirectly. What may have been his reason for this distinction?

2. Davenport devotes 20 lines to the flaws in "Trees" and to others' criticism of it but only three lines to praising it. What may have been his reasons for placing the negative criticism first and for making the praise so brief?

3. After the four-paragraph narrative that begins the essay, almost every para- graph begins with its topic sentence. Which sentence gives the topic of the ninth paragraph?

4. How has Davenport constructed the final paragraph to make it build up to a sort of climax?

5. Check the etymology, denotation, and connotation of *taradiddle, "having at" someone, verities, transcendentally, rendering down.*

7-B	Sex and the Split Brain

Carol Johmann

This essay, here complete, first appeared in *Omni* in 1983. Throughout, the author uses summary, paraphrase, and quotation to present recent scientific research on the differences between men's and women's brains.

When she was a Ph.D. student at Columbia University, physical anthropologist Christine De Lacoste-Utamsing was dissecting human brains as part of her research. In the course of her work her attention was drawn to a flat bundle of nerve fibers, called the corpus callosum, that connects the right and left hemispheres of   5
the brain. After examining specimens from nine men and five women, she noticed an odd thing: On average, the corpus callosum was larger and more bulbous in women's brains than in men's. Intrigued by this, she has since gone on to study more specimens, including the brains of both adults and fetuses. Her   10
data have led her to one conclusion: The brains of men and women are physically different.

De Lacoste is still fascinated by her work and loves to talk about it, but she is concerned that people might jump to the wrong conclusions. She worries that her discovery might be used to   15
support a controversial hypothesis that women's brains are less specialized than men's, a theory often cited by some researchers to explain why men tend to outperform women in such visual-spatial disciplines as geometry or engineering.

"Studying areas of the brain is very exciting," says De Lacoste,   20
now at the University of Texas's Health Science Center, "but [my findings] can be twisted in a very sexist way. All I've shown is that there is a difference in the number of connections between hemispheres."

"What gets me is the leap some people make," adds City Uni-   25
versity of New York psychologist Florence Denmark, who has been following this research. "They assume that brain differences

between the sexes always indicate differences in intelligence and ability. And somehow men always come out on top."

Such concern is hardly unwarranted. The notion that "biology is destiny" has been used repeatedly over the years to support a variety of racist, sexist, and other prejudicial attitudes. In his book *The Mismeasure of Man,* Harvard paleontologist Stephen Jay Gould points out how vulnerable a topic the brain is for misguided use of research. Bigots have long manipulated I.Q.-test results and comparative studies of brain size to support their views. What De Lacoste and others are trying to do is to put the new brain discoveries into the proper perspective before something similar happens with those findings.

Since the early Seventies there has been an increasing body of evidence that the brains of males and females differ. Studies of rat brains, for example, disclosed structural brain differences between the sexes in the hypothalamus—the section of the brain that regulates sex drive, body temperature, and blood pressure—and in the cerebral cortex, the control center for thinking, the senses, and movement. De Lacoste's research showed that there were sex-related differences in the human brain as well.

Brain researchers now assume that a larger corpus callosum means there is more communication between the right and left halves of the brain. This assumption and data from De Lacoste's research are significant when we realize how divided the brain is in its abilities, especially when we consider how that split may differ between the sexes.

The human brain is split in two ways. First, each hemisphere controls the movement of, and receives sensory input from, the opposite side of the body. Second, each half is specialized, or lateralized, as scientists like to say. The left brain handles information in an analytical, sequential manner. It is concerned with problem solving, and it excels in language skills. We use it to understand spoken instructions, for example. By contrast, the right brain appears to process information holistically; that is, more intuitively and perceptively. This is the brain half used to recognize visual patterns and three-dimensional objects.

By connecting the two halves and letting them act as a whole, the corpus callosum keeps us from feeling like some kind of two-headed, or at least two-minded, beast. So if the female's larger corpus callosum allows for more of this cross-communication, her brain may be more balanced than a man's. In short, women's brains may be less lateralized, or specialized in what they can do.

Some researchers even argue that this could help explain why boys do better in math and spatial-reasoning tasks involved in

geometry but have more trouble learning how to read. With less
communication going on between their hemispheres, men may
have the edge on women when it comes to who uses the right side   75
of the brain more exclusively.

In fact, several observations other than De Lacoste's suggest
that the sexes are *not* created equal when it comes to lateralization. After a stroke has damaged the brain's speech center, a
woman is more apt to recover the ability to speak than a man. In   80
theory, this is because the other side of her brain can take over
more easily. Another piece of evidence comes from what we
know of human development. The process of becoming lateralized begins in the fetus. At what point lateralization begins is not
clear, although in her study of fetal brains, De Lacoste has found   85
structural differences in fetuses as young as 26 weeks. And this
process isn't finished until the onset of puberty. Since girls reach
puberty before boys do, their brains may have less time to lateral-
ize.

Brains as well as bodies are shaped by sex hormones; so a   90
difference in specialization should not be at all surprising. If a
male rat is castrated at birth, for example, his hypothalamus will
develop into one that resembles a female's. If a female rat is given
the male hormone testosterone at birth, her hypothalamus will
take on male characteristics. Remove her ovaries, the source of   95
the female hormones estrogen and progesterone, and the female's cerebral cortex will become malelike.

As De Lacoste points out, when the human brain was evolving,
males and females occupied different ecological niches. Female
hominids gathered food and nurtured babies; males hunted.   100
These activities, each requiring different skills, could have put
different adaptive pressures on brain development. Females, for
example, may have needed a more integrated understanding of
the world, while males might have required more specialized
skills like the ability to hold three-dimensional images in their   105
minds (perhaps for mapmaking). Pressures like these, De Lacoste
speculates, may have been the environmental forces that shaped
women's brains so that they became less lateralized.

"But don't misunderstand," she adds. "We don't have two
brains evolving separately, just one brain that reflects the differ-   110
ences in sex hormones and reproductive functions." More important, she adds, one shouldn't misconstrue what sex-linked brain
differences mean. In itself lateralization says nothing about an
individual's innate intelligence and mental capability.

"We're talking about differences in the way men and women   115
screen information," De Lacoste explains. "Women seem to have
a bias toward picking up information presented in a verbal fash-

ion; men, in a visual-spatial way. Once information is selected, though, their brains function in the same way with the same potential."   120

Neither approach is better than the other, says Denmark. "It's assumed that if males have more lateralization, then it's the thing to have. But you can interpret it another way. Perhaps women have larger areas of the brain from which to draw skills."

Ultimately, both interpretations are equally irrelevant, she con-   125
cludes. Why? Because when it comes to human behavior and intelligence, biology is *not* destiny. "Regardless of structural differences, the cultural factors are enormous," explains De Lacoste. Research shows that our genes may determine which sex hormones course through our bodies, and those hormones may help   130
sculpt our brains. But as De Lacoste points out, it is the constant interplay between this genetic potential and our environment that defines our talents and abilities, and determines what we learn.

1. There are six direct quotations and many more indirect ones and summaries in this essay. What reasons may Johmann have had for quoting those six statements directly instead of quoting them indirectly or summarizing them?

2. Where does Johmann summarize opinions? What may have been her reasons for summarizing instead of quoting them?

3. Check the etymology, denotation, and connotation of *unwarranted, paleontologist, bigot, holistically, lateralized, fetus.*

7-C   To Deal and Die in L.A.

Aldore Collier

In this essay, first published in *Ebony* in 1989, the writer reports on his firsthand observations of young people being destroyed by the temptations of the drug trade. His use of direct quotation and specific detail make his report convincing and forceful.

As the Compton, Calif., gang unit police car pulls into an alley, Ronald, a 22-year-old drug dealer, tries to hide a small plastic packet. His customers slowly disperse, desperately trying to appear innocent to Lt. Hourie Taylor, head of the unit.

Taylor takes the packet and sees that it contains only pebbles.   5
In a fatherly tone, he admonishes Ronald that he could get killed for selling rocks for up to $35 each.

Ronald is glassy-eyed from the drugs he has taken. His speech is slurred as he talks in a boastful tone about having just gotten out of the penitentiary. He earns about $400 a day on the streets of this mostly Black suburb of Los Angeles, selling cocaine—real and fake.

When asked what he does with his earnings, he looks up at the sky thoughtfully. "Let's see," he says, "I buy clothes, bought a car, whatever I want. I give my mama some when she needs it."

Although he is one of the few in his gang who have not been injured by gunfire, Ronald has been shot at often. Still, he has no fear of death. "If it happens, it just happens. If I die, then I'm dead," he says. "I ain't worried about that. I never let that enter my mind." Selling drugs since he was 14, he has considered quitting but, so far, it hasn't gone beyond the thinking stage.

Ronald is one of some 80,000 young adults in the Los Angeles area who are gang members, lured into the world of violence and drugs by visions of riches and excitement. The L.A. area has twice as many gang members as any other city in the U.S., according to the Justice Department and Los Angeles-area law enforcement statistics.

Explains Lt. Taylor: "With the cocaine explosion in 1982, all of a sudden there is a lot of money to be made selling drugs, specifically cocaine and PCP. So the gangs that had been involved in property offenses said, 'Wait a minute! Why risk our lives robbing a gas station when we can go out and sell cocaine and make a lot more money?' These kids unfortunately are attracted by the glamor that goes with it—the money, the girls, the jewelry and the travel. You get a 15- or 16-year-old who never went anywhere and all of a sudden he's in Seattle or Kansas City. It's mind-boggling.

"How can you tell the kid who dropped out of school to go and find a job somewhere that pays minimum wage when he can make $200 a day selling drugs? He is going to laugh at you. He'll say he can make money for himself, plus help his mama out. A lot of these kids are being hired at an early age, like eight or nine, and given $100 to be lookouts."

Often parents go to the police station to claim the money taken from their children who are arrested with drugs, says Lt. Taylor, who adds that some become quite indignant. "I had a case where we arrested a guy and he called his mother and said, 'Hey, mama, go look in my dresser drawer and you'll find $5,000. Come bail me out.' This guy was in his teens."

Law enforcement officials and various area businessmen tell stories of how children as young as 12 years old attempt to buy

cars, expensive guns, stereos and TV sets with cash. One car
dealer says the young gang members get willing adults to purchase the items that won't be sold to them.

Sometimes, though, money has absolutely nothing to do with   55
selling drugs. For 16-year-old Keith Houston, joining a gang and
selling drugs was simply a way of fitting in. "I joined because
everybody else was doing it. The money [for selling drugs] was
good but I wasn't really in it just for the money," he says. "I make
about $400 or $500 a day, maybe a little more. I use the money   60
to buy clothes, food, drinks and PCP. I give my mom some so she
can do what she wants. The rest I just spend on PCP and stuff like
that."

Jallay Hall, 15, joined the Westside Rolling Forties at the age
of eight because gangs were the only way of life in his neighbor-   65
hood. "I didn't want to sell drugs but I did and it just got bigger
and bigger. I was netting $350 a day. I'm not rolling in money
or nothing. There are eight of us in the dope house taking turns
doing what we got to do."

Drug dealing in Southern California is by no means restricted   70
to males. Ta-Tanisha Scott, 16, makes upward of $500 a day,
depending on how long she feels like selling. "I'm always scared
about selling, but it's just a chance you have to take," she says.
"I keep doing it because the money is good. My mother needed
stuff. I still help out at home a lot."   75

Her family worries a lot about her, she says, especially since she
was shot in the leg last year and has been shot at several times.
She has also been arrested for auto theft. "Everybody in jail says,
'I'm gonna do this or that when I get out.' That's just a line. When
they get out they are back to the same thing. I want to change my   80
life, but if the money is still out there, I'm going to do it. I'm not
making those people come to me and get dope. I am going to stop
some day. I know it's wrong, but they still want to do it. They
made that choice to do that with their lives, not us." Unlike many
of her fellow gang members, Ta-Tanisha has managed to save   85
much of her money.

Despite the large sums of money to be made daily, the drug-
oriented life-style is losing some of its appeal to some, but not
because of escalating violence or the police presence. Some point
to the simple, intangible desire to try something new and less   90
dangerous. Also, the L.A. market is reported to be saturated with
cocaine and the price is starting to drop.

Ta-Tanisha, Jallay and Keith are among 60 current and former
gang members participating in the Community Youth Sports and
Arts Foundation program. The foundation, funded by the City of   95

Los Angeles, is headed by Chilton Alphonse and provides students with educational programs, counseling, field trips and athletic activities.

Also, a growing number of religious leaders, such as the Rev. Charles Mims Jr., who organized a gang summit last year, are   100 slowly getting their message of a better life within the law to some violence-weary gang members.

Rev. Mims organized other ministers to provide counseling to gang members and to encourage businesses to train and hire them.   105

The life she has chosen to live has provided Ta-Tanisha with money to buy any and everything she wants except peace of mind and, above all, self-respect. Now, she wants those as well and is determined to get them. She also is encountering many on the south side of L.A. who are genuinely interested in the welfare of   110 area youngsters. That attention is helping her slow down her dollar-chasing ways. "I'm going to school now, getting my education, and I'm going to be somebody," she says in a loud, convincing tone. "I'm going to do something with my life."

Locate the following in Collier's essay: eleven direct quotations, three direct quotations contained in quotations; three summaries of spoken remarks; an explanation inserted in a direct quotation.

ASSIGNMENTS

1. Compose a paraphrase of the three-paragraph passage of Johmann's essay that begins "As De Lacoste points out." Assume that your readers are other students who have not read the essay.
2. Study the three summaries on pages 158–159 carefully, comparing each with the original essay and with each other. Notice in each what is saved in space and what is lost in detail.
3. Compose a summary of the essay by Johmann in about 200 words. Consider your paragraphing carefully; remember that the number of paragraphs you use should indicate the number of main points in the original but may not be related to the number of paragraphs Johmann uses.
4. Reduce the summary you composed for assignment 3 to one paragraph of not more than 100 words; then reduce that paragraph to a single sentence of not more than 50 words.
5. Combining quotation, paraphrase, and summary, as necessary, compose a detailed account of an editorial in a recent newspaper. Include your opinion of the writer's views, and assume that your readers are classmates who have not read the editorial.

UNIT 8

Outlines

An outline lets you see a whole essay or lecture at a glance. It not only records the main ideas–any notes can do that–but it also arranges them on the page to show their relative importance and their connections with each other. An outline can therefore give you essential help in studying and writing. Which of these versions would be more helpful if you were reviewing the information for a test or planning to use it in a report?

1. This version presents the information in a rough summary:

History is divided into two periods—prehistoric, before writing, and historic, after writing. Prehistoric, known by remaining weapons and utensils, is divided into four stages: Old Stone (rude and primitive), New Stone (more advanced), Copper-Bronze (first use of metals), and Iron. Historic age is much better known through written records.

2. This version presents the same information in a rough outline:

History is divided into two periods:
 Prehistoric—before writing—known by weapons and utensils
  Old Stone (rude and primitive)
  New Stone (more advanced)
  Copper-Bronze (first use of metals)
  Iron
 Historic—after writing—much better known, through written records

The formal outline is merely a conventional, labeled arrangement of logical indentations like those shown in the second version. It may be more elaborate and precise than you can work out in detail while listening to a lecture, but you can apply the general principles even when in a hurry. Besides helping you to see how the writers and lecturers organized their main ideas, it will help you to organize your own ideas. Every time you plan a paper, you will have occasion to work out a rough outline like those in Part I, Unit 1, "The Fundamentals of Writing: Composing. . . ."

Two systems are widely used for labeling the parts of an outline to indicate their connections and their relative importance. The standard system for work in the humanities combines Roman and Arabic numerals with upper- and lower-case letters. The standard system for the sciences, social sciences, business, and engineering uses only Arabic numerals. The method of indentation is the same in both systems.

An outline labeled for use in the humanities would look like this:

Thesis statement: Brief statement of topic and of conclusions drawn

   I. First major point
     A. First point to illustrate or explain I.
     B. Second point to illustrate or explain I.
       1. First subpoint to illustrate or explain B.
         a. First sub-point to illustrate or explain I.B.1.
         b. Second sub-subpoint to illustrate or explain I.B.1.
       2. Second subpoint to illustrate or explain I.B.
  II. Second major point
     A. First point to illustrate or explain II.
     B. Second point to illustrate or explain II.

You are not likely to need subdivisions beyond the level of *a.,* but if you do need further subdivisions, label the first level below *a.* as (1), (2), and so on, and label subdivisions of those (a), (b), and so on.

Notice how the indentations help to emphasize thought relationships by grouping points visibly according to their relative importance. The more important a point is, the closer it should be to the left margin.

An outline labeled for use in the sciences would look like this:

Thesis statement: brief statement of topic and conclusions drawn

    1. First major point
      1.1 First point to illustrate or explain 1.
      1.2 Second point to illustrate or explain 1.
         1.2.1 First subpoint for 1.2
         1.2.2 Second subpoint for 1.2
    2. Second major point
      2.1 First point to illustrate or explain 2.
      2.2 Second point to illustrate or explain 2.

And so on.

The two labeling systems work equally well for both sentence and topic outlines. A topic outline presents each point in a phrase or a single word; a sentence outline presents each point in a complete sentence. For your own use and for readers who need only an overview of your essay, a topic outline is preferable because it can be seen at a glance. For readers likely to find your material unfamiliar or complex, a sentence outline is more helpful. When an instructor asks you to submit an outline of your essay, be sure to determine which type to prepare.

∴ ∴ ∴

Making a reading outline is an excellent way to study anything you want to remember, and later the outline will help you to review the reading quickly. Follow these steps:

1. **What is the main idea?** Read the entire piece through carefully— you would outline a book by chapters or other manageable units, not as a whole. Then reduce its central meaning to a single comprehensive sentence. This is the main idea or thesis and should always appear at the head of your outline, for it represents the "essay as a whole." This thesis sentence should express content, not purpose, and be long enough to indicate the major divisions of your plan. Omit all unnecessary expressions, such as "the author says."

2. **What are the main divisions of the author's thought?** These are the major sections into which the lesser points are grouped. If you find eleven, say, or seventeen, reconsider. You are probably "failing to see the forest because of the trees in the way" and are treating small details as important items. A single chapter or essay cannot manage so many main points—probably, in fact, not more than a half-dozen at most. Remember that there will be at least two, however; since outlining is a process of breaking down, a one-point outline is not an outline at all. If at first you think you have

only one, it is the main idea, and you must break it down into points I, II, and so on.

3. **Make the main points comparable.** The material of each should have about the same level of importance as that of the others. If not, that point does not deserve equal rank in the outline. Whenever you can, make such equality clearly evident through parallel wording (see A and B under I in the preceding examples).

4. **Break down each main section into its own smaller parts.** Thus you arrive at the secondary divisions, which you indicate by capital letters and an indented position.

5. **Finish outlining each main section before moving on.** It is better not to start on items of the third rank, however, until you have worked out all the second-rank items for that section, or on the fourth until the third is completed, and so on. Otherwise, you may lose perspective and give too much importance to trifling points. Be sure that within every level your points are logically of equal importance, and continue to indicate the fact not only by similar symbols and indentations but, wherever possible, by parallel wording as well.

6. **Make your outline follow a deductive order.** Proceed from the general to the particular, from the main point to the subpoints beneath it. Even if the author has deliberately reversed the order of the material for emphasis by giving the particulars first and arriving at the main point only through them, your outline must nevertheless present the author's points deductively.

7. **Omit everything irrelevant to the main plan.** Rhetorical questions, figures of speech, elaborate descriptions, repetitions for effect—reduce them all to the basic points they illustrate or emphasize. The college lecturer who advised students, "Take down the point I am trying to make, not the funny story I tell you in making it," was right—although you might mention such a story in its properly subordinate position as a subpoint under the superior point it illustrates.

8. **Use as many levels as you find suitable.** The purpose of your outline will determine how much detail you should include. For example, you may or may not choose to list under a point the three subpoints composing it, but if you mention one subpoint you are duty bound to give the others of the same rank.

9. **Avoid the meaningless single subpoint.** If the information on a point is not divisible into at least two subpoints, it has no subpoint at all. For instance, if the only example that you are going to give under the main heading "A. Trees" is "1. Oak," your main heading should be "A. Oak trees" because you do not have a subpoint. There is only one exception to

this rule. If you have information for two or more subpoints under one heading (for example, "A. Dogs, 1. Beagles, 2. Poodles, 3. Boxers") but for only one under a matching heading, you may list that as "1" under "B" (for example, "B. Cats, 1. Siamese") to show that it is parallel with the subpoints under A and not with the more general heading of "A." Otherwise, incorporate the example into your statement of its superior point.

10. **Check your work to see that it is entirely logical.** Remember that your main-idea sentence must cover, briefly but definitely, the thought contained in the main points of the essay, and point "I" must read so as to include logically its own "A," "B," and "C," and so on. Similarly, each set of subpoints must add up to the main point under which it appears: "a," "b," and "c" must compose "1," "1" and "2" must compose "A," "A" and "B" must compose "I," and "I," "II," "III" (plus the Introduction and Conclusion) must compose the main idea. (Sometimes a change in wording can correct a flaw in logic. If "a," "b," and "c" fit logically under "2," but "d" does not, you may be able to keep "d" by narrowing its scope or by enlarging the scope of "2" to include it.)

11. **Be consistent.** Whichever type of outline you choose for a particular purpose, do not mix it with the other type. Do not use single words or phrases to present any items in a sentence outline. Do not use any sentences in a topic outline.

EXAMPLES

8-A   The Fifth Freedom

Seymour St. John

This essay was first published in the *Saturday Review* in 1955, but the writer's criticism of American education is still widely applicable. Note, for example, William Zinsser's plea in 1977 that students be allowed the "right to fail" (15-E).

Important: For your convenience, the paragraphs are numbered. These numbers are repeated in the margin of the sentence and topic outlines to emphasize their relationship with the essay.

[1] More than three centuries ago a handful of pioneers crossed the ocean to Jamestown and Plymouth in search of freedoms they were unable to find in their own countries, the freedoms we still cherish today: freedom from want, freedom from fear, freedom of speech, freedom of religion. Today the descendants of the   5

early settlers, and those who have joined them since, are fighting to protect these freedoms at home and throughout the world.

[2] And yet there is a fifth freedom—basic to those four—that we are in danger of losing: *the freedom to be one's best.* St. Exupéry describes a ragged, sensitive-faced Arab child, haunting the streets of a North African town, as a lost Mozart: he would never be trained or developed. Was he free? "No one grasped you by the shoulder while there was still time; and nought will awaken in you the sleeping poet or musician or astronomer that possibly inhabited you from the beginning." The freedom to be one's best is the chance for the development of each person to his highest power.

[3] How is it that we in America have begun to lose this freedom, and how can we regain it for our nation's youth? I believe it has started slipping away from us because of three misunderstandings.

[4] First, the misunderstanding of the meaning of democracy. The principal of a great Philadelphia high school is driven to cry for help in combating the notion that it is undemocratic to run a special program of studies for outstanding boys and girls. Again, when a good independent school in Memphis recently closed, some thoughtful citizens urged that it be taken over by the public-school system and used for boys and girls of high ability, that it have entrance requirements and give an advanced program of studies to superior students who were interested and able to take it. The proposal was rejected because it was undemocratic! Out of this misunderstanding comes the middle-muddle. Courses are geared to the middle of the class. The good student is unchallenged, bored. The loafer receives his passing grade. And the lack of an outstanding course for the outstanding student, the lack of a standard which a boy or girl must meet, passes for democracy.

[5] The second misunderstanding concerns what makes for happiness. The aims of our present-day culture are avowedly ease and material well-being: shorter hours; a shorter week; more return for less accomplishment; more soft-soap excuses and fewer honest, realistic demands. In our schools this is reflected by the vanishing hickory stick and the emerging psychiatrist. The hickory stick had its faults, and the psychiatrist has his strengths. But the trend is clear: *Tout comprendre c'est tout pardonner* [To understand everything is to excuse everything]. Do we really believe that our softening standards bring happiness? Is it our sound and considered judgment that the tougher subjects of the classics and mathematics should be thrown aside, as suggested by some educators, for doll-playing? Small wonder that Charles Malik, Lebanese delegate at the U.N., writes: "There is in the West [in the United

States] a general weakening of moral fiber. [Our] leadership does not seem to be adequate to the unprecedented challenges of the age."

[6] The last misunderstanding is in the area of values. Here are some of the most influential tenets of teacher education over the past fifty years: there is no eternal truth; there is no absolute moral law; there is no God. Yet all of history has taught us that the denial of these ultimates, the placement of man or state at the core of the universe, results in a paralyzing mass selfishness; and the first signs of it are already frighteningly evident.

[7] Arnold Toynbee has said that all progress, all development come from challenge and a consequent response. Without challenge there is no response, no development, no freedom. So first we owe to our children the most demanding, challenging curriculum that is within their capabilities. Michelangelo did not learn to paint by spending his time doodling. Mozart was not an accomplished pianist at the age of eight as the result of spending his days in front of a television set. Like Eve Curie, like Helen Keller, they responded to the challenge of their lives by a disciplined training: and they gained a new freedom.

[8] The second opportunity we can give our boys and girls is the right to failure. "Freedom is not only a privilege, it is a test," writes De Nöuy. What kind of a test is it, what kind of freedom where no one can fail? The day is past when the United States can afford to give high school diplomas to all who sit through four years of instruction, regardless of whether any visible results can be discerned. We live in a narrowed world where we must be alert, awake to realism; and realism demands a standard which must either be met or result in failure. These are hard words, but they are brutally true. If we deprive our children of the right to fail we deprive them of their knowledge of the world as it is.

[9] Finally, we can expose our children to the best values we have found. By relating our lives to the evidences of the ages, by judging our philosophy in the light of values that history has proven truest, perhaps we shall be able to produce that "ringing message, full of content and truth, satisfying the mind, appealing to the heart, firing the will, a message on which one can stake his whole life." This is the message that could mean joy and strength and leadership—freedom as opposed to serfdom.

8-B Sentence Outline of "The Fifth Freedom"

The numbers in brackets near the left margin correspond to the paragraph numbers in the essay. Within the outline, the italicized sentences in brackets are not part of the outline; they give explanations of the outline structure.

Main idea: Besides the four freedoms we cherish, there is a fifth, the freedom to be one's best, which we are in danger of losing through our misunderstandings but which we must preserve and pass on to our children by challenging them.

[1]   I. Today we cherish four freedoms.
        A. The pioneers came to America to find them.
            1. One is freedom from want.
            2. Another is freedom from fear.
            3. Another is freedom of speech.   5
            4. Another is freedom of religion.
                [*These are a common kind of subpoint, a simple
                enumeration. Here they are written out more fully
                than in the essay, to satisfy the requirements of the
                sentence outline.*]   10
        B. Today we fight to protect them.
            [*A and B are parallel subpoints as cause and effect
            of the introductory statement; note the balanced word-
            ing.*]

[2]   II. The fifth freedom is freedom to be one's best.   15
        [*Now the subject of the essay, indicated by the title, begins;
        the first main section prepared the way for it.*]
        A. It is basic to the other four.
        B. We are in danger of losing it.
            [*The incident of the Arab child, being only an illus-   20
            tration, may be omitted from a brief outline.*]

[3–6] III. We are losing this fifth freedom through three mis-
        understandings.
        [*A question like the one that begins ¶3 is rhetorical and
        should never appear in the outline in that form. Here,*   25
        *moreover, half the answer doesn't appear until the next
        point, beginning in ¶7.*]

[4]   A. The first misunderstanding is of the meaning of
            democracy.

    1. We think that democracy in education   30
means gearing all courses to the middle
level.

    2. We reject special programs and schools for
superior students as undemocratic.

        a. In Philadelphia a special program for su-   35
perior students was attacked.

        b. In Memphis a proposed special school for
superior students was rejected.

*[Here, a and b are examples supporting 2
which in turn supports A and therefore should*   40
*be included, unlike the illustration in II. No-
tice both the continued reduction of the original
wording and the parallel sentence structures
for parallel points.]*

[5]   B. The second misunderstanding is of the meaning   45
of happiness and results from our stress on comfort rather than on accomplishment.

    1. Our schools try to excuse children rather
than discipline them.

    2. They try to amuse children rather than edu-   50
cate them.

*[Details such as shorter hours and metaphors
such as the hickory stick are omitted, the outline stripping the essay down to its bare ideas.]*

[6]   C. The third misunderstanding is of ultimate val-   55
ues.

    1. These values have been denied in recent
teacher education.

        a. Eternal truth is denied.   60

        b. Absolute moral law is denied.

        c. The existence of God is denied.

*[Subpoints at this level could be omitted, but if
we include one we must include all.]*

    2. The inevitable result in mass selfishness is   65
already evident.

[7–9]   IV. To assure our children the freedom to develop, we
must challenge their abilities.

*[Toynbee's statement is a further illustration so that we
can omit it from the outline.]*   70

[7]   A. We can give them a demanding curriculum.

    1. Michelangelo did not learn to paint by doo-
dling.

    2. Mozart did not become a pianist by watching
television.   75

3. They, like Eve Curie and Helen Keller, were challenged by disciplined training.

[*1 and 2 are negative examples and 3 is positive, but they are on the same level.*]

[8] B. We can give them the right to failure. 80

[*De Nöuy's statements, like Toynbee's, can be omitted.*]

1. We must not give high school diplomas without regard to merit.

2. We must be realistic about failure to meet 85 standards and must teach our children realism.

[*Again, 1 is a negative statement and 2 a positive one, but they are parallel points.*]

[9] C. We can give them the best values we know. 90

1. We can show them what history has taught us to be true.

2. These truths may inspire us to make a "ringing message" that could mean true freedom for them. 95

[*Although 1 is the means and 2 is the end in view, they are parallel points under C.*]

Note the following points about the preceding outline:

1. The statement of the main idea makes specific reference to the four main points and is therefore a *one-sentence summary* of the essay; but it does not attempt to jump a level and include any of the supporting points.

2. The four sentences stating the main points, I, II, III, and IV, when taken together, form a slightly longer summary of the essay. We can, in turn, expand this by including the sentences for points A, B, and C.

3. These summaries would seem stiff if compared to the summary of the essay on page 158. Sentence designations in the outline have replaced the transitions used in the summary, and the effort to keep parallel points in parallel wording has eliminated sentence variety. As a piece of writing, the summary is obviously better; as a view of the writer's organization, the outline is better.

4. Starting with the lowest level of subpoints (in this example, designated "a," "b," and so on), check for two things: first, to see that all statements having designations of the same level are actually comparable in importance; second, to see that all subpoints, at every level, are actually logical under the superior point of which they are the divisions.

8-C   Topic Outline of "The Fifth Freedom"

Main idea: Besides the four freedoms we cherish there is a fifth, the freedom
to be one's best, which we are in danger of losing through our
misunderstandings but which we must preserve and pass on to
our children by challenging them.

[1]   I. Four cherished freedoms—from want, from fear, of
speech, of religion
A. Sought by early settlers
B. Protected by our efforts today

[2]   II. Fifth freedom—to be one's best   5
A. Basic to other four
B. In danger of being lost

[3–6]   III. Three misunderstandings of fifth freedom
A. Democracy
1. Education geared to middle level   10
2. Special education for superior students considered undemocratic

[5]   B. Happiness
1. Children excused, not disciplined
2. Children amused, not educated   15

[6]   C. Values
1. Denial of all ultimate values
2. Mass selfishness as result

[7–9]   IV. Challenge necessary for children's development
[7]   A. Demanding curriculum   20
1. Michelangelo
2. Mozart
3. Eve Curie and Helen Keller

[8]   B. Right to failure
1. High school diplomas on merit only   25
2. Realistic view of failure

[9]   C. Our best values
1. Teachings from history
2. Inspiration to be truly free

Compare this topic outline with the sentence outline preceding it. What
differences do you see in wording and arrangement? The brevity here results
not only from using fewer words in each item but from using fewer low-order
subpoints. Although a topic outline can have as many subdivisions as a
sentence outline, in practice it usually has fewer.

8-D Clutter

William Zinsser

Often, what you plan to outline will not have convenient transitional words like "First," "Second," and "Finally" to guide you to the divisions and subdivisions of the material. The third chapter from *On Writing Well* (1980), quoted here in full, lacks such markers, but often the first sentence of a paragraph is a guide to that paragraph's relation to the rest of the discussion. Zinsser develops here the claim he made earlier in his book that "Clutter is the disease of American writing. We are a society strangling in unnecessary words, circular constructions, pompous frills and meaningless jargon."

The numbers and letters in the margin correspond to those of the topic outline that follows.

I.

[1] Fighting clutter is like fighting weeds—the writer is always slightly behind. New varieties sprout overnight, and by noon they are part of American speech. It only takes a John Dean testifying on TV to have everyone in the country saying "at this point in time" instead of "now." 5

II.
  A.
    1.
    2.

[2] Consider all the prepositions that are routinely draped onto verbs that don't need any help. Head up. Free up. Face up to. We no longer head committees. We head them up. We don't face problems anymore. We face up to them when we can free up a few minutes. A small detail, you may say—not worth bothering about. It *is* worth bothering about. The game is won or lost on hundreds of small details. Writing improves in direct ratio to the number of things we can keep out of it that shouldn't be there. "Up" in "free up" shouldn't be there. Can we picture anything being freed *up?* The writer of clean English must examine every word that he puts on paper. He will find a surprising number that don't serve any purpose. 10 15 20

  B.
    1.
    2.

[3] Take the adjective "personal," as in "a personal friend of mine," "his personal feeling" or "her personal physician." It is typical of the words that can be eliminated nine times out of ten. The personal friend has come into the language to distinguish him from the business friend, thereby debasing not only language but friendship. Someone's feeling *is* his personal feeling—that's 25

what "his" means. As for the personal physician, he is
that man so often summoned to the dressing room of a
stricken actress so that she won't have to be treated by   30
the impersonal physician assigned to the theater. Someday I'd like to see him identified as "her doctor."

3.

[4] Or take those curious intervals of time like the
short minute. "Twenty-two short minutes later she had
won the final set." Minutes are minutes, physicians are   35
physicians, friends are friends. The rest is clutter.

C.

[5] Clutter is the laborious phrase which has pushed
out the short word that means the same thing. These
locutions are a drag on energy and momentum. Even
before John Dean gave us "at this point in time," people   40
had stopped saying "now." They were saying "at the
present time," or "currently," or "presently" (which
means "soon"). Yet the idea can always be expressed by
"now" to mean the immediate moment ("Now I can see
him"), or by "today" to mean the historical present   45
("Today prices are high"), or simply by the verb "to be"
("It is raining"). There is no need to say, "At the present
time we are experiencing precipitation."

III.

[6] Speaking of which, we are experiencing considera-
ble difficulty getting *that* word out of the language now   50

A.

that it has lumbered in. Even your dentist will ask if you
are experiencing any pain. If he were asking one of his
own children he would say, "Does it hurt?" He would,
in short, be himself. By using a more pompous phrase in
his professional role he not only sounds more important;   55

B.

he blunts the painful edge of truth. It is the language of
the airline stewardess demonstrating the oxygen mask
that will drop down if the plane should somehow run out
of air. "In the extremely unlikely possibility that the
aircraft should experience such an eventuality," she be-   60
gins—a phrase so oxygen-depriving in itself that we are
prepared for any disaster, and even gasping death shall
lose its sting. As for those "smoking materials" that she
asks us to "kindly extinguish," I often wonder what materials are smoking. Maybe she thinks my coat and tie are   65
on fire.

C.

[7] Clutter is the ponderous euphemism that turns a
slum into a depressed socioeconomic area, a salesman
into a marketing representative, a dumb kid into an underachiever and garbage collectors into waste disposal   70
personnel. In New Canaan, Conn., the incinerator is now

the "volume reduction plant." I hate to think what they call the town dump.

D.   [8] Clutter is the official language used by the American corporation—in the news release and the annual report—to hide its mistakes. When a big company recently announced that it was "decentralizing its organization structure into major profit-centered businesses" and that "corporate staff services will be aligned under two senior vice-presidents" it meant that it had had a lousy year.

    [9] Clutter is the language of the interoffice memo ("The trend to mosaic communication is reducing the meaningfulness of concern about whether or not demographic segments differ in their tolerance of periodicity") and the language of computers ("We are offering functional digital programming options that have built-in parallel reciprocal capabilities with compatible third-generation contingencies and hardware").

E.   [10] Clutter is the language of the Pentagon throwing dust in the eyes of the populace by calling an invasion a "reinforced protective reaction strike" and by justifying its vast budgets on the need for "credible second-strike capability" and "counter-force deterrence." How can we grasp such vaporous double-talk? As George Orwell pointed out in "Politics and the English Language," an essay written in 1946 but cited frequently during the Vietnam years of Johnson and Nixon, "In our time, political speech and writing are largely the defense of the indefensible. . . . Thus political language has to consist largely of euphemism, question-begging and sheer cloudy vagueness." Orwell's warning that clutter is not just a nuisance but a deadly tool did not turn out to be inoperative. By the 1960s his words had come true in America.

IV.   [11] I could go on quoting examples from various fields—every profession has its growing arsenal of jargon to fire at the layman and hurl him back from its walls. But the list would be depressing and the lesson tedious. The point of raising it now is to serve notice that clutter is the enemy, whatever form it takes. It slows the reader and robs the writer of his personality, making him seem pretentious.

A.   [12] Beware, then, of the long word that is no better than the short word: "numerous" (many), "facilitate" (ease), "individual" (man or woman), "remainder"

(rest), "initial" (first), "implement" (do), "sufficient"
(enough), "attempt" (try), "referred to as" (called), and
hundreds more. Beware, too, of all the slippery new fad

B.   words for which the language already has equivalents:
overview and quantify, paradigm and parameter, input   120
and throughput, peer group and interface, private sector
and public sector, optimize and maximize, prioritize and
potentialize. They are all weeds that will smother what
you write.

C.   [13] Nor are all the weeds so obvious. Just as insidious   125
are the little growths of perfectly ordinary words with
which we explain how we propose to go about our explaining, or which inflate a simple preposition or conjunction into a whole windy phrase.

1.   [14] "I might add," "It should be pointed out," "It is   130
interesting to note that"—how many sentences begin
with these dreary clauses announcing what the writer is
going to do next? If you might add, add it. If it should
be pointed out, point it out. If it is interesting to note,
make it interesting. Being told that something is interest-   135
ing is the surest way of tempting the reader to find it dull;
are we not all stupefied by what follows when someone
says, "This will interest you"? As for the inflated preposi-

2.   tions and conjunctions, they are the innumerable phrases
like "with the possible exception of" (except), "for the   140
reason that" (because), "he totally lacked the ability to"
(he couldn't), "until such time as" (until), "for the purpose of" (for).

V.   [15] Clutter takes more forms than you can shake
twenty sticks at. Prune it ruthlessly. Be grateful for every-   145
thing that you can throw away. Re-examine each sentence that you put on paper. Is every word doing new
and useful work? Can any thought be expressed with
more economy? Is anything pompous or pretentious or
faddish? Are you hanging on to something useless just   150
because you think it's beautiful?
       [16] Simplify, simplify.

8-E   Topic Outline of "Clutter"

Main idea: To write effectively we must reduce clutter in our use of language.

[1]   I. Problem of rapid growth of clutter
             II. Redundancies
[2]   A. Prepositions
                      1. Unnecessary ("head up")
                      2. Illogical ("free up")   5
[3–4]   B. Adjectives
                      1. Unnecessary ("personal friend/feeling/
                         physician")
                      2. Debasing meaning ("personal friendship")
                      3. Illogical ("short minutes")   10
[5]   C. Longer words and phrases
[6]   III. Euphemisms and jargon to conceal unpleasant
                  truths
                  A. Physical pain
                  B. Danger   15
[7]   C. Social discrimination
[8–9]   D. Bad business news
[10]   E. Government action
             IV. Other redundancies
[11–14]   A. Long words and phrases ("numerous" for   20
                     "many")
                  B. Fad words ("optimize")
                  C. Ordinary words
[15]   1. Unnecessary explanations
[16]   2. Inflated prepositions and conjunctions   25
             V. Need for ruthless editing: simplify

    1. In "The Fifth Freedom" every paragraph received an outline designation of either the first or second level (I and II, and III. A, B, C, and IV. A, B, and C). How does the relationship between the paragraphs and the outline designations of "Clutter" differ from this?

    2. What are the reasons for the differences?

    3. Why do paragraphs 4 and 9 have no corresponding designations in the outline?

4. How is paragraph 13 related to the rest of the essay?

5. In the outline II.A and II.B are subdivided, but II.C is not. Why?

6. Make a sentence outline of "Clutter."

ASSIGNMENTS

1. Before you start work on outlining the ideas in an essay, test your knowledge of numbering and arrangement and your sense of logical relationships by putting into proper topical outline form the items in the following unorganized list. Use as many main points and as many degrees of subordination as the material seems to you to require, but limit yourself to these words.

caves	meat	sandals	chicken
clothing	tents	Irish potatoes	fruit
sausage	vegetables	pork	sneakers
potatoes	lemons	boots	shelter
food	suits	oranges	hats
cabins	cottages	hamburger	beans
apples	lima beans	sweet potatoes	houses
sauerkraut	cole slaw	slippers	corn
pineapple	bacon	grapefruit	beef
caps	bungalows	berets	headgear
footwear	navy beans	T-bone steaks	cabbage

2. a. Assuming common agreement as to the definition of each term, there can be no disagreement as to two aspects of the completed arrangement: the items that will appear in a single group at a given level (such as oranges, lemons, etc.) and the subpoints that will appear under a given main point (such as oranges, lemons, etc., under fruit), for this much is logically inherent in the material.

   b. However, the arrangement of the items within a single group at any level will vary according to purpose. Consider, for example, the differing orders of the five items under the larger heading of fruit that may result, depending on whether the issue is size, color, type, price, scarcity, area of production, popularity, or nutritive value. Justify, according to some such purpose, the order within each group in your own arrangement. Will the same purpose determine the order within each?

   c. Under what main idea might all these items appear?

3. Choose a magazine article, a book chapter, or an essay from a unit in this book and compose an outline in each style based on it. These should be good for your first efforts: Unit 4-H, 6-E, 12-D, and 15-C. These are more challenging: Unit 4-I; 6-B; 10-D; 12-B and G; 13-H; 15-I; 16-A, F, and J; and the speeches by Frederick Douglass, John F. Kennedy, and Martin Luther King, Jr., in "Essays for Further Reading."

PART III

Supporting the Thesis:
Logical Methods

UNIT 9

Process

What's the shortest route to your house? How is lead-free gasoline produced? How can I become a better chess player? How do you start to housebreak a puppy? How do beginning writers get their books published? How do American political parties choose candidates? How are stocks sold in the over-the-counter market? How do you apply for a bank loan?

Some of these questions arise from a practical need for directions, others from a desire for more information or from simple curiosity. The answer to each requires the analysis of a process—of a series of related actions serving a particular purpose or leading to a particular goal. You have already had many occasions to answer such questions orally, and you will have many occasions to give written answers on examinations, in reports, and in your career.

In writing a process analysis, you should draw particularly on your training in *description* and *narration* because you will be describing a series of actions in chronological order. You will also need your training in *organizing* to help you decide where to give background information and, when you must describe two or more simultaneous actions, which one to take first. Most of all, you will need your training in *accurate observation.* An error on your part could make your readers take the wrong road, lose a chess game, spoil a formula, or misunderstand the operation of a machine.

Ordinarily, you will write a process analysis in answer to a question that someone else asks you, and the nature of the question will determine your specific topic. For a practice paper, however, you should choose your own topic because it must be one about which you have special knowledge. For a paper giving directions on how to do something that your readers may want to do themselves, such as housebreak a puppy, choose a process that you have performed yourself several times so that you are thoroughly familiar with it from a performer's point of view. For a paper giving your readers information on how something is done, such as launching a spacecraft, choose a process that particularly interests you and that you have observed closely or read a great deal about so that you will be able to give all the necessary details.

When you have chosen a subject and decided on your purpose—to give your readers directions to follow or information to satisfy their curiosity—follow these steps in planning and writing your paper:

1. **Think through the procedure from start to finish** so that you see it as a whole. An overall view will help you with all the other steps in planning the paper.

2. **Ask yourself what background information, if any, your readers need** as an introduction to the process, such as its past history, in what locations and under what conditions it is usually performed, and so on. If time and space permit, include background information that is interesting for its own sake even though not necessary for an understanding of the process.

3. **Divide the process into steps.** Your practice in making subdivisions and sub-subdivisions in outlines will help you here.

4. **Describe each step in the process in complete detail.** You are something of a specialist in the subject you have chosen, but your readers are not. Remember that specialists are often unclear in explaining their specialties because they forget to see them from the viewpoint of the untrained person. For example, in giving the recipe for a sauce, an experienced chef may omit a detail that other chefs would take for granted, but without it an amateur will produce something that tastes like glue. Be careful not to talk down to your readers, but always assume that they are ignorant of your subject.

5. **Include in your description the reasons for each step you describe.** Clear directions should result in success, but your readers will appreciate warnings and explanations of *why* a certain step is necessary as well as *how* it is to be taken. "Always work with the knife blade turned away from you so that you will not cut yourself if it slips." "Let the milk cool before adding the beaten egg, which otherwise will cook into lumps before you can stir it in."

6. **Define any special terms you use.** Words that have become familiar to you may be stumbling blocks to readers unfamiliar with your subject. Every field has its own vocabulary—special words or special meanings attached to common words. Words and phrases such as "empennage," "shim," and "clarify the butter" will be immediately understood by the aeronautical engineer, the carpenter, and the cook, respectively, and may be used freely by one craftsman writing for another. But for general readers, you must carefully define such terms or substitute more familiar ones.

7. **Use illustrative aids whenever appropriate.** Make your descriptions as definite and concrete as you can. Even a hastily drawn map is more useful than a page of written instructions on how to go somewhere. A simple sketch or diagram will clarify a complicated procedure, as will verbal images such as, "The standard gearshift moves in an H pattern."

8. **Check and doublecheck what you write for accuracy and clarity.** One or two small factual errors or ambiguities may not do serious harm in some kinds of writing, but when you tell readers how to do something, they depend on you for their success.

∴   ∴   ∴

The **organization for both types of process paper,** giving directions or giving information, is the same—the chronological pattern. Time is always involved in doing things. The sequence of parts, then, takes care of itself. But you must choose how to group many small, separate steps in a few clear, manageable units. Four suboperations of five steps each, for instance, are far easier to follow and remember than twenty single steps. The basic methods for outlining, which we applied to the imaginary topic in Unit 1 and examined in more detail in Unit 8, are the ones to use here.

However familiar you may be with the process of starting a new lawn, for example, you must first think through the decisions and motions involved in that procedure before you can write a process paper on it. You may decide that these steps should be mentioned:

(1) Weeding   (6) Seeding
(2) Digging to loosen soil   (7) Raking to distribute seed
(3) Liming   (8) Rolling
(4) Fertilizing   (9) Watering
(5) Raking to distribute chemicals

When you look over these steps carefully, however, you realize that they are not equal in importance. You can group them in a few main units, each consisting of several related steps:

I. Preparing the soil   III. Planting seed
   A. Weeding   A. Seeding
   B. Digging to loosen soil   B. Raking to distribute seed
II. Adding chemicals   C. Rolling
   A. Liming   IV. Watering
   B. Fertilizing
   C. Raking to distribute
      chemicals

You are at last ready to start. Cover this skeleton plan with the flesh of words and phrases; the bones should never stick out in the body of your finished prose. Your paper is more than a sentence outline; instead, your plan should give your readers a pleasant sense of meaningful order. Determine the amount of space needed for each main division and develop your paragraphs accordingly. Use transitional devices to hold them together and especially to clarify any shift from one division of your subject to another, but vary these devices. Do not overdo the easy but monotonous "then" and "the next step."

·: · ·: ·:

Catching your readers' interest can be important in a process essay. To write everyday cookbook kinds of direction-giving, you need only clarity and logical order. Someone trying to operate an unfamiliar washing machine wants brief, clear, numbered directions, but readers of an essay expect more.

Consider what attitude you should take toward your material—what tone to adopt for your intended readers. In giving directions, do not limit yourself to the formal "One does this" or the more direct "Do that." You may instead present your directions in a personal narrative and, by saying something like "I did this," add human interest. Rather than plunging directly into the first step of the procedure, you may begin in a leisurely fashion—with an account of how you came to be familiar with the process, or why you consider it worth doing. Instead of ending with the final step, you may give an account of the results of the procedure and their significance—not an essential part of direction-giving as such but often adding reader interest.

In giving general information, try to make it lively as well as intelligible. *Take advantage of the arts of description, narration, and exemplification as aids to exposition.* Enliven your account of a spacecraft launching with vivid descriptions of the equipment and the people involved, or with your own reactions to the scene, so that your readers feel that they are there, sharing the experience with you. Also, give special thought to composing an attention-getting beginning and a memorable ending.

EXAMPLES

A process is a major feature in each of the following selections. Other selections in which a process is important are Nemy's "Business Status" (11-G), Peeples' "Branch Libraries" (12-B), Burgess's "Splitting the Word" (12-H), Conza's "Christmas Eve" (12-I), Conroy's "Death of an Island" (13-B), Keremes's "The Passing of Little Gibbs Road" (15-J), Sullivan's "Cyclones" (14-A), Bean's "No Easy Job" (14-C), and Swift's "A Modest Proposal" ("Essays for Further Reading"-A).

The first selection in this unit is an example of completely impersonal direction-giving. Notice how the second writer, while describing the same basic process as the first, gives her directions a highly personal tone. In the other examples, the personalities of the writers color their descriptions in varying degrees and by varying methods.

9-A   Baked Beans

This is a standard recipe from a cookbook.

Soak 2 cupfuls of dry beans overnight. In the morning, boil until soft, and drain. Put them into a covered bean pot with ¼ lb. salt pork. Mix into ½ cup of boiling water the following: ½ tsp. baking soda, ¼ tsp. mustard, ¼ cup molasses, and salt and pepper to taste. Pour over beans, adding enough more water to cover. Bake for 6 hours in a slow oven, uncovering during the last half hour to brown.   5

9-B Baking Beans

Louise Dickinson Rich

This selection comes from *We Took to the Woods* (1942), an autobiographical account of the author's experience after she and her husband left their city home for what they hoped would be the "simple life" in Maine.

Now consider the baking of the beans. Baked beans have to be baked. That sounds like a gratuitous restatement of the obvious, but it isn't. Some misguided souls boil beans all day and call the lily-livered result baked beans. I refrain from comment.

We use either New York State or Michigan white beans, be-   5
cause we like them best, although yellow-eyes are very popular, too. I take two generous cups of dry beans, soak overnight and put them on to boil early in the morning. When the skins curl off when you blow on them, they've boiled long enough. Then I put in the bottom of the bean pot, or iron kettle with a tight-fitting   10
cover, a six-by-eight-inch square of salt pork with the rind slashed every quarter of an inch, a quarter of a cup of sugar, half a cup of molasses, a large onion chopped fairly fine, and a heaping teaspoonful of dry mustard. This amount of sugar and molasses may be increased or cut, depending on whether you like your   15
beans sweeter or not so sweet. This is a matter every man has to decide for himself. The beans are dumped in on top of this conglomerate, and enough hot water is added to cover, but only cover. The baking pot should be large enough so there's at least an inch of freeboard above the water. Otherwise they'll boil over   20
and smell to high heaven. Cover tightly and put into a medium oven—about 350° is right. They should be in the oven by half past nine in the morning at the latest, and they should stay there until supper time, which in our family is at six.

So far there is no trick in making good baked beans. The trick,   25
if it can be dignified by such a term, lies in the baking, and like a great many trade tricks, it consists only of patience and conscientious care. You have to tend the beans faithfully, adding water whenever the level gets down below the top of the beans, and you have to keep the oven temperature even. If you're lazy, you can   30
put in a lot of water and not have to watch them so closely. But to get the best results, you should add only enough water each time to barely cover the beans. This means that you'll give up all

social engagements for the day, because you can't leave the baby
for more than half an hour at a time. I think the results are worth   35
it—but then, I haven't anywhere special to go anyhow. My beans
are brown and mealy, and they swim in a thick brown juice.
They're good. I always serve them with corn bread, ketchup and
pickles.

1. Where and how does the writer give her opinions?

2. In Example A, if anything were omitted from the directions, they would be
incomplete. What could be omitted here and still leave us with adequate directions
for baking beans? What would such omissions do to the overall effect?

3. Check the etymology, denotation, and connotation of *gratuitous* and *conglomerate*.

9-C   Taking Care of Contacts

Marjorie Sybul *(student)*

Except for the light touch just before the end, this is straightforward direction-
giving.

ANALYSIS
I. General
   problem

  A. General
    proce-
    dure #1
  B. General
    proce-
    dure #2

       Contact lenses are a big investment. Before you decide
to buy a pair, you should realize that hard contact lenses
require much more care than does an ordinary pair of
glasses. A definite procedure must be followed daily for
your own safety. Unlike a pair of glasses that is casually   5
put on and taken off, contact lenses must be prepared for
insertion and, when not in use, must be stored in a liquid.
You must use two special solutions: a wetting agent to
prepare the lenses for insertion, and a soaking agent to
keep the lenses pliable.   10

II. Specific
  proce-
  dures:
  nine steps
  before
  insertion

       Before touching your contact lenses, wash your hands
thoroughly; bacteria trapped between the lens and the
eye can cause infection. Then uncap the bottle of wetting
solution and set it aside. Close the sink drain to prevent
the loss of a lens if you accidentally drop it. Open the left   15
chamber of the lens case. The concave surface of the lens
will be facing you. Touch the lens very gently; it will stick
to your wet finger. Place it between your thumb and

forefinger, and carefully rinse it with water. Now, holding the lens at its edges, squeeze one drop of wetting   20
solution on each side. Rub the lens gently and rinse
again. Put another drop on the concave surface. The lens
is now ready for insertion.

III. Specific   At first, inserting the lens will seem very difficult, but,
    proce-   like many other things, it becomes easier with practice.   25
    dures;   Balance the lens on the tip of your middle finger and
    four   slowly raise your finger to your eye. At the same time,
    steps for   be sure to cup your other hand underneath to catch the
    insertion   lens should it drop from your finger. Look straight ahead
                 and bring the lens to your iris. At the slightest touch, the   30
                 lens will pop into place. Now follow the same procedure
                 with the other lens.

IV. Specific   Removing the contact lens is fun. First open the appro-
    proce-   priate chamber of your lens case. Then bend your head
    dures;   down and place one cupped hand under your eye. With   35
    six steps   the other hand, pull the outer edge of your eyelid to one
    for   side as though you were imitating the shape of an Orien-
    removal   tal eye. Blink, and the lens will pop into your hand. Place
                 the lens in the lens case with the concave side facing you.
                 Squeeze a few drops of soaking solution over it and close   40
                 the chamber. The soaking solution will be rinsed away
                 the next time you reinsert the lens.

V. Benefits   This entire procedure takes only a few moments, and
                 every step must always be followed. There are several
  A. Benefit   large benefits. When any of your lensless friends happen   45
     #1   to see you popping your lenses in or out, they are sure
                 to be impressed and fascinated by your courage and will
  B. Benefit   probably gasp and groan. When you meet another lens
     #2   wearer, you will immediately have a great bond in com-
                 mon and will be able to swap stories about the time you   50
                 lost a lens in the middle of the decisive game in a tennis
                 match or on a crowded dance floor. More seriously, the
  C. Bene-   small sacrifice in time and effort required to learn these
     fits #3,   procedures and follow them faithfully will be more than
     4   repaid by the great improvement in your appearance and   55
                 in your peripheral vision.

| 9-D | In Praise of the Archenemy |

Jonathan Richardson

In this essay, here complete, a professor of biology explains a process of natural growth that has inspired his respect for a common weed, the dandelion, and answers his own question, "How does this escape artist defy the guillotine?" or, in more direct terms, "What does a dandelion do to survive and how does it do it?"

Is it un-American to admire the archenemy? I speak of *Taraxacum officinale,* that impudent yellow face in every green carpet of grass. Surely you can't wholly hate such a spunky antagonist, especially one with the survival tricks of a Houdini. From spring to fall it performs its weekly escape act, and if a poll were taken   5
among suburbanites to nominate the weed most impervious to lawn mowers, *Taraxacum*—the dandelion—would no doubt sweep the election.

But Subversive I may be, but I can't resist applauding a species that defies man's best efforts to eradicate it. A well-manicured lawn is   10
a thing of beauty; but, if considered without prejudice, so is a dandelion. Consequently I have never let the counterattack of *Taraxacum* ruin my weekends, though it has not always helped my mood. Who, after all, enjoys being ridiculed? And how else can one feel when, after a muscular session with the mower, one   15
is greeted the next day by a throng of yellow faces and silver bonnets towering over the close-cropped turf?

How does this escape artist defy the guillotine? Part of its strategy is obvious at a glance. In any well-kept lawn the leaves of dandelions emerge at ground level rather than from a stalk and   20
elude damage by lying flattened to the ground. Indeed, the more often you mow, the flatter the leaves lie. The only stalk is the naked one that hoists the flower and later the seed ball aloft.

But it is precisely these elevated parts, reminiscent of a thumb held to an urchin's nose, that most enrage the lawn perfectionist.   25
One gloomy Sunday, having been mocked yet again, my irritation gave way to curiosity. How could those stalks have escaped the blade that on Friday was whirring so low? Curiosity, as it too rarely does, gave rise to investigation; over the next several weeks, armed with ruler, pencil, and paper, I recorded the   30
growth of individual stems. *Voilà!* The cleverest element in *Taraxacum*'s strategy was revealed in all its simplicity.

My measurements showed that the potentially vulnerable head of a dandelion is not thrust skyward at a constant rate but in bursts. For many days after a bud appears it has no stalk at all, but nestles in its flat rosette of leaves like the centerpiece of a salad platter, well below the lowest setting of my mower. Only when the bud is ready to open does the stalk suddenly begin to grow. Then, high above its basal leaves for just a day or two, the flower advertises boldly to passing insects. When the bloom closes, the stalk cannot undo its previous growth but becomes flaccid and collapses, so that while its seeds mature, the aging flower head again lies close to the ground. A mower at this time will pass right over it again. Then the stalk stiffens and there is another spurt of growth. Within a day or two the head may be raised five or six inches, and the ripe seed ball becomes an easy target for wind (or the breath of helpful children), which disperses the seeds on their gossamer parachutes.

Thus for only two brief periods in a dandelion's growth cycle— when the flower opens and when the seeds are ready for dispersal—is it vulnerable to a marauding mower. Given a plant's need to attract pollinators and disseminate its offspring, one can scarcely imagine a more perfect strategy.

But even now a more evasive strategy is in prospect. *Taraxacum* no longer really needs insects to effect pollination; it has evolved the ability to set seed and to germinate without cross-fertilization (even, in many cases, without fertilization at all—a phenomenon known as apomixis). This being so, the first growth spurt of the stalk, the function of which is surely to make the flower conspicuous to pollinators, seems now an unnecessary evolutionary anachronism. The next step in adaptation may be to delay stalk growth until after flowering is completed and the seeds are ready for dispersal. This would leave but one brief phase of vulnerability to the blade in each reproductive cycle.

Vulnerability, however, is a relative term. If a few of the many dandelions in my lawn unluckily raise their heads before I start mowing, they still have the last laugh. Decapitation is not the end, for the energy-packed root and leaves survive, and in time another bud will appear. Painstaking application of herbicides to individual plants seems the only way to produce a lawn without dandelions—and my sense of fair play has always deterred me from this approach. Besides, a lawn full of blackened, chemical-blasted weeds is, at least temporarily, far less attractive than a lawn full of healthy ones.

Like many others, *Taraxacum* is not an American weed but an import from the Old World. Its introduction may have been intentional, because dandelions were once considered useful food

plants. But it is more likely that the first seeds arrived uninvited
in the baggage of some unsuspecting European immigrant. Let us
hope the carrier found the New World as bountiful as did the   80
hitchhiker!

The marvelous dispersal powers of weeds couple with the travels of humankind to transport these plants to almost every spot
where one can conceive of them growing. A few years ago, while
enjoying a sabbatical leave in Australia, I prematurely concluded   85
that this land of isolation, famous for its distinctive flora and
fauna, had managed to escape the dandelion. Of course I was
mistaken. In Canberra, my sabbatical home, the climate is drier
than *Taraxacum* likes, and I had arrived in the cool of midwinter.
So it is not surprising that I did not see the familiar yellow heads   90
during my first weeks Down Under. Where did I finally find
them? Where else but in the close-clipped, well-watered lawns of
the American embassy!

In truth, frequent mowing is precisely the reason that dandelions are so successful in lawns. If the grass is allowed to grow tall, 95
these ground-hugging plants will soon be shaded out, as one can
appreciate by comparing their numbers in lawns and nearby un-
mown meadows. In a meadow one can find a few dandelions
reaching for the sun as best they can—their leaves larger and no
longer prostrate, their stalks longer than those in your lawn—but   100
the competition of larger plants is not friendly to *Taraxacum.*

Doubtless the dandelion's lawn-mower strategy appeared long
before the first lawn, for such a strategy also is ideal in pastures
and heavily grazed natural grasslands. In an earlier, more rural
America dandelions flourished primarily in barnyards and pas-   105
tures. Here, as in a lawn, competing plant species are cropped
short while the low-lying dandelion is spared. Indeed, certain
features of *Taraxacum*—for example its toothed, thistle-mimick-
ing leaves and bitter white sap—make sense as adaptations to
grazing animals, not to mechanical grazers.   110

The spread of urbanization at the expense of rural America has
not checked the spread of the dandelion. Indeed, its growth may
be nearly as rampant as ours. For each year we create for our
pretty adversary countless additional acres of the finest *Taraxacum*
habitat of all—suburban lawns!   115

1. What examples of figurative language, especially personification, can you
find?

2. What does the personification suggest as to the writer's attitude toward
dandelions?

3. Dandelions are well adapted to escape being killed by lawnmowers, but what does the writer suggest caused that adaptation?

4. Check the etymology, denotation, and connotation of *impudent, antagonist, impervious, flaccid, gossamer, germinate, anachronism, sabbatical, prostrate, rampant.*

9-E How Dictionaries Are Made

S. I. Hayakawa

This is a complete subdivision of a chapter in *Language in Thought and Action* (4th edition, 1978). The author is a semanticist, a specialist in the development and changes in the meanings of words.

It is an almost universal belief that every word has a "correct meaning," that we learn these meanings principally from teachers and grammarians (except that most of the time we don't bother to, so that we ordinarily speak "sloppy English"), and that dictionaries and grammars are the "supreme authority" in matters of 5
meaning and usage. Few people ask by what authority the writers of dictionaries and grammars say what they say. The docility with which most people bow down to the dictionary is amazing, and the person who says, "Well, the dictionary is wrong!" is looked upon with smiles of pity and amusement which say plainly, "Poor 10
fellow! He's really quite sane otherwise."

Let us see how dictionaries are made and how the editors arrive at definitions. What follows applies, incidentally, only to those dictionary offices where first-hand, original research goes on—not those in which editors simply copy existing dictionaries. The task 15
of writing a dictionary begins with the reading of vast amounts of the literature of the period or subject that it is intended to cover. As the editors read, they copy on cards every interesting or rare word, every unusual or peculiar occurrence of a common word, a large number of common words in their ordinary uses, 20
and also the sentences in which each of these words appears, thus:

> pail
> The dairy *pails* bring home increase of milk
> Keats, *Endymion*
> I, 44–45

That is to say, the context of each word is collected, along with the word itself. For a really big job of dictionary writing, such as the *Oxford English Dictionary* (usually bound in about twenty-five volumes), millions of such cards are collected, and the task of editing occupies decades. As the cards are collected, they are alphabetized and sorted. When the sorting is completed, there will be for each word anywhere from two or three to several hundred illustrative quotations, each on its card.

To define a word, then, the dictionary editor places before him the stack of cards illustrating that word; each of the cards represents an actual use of the word by a writer of some literary or historical importance. He reads the cards carefully, discards some, re-reads the rest, and divides up the stack according to what he thinks are the several senses of the word. Finally, he writes his definitions, following the hard-and-fast rule that each definition must be based on what the quotations in front of him reveal about the meaning of the word. The editor cannot be influenced by what he thinks a given word ought to mean. He must work according to the cards, or not at all.

The writing of a dictionary, therefore, is not a task of setting up authoritative statements about the "true meanings" of words, but a task of recording, to the best of one's ability, what various words have meant to authors in the distant or immediate past. The writer of a dictionary is a historian, not a lawgiver. If, for example, we had been writing a dictionary in 1890, or even as late as 1919, we could have said that the word "broadcast" means "to scatter," seed and so on; but we could not have decreed that from 1921 on, the commonest meaning of the word should become "to disseminate audible messages, etc., by wireless telephony." To regard the dictionary as an "authority," therefore, is to credit the dictionary writer with gifts of prophecy which neither he nor anyone else possesses. In choosing our words when we speak or write, we can be guided by the historical record afforded us by the dictionary, but we cannot be bound by it, because new situations, new experiences, new inventions, new feelings, are always compelling us to give new uses to old words. Looking under a "hood," we should ordinarily have found, five hundred years ago, a monk; today, we find a motorcar engine.

1. What larger expository purpose than is indicated by the title does this selection serve? Where is it discussed? Write a sentence that expresses what you believe to be the main idea of the whole essay.

2. Which paragraphs actually tell how dictionaries are made? Make a numbered list of the main steps in the process.

9-F   The Photovoltaic Cell

Tracy Kidder

This description of the process by which two wafers of silicon can be made to produce electricity appears in *The Soul of a New Machine* for which Tracy Kidder won a Pulitzer Prize in 1982.

In solid-state physics lies a fundamental surprise, like the rabbit inside a magician's top hat. This is the recognition that the apparently quiescent, lumpish things of nature may be veritable carnivals of change and motion on the inside. Most solar cells on the market today are made of silicon, which along with oxygen is   5
found in ordinary sand and is the second most abundant element on earth. A few complex, expensive processes tear the silicon away from the oxygen and convert it into a very thin wafer of crystal. Sunlight penetrating such a crystalline wafer will transfer some of its energy to some of the atomic particles inside—specifi-   10
cally, to the little bits of matter called electrons. (As high school courses in physics teach, electrons are what make electricity; a flow of electrons *is* an electrical current.) In effect, the light that enters the wafer of silicon will knock some electrons away from their atoms and set them free.   15
But to manage this small internal ferment, to make the electrons move in an orderly, useful fashion, the manufacturer must turn the silicon wafer into a sandwich. Imagine two slightly different slices of material fused together face to face. In a sense, a very rough and incomplete one, this sandwich is a battery, one   20
slice representing the positive pole, the other the negative; an external wire connects the two open faces. Put this contraption out in the sun. The light passes through one slice of the sandwich and, reaching the area where the two slices meet, breaks chemical bonds, releasing electrons. If the wafer were not a sandwich but   25
all of a piece, the freed electrons would quickly return where they came from, and that would be the end of it. But by giving the wafer two sides, imbued with opposite electrical properties, the manufacturer has created an internal pressure which forces the loosened electrons to one side of the sandwich and the broken   30
bonds to the other. The broken bonds and electrons are of opposite charges. They are attracted to each other. But they cannot

flow back the way they came: the pressure is one-way. So the
electrons take the path of least resistance, and flow outward to the
open face on their side of the wafer and into the external wire.   35
Attach to this wire a small bulb and it should light up.

1. Where does the writer use a simile and metaphors to help explain the
process?

2. Where does he use an analogy?

3. Check the etymology, denotation, and connotation of *quiescent, silicon, wafer,
particle, electron, ferment, fused, imbued.*

9-G   How to Have Free
                Entertainment with Your Meal

Cynthia Hoffman *(student)*

The writer uses satire to point out the selfish rudeness of some restaurant
patrons. Compare her opinions with Natsuko Uesugi's in "Greed" (Unit 12-D).

Dining out is popular these days. Magazines are devoted to
exploring the best places to dine. Newspapers and local television
programs frequently carry critiques of restaurant cuisine and am-
bience. Miss Manners gives advice on the proper fork for each
course of the meal. Yet one important aspect of patronizing res-   5
taurants is often overlooked: the free entertainment portion—the
abuse of the waitress.

It's best to start the comedy right off, when your server makes
her first appearance at your table. As she introduces herself and
begins to relay such trivia as the daily specials and the soup du   10
jour, take this as your cue to begin a conversation with others in
your party. To ensure a successful evening, under no circumstances should you make any acknowledgment whatsoever of her
presence. Only when she has gotten five feet away from your
table should you grant her recognition and summon her back to   15
order cocktails. Use the finger-snapping method of getting attention; it is the most common and most effective.

Now we raise the curtain for Act II, ordering the meal. Ask as
many questions as humanly possible. An inquisitive customer is
a happy customer, especially while you watch the waitress cringe   20

as each member of your group asks her to repeat the list of salad dressings ad infinitum. This questioning should continue for no less than ten minutes before you actually order anything from the menu. And do not order right away what you really want to eat; as a patron, changing your selection as frequently as possible is   25 your prerogative and your duty. Besides, it's so much fun to watch the server as she frantically tries to amend the order correctly.

Act III, the arrival of the food, is my favorite portion of the evening and the most entertaining. You are now able to see   30 whether you confused the waitress successfully during Act II. If the food you ordered is placed before another person or if the whole order is completely amiss, take a bow. You have a potential hit on your hands. Once the plate-switching has ceased, the plot truly begins to thicken. Insist that your steak is too well done   35 when you distinctly indicated that you wanted it rare. (Never mind the actual order.) The other veteran members of the troupe will then use this as a signal to do the same. Twice each should be sufficient.

Receiving the check is not necessarily the final curtain for the   40 production. The modus operandi may take various forms—anything from insisting on an error in the addition to ordering more food or drink. The option is all yours. But as a final curtain call, the crowning glory of the evening, remain seated without paying the bill until they begin turning off the lights.   45

Eating out can be much more enjoyable this way. If there is a sudden lull in the conversation, why, just send back your salad. It's guaranteed to get a few laughs and arouse good feelings. And for those diners who believe that all of this is reminiscent of the Marquis de Sade, well, why do you think the waitress receives a   50 tip?—for the entertainment, of course. Besides, the customer is always right.

ASSIGNMENTS

1. Look through the selections in this unit for examples of the four points of view from which directions can be presented: the first-person "I (or we) do this," the second-person "You do that," the indefinite third-person "One should do thus and so," and the impersonal passive "Such and such should be done." Compare the effects produced. Will your choice of method be governed by your material, your attitude toward it, or your reader?
2. Some of these selections have strictly informative titles. Try supplying more stimulating ones for some of them (see Unit 1, page 22).

3. For a direction-giving paper do not choose an involved subject, like how to cure inflation, or a complicated procedure, like how to play bridge, but rather some simple process for which you can give directions that will actually direct. You need not limit yourself, however, to a procedure that can be done perfectly on the first attempt; you may assume the necessity for repeated practice, as in how to perform the crawl stroke.

Suitable subjects include how to perform a card trick, use a jigsaw, prepare a favorite dish, cast for trout, treat a snakebite, learn to ride a bicycle, write a theme, paddle a canoe, sail a boat, go waterskiing or skin diving, repair a leaky faucet or an electrical connection, shoot free throws, make an archer's bow, build a model airplane, caddy, run a trap line, develop films, drive a car, administer artificial respiration, conduct a business meeting. These topics, however, like those in other units, are meant merely as *suggestions,* to be used if you wish, but preferably to remind you of other suitable ones on which you may be even better equipped to write. When you have chosen a subject:

a. Present it as a list of numbered steps (pages 191–192).

b. Make a rough outline in which you arrange these steps logically into larger related units (page 192).

c. Write out the procedure as briefly as possible, limiting yourself to a simple straightforward account of how to do it and working from this outline.

d. Write a second essay in which you add as much reader interest as you can—this will involve decisions as to the purpose of your paper, the kind of reader to whom it is addressed, and the attitude you wish to assume toward your subject.

4. For your informative process paper choose a subject that is so familiar to you that you can explain it accurately and interestingly to those less well informed. Remember that you can choose a larger field than for assignment 3, since you will not need to go into the exact details necessary to direction-giving. Suggested topics: How a drug store is run (compare "How to Make an Ice Cream Soda" in scope), how a fish (bird, insect, animal) lives, how an election is conducted, how calves (chickens, pigs) are raised, how something is mined or grown or harvested, how some business is run, how an airplane flies, how a ball team is managed, how a factory process (such as the manufacture of lead pencils) is carried on, how a newspaper is published, how a paper route is managed, how an amateur play is produced, how puppets are handled.

Your subject chosen, proceed as before: Think through your material and jot down the important phases of the procedure in their proper sequence; determine the larger units into which they fall and make a rough outline; decide on your attitude toward your material—your purpose in presenting it. As an account of something with which you have had some experience, your paper will probably be cast into the form of a first-person narrative like several in this unit. But do not be distracted into writing pure narration; an account of how a summer camp is run should not be sidetracked, for example, into the more exciting story of a near-drowning that once occurred there.

UNIT 10

Comparison and Contrast

Is Mark as good a skier as Bill? Which small car gets the best mileage? Is Dorado Beach as beautiful as Paradise Island? Who is best suited to be the next president of the United States? Which sweater will wear longer? Which graduate school has the best program in astrophysics?

Questions like these may range from the most important topics to the most trivial, but the answer to each involves making a comparison. Whenever we are faced with a choice, we view the various possibilities, noting the **similarities** and, even more important, the **differences**, because the differences will ultimately determine our decision.

Comparison as a pattern of thought involves holding up two similar but not identical objects, situations, people, ideas, and so on, to determine in detail their likenesses and differences (a thorough comparison must always include contrast to be complete). We follow this pattern in selecting brand-name goods, in determining contest winners, in choosing a candidate or a way of life—in any situation that involves weighing and judging.

In examinations and writing assignments of many kinds you will often be asked to reach conclusions on a choice of objects, people, issues, or theories by comparing them. Your purpose in writing an essay of comparison may be only to determine similarities and differences or it may be to convince your readers of the superiority of one of the things you are presenting. Whatever your subject and purpose, the general mental process will be the same.

In planning and composing your paper, follow these steps:

1. **Choose two things as your subject.** More than two may have been involved in your original view, but we usually eliminate choices by examining them two at a time so that reaching a decision is essentially a matter of alternatives. For example, in deciding which of several cameras to buy, you will probably narrow your choice by weighing and eliminating until you arrive at the two likeliest, which you will then compare to each other in every detail.

2. **Choose two things alike but different.** They must be alike enough to be genuinely comparable, different enough to make the comparison fruitful through contrast. Two cars of the same make, year, and model may have some differences, despite standardized production, but such variations are usually unimportant. On the other hand, although a school bus and a space shuttle are both vehicles, they are probably too dissimilar for a comparison of them to be worthwhile.

3. **Organize your information on the two things in similar ways** so that your readers will easily see the basis for the comparison. The methods you learned in outlining will give you essential help in forming a pattern. If you mention a certain type of detail about one, be sure to include it or to note the lack of it in your discussion of the other. For example, if leg room is important in your choice of a car, consider that feature in both cars you are comparing.

Two patterns are appropriate for organizing information in a comparison: the opposing pattern and the alternating pattern.

a. **Opposing pattern.** Suppose you decide to compare education as you experienced it in high school with what you have found in college. Your chief concern will probably be to paint a vivid picture of life in each area, and your paper will consist of two main divisions: education in high school and education in college. Where you place the parts will depend on which you wish to emphasize—the more important one should be last.

To compare the two thoroughly, you must examine essentially the same phases of experience in each. Your subpoints under each main division are therefore likely to be similar—for example, activities, teachers, classes. Determine the order of these subpoints logically and then maintain it under each heading. If you decide to emphasize your experience in college, your skeleton outline for the main body of your paper may look like this:

I. Education in high school
   A. Teachers
   B. Classes
   C. Activities

II. Education in college
   A. Teachers
   B. Classes
   C. Activities

As you write, you may merely paint two pictures, leaving your readers to draw their own conclusions; or, in your second picture, you may often point out comparisons and contrasts with the first; or you may write a conclusion tying them together and making clear your purpose in discussing them.

b. Alternating pattern. If, however, you wish to emphasize the details of the comparison instead of the larger differences, you will find an alternating arrangement more useful. In this, the levels of the points are the reverse of those used earlier, emphasizing the aspects of each way of life instead of the area. Your previous subpoints become main divisions; your main divisions, subpoints. Your skeleton outline for the main body of your paper will then look like this:

I. Teachers
   A. High school
   B. College

II. Classes
   A. High school
   B. College

III. Activities
   A. High school
   B. College

Which pattern you choose for a given paper will depend on your particular subject. For the topic of high school versus college, the first would probably be better since it emphasizes the contrast between the two pictures as a whole. But when you wish to emphasize the particular points of a comparison—one beach resort versus another, for instance, as to climate, hotels, and amusements—the second type of pattern would be better. If you completed the discussion of one resort before you started on another, the details of the first might have faded from your readers' minds before they were halfway through the second.

Notice how the patterns are used in the following examples. In the first, on two often confused objects, the *opposing pattern* emphasizes differences.

The beginner has some trouble in distinguishing the planets from the stars, but the following difference in appearance may help. The stars are so distant that they shine only as points of light even through the largest telescopes. In consequence, their light is unsteady because of disturbances in the Earth's atmosphere, such as the rising of warm currents and the falling of cold currents. Thus the stars twinkle. The planets, on the other hand, are very much nearer—so near that with the exception of Pluto they show as discs in our large telescopes, and not as single points of light. Therefore their light is not so much affected by disturbances in our atmosphere. It is usually said that planets do not twinkle, but shine with a steady light. (Clyde Fisher, *Exploring the Heavens.*)

Introduction. Planets and stars

I. Stars   II. Planets
  A. Very distant   A. Less distant
  B. Result—twinkling   B. Result—steady light

The treatment of each part of the subject is so brief that there is no paragraph break before the second one appears in sentence 5, but "on the other hand" is a valuable transition between the two. Notice, too, the balance of "in consequence" (sentence 3) and "therefore" (sentence 6), transitions introducing in each part the comparable material on results.

The even briefer paragraph that follows is an equally clear example of the *alternating pattern.* Here, two people are compared, detail by detail.

Irène was, like Eve, a brilliant, courageous bearer of the great Curie name, yet in every other respect the two sisters were far apart. Where Eve was a Gaullist, Irène was pro-Communist. Eve was chic and smart; Irène lived in a gray chemist's smock. Eve traveled the world and mingled with the mighty; Irène's world was the laboratory of the Curie Institute and she mingled with molecules and atoms, whose power was less visible if mightier. (David Schoenbrun, *As France Goes.*)

Introduction. Irène and Eve Curie

I. Politics   II. Dress   III. Experience
  A. Eve—   A. Eve—   A. Eve's—wide and
     Gaullist   fashionable   important
  B. Irène—pro-   B. Irène—   B. Irène's—narrow
     Communist   workaday   but more impor-
                                             tant

To see more precisely how the effects of these patterns differ, rewrite each paragraph according to the other pattern. The changes you find will be much greater in longer pieces.

Each pattern has limitations. The opposing pattern is not suitable for papers of more than a thousand words. Readers would forget the first part of the subject long before they finished the second part. But a writer may use the opposing pattern briefly at many points in a paper or book of any length. The alternating pattern may be as monotonous as a swinging pendulum if many of the parts are the same length. This pattern is most effective when the alternation varies from a contrast within a sentence, to one between sentences, or to one between paragraphs, depending on what is most appropriate for the particular material.

∴　∴　∴

An **analogy** is like a figure of speech because its only purpose is to make something vivid and understandable. Unlike most figures of speech, however, it is always based on several points of comparison. Also, since the purpose is always practical, it appeals primarily to our sense of logic rather than to our emotions.

A familiar analogy is the description of a pump to explain the heart: The heart with its valves forcing blood through the body is compared to a pump with its valves forcing water through a system of pipes. These are two very different things—one anatomical, the other mechanical—but the relationship of their parts is comparable at point after point, and the working of the complex and unfamiliar becomes clearer through analogy with the relatively simple and familiar.

Analogies can be particularly helpful in translating measurements of some kind into familiar terms. For example, an advertisement for an airline caught the eye with "Last week we moved Chicago to Dallas." The advertisement continued: "In an average week, U.S. scheduled airlines carry three-and-a-half million passengers an average of 800 miles. That's the equivalent of picking up every man, woman, and child in Chicago and transporting them to Dallas." The advertisers made their point.

Do not expect an analogy to prove anything. The action of a pump can be used to explain that of the heart, but it does not follow that a heart is a machine whose parts can be replaced easily or that a plumber could perform open-heart surgery successfully.

∴　∴　∴

Balanced sentence structure will give you special help in writing a comparison. It emphasizes the similarity of ideas by presenting them in similar grammatical patterns, as in "government of the people, by the people, and for the people." When the ideas are contrasting, the balance is called *antithesis* because the first part states a point, or thesis, which the second opposes or contradicts to some degree by a contrast. Two examples are "Give me liberty or give me death" and "Let us never negotiate out of fear, but let us never fear to negotiate"—sentences in American history as memorable for expression as for thought. Note the examples of antithesis in the selections that follow, especially in A and B.

EXAMPLES

The writers of these selections make comparison a major feature, but you will find it used in varying degrees in many other selections in this book: Thomas's "On Societies as Organisms" (3-C), Raiano's "Remembering the Child" (4-G), Cardeli's "My Son Jonah" (4-H), Granville's "A New Life" (5-C), Tysoe's "Do You Inherit Your Personality?" (6-E), Johmann's "Sex and the Split Brain" (7-B), all the essays in Unit 11, Sithole's "When Blacks Rule in South Africa" (12-E), Shoglow's "Two Imperatives in Conflict" (12-F), Satriale's "Dix Hills" (13-E), Hall's "Bring Back the Out-Loud Culture" (13-G), The New Yorker's *"Three Incidents" (15-A), Cohen's "The Language of Uncertainty" (15-C), Montagu's "Parentage and Parenthood" (14-B), Bagnall's "The Importance of Not Being Smith" (15-B), Tudge's "They Breed Horses, Don't They?" (16-B), and Woolf's "The Patron and the Crocus" ("Essays for Further Reading"-C).*

The following examples all have some form of the alternating pattern. It is more flexible than the opposing pattern and therefore more useful.

10-A   The Seventh Continent

These paragraphs are from a travel agency's brochure on cruises to Antarctica. Notice that as the paragraphs grow longer, we move from a single sentence covering both regions to separate sentences for each, and then to more than one sentence.

Antarctica differs from the Arctic regions, which are better known to us and easier to reach. The North Pole is crossed daily by commercial airlines, whereas not a single commercial airliner operates over Antarctica.

The Arctic is an ocean covered with drifting ice and hemmed   5
in by the continents of North America, Asia and Europe. The Antarctic, on the other hand, is a continent as large as Europe and the United States put together, and surrounded entirely by oceans—the Atlantic, the Indian, and the Pacific.

More than a million persons live within 2,000 miles of the   10

North Pole and the area is rich in forest and industry. There are
animals and birds of many varieties. Within the same distance of
the South Pole, there are no settlements apart from scientific
stations which are entirely dependent on outside supplies for
every need. There is not a single tree and not a single animal. It   15
takes 70 to 80 years to grow an inch of moss.

1. What do these two regions have in common that makes them comparable?
In how many and what respects are they compared?

2. Rewrite this description as a comparison organized in the opposing pattern.

3. Explain the advantages and disadvantages of the two patterns in presenting
this particular information.

4. What transitional devices did you use to link the parts of your comparisons?
What devices are in the example?

10-B   Tolstoy's Contradictions

Henri Troyat

After two introductory sentences, this short paragraph from an article in the
Literary Guild Magazine (1968) is the ultimate in balanced construction: All the
remaining sentences match, each forming an antithesis whose parts are marked with
"He preached" and "but he. . . ."

Who is Tolstoy? For me, he suffered his whole life long from
an inability to match his thoughts with his actions. He preached
asceticism and chastity, but he gave his wife thirteen children. He
preached the joys of poverty, but he never lacked for anything.
He preached the need for solitude, but he was the most sur-   5
rounded and the most adulated man of his times. He preached
hatred of the government, but he never suffered any curtailment
of his freedom, while his followers went into exile.

1. Rewrite this paragraph to make a comparison in the opposing pattern.

2. Explain the advantages and disadvantages of the two patterns in presenting
this particular information.

10-C   The Downfall of Christmas

William Kirchoff *(student)*

Not all essays of comparison are patterned as neatly as the first two, which show the alternating pattern in its clearest and simplest form. In longer pieces the pattern can be used more freely, as shown in this essay, written over thirty years ago. Compare the opinions expressed here with those in Conza's "Christmas Eve" (12-I) and your own impressions of celebrating Christmas.

ANALYSIS
General
topic

I. First
   example
   A. Then

B. Now

II. Second
    example
    A. Then
    B. Now

Christmas is gone. The American people have stood Christmas up against a wall and executed it, and from its grave a ghost has arisen. Strangely enough, this ghost is also named Christmas. This new Christmas is different, much different, from the one I knew not too long ago. 5 Most of the things that to me meant Christmas are gone. A little change here and a little change there have made Christmas a ghost of its former self.

A noticeable change has taken place in the tree. As I remember our trees, they were green, a green that could 10 not only be seen, but smelled. The ornaments were bright, but not gaudy. The lights were few and plain. I remember I used to have a favorite light each year, one that was in just the right place, and just the right color. All this sentiment was old-fashioned, though, and Amer- 15 ica was progressive. Manufacturers told us that we must always keep ahead of the Joneses and that we must always be new and unique. It is now no longer fashionable to have a green tree. One must have a silver one, a white one, a pink one, or a blue one. One must have a tree with 20 music tinkling from a hidden music box. The ornaments are no longer simple. They are now all hideous sizes and shapes, splashed with color, signifying nothing. They are all silver and sparkle, and no sentiment. The lights must bubble, flash, blink, glimmer, and do a million other 25 things. The Christmas tree is now an over-glorified monstrosity that smells suspiciously like machine oil.

Christmas songs have likewise undergone a disastrous change. It seems that no one was satisfied with "Silent Night." Now we have such pieces of trash as "I Saw 30 Mommy Kissing Santa Claus" and "Santa Rides a Straw-

berry Roan.'' Then there is the song that has done the
most toward ruining Christmas, and that is ''Santa Baby.''
It is my opinion that that is the lowest depth to which any
songwriter can stoop. The modern songwriter is succeed-   35
ing in his attempts to make a farce out of Christmas songs.

III. Third example
A. Then
B. Now

Poor old Santa has really been through the mill. He is
no longer the kindly old gentleman who puts candy in
children's stockings. He is now the man in the nylon
acetate beard and the red satin costume (which sells for   40
twelve dollars and ninety-five cents at most downtown
stores) who tells children to buy such and such from this
or that store. He is now the man who comes riding into
town surrounded by twenty-five Hollywood models in
skimpy costumes, about a month early. Like everything   45
else, Santa has gone commercial.

IV. Fourth example
A. Then
B. Now

Even the Christmas season is different. Instead of a day
or a week, it is now a month long and growing every
year. It starts when Santa arrives in town accompanied by
television and movie stars. It gets well under way when   50
Santa is starred on some program and tells gullible children what to buy and from whom. The person who
sponsors his show must feel very proud of himself.

V. Individual illus- tration

Merry Christmas, everybody; Peace on Earth, good
will toward men, and see whose house decorations can   55
be the gaudiest. Mr. Smith is full of Christmas spirit. His
house has 200 strings of light bulbs spelling out the first
verse of ''Jingle Bells.'' It looks as if no one will have a
white Christmas, except Mr. Jones, who sprays his whole
front lawn with 50 gallons of artificial snow.   60

Conclusion Summary of ''now''

Well, in short, that is the Christmas of today, a mere
ghost of the Christmas that used to be. All the feelings
are gone. Like almost everything made in this country,
it smells and tastes like tin cans. It looks like a gaudy
fireworks display, and sounds like Tin Pan Alley. Worst   65
of all, the feeling of Christmas is like the feeling of any
other holiday when no one works. The one day of the
year that was set aside for tradition is ruined by the
American people who know no tradition. One day out of
three hundred and sixty-five, and we had to go and ruin   70
it. Christmas is gone. It died when the true meaning of
Christmas was all but forgotten, when Rudolph the red-
nosed reindeer took the place of Dasher, when Mommy
kissed Santa Claus, when a chorus girl in a low-cut evening gown sang ''Silent Night'' with a glycerin tear in her   75
eye.

1. Why are the "now" sections longer?

2. Is the writer's use of colloquial words and phrases appropriate to his purpose?

3. Compare the celebration of Christmas with present celebrations of Independence Day, Memorial Day, and other public holidays.

10-D The Aquarium and the Globe

Mary Catherine Bateson

This selection forms the introductory chapter of *With a Daughter's Eye,* the author's memories of her famous parents. Her mother, Margaret Mead, was one of the best known anthropologists of this century and the author of many books, most notably *Coming of Age in Samoa* (1928), *Growing Up in New Guinea* (1930), and *Male and Female* (1949). The author's father, Gregory Bateson, also a noted anthropologist, was the author of several books, among them *Steps to an Ecology of Mind* (1972) and *Mind and Nature* (1979).

My parents, Gregory Bateson and Margaret Mead, were scientists and teachers, not only in the wider community in which they worked and published, each becoming famous in different ways and touching many lives, but in the domestic circles of family and friendship as well. For them, the intimate was projected on the widest screen, even as knowledge from far places was worked into the decisions of everyday life. The minds of both sought patterns of completeness, wholes, and so they thought of worlds entire, whether these worlds were minute images of microscopic life within a drop of water or the planet wreathed in cloud.

They thought of worlds and drew me into them. There were worlds to be built and worlds to be imagined, worlds to be held and cherished in two hands and worlds of abstract argument, in spherical tautology. The small primitive societies in which each did ethnographic work were worlds of one kind, complete communities to be described and understood, but along with these there was the challenge to construct and be responsible for the wholeness of family, a world for a child to grow in, a biosphere to protect, the possibility of the bright sphere shattered. Growing up was a passage from the microcosm, a motion through concentric metaphors. Even in the smallest of shared spaces, a camera or a notebook stood for a possible opening up to the macrocosm.

A child moves out through concentric worlds even with her first steps, but whether these worlds are encountered as wholes

or as fragments and whether they provide an entry to other   25
spheres of imagination and experience depend on how they are
presented, how attention is gradually shaped and the cosmos
gradually unfolded.

In Holderness, New Hampshire, where we spent many sum-
mers, a long field runs down toward the lake. At the bottom, just   30
short of the strip of woods that shields the shore, there lies a broad
patch of spring moss, like a bright green eiderdown spread out
under the trees. This was a place my mother had picked to be
alone with me in counterpoint to the large household in which
we stayed. We used to wander there for an hour or so, especially   35
in the early morning. Sometimes we found spiderwebs stretched
flat above the moss between protruding grass stems, with dew-
drops still shining on them. These she showed to me as fairy
tablecloths, the damask spun by tiny fingers, with crystal goblets
and silver plates still spread out, for the feckless fairies went off   40
to sleep at dawn without cleaning up. Then she showed me red-
tipped lichens as small as a pinhead—fairy roses—and searching
along the ground we found their serving bowls, the bases of
acorns.

My great-grandmother had taught my mother how to identify   45
and draw all the plants of her Pennsylvania childhood, but for me
the flowers had only colloquial names and were lenses of fantasy:
Indian paintbrush, black-eyed Susan, milkweed, Jack-in-the-pul-
pit. "I know," she sang, "where the fringed gentians grow."

My father had the English habit of latinizing in the woods or   50
in the garden. The intricacies he showed me between the grass
stems were of another sort, perhaps a beetle or a moth living out
quite different dramas. When I look at the field with his eyes, I
see it as a series of complex symmetries and relationships, in
which the position of the spiderweb above the moss hints at the   55
pathways of foraging insects. The petals of daisies can be used to
count—"He loves me, he loves me not"—because they are not
true petals but flowerets—otherwise their number would be set
in the precise morphology of the flowering plants.

"Once upon a time," my mother would narrate as the sun   60
moved higher in the sky, "in the kingdom between the grass
stems, there lived a king and a queen who had three daughters.
The eldest was tall and golden-haired and laughing, the second
was bold and raven-haired. But the youngest was gray-eyed and
gentle, walking apart and dreaming." The story varies but the   65
pattern remains the same, woven from the grass of the meadow
and the fears and longings of generations. For this king and queen
lived in no anarchic world, but in a world of rhythm and just

symmetries. Their labors, quests, and loves grew out of each
other with the same elegance that connects the parts of a flower-   70
ing plant and its cycles of growth. At their court, as at the fairies'
banquets, crystal goblets and courtly etiquette reflected a social
order. Prince and princess find one another in a world of due peril
and challenge and happiness ever after. The flower is pollinated,
seed is formed, scattered, and germinated. Look! The silk in the   75
milkweed pods is what the fairies use to stuff their mattresses.
Blow on the dandelion down to make a wish, anticipating the
wind. Pause in the middle of fantasy to see the natural world as
fragile and precious, threatened as well as caressed by human
dreaming.   80

W orlds can be found by a child and an adult bending down and
looking together under the grass stems or at the skittering crabs
in a tidal pool. They can be spun from the stuff of fantasy and
tradition. And they can be handled and changed, created in little
from all sorts of materials. On a coffee table in the center of our   85
living room, which often held toys and projects of mine, I constructed a series of worlds on trays. One of these was meant to
depict a natural landscape, built up from rocks and soil, with
colored sand and tinted strawflowers set into it. Another was
inspired by a book my father had read to me in which a child   90
constructs a city with cups, dishes, and utensils from the kitchen
and then visits it in his dreams. My mother, in that same period,
was fascinated by the World Test of Margaret Lowenfield, an
English child analyst. This projective test consists of a tray of moist
sand and a vast array of miniatures: people and animals, trees and   95
houses and vehicles. In using the test, one molds the soil and
handles the objects, arranging and changing them, and then
weaves narratives within the world one has created, so that the
creation of a microcosm becomes the expression of an inner,
psychic world, a world that embodies pain and perplexity as well   100
as symmetry.

The other kind of world that I constructed as a child was
represented by a series of aquaria set up with my father. An
aquarium is bounded, like a city or a landscape built on a tray, but
the discipline that goes into building it is different, for it is alive.   105
In the fantasy world, the discipline is primarily aesthetic: here is
the forest and here the open valley; here the dragon lurks and
here the river runs. In any aquarium it is necessary to balance the
needs of living creatures and their relationships with each other,
the cycles of growth and respiration and decay. Here among the   110
thicker water plants, newly spawned swordtails shelter lest they
be devoured. The snails that move sedately on the grass control

the algae, and on the sandy bottom catfish prowl continually, scavenging the pollution of living that never occurs in fairy tales.

It is not easy to give a child a sense of the integrity of the   115
biosphere. Even today there seem to be few who see themselves
as living within and responsible to a single interconnected whole.
As a very small child, asked what I wanted for Christmas, I am
supposed to have answered that I wanted the world, and my
parents gave me a globe. I do not know now whether I found the   120
hollow painted sphere a very satisfactory present. I remember it
standing at one end of the long living room for years, next to the
aquarium, and yet I am sure that none of us in those days saw the
two as metaphors, each of the other, a metaphor that we now can
easily make through the mediating symbolism of the picture of   125
the earth as seen from space.

Through my mother's writing echoes the question "What kind
of world can we *build* for our children?" She thought in terms of
building. She set out to create a community for me to grow up
in, she threw herself wholeheartedly into the planning and gov-   130
ernance of my elementary school, and she built and sustained a
network of relationships around herself, at once the shelter in
which I rested and the matrix of her work and thought. Not so
my father, for the most complex actual worlds I knew him to set
out to build have been aquaria and conferences, temporary con-   135
stellations of people who learn to think in counterpoint to each
other, moving toward a unity of mental process. He was less free
than my mother to build and imagine, but I remember him for
creating moments of attention when the patterned wonder of
some wild place or human interaction became visible.   140

1. Bateson says that her parents "thought of worlds and drew me into them." What were these worlds?

2. How did her parents differ in their reactions to nature?

3. Check the etymology, denotation, and connotation of *tautology, ethnographic, biosphere, macrocosm, cosmos, eiderdown, counterpoint, damask, lichens, latinizing, foraging, morphology, pollinated, germinated, spawned, algae, matrix.*

10-E   It's Not That I Don't Like
               Men

Anna Quindlen

This essay, here complete, was first published in a newspaper as part of a series by the writer on her experiences as a woman in her thirties—the years between youth and middle age. Notice her use of examples to support her thesis, which she states at the end of the second paragraph.

My favorite news story so far this year was the one saying that in England scientists are working on a way to allow men to have babies. I'd buy tickets to that. I'd be happy to stand next to any man I know in one of those labor rooms the size of a Volkswagen trunk and whisper "No, dear, you don't really need the Demerol; just relax and do your second-stage breathing." It puts me in mind of an old angry feminist slogan: "If men got pregnant, abortion would be a sacrament." I think this is specious. If men got pregnant, there would be safe, reliable methods of birth control. They'd be inexpensive, too.

I can almost hear some of you out there thinking that I do not like men. This isn't true. I have been married for some years to a man and I hope that someday our two sons will grow up to be men. All three of my brothers are men, as is my father. Some of my best friends are men. It is simply that I think women are superior to men. There, I've said it.

This is my dirty little secret. We're not supposed to say it because in the old days, men used to say that women were superior. What they meant was that we were too wonderful to enter courtrooms, enjoy sex or worry our minds about money. Obviously, this is not what I mean at all.

The other day a very wise friend of mine asked: "Have you ever noticed that what passes as a terrific man would only be an adequate woman?" A Roman candle went off in my head; she was absolutely right. What I expect from my male friends is that they are polite and clean. What I expect from my female friends is unconditional love, the ability to finish my sentences for me when I am sobbing, a complete and total willingness to pour their hearts out to me as well as the ability to tell me why the meat thermometer isn't supposed to touch the bone.

The inherent superiority of women came to mind just the other day when I was reading about sanitation workers. New York City has finally hired women to pick up the garbage, which makes sense to me, since, as I've discovered, a good bit of being a woman consists of picking up garbage. There was a story about   35
the hiring of these female sanitation workers, and I was struck by the fact that I could have written that story without ever leaving my living room—a reflection not upon the quality of the reporting but the predictability of the male sanitation workers' responses.   40

The story started by describing the event, and then the two women, who were just your average working women trying to make a buck and get by. There was something about all the maneuvering that had to take place before they could be hired, and then there were the obligatory quotes from male sanitation   45
workers about how women were incapable of doing the job. They were similar to quotes I have read over the years suggesting that women are not fit to be rabbis, combat soldiers, astronauts, fire-fighters, judges, ironworkers and President of the United States. Chief among them was a comment from one sanitation worker   50
who said that it just wasn't our kind of job, that women were cut out to do dishes and men were cut out to do yard work.

As a woman who has done dishes, yard work and tossed a fair number of Hefty bags, I was peeved—more so because I would fight for the right of any laid-off sanitation man to work, for   55
example, at the gift-wrap counter at Macy's, even though any woman knows that men are hormonally incapable of wrapping packages or tying bows.

I simply can't think of any jobs any more that women can't do. Come to think of it, I can't think of any job women *don't* do. I   60
know lots of men who are full-time lawyers, doctors, editors and the like. And I know lots of women who are full-time lawyers and part-time interior decorators, pastry chefs, algebra teachers and garbage slingers. Women are the glue that holds our day-to-day world together.   65

Maybe the sanitation workers who talk about the sex division of duties are talking about girls just like the girls that married dear old dad. Their day is done. Now lots of women know that if they don't carry the garbage bag to the curb, it's not going to get carried out either because they're single, or their husband is   70
working a second job, or he's staying at the office until midnight, or he just left them.

I keep hearing that there's a new breed of men out there who don't talk about helping a woman as though they're doing you a favor and who do seriously consider leaving the office if a child   75 comes down with a fever at school, rather than assuming that you will leave yours. But from what I've seen there aren't enough of these men to qualify as a breed, only as a subgroup.

This all sounds angry; it is. After a lifetime spent with winds of sexual change buffeting me this way and that, it still makes me   80 angry to read the same dumb quotes with the same dumb stereotypes that I was reading when I was 18. It makes me angry to realize that after so much change, very little is different. It makes me angry to think that these two female sanitation workers will spend their days doing a job most of their co-workers don't want.   85

1. Where does the writer use specific examples to illustrate her main point, that in her opinion women may be superior to men?

2. Where does the writer compare the present with the past?

3. Throughout her essay, the writer uses a very informal style with contractions such as "I'd," "We're," and "isn't," with slang such as "Make a buck," and with informal expressions such as "Come to think of it." In your opinion, does her informality strengthen or weaken the effectiveness of her presentation?

10-F   Who Am I?

Caroline Bajsarowicz *(student)*

Which "me" shall I be today? This question confronts me every time I stand before my closet searching for something to wear.

Shall I dress like a JAP, a "Jewish American Princess"? (This style has become very popular around my affluent suburban neighborhood.) I could wear my black formal pantsuit and exqui-   5 sitely colored scarf, a gold pendant, a charm bracelet, and 14-carat gold hoop earrings. My richly colored, dark brown platform shoes and coordinating handbag would accentuate this polished outfit. My short brown hair would be blown dry so that it could lie perfectly. Then in front of my vanity mirror, I'd spend an hour   10 polishing my nails, spraying a light mist of my favorite perfume, and most important, applying my cosmetics: first foundation and blush, then eyeshadow and mascara. This outfit, with my dark green pants coat trimmed with fur, gives me the appearance of a high class snob. I become the stereotyped "rich student." (I have   15 also been called a bitch when I dressed like this.)

At the other end of the closet there is a distinct odor of pine

trees and outdoor freshness. My faded blue jeans with the old
turtle patch in the center of twenty other brightly colored patches
hang here on a peg. With them I wear a stained red T-shirt two   20
sizes too large, old white sweat socks, and dirty hiking boots. My
hair is generally tousled and hidden under a blue bandanna. I pay
no special attention to my appearance and use no nail polish or
makeup. I throw on a shocking, bright green down jacket and pull
on a pair of blue and gold checked mittens. My ghastly outfit   25
presents me as a nonconformist.

Like the contents of my closet, the contents of my small but
cluttered bedroom show my two personalities. All my brushes,
cosmetics, and powders are neatly arranged on a large, mirrored
vanity next to my bed. The bed is draped with a lacy orange   30
bedspread and is covered by a dozen stuffed animals. The three
scalloped shelves above my bed are filled with my collections of
dolls, figurines, and souvenirs. Across the room, there is a modern, bright yellow sewing chest. But above this hangs a poster of
a snowcapped mountain and a cloudless blue sky. Under my bed,   35
hidden by the sides of the bedspread, is a down sleeping bag. My
green Trailways backpack hangs next to my handbag. In my photo
album, a picture of my friends at a beer party is pasted next to a
photograph of an altar of ice carved on a cliff.

My dual personality complicates my social life. Half of me gets   40
along with most of the other students. I attend the many functions
sponsored by the university, cheer for our sports teams, attend
club meetings, and spend Friday nights dancing in the Rathskeller
at the weekly Beer Blasts. I ask myself, though, "Is this what
everybody calls fun? Is this having a good time?" I may be smil-   45
ing, laughing, joking, and acting out the gestures of amusement
so that I'll seem to fit in with the group of people I'm with, but
part of me doesn't want to be there. There are so many more
constructive activities I'd rather be doing, such as learning about
musical instruments, making a needlepoint pillow, or taking a   50
solitary walk through a park.

At summer orientation for freshmen, when we were given a list
of all the clubs and sports in the university, I had many problems
deciding which ones I wanted to join. The more popular clubs,
such as the sororities, appealed to me because I could meet so   55
many girls in the school. I would have such privileges as exclusive
rights to a table in the cafeteria and free passage into the Panhel-
lenic Suite. But I also wanted to join the Outing Club. Although
it has only four members, they appreciate those other things I like.

I'm a freshman with only three years left before I must answer   60
that infamous question, "What do you want to be when you grow

up?'' I have spent many long hours trying to decide. How I would love to fulfill my mother's dream by marrying a wealthy doctor. My husband and I would live in an upper-middle-class, suburban neighborhood and own a boat, two cars, and several pairs of skis. Probably, we would compete with the Joneses. Every time our neighbors bought something or went on a vacation, we'd buy something bigger and go to a more exclusive resort or on a more exotic cruise. It would be comfortable to settle down to familiar routine with only superficial worries.

But the rebellious me doesn't want this routine. That part of me would much rather go through life without ever settling down. Some people may say this free style of living is that of a bum or hippie, but I want to be independent and unrestrained so that I can see the many splendors of this world. The rebellious me doesn't want to be tied down with a job or a home, nor does it want to worry about the Joneses.

How can these two very different personalities exist in one person? I have three years left to find the answer. . . .

1. Why does the author give somewhat more attention to her conventional "rich student" self than to her rebellious self?

2. Why does the author give the descriptive details of her clothes and room first rather than the larger problem she faces?

10-G   The Odd Couple

Lisa Giacomo *(student)*

Compare this humorous description of two very different parents with a serious treatment of the subject in Mary Catherine Bateson's "The Aquarium and the Globe" (Unit 10-D).

I have always wondered how my parents were attracted to each other. Their physiques, personalities, temperaments, and attitudes toward money are all opposite. The saying that "opposites attract" certainly holds true for them.

My mother is 5'2" and weighs about 125 pounds, but my father is 6' and weighs 225 pounds. They are like Alice and Ralph Kramden of "The Honeymooners."

Their personalities differ as much as their physiques. My
mother is outgoing and vivacious. She enjoys people because, to
her, they are the most interesting form of life. When she meets   10
new people, she greets them as if they were old friends, whether
they are first-time clients at her beauty shop or acquaintances of
someone she already likes. She loves to socialize. Making conversation with any type of personality comes easily to her—it's a
natural quality.   15

My father, on the other hand, is conservative and shy. Socializing is not easy for him. His shyness may give the impression that
he's cold, but once he gets to know you, his warmth, sensitivity,
and strong sense of values emerge.

When it comes to controlling one's temper, my mother clearly   20
exceeds my father. She will tolerate a lot before she gets angry
and prefers to rationalize rather than lose her temper. However,
my father's temper is like a short fuse on a stick of dynamite. He
will flare up immediately when something is said or done improp-
erly. Also very stubborn, he always insists that he is right. Our   25
dinners often turn into debates, with the issue usually being
money.

My mother is not the bargain shopper. She does not cut out
coupons or compare products or prices; she is impatient—if she
likes something, she buys it. My father, therefore, has always   30
done our food shopping. He compares products and prices, looks
for sales and bargains, and buys only what he needs. He has also
always taken care of all our household finances and is the book-
keeper, banker, and accountant of the family. My father says that
my mother has champagne tastes with a beer pocketbook, and she   35
says that he's cheap, but there is a happy compromise—she spends
and he saves.

"It must be love," I say about this odd couple. They may be
very different, but they are also very compatible. Learning from
each other insures the success of their partnership.   40

ASSIGNMENTS

1. Write an essay of comparisons, choosing as your subject two things enough alike
   to be comparable but with enough differences to make the comparison worthwhile. There are two chief types of topics: (1) a comparison based on periods of
   time—"then and now" or "now and later," and (2) a comparison based on two
   coexistent things—"this and that."

   Suggestions for the first type: horse and automobile, washboard and washing
   machine, clothing styles, early and contemporary cars, kindergarten and grade
   school, high school and college, your parents' childhood and yours.

Suggestions for the second type: gasoline and diesel engines, city life and suburban life, suburban life and farm life, community colleges and universities, football and soccer, a camping vacation and a resort vacation, your home and that of a friend, your bedroom and that of a brother or sister, a book or play and the movie version, two different singers, two makes of automobile, two breeds of dogs, two TV situation comedies, two TV news analysts.

After choosing a subject, decide which type of organization will be better for it, and make an outline showing the main points and subpoints you intend to develop.

2. Analyze the use of comparison in examples in other units, notably Unit 3-C, 4-H, 5-C, 6-C, 12-A, and 13-B.

3. Compare the opinions expressed here with those in Conza's "Christmas Eve" (12-I).

UNIT 11

Classification

"Oh, so *that's* where you keep the salt!" you exclaim after a long search. In your own home the salt is next to the stove because everyone in your family likes it in most foods, but your friend keeps it in a cupboard with garlic powder, nutmeg, and other seasonings. *"Where* did you say I could find a safety pin?" In your home the safety pins are with needles and thread in your mother's sewing box, but your friend keeps them in a desk drawer with paper clips, a stapler, and thumb tacks.

You and your friends are applying logical principles of classification in choosing where to keep salt and safety pins, and your basic methods of reasoning are the same, but your criteria for establishing the classes differ. You classified the salt according to frequency of use, but your friend classified it according to purpose. You classified the safety pins according to a single purpose, fastening fabrics, and your friend classified them in the more general category of small fasteners for any purpose, but you both used classification to keep track of the salt and safety pins.

Sharing criteria for classification is like sharing a language. Without it we often have difficulty understanding each other. Scientists depend on shared criteria to communicate with other scientists. For example, biologists divide all living things into the animal, vegetable, and protist kingdoms; each kingdom is divided into phyla, each phylum into classes, each class into orders, and so on down through the family, genus, species, and variety. Anthropologists classify people according to race; businesses classify their creditors according to degrees of risk; college grading systems classify students as A's, B's, and so on.

To classify any group formally and completely involves considering every representative of that group and breaking down classes into subclasses, sub-subclasses, and so on, until the ultimate in division is reached. For most purposes, however, we need to consider only the main classes into which we can divide a given subject and to treat only the main subclasses, with perhaps a few sub-subclasses. An essay on musical instruments, for example, intended for the general reader need not have classifications covering every rare or ancient piece but may consider only those commonly used by the modern orchestra. Once the writer has divided and grouped them into kinds and described the outstanding instruments of each kind, the task of classification is, for practical purposes, complete. The purpose of such an essay is usually not total thoroughness; the writer uses classification to bring out some other point in an orderly manner.

⁘ ⁘ ⁘

To find an appropriate topic for a paper in which you use classification, follow these steps:

1. **Choose a limited group.** It should be small enough for you, in a brief paper, to go into some detail in describing the subgroups. "People" is too much to handle; "taxi drivers" might do nicely.

2. **Choose a group with three or more subgroups.** A classification with only two classes will give you the same practice in organizing as the essay of comparison in Unit 10. Classifying people into "types I like" and "types I dislike" is an example of a rather pointless division of a subject that is too large.

3. **Look for a personal and original development.** Many classifications already exist; for example, scientists divide meteorites into three types according to their composition: iron, iron and stone, and stone. But you may get—and give—more enjoyment with an original approach such as that of the girl who classified her dates according to the reasons for her choices into the "old school friend type," the "he drives a sports car" type, and the "he's a

good disco dancer" type. (Beware of the "good-bad-average" kind of classification, which is likely to produce little originality.)

4. **Choose and apply a single principle of classification.** Your principle will determine the classes to be discussed. Engines may be classified
according to maker, use, speed, number of cylinders—but only one at a time.
An attempt to classify drivers into women drivers, truck drivers, and good
drivers is no classification at all, merely a loose and purposeless discussion.
The topic "women drivers" announces that the principle guiding the division
is sex; "truck drivers" changes the principle to the type of vehicle driven; and
"good drivers" changes it once more, this time to driving skill. Actually,
there are the beginnings here of three distinct classifications:

> according to sex (women, men—one of those two-part, ready-made
> schemes)
> according to vehicle driven (truck, taxi, camper, van, passenger car)
> according to proficiency (good, bad, average)

5. **Do not let your classes overlap.** In the scheme just presented, for
example, a truck driver might also be both a woman and a good driver.

6. **Make your classification reasonably complete.** As mentioned
earlier, your essay need not be exhaustive, but it should be adequate for your
purpose. In classifying hunting dogs by breed, you might omit certain rare
varieties, but you would be obliged to consider all those commonly known.
To discuss horror movies you dislike and those you enjoy, you must include
those you tolerate; then your classification, based on the principle of your
reactions, would be adequate.

7. **Introduce subclasses as needed.** If there are finer divisions of any
of the subgroups into which you divided your original group, you may wish
to include them. In classifying students according to religious faiths—for
example, as Jews, Christians, Moslems, and so on—you may want to subdivide at least the Christians into subgroups as Catholics and Protestants and
the Protestants into sub-subgroups, such as Methodist, Presbyterian, Baptist,
and so on. But be sure to keep such a sub-subgrouping in its place, and do
not allow your reader to confuse it with the larger classification on which
your paper is based.

∴   ∴   ∴

Your **organization**—the order in which to discuss the main classes
(categories) in your classification—is the next question to consider. Sometimes this order is natural because it is inherent in your subject, leaving you
no choice; sometimes you will have to decide among several possibilities, all

logical. Choose the one that best suits your purpose and is likely to be clearest to your readers.

To discuss students according to their college year, you would probably use a chronological order, starting with freshmen and finishing with seniors. To classify them according to religions, you have at least three choices: (1) the chronological order in which the religions were founded; (2) the numerical size of the groups on your campus or in the nation; or (3) your own interest in them, saving until last the one you consider most interesting or important so that you can make a strong final impression on your readers and placing first the one most likely to attract your readers' attention.

Remember that the divisions and subdivisions in your outline indicate comparable groups of topics, just as they did in your essay of comparison. Each group should therefore receive similar treatment. If you write on the American Kennel Club's official classification of dogs (a somewhat arbitrary sorting into six groups: sporting, hound, working, terrier, toy, nonsporting), and if you give information on breeds, uses, and popularity for sporting dogs, your readers will expect you to cover the same areas, probably in the same order, for the other five categories. Notice that the first section suggested—breeds—will involve the kind of subclassification that a classification often includes (see section 7 on page 228 in the discussion of finding an appropriate topic).

Balanced sentence structure can help you to emphasize comparable topics and subtopics, as it could in writing an essay of comparison. Study the writer's use of it in this paragraph:

> The distinctions I am making among three different kinds of culture—*postfigurative,* in which children learn primarily from their forebears, *cofigurative,* in which children and adults learn from their peers, and *prefigurative,* in which adults learn also from their children—are a reflection of the period in which we live. Primitive societies and small religious and ideological enclaves are primarily postfigurative, deriving authority from the past. Great civilizations, which necessarily have developed techniques for incorporating change, characteristically make use of some form of cofigurative learning from peers, playmates, fellow students, and fellow apprentices. We are now entering a period, new in history, in which the young are taking on new authority in their prefigurative apprehension of the still unknown future. (Margaret Mead, *Culture and Commitment.*)

Notice that the three kinds of culture Mead names are listed in her first sentence as a parallel series, each named, then followed by an "in which" definition. The three sentences that follow take up these kinds in the same order, explaining where each is found. Not all essays of classification will or should show such complete balance, especially the longer and more informal ones. But similar treatment is essential. The preceding quotation is the opening paragraph of a small book that Mead divides into three chapters, "The

Past," "The Present," and "The Future," presenting her thoughts about these three kinds of culture one by one in the order in which she introduced them. These long chapters do not, of course, match in wording—but they do in purpose and accomplishment.

∴   ∴   ∴

Your outline will give you essential help in organizing a logical essay, but remember not to let it obtrude awkwardly. A formal classification that never goes beyond the outline stage remains a mere listing under appropriate headings and subheadings and will not interest your readers. Make your classification, like your essays on previous assignments, both logical and readable.

EXAMPLES

In each of these selections, classification is essential to the main point. Other selections in which the writers use classification are Thomas's "On Societies as Organisms" (3-C), Bucello's "Pop Fly to Short" (3-D), Cumming's "Dottle and the Bottle with a Punt" (3-F), Kakutani's "Dashers and Dawdlers" (6-D), McBee's "Gobbledygook" (6-G), Zinsser's "Clutter" (8-D), Kirchoff's "The Downfall of Christmas" (10-C), Peeples' "Branch Libraries" (12-B), Sithole's "When Blacks Rule in South Africa" (12-E), all the selections in Unit 14, and Mahood's "Puns and Other Wordplay" (17-C).

With each selection in this unit, be sure to observe the subject being classified, the principle used, the number of classes that result, and the order in which they are presented. Also notice the transitions that connect the discussions of the various classes.

11-A   Book Owners

Mortimer J. Adler

This excerpt comes from an essay, "How to Mark a Book," first published in the *Saturday Review* in 1940.

There are three kinds of book owners. The first has all the standard sets and best-sellers—unread, untouched. (This deluded individual owns woodpulp and ink, not books.) The second has a great many books—a few of them read through, most of them

dipped into, but all of them as clean and shiny as the day they 5
were bought. (This person would probably like to make books his
own, but is restrained by a false respect for their physical appearance.) The third has a few books or many—every one of them
dog-eared and dilapidated, shaken and loosened by continual use,
marked and scribbled in from front to back. (This man owns 10
books.)

1. What is the principle of classification involved here? Do these three classes
constitute a "reasonably complete" discussion of the subject?

2. Notice the almost perfect parallelism of the treatment of the three classes,
similar to the kind of balance we found in the development of the essay of comparison. But like the antitheses of Example B in Unit 10, this could not be sustained at
length. Compare the high degree of organization here with the greater freedom in
the longer selection that follows.

3. Check the etymology, denotation, and connotation of *deluded* and *dilapidated.*

11-B   The Ones Left Behind

Rebecca Lanning *(student)*

The Cullowhee Exodus, so much a part of the average WCU
student's Friday life, begins around noon and by three o'clock is
in full swing. Almost everyone who can possibly do so has
wedged himself into a homeward-bound car, leaving behind only
those who couldn't find a ride, those who feel they have too much 5
studying to do, and those rare and inexplicable souls who seemingly enjoy a weekend on a temporarily almost deserted campus.

The most bitter of those left behind are the No-Way-Homers.
These are made up of individuals unlucky enough to have a
four-o'clock class and to find no driver willing to wait until 4:50, 10
and those who live too far away from the university to be able to
travel there and back in a weekend. These two groups spend their
weekend with appropriate differences: the first complaining end-
lessly about the stupidity of the computer that gave them such a
lousy schedule, the second moaning to anyone within earshot of 15
the folly of having any institution for higher education located so
far from civilization.

The largest group of these campus weekenders, the Studiers,

are less bitter than the No-Way-Homers but more disgusted. In
fact, they are running over with disgust because, having wrestled   20
with the books all week, they must now continue the match
throughout the weekend. Most of the Studiers are chronic pro-
crastinators; some are the lucky people to whom Professor Smith
has given one of his little over-the-weekend take-home fifty-ques-
tion "opportunity" quizzes; and the rest are the students of Sand-   25
box 2331, who were informed in class on Friday of a term paper
due the following Monday.

On Saturday afternoon the library is full of sleeping Studiers
who had stayed awake far into Friday night. Some of them were
scheduling their Saturday study time; others were plotting the   30
arsenic murder of Professor Smith and his ilk. Quickly the weekend flies by, and with it the intentions of the Studiers, who when
questioned later about how they spent their time, mutter something unintelligible about how much work they accomplished. In
all truth, however, the only thing they really did was getting   35
ready to get ready to study.

Neither bitter nor disgusted is the third, final, small, and entirely atypical group of those remaining behind, the Enjoyers.
These rare people seem actually to relish life on an almost empty
campus. They spend the entire weekend looking cool and de-   40
tached as they sit drinking cokes in the Town House or strolling
along the ivy-bordered walks, showing off their wonderful dispo-
sitions and making enemies right and left. The Enjoyers are considered by everyone else to be either remarkably school-spirited
or downright crazy—but maybe they actually do enjoy the atmo-   45
sphere of a simulated Siberia.

Time marches on (to coin a phrase), and soon it is Monday.
Back troop the rest of the student population, and the No-Way-
Homers, the Studiers, and the Enjoyers all blend into the re-
newed hustle and bustle for another busy college week. One   50
thought, however, runs continually through most of their minds:
"Just wait till next weekend; wild horses couldn't keep me here."

1. What determines the order of the three major classes of "those left behind"?

2. What subclasses and sub-subclasses are identified in the second, third, and
fourth paragraphs?

11-C   Mental Depression: The
                  Recurring Nightmare

Jane E. Brody

This excerpt forms the first two-thirds of an article by a writer who regularly covers health news for the New York Times. The rest of the article describes various treatments for depression.

ANALYSIS
Introduction

The feeling is familiar to almost everyone—nothing seems satisfying, things don't work out, you can't get yourself to do much of anything and your mental landscape is bleak. It's called depression, and few of us get through life without experiencing it at one time or another. 5

Major class
#1

Many things can get a person "down," including the weather (midwinter doldrums are an annual event for some), the letdown after the excitement and activity of the holidays, insufficient sleep, too much work and too 10 little time in which to get it done. The ordinary everyday "blues" are fortunately usually brief and self-curing and, although they take the edge off life, are not terribly incapacitating.

Major class
#2

However, for millions of Americans, depression is a 15 far more serious, sometimes even life-threatening, situation. Most serious depressions are reactions to stressful life events—loss of a job or a spouse, serious financial setback, a serious illness or injury, the end of a love affair. After a reasonable number of weeks or months, most 20 such depressions lift and the world and life begin to seem brighter.

Major class
#3

But for some people, depression is a recurring phenomenon that is provoked by events that others seem to weather with little difficulty or get over very quickly. 25 And for others, depression happens "out of the blue," unrelated to any particular situation, and totally incapacitates the victims. Many accomplished people suffered from severe depression, including Sigmund Freud, Abraham Lincoln, Nathaniel Hawthorne, Winston Churchill 30 and the astronaut, Edwin E. Aldrin.

Importance of major class #3	The National Institute of Mental Health estimates that each year between 4 and 8 million Americans suffer depressions severe enough to keep them from performing their regular activities or compelling them to seek medical help. Perhaps 10 to 15 million others have less severe depressions that interfere to some extent with the performance of normal activities.

All told, depression is clearly "the mental illness of our time," rivaling schizophrenia as the nation's number one mental health problem and currently increasing significantly among people below the age of 35.

Theories on causes of major class #3

Some experts say the social tensions of the times—the erosion of trust, diminished personal impact, unrealistically high expectations for success, disintegration of the family, social isolation and loss of a sense of belonging to or believing in some stable, larger-than-self institution— foster a society especially prone to depression.

Subclasses of #3 Subclass #1

Recognizing depression, should it strike you or someone you know, can sometimes be very difficult. In its classic, undisguised form, depression has three main characteristics:

Sub-subclass #1

¶Emotional—A dull, tired, empty, sad, numb feeling with little or no pleasure from ordinarily enjoyable activities and people;

Sub-subclass #2

¶Behavioral—Irritability, excessive complaining about small annoyances or minor problems, impaired memory, inability to concentrate, difficulty making decisions, loss of sexual desire, inability to get going in the morning, slowed reaction time, crying or screaming, excessive guilt feeling;

Sub-subclass #3

¶Physical—loss of appetite, weight loss, constipation, insomnia or restless sleep, impotence, headache, dizziness, indigestion and abnormal heart rate.

Subclass #2

But in many cases, the symptoms of depression are "masked," disguised in a form that makes recognition by the depressed person, his family, friends and even his physician difficult. "The exhausted housewife, the bored adolescent and the occupational underachiever are often suffering from depression just as truly as the acutely suicidal patient or the one who refuses to get out of bed," according to Dr. Nathan Kline, a New York psychiatrist.

The patient with disguised depression may complain of headache, backache or pains elsewhere in the musculoskeletal system. He may have a gastrointestinal disorder,

such as chronic diarrhea, a "lump" in the throat, chest
pain or a toothache.

Or his depression may be disguised in sexual promis-
cuity, overeating, excessive drinking or various phobias.

Depression in children is usually masked, presenting   80
symptoms like restlessness, sleep problems, lack of attention and initiative.

Other causes   In addition to stressful events that cause depression
of major   (called "reactive" or "exogenous" depression), and un-
class #3   known internal, probably biochemical, causes (called   85
"endogenous" depression), depression can result from
organic diseases, including viral and bacterial infections,
such as hepatitis, influenza, mononucleosis and tubercu-
losis; hormonal disorders, such as diabetes and thyroid
disease, and such conditions as arthritis, nutritional defi-   90
ciencies, anemia and cancer.

1. Why is "Masked" not listed as a fourth classification of the symptoms of
depression, after "Emotional," "Behavioral," and "Physical"?

2. What distinction is the author drawing between "emotional" and "behavioral" symptoms?

11-D   The South Africans

E. J. Kahn, Jr.

The following paragraphs are from *The Separated People* (1968), a study of South
Africa, and were first published in *The New Yorker.* For a more recent comment on
troubled racial relations in South Africa, see Sithole's "When Blacks Rule in South
Africa" (12-E).

The peculiar composition of South Africa's population . . . has
given the country its character and its controversiality. There are
four principal kinds of South Africans. Largest in number and
least in influence are its twelve and a half million black-skinned
people. There are almost two million others, of mixed blood, who   5
are known as "Colored." Their skins range in hue from white to
black, but whatever a Colored man's color, his rights are meager.
There are slightly more than half a million Asiatics, most of them

of Indian ancestry and all of them second-class citizens. First class
is reserved for three and a half million Whites, who, as they never   10
forget, constitute the largest concentration of white people in
Africa. Johannesburg, the Republic's main metropolis, with a
total population of 1,250,000, has the biggest white population
of any city on the continent. Johannesburg also has the biggest
black population. It is in large part because of such unique distinc-   15
tions that contemporary South Africa is so uniquely vexed.

The mere identification of the various categories of South Africans can confuse outsiders. The Whites—who rarely have anyone
else in mind when they use the term "South African"—are often
known as "Europeans," although in fact most of them have firm   20
African roots; some of their family trees were planted in African
soil a dozen generations ago. (The few Japanese in South Africa
also rate as Europeans, because most of them are businessmen and
it suits the South African government to treat them—although
Chinese do not get the same break—as honorary Whites.) In the   25
Transvaal province—wherein are located both Johannesburg and
Pretoria, the country's administrative capital—"non-European"
means "non-White." In the province of the Cape of Good Hope,
however, wherein lies Cape Town, the country's legislative capital (the highest judicial body sits in still another province, at   30
Bloemfontein in the Orange Free State), the only non-Whites
considered non-European are the Coloreds, most of whom live in
the Cape. Throughout South Africa the darkest and most down-
trodden of its residents are called either Africans, as they themselves prefer to be designated, or Bantu, as the government pre-   35
fers to designate them (in many African languages, "Bantu"
means "people"), or natives, or kaffirs, a word of Arabic origin
that means infidels and is akin to the American "niggers." Only
bigots and Africans use "kaffir."

South Africa is extremely conscious of the variety and disparity   40
of its inhabitants. Where else on earth would the head of a government refer, as Prime Minister Balthazar John Vorster did in
the winter of 1967, to "my country and my *peoples*"?

1. This selection suggests some of the need for and difficulties of classifying.
What is the principle of classification here?

2. How do you account for the order in which the classes are presented? Could
it have been reversed?

3. Check the etymology, denotation, and connotation of *unique.* How does it
differ from *unusual* and *rare?*

11-E The Button

John Berendt

The writer combines history, specific detail, and some humor to add interest to his discussion of buttons—objects that most readers are likely to have taken for granted. This essay, here complete, first appeared in Esquire.

It was in the thirteenth century—the age of Marco Polo, Genghis Khan, Dante, and Saint Thomas Aquinas—that an anonymous individual invented one of the simplest but most useful devices of all time: the buttonhole. The surprising thing is that no one thought of it sooner, because buttons had existed for thousands   5 of years. Prebuttonhole buttons were fastened by loops. The advent of buttonholes simplified things and also profoundly influenced the styling of clothes. Men started wearing tailored, front-opening garments. The modern coat, for instance, replaced the age-old tunic pullover. Of necessity, the tunic had been loose-   10 fitting and shapeless, because it had to be pulled over the shoulders. Coats did not present that problem; they wrapped around the body and could be buttoned snugly up the front.

The immediate response to the invention of the buttonhole was a sort of buttonmania. You can see from paintings and carved   15 effigies of the period that people soon began to wear slim-fitting garments, with an almost solid row of buttons from chin to waist and from elbow to cuff. As time went on, buttons became more and more elaborate and decorative. The relative grandeur of a man's buttons often served to indicate his rank in society, and   20 some countries enacted sumptuary laws stipulating who could wear what kind of button. Louis XIV had so many bejeweled buttons that, according to Saint Simon, "he sank beneath the weight of them."

The apogee of button artistry was achieved in the eighteenth   25 century, at which time button makers were turning out embroidered buttons, engraved buttons, stamped buttons, buttons encrusted with gemstones, cameo buttons carved in ivory, and picture buttons with miniature paintings mounted under glass. A legendary suicide note of the era heaved a sigh of transcendent   30 weariness at "all this buttoning and unbuttoning."

By the twentieth century, buttons were primarily utilitarian

devices with only minor decorative value. But the passion for
buttons lives on, especially in the hearts of collectors such as
Diana Epstein, the coproprietor of a shop in New York called   35
Tender Buttons. Epstein has thousands of buttons in her shop,
including a large stock of the three very simple types of buttons
that men tend to wear most often today: horn buttons for suits and
jackets, white mother-of-pearl for shirts, and metal buttons for
blazers. These are classic buttons; they've been made for hun-   40
dreds of years. Their quality can vary considerably, however, and
the news is not good.

　　Horn buttons are made from the hooves and horns of buffalo
and cows, and lately these animals have been grazing on inferior
grass, the result being smaller buttons that are not very vivid in   45
color. "There used to be an infinite variety of markings in horn
buttons," says Epstein. "But not anymore. The ones you see today
are murky. They don't have good streaks. They only come in light
brown or dark brown. That's all. Gray is out.

　　"Part of the problem is the lack of human involvement. Old-   50
style button making is a dangerous, largely unsung profession.
The horn has to be held against an abrasive wheel—people have
been known to lose fingers doing it. It's the same with mother-of-
pearl buttons. Somebody has to dive for the mollusk shells, and
then someone else has to hand-carve the buttons and select match-   55
ing grains. Genuine mother-of-pearl buttons cost a dollar or more
today, which is why you see so many plastic ones—but they aren't
the same. They don't have that luminous quality. It's sad. Most
of the great button companies in the U.S. and England have had
to close down. I mean, who can afford to pay somebody to sit   60
around all day sorting out buttons with matched markings?"

　　And what about blazer buttons?

　　"The new ones are stamped out of lighter metal," Epstein says.
"Remember the old foxhead buttons? The foxes were sharp-eyed
and heroic. Now they look like muppets."   65

　　1. What types of buttons does the author list as fashionable in the eighteenth
century?

　　2. According to what principle does the writer classify these types?

　　3. Before buttonholes were invented, how did buttons fasten anything?

　　4. Why are good buttons of horn or mother-of-pearl hard to find now?

　　5. Check the etymology, denotation, and connotation of *sumptuary, stipulating,
apogee, cameo, transcendent, abrasive, mollusk, luminous.*

11-F   Outer Limits

Jane Panzeca *(student)*

The writer finds an imaginative basis for classifying students and combines narrative and analogy to make her point.

A good student need not be on the honor role or a whiz at taking tests. He or she must, however, view learning as a way to expand and grow as a human being and as a way to contribute to society.

There are four basic types of students: Regurgitators, Magi-   5
cians, Sluggards, and Generators. The Regurgitators are the ones who cough up information as it was dictated to them. They do well on tests but never offer an opinion or idea of their own. The Magicians are the deceivers; they view schooling as a means of getting a high-paying job. They are the master cheaters who pull   10
top grades from midair but who perform a disappearing act when the going gets tough. The Sluggards are habitually lazy. They lack motivation and regard school as useless. They must be pushed to learn, even though they have the ability to do well. The Generators are the dedicated students who take part in all class discus-   15
sions. They see learning in a different light. Although they are not all honor students, they are curious and in touch with the world around them. They will view even the most common things differently from their peers.

If one representative of each group were taken by an instructor   20
to a stream and asked to throw a pebble into the water and then to express a thought, each would react differently. The Regurgita-
tor might say, "Well, what is *your* opinion?" The Magician might reply, "Are we going to be asked this on a test?" The Sluggard might say, "I'm not going to throw the stone; you throw it for   25
me!" The Generator might reply, "I get the idea! It reminds me of an earthquake. The rock hitting the water generates ripples. Earthquake waves are like the vibrations in the water."

A student who is curious and interested will see even very ordinary devices in a provocative way. For such a student, learn-   30
ing is like the pebble causing circular waves, a never-ending process; for, after all, learning has no limits.

11-G   Business Status—How Do You
                        Rate?

Enid Nemy

This article, given here almost complete, appeared in the *New York Times* (August 1980). The writer's tone is half-joking; how accurate do you think her observations are?

You arrive for a business appointment. First you spend twenty minutes in the waiting room, leafing through January's *Reader's Digest* and the April *New Yorkers.* Then the receptionist tells you to go in—the first corridor on the right, the fifth door on the left.

Right then, you should know that you don't rate. According to   5
unofficial office protocol, you're a one or two on a scale of 10. Not quite the bottom of the totem pole—a zero wouldn't have been granted an appointment at all—but next thing to it.

Still, if it's any comfort, you may find that the person with whom you have the appointment isn't a 10 either, or even a six   10
or seven. His rating, or hers, may be just as pathetic as your own.

There are two distinct aspects to business status. The first encompasses the actual office space you occupy, and the second is how you are treated and greeted when you arrive in someone else's office for an appointment.   15

In the matter of office space, it is as well to know that anyone without an office, that is, a physical space with walls, is probably not worth wasting time on. This includes all or most newspaper reporters.

Cubicles also aren't worth much. At most, they're half a step   20
up, but that's only if they have doors. Cubicles without doors are considered about as impressive as Princess telephones.

It is, however, in the genuine private offices that the status game is played seriously. For example, it's a good thing to be on friendly terms with men and women who have suites of rooms on   25
high floors. Executives of this ilk can be very useful. As can the occupants of large corner offices with two walls of windows or, at the very least, with lots of window, or even one big window.

Windows, in fact, apparently are as essential to office prestige as Christmas is to retailing. Even at the United Nations, where   30
legend has it that the building was designed so that there could

be no corner offices, the expanse of glass in individual offices is said to be a dead giveaway as to rank. Five windows are excellent, one window not so great.

In addition to a lofty floor number and windows, a carpet is   35
another feature to look for. At a certain corporate level, offices almost always have carpets. If they don't, the assumption is that the occupants don't wish to have them. But they practically all do, so there is rarely need to assume.

As though all this weren't enough, some cities have additional   40
hierarchical clues. There are Washington officeholders who would hang their heads in shame if they didn't have a big flag and a personally inscribed picture of the President. And areas, best unnamed, where an office without a bar and refrigerator is, well, naked.   45

As for visiting other offices, the signals are equally clear. An important visitor is not kept waiting after his presence is made known. He is met and escorted to the inner office by a private secretary. That is about as well as most people can do, other than the few who rate the big gun himself or herself coming out to the   50
reception area to do the escorting personally. This treatment usually entails a similar kind of farewell—the caller is escorted right out to the elevator by his host.

Assuming that one doesn't rate the biggie greeting, but the scene of the appointment is finally reached, what happens then?   55
It's a bad sign if the person is talking on the telephone and indicates with a casual wave of a hand that you be seated. Better, much better, if the telephone conversation is terminated immediately, and the greeting is done by a figure at least on its feet.

The nuances are endless. For example, once a business meeting   60
has begun, it's a sign of the visitor's importance if there are no interruptions. This generally means that the outside office has been told to hold telephone calls. If calls are accepted, the situation still isn't hopeless so long as the conversation is confined to saying that the call will be returned later.   65

If you're kept waiting in the reception area, told how to find the right office yourself, are faced with a hand holding a telephone and another hand waving you to a chair and are constantly interrupted by long telephone conversations, be advised: There is nowhere to go but up.   70

1. The writer has two main classes: How does she arrange the subclasses of each?

2. Check the etymology, denotation, and connotation of *protocol* and *entails*.

3. What is the effect of the writer's occasional use of such colloquialisms as *dead giveaway,* *big gun,* and *biggie?* What other colloquial words and phrases do you find?

ASSIGNMENTS

1. For an essay of classification you have a wide choice of subject matter. For example, you may write of classes already existing in guns, boats, airplanes, engines, welding processes, ways of preparing food, swimming strokes, trees, crops, cattle, pets, advertising, music, musical instruments, mathematics, curricula. Some of these subjects also lend themselves to more original handling, depending on the principle of classification you adopt and on the attitude you take toward the material. But more likely to demand originality of treatment are subjects such as love, patriotism, weather, television commercials, books, movies, fraternities.

2. You may especially enjoy a personal and original classification of some limited group of people: students, teachers, "dates," pledges, grandparents, salespeople, customers, employers, dog lovers, service-station attendants, taxi drivers, bridge players, pilots, amateur fishermen, news commentators, ballplayers, sports fans, dancers, hitchhikers.

3. Having chosen your subject, decide on a single principle of classification and keep it firmly in mind as you jot down the classes that you will include, making sure that they represent a reasonably complete treatment of the subject. Next, determine the most effective order in which to present these several classes, and then make a brief outline, indicating not only the classes and their order, but, with subpoints, the kind of information that you will include under each. (Remember that the information should be approximately the same and presented in approximately the same order for each class.)

UNIT 12

Analysis

What did you put in this soup? How is the city government organized? What are the structural patterns of Rembrandt's *The Night Watch?* What are the departments in this engineering company? What chemicals are in aspirin? What are the parts of a sonata? What materials are in this sweater?

The soup eater, the city resident, the art student, the business employee, the medical student, the music lover, the clothing shopper, have different questions, but they are all asking for an analysis. They share the need to know in detail the parts, whether tangible or intangible, that make up a whole so that they can understand and use both the whole and its parts intelligently. There are several methods to apply, singly or in combination, to analyze anything.

1. **Division** The simplest kind of analysis is a form of division—we split a subject in the way we section an apple, to make it yield comparable parts. The results are not like those of classification (Unit 11), however,

because they come from breaking down a single thing rather than a group. Apples in the mass may be classified—into sizes, colors, varieties; but one apple will be divided into halves or quarters. We use division when we think of a year as twelve months or of a day as morning, afternoon, and evening. We use it when we think of the world as composed of continents, or of a nation as composed of states.

2. **Dissection** The process that we shall for convenience call dissection operates on a deeper level of analysis than division. Dissection yields not similar sections of the apple but its different components: skin, flesh, core, stem. Some subjects lend themselves to either kind of breakdown. We divided the day into comparable time periods, but we can dissect it into logical rather than chronological components: classes, outside activities, recreation (see pages 14–15). Many subjects that can be analyzed by dissection would not lend themselves to division. A pencil could be dissected into graphite, wood, and paint, or divided into inch-long pieces: but although you can easily dissect a radio, you cannot divide it.

The analytical process, however, goes far beyond apples and radios. You may use it, of course, in the relatively simple matter of explaining the parts composing a given mechanism (it will then be similar to the simple informative type of description discussed in Unit 4, but you may also use it in the far more difficult task of discovering the issues in a complex problem. You may be interested in listing the components of a diesel engine or in setting forth what you believe to be the elements of Homer's greatness as an epic poet. In either task, the process of analysis by dissection is essentially the same.

3. **Enumeration** How often in serious discussions do we find expressions like these: "Three questions remain to be considered"; "Five courses of action are possible"; "Two reasons for his success emerge"; "Several misconceptions must be corrected."

When we analyze by division or dissection we determine the number of parts or phases of our subject and examine them one by one. How many there are will be determined largely by the subject and our purpose, but there are limits. We can never divide it in less than two, since by definition analysis implies a breaking down, and we are not likely to need more than five or six, since a larger number becomes unwieldy. Reasonable completeness, in analysis as in classification (page 228, item 6), will suffice.

Here, too, it is of prime importance to choose a principle to guide you through the breakdown of your subject so that your result will be neatly ordered pieces making up a logical whole. Whether they are parts of a simple mechanism or abstract qualities making up a reputation, they must be comparable. The tone is not an item in enumerating the parts of a radio, although it is the result of the parts; nor is the title "General" one of the qualities of Washington's character that you may list as contributing to his greatness. Recognize elements that are logically similar and omit the unrelated.

The order of the parts you finally choose as suitable will be determined, of course, by the usual patterns of arrangement for emphasis (see pages 13–19). Because the parts are comparable, you may often find that numbers make the best transitions: "1," "2," "3," or "first," "second," "third," and so on (the forms "firstly," "secondly," "thirdly" are no longer popular). Other transitions like "next" and "another" may also serve to emphasize your arrangement.

4. **Focusing on a problem** Your analysis need not stop with an enumeration of parts. You can apply it as a logical process in problem solving. To find a solution, you must discover the exact nature of the problem; to discover its nature, you must break it down into its component parts. Whether you are hunting for an error in your bank balance, choosing a career, or settling one of the world's major ills, the general procedure will be the same.

You may make a preliminary analysis in order to eliminate any aspects of the subject that are irrelevant to your view of the problem, just as when, asked to determine the chemical composition of an unknown substance, you rule out rapidly the more unlikely possibilities. Martin Luther King described doing this in *Stride Toward Freedom.* Having found three ways in which oppressed people might react to oppression—by acquiescence, violence, and nonviolent resistance—he ruled out the first two as unsuitable and concentrated on the third. You may analyze the psychological pressure on the average student, for instance, into the academic, economic, and social aspects, and decide to eliminate the first two from your discussion in order to devote yourself to the third, the one over which the student has most control. You will then proceed to break down the chosen part of the problem into its subordinate parts (dormitory life, dating, extracurricular activities, etc.), and on the basis of these parts, clearly stated, you will work through to a logical solution of the problem.

Although such an analysis is often applied to problem solving, it does not necessarily include a solution. It may imply an answer, or it may merely lay bare the issues for the reader's consideration; clarification is the central purpose of the analytical process.

5. **Stating the essentials** To help your readers understand the parts of an analysis and see how they fit together, you may begin by summing up instead of breaking down—by setting forth the essence, the root principle, the key to the whole subject. This procedure may not seem to be "analysis" at all, in the sense in which we have been using the word; but in a wider sense it is one of the most valuable parts of this logical process. Analysis may mean not only dissection, a breakdown into parts, but also a reduction to a simpler form—to the bare essentials. Such a reduction is likely to precede the normal taking-apart process (especially in the handling of abstract and complex subjects) to give the dissection clarity and purpose.

A writer might, for example, begin an analysis of the depression of the thirties by reducing that complex economic phenomenon to a basic description, such as starvation in the midst of plenty, before breaking it down into its causes, results, manifestations, or whatever other aspects interest the writer. The essentials will serve as a unifying guide among the aspects. One writer reduces the greatness of Lincoln to the fact that he was able to make such a reduction out of the confusion of his time:

> The greatness of Lincoln consisted precisely in the fact that he reduced the violence and confusion of his time to the essential moral issue and held it there against the cynical and worldly wisdom of the merchants of New England and the brokers of New York and all the rest who argued for expedient self-interest and a realistic view. (Archibald MacLeish, *A Time to Act*)

EXAMPLES

Analysis has a major role in all the selections in this unit. It is also a contributing factor in almost all the other selections in the book, most notably in Thomas's "On Societies as Organisms" (3-C), Jackson's "Challenge" (3-E), Klein's "Small Town Summer" (4-I), all the selections in Unit 6, St. John's "The Fifth Freedom" (8-A), Davenport's " 'Trees' " (7-A), Troyat's "Tolstoy's Contradictions" (10-B), Bateson's "The Aquarium and the Globe" (10-D), Quindlen's "Why I Don't Like Men" (10-E), Bajsarowicz's "Who Am I?" (10-F), and all the selections in Units 13, 14, 15, 16, and 17.

12-A   The Structure of a Comet

C. C. Wylie

This example of objective description, analyzing a comet, is taken from *Astronomy, Maps and Weather* (1942), a book intended for the general reader.

The head of a comet is a hazy, faintly shining ball. This head, or *coma,* is the essential part of the comet and gives it its name. Inside the coma there is usually, but not always, a *nucleus.* The nucleus is formed as the comet approaches the Sun and is seen as a starlike point near the center of the coma. Naked-eye comets   5 always, and telescopic comets often, form a *tail* as they approach the Sun. The tail is formed by matter streaming off in a direction opposite to the Sun. Usually the tail attains its maximum length and brightness a little after the comet passes perihelion.

In volume, comets are the bulkiest members of the solar sys-   10

tem. The head, or coma, is rarely smaller than the Earth in diameter, and for one or two comets the diameter of the head has
surpassed that of the Sun. The length of the tail of a spectacular
comet may be as much as one hundred million miles, or about the
same as the distance of the Earth from the Sun.   15

The mass of any comet is exceedingly small—so little that it
cannot be measured directly. Calculations from the amount of
light reflected indicate that the mass of Halley's Comet, one of the
most spectacular, was a little less than that of the rock and dirt
removed in excavating the Panama Canal. From its mass and   20
volume the density of the head of Halley's Comet was estimated
as being equivalent to twelve small marbles per cubic mile. It is
believed that the head of a comet is composed of dust and small
particles surrounded by gas. The density of the tail of a comet is
almost inconceivably small. For Halley's Comet the density has   25
been calculated as equivalent to one cubic centimeter of air at sea
level pressure expanded to two thousand cubic miles.

1. What principle of organization has the writer used?

2. Can you think of a different method of organization that would make the
material as clear?

3. What similarities and differences do you find in purpose, organization, and
general style between this example and Unit 4-D, Unit 6-E, and Unit 10-A?

4. Check the etymology and denotation of *perihelion.*

5. Where and how does Wylie use figures of speech to make his description
clear?

12-B   Branch Libraries

Edwin A. Peeples

The writer uses comparison, contrast, and classification in his analysis of trees
to explain his very personal conclusions. The essay, here complete, appeared in
Country Journal in 1989.

ANALYSIS   Ever since the inception of the written word, one of
Introduction   the best places to read has been under a tree. Here in the
stating the   shade one can quietly peruse a book without any com-
essentials   panions except the leaves that rustle softly like so many
                pages turning over in a library. A good tree either nur-   5

tures soft, cool grass beneath it or exposed, twisting roots large enough to sit on and filled with crevices to hold bookmarks, cast-aside sneakers, and a glass of lemonade.

background
Artists Maxfield Parrish, Milo Winter, Norman Rockwell, and N. C. Wyeth loved to paint people reposing under trees, books open beneath their eyes. Scientists have acknowledged that trees are guardians of students by accepting the vernacular name for *Sophora japonica*— the scholar tree.

humorous side issue
Television has drawn people away from reading beneath trees—and everywhere else for that matter. Don't try to make amends to neglected trees by trying to view television under them. There's no place to plug your set in, no aerial, too much light, and a heck of a long stretch for the cable cord.

One can hope that the atavism that is drawing people back to the country and to simpler pleasures like watching bees and butterflies, will encourage them to return to outdoor reading. Then they can rediscover a joy too long neglected.

focusing on the problem
A good tree to read under is like a good book—friends and acquaintances may praise one to the heavens, but only your own examination will tell the true tale. And just as you can't judge a book by its cover, you can't always judge a reading tree by its appearance.

Division I: unsuitable trees Dissection: 1. foliage
Pines, firs, hemlocks, and larches are nice to have nearby for fragrance, but their limbs grow too near the ground to leave reading space beneath them, and their foliage is so dense it shuts out most of the light. A Southern magnolia has plenty of room beneath it, but its foliage, lapped tight as shingles, shuts out all of the light. You might as well try to read in a cave or at the bottom of a well.

Oaks and maples have high crowns and plenty of space, but be sure to choose among them wisely: Sometimes their foliage is too dense to let in enough light. Besides, inchworms love these trees and for almost all of the month of June drizzle down on their spiderweb threads to measure their way across your page or across the back of your neck.

additional problem

2. location
The weeping willow can be a good reading place. Its leaves let in plenty of light yet provide a theatrical curtain that descends to the ground on all sides and lends privacy.

10

15

20

25

30

35

40

45

additonal
problem

The willow has the drawback of liking to grow in wet   50
places (as do mosquitoes). Other willows mist down a
bath of sticky sap at times and, at other times, clouds of
seeds like small, loose feathers. Such showers do not
improve the flavor of Shakespeare or of Proust.

3. droppings

Such effusions also cause some to complain of *dirty*   55
trees, as if one group of trees were messier than others.
All trees drop three things: flower parts like petals; fruit,
nuts, or seeds; and leaves. Fruit trees like mulberries and
wild cherries are not good for reading under when they
are in fruit because they inundate you with harvest.   60
Fallen berries are squishy and sticky.

Division II:
good trees
Dissection:
1. nut tees
dropping
foliage

Among the best trees to read under most of the year
are nut trees: walnuts, hickories, pecans, and filberts. The
blossoms of these trees mature long before good reading
weather. The drop of flower petals and parts is over well   65
before time to take up reading residence. The leaves of
these trees are slender and airy, letting in lots of sunlight.

counter-
argument

Having a nice green lawn beneath you while reposing
is a plus. Unfortunately, while the reading weather is still
good, these trees will litter that grass with nuts. When   70
this begins, you will have to wear a football helmet to sit
beneath one. A black walnut is almost as large as a tennis
ball and hard as a baseball. Getting hit by one that has
fallen 40 feet will surely drive you back to the TV room.

2. catkins

foliage
dropping

I would choose a tree that produces catkins: black   75
locust, filbert, birch, scholar, or yellowwood. All of these
are high crowned and allow enough light to encourage
grass. The catkins drop long before the weather is warm
enough for outdoor reading. Only the filbert drops nuts,
and these are little larger than acorns. All drop leaves as   80
the weather cools.

3. sycamore

dropping
foliage

Finally, there is the long-armed sycamore. Its limbs
often measure 30 feet and have several elbows and knees
in case you want to climb a bit between chapters. The
sycamore produces a nutlike fruit that hangs like a Christ-   85
mas tree ornament. The fruit doesn't drop until the following spring. The leaves are large and numerous but
widely enough spaced to let in plenty of light.

related topic
analytic
question
division

And what chair should one select to place beneath the
reading tree (assuming one is no longer young enough   90
to read lying prone upon the grass)? Many like ham-
mocks to curl into. A cushioned chair is nice, but can be
too straight. My preference is the chaise longue with the

cartridge belt cushion that allows the reader to adjust his
posture from supine to sitting. On one of these beneath   95
a grove of three paper birches, I spent time on many a
summer morning sipping coffee and reading before I
went to work.

Conclusion   The most delightful memory of summer shade tree
personal   reading I have is of enjoying Stuart Gilbert's volume of   100
narrative   the letters of James Joyce. It took me from beneath my
tree to France and Italy and Trieste where Joyce traveled
and lived.

As I read, the sunlight sifted through the trees, a bird
sang "Larch, larch, larch!" and the wind gave the leaves   105
a voice that said: "Gleeee."

I was, I felt, in just the right place—a spot where, for
a moment, the world stood still.

1. What characteristics does the writer look for in a tree when he wishes to read
outdoors?

2. What are the chief hazards of reading under a tree?

3. Check the etymology, denotation, and connotation of *inception, peruse, nurtures, crevices, vernacular, atavism, inundate, catkins, prone, supine,* and the colloquial
words *heck* and *squishy.*

12-C   A Sense of Self

Edwin Ortiz *(student)*

This essay was written in class on an assigned topic: Describe an event that made
an important difference in your life.

Many experiences have given me insights directly affecting my
sense of self. An experience during my senior year of high school
in Puerto Rico proved particularly illuminating. It caused me to
come to a conclusion about myself.

My civics teacher had recommended me as an appropriate and   5
deserving participant in the Presidential Classroom, which was a
yearly seminar held in Washington, D.C. Senior and junior high
school students from across the United States attended this seminar to learn about the federal government and what supposedly
enables that government to function. I, with about 300 other   10

students, spent a week listening to dozens of speakers, visiting
government facilities, and being educated about the important
issues of the day.

I and five others were from Puerto Rico, while the rest of the
students were from the mainland, so to speak. Unlike the five   15
other Puerto Rican students who had been born and raised on the
island, I had been living in Puerto Rico for only three years after
having moved from New York. This information is important in
explaining the significance of the episode I am about to describe.

I was walking through the Washington National Zoo with a   20
new acquaintance, a young Puerto Rican woman from New York
who was also attending the Presidential Classroom. We had arrived at the zoo after having visited several monuments. During
all the time we spent together, I spoke only of the great symbolism of the nation's capital. I even told her that I wanted to be   25
President of the United States. After having listened to me all
day, she finally looked me directly in the eye and said, "You
would rather be an American, wouldn't you?" I answered,
"Yes."

There is not enough time or paper to describe all the conflicting   30
emotions which I experienced at that moment. I began to realize
that I had never truly been in touch with my own heritage. Being
Puerto Rican had never had any deep meaning. However, I knew
what it was like to be an American. I was born and raised in New
York and spoke English nearly exclusively, almost ignoring my   35
opportunity to be bilingual. My world was American.

During the years following the incident at the Washington
National Zoo, I have spent much time trying to reorient my
perspective and to reconcile the Americanism with which I had
grown up and my still emerging identification as a person of   40
Puerto Rican heritage living in the United States. I have had to
struggle to improve my Spanish and to expand my knowledge of
the Puerto Rican community in New York. It has been difficult
learning to think in two languages.

Despite those difficulties, my experience has helped me to   45
grow—culturally, politically, and as a human being. I have
become more aware of my surroundings, more understanding of
human foibles, and more determined to be a part of the political
and economic struggles which are taking place today.

Besides analysis, which of these methods does the writer use to present his ideas
and where does he use them: description, narration, exemplification, quotation, comparison and contrast, classification?

12-D   Greed

Natsuko Uesugi *(student)*

Compare this writer's direct criticism of contemporary behavior with the implied criticism in Cynthia Hoffman's "How to Have Free Entertainment with Your
Meal" (9-G).

"All you can eat for $6.99," announced the girl with a perfect
set of teeth, sparkling her smile enthusiastically into the eyes of
millions. Dancing tomatoes and cucumbers twirled around her,
displaying dishes of glossy turkey and impeccable gravy with no
lumps. Simultaneously, the concentration level of the viewers   5
increased as they focused their attention on the television screen.
Before the jingle for the family restaurant is finished, they are in
a mad rush to get to their cars. Such swift action can only be the
product of a great American virtue, greed.

Greed is a popular and sophisticated quality frequently dis-   10
played by such role models on television series as Alexis on
Dynasty and J.R. on *Dallas.* The skill with which they find ways
to benefit themselves in any situation is truly magnificent. They
stress the importance of self, which is the principle of greed.
Although Alexis and J.R. are professionals in this field, ordinary   15
people can strive to achieve their level of greediness, for everybody has the potential of being greedy. Such potential can be
observed in public places like the local expressways, shopping
malls, and restaurants, where greed prompts competition with
others.   20

Expressways are usually infested with greedy drivers. Upon
entering an expressway, greedy drivers usually drive at full speed
to the end of the merging area to get ahead of as many cars as
possible. Greed does not allow them to be patient because patience
deprives them of time. The faster they get to their destinations, the   25
more advantage they have over others with the same goal. Once on
an expressway, greedy drivers make sure that no one passes them
from behind. If someone has the audacity to pull alongside, greedy
drivers usually increase their speed so that it will be impossible for
the other driver to occupy the space in front. Greed does not allow   30
them to be generous because generosity gives others an opportunity to surpass them. Greedy drivers also prevent this from happening by omitting turn signals completely. Turn signals would
allow others to see where greedy drivers were headed, which

might prompt others to take the opportunity to move ahead.   35
Therefore, greedy drivers sneak in front of other drivers without
signaling. By such clever maneuvers greedy drivers gain maximum advantage over others on the road.

Shopping malls provide a place for greedy shoppers to practice
their skills. To get the best parking spaces, they usually come early   40
in the morning. When the most desirable spaces are taken, greedy
shoppers invent their own imaginary parking spaces at the front
of each row. Walking a long distance between parking areas and
shopping malls is a waste of energy and time, which should be
devoted to shopping.   45

Greedy shoppers are most visible during the holiday season, a
time when the price of Christmas wrapping paper and calendars
may drop drastically within days. Greedy shoppers come prepared with accomplices, usually spouses or children, who will
keep their places in busy register lines while they exhibit strength   50
and agility in grabbing, shoving, and pushing for the most and the
best selections within reach. Greed helps sharpen athletic abilities
tremendously.

In restaurants, greedy eaters display intelligence in knowing
which selections provide the greatest quantity at the lowest price.   55
Especially in restaurants that offer buffet and "all you can eat"
menus, greed prompts them to take in as much food as possible,
even if it means not being able to move out of their chairs for a
few hours afterwards. Complimentary breadsticks and after-din-
ner mints always find their way into the pockets and purses of   60
greedy eaters.

Taking advantage of situations like these is an important aspect
of greed. Greed sets priorities in their rightful order: self always
comes first. At times, others may object to this idea, but it is only
because they do not understand the importance of taking all that   65
one can get without the hassles of thinking about others. After all,
greed is a great American virtue.

Meanwhile, back at the family restaurant, a lifesize poster of the
girl with the perfect set of teeth stands ever so innocently over
the crowded buffet counter, which is under attack by anxious   70
hands grabbing the biggest helpings of salads and poultry while
skillfully balancing a pyramid of food on their plates. Ah, a picture
of the beauty of greed.

1. How has the writer organized her material? Into what subdivisions does she
divide the general topic of greed?

2. By what methods does she make the examples of greed vivid?

12-E   When Blacks Rule in South
Africa

Masipula Sithole

The writer is a professor of political science at the University of Zimbabwe, and his brother founded the Zimbabwe African National Union. In this essay, here complete, Sithole analyzes the thinking of Afrikaners, who are opposed to granting political power to blacks, and finds cause to hope for a peaceful outcome for the black struggle for recognition. In 1989 the white population, which controls South Africa, was only 4.5 million, whereas the black population was 23 million.

At the Crossroads near Cape Town, blacks backed by white police battle black activists, and the level of militancy increases. In Pretoria, members of the Afrikaner Resistance Movement are more vocal; white backlash increases as the pressure for change in South Africa mounts. The voice of reason, of the moderate   5
middle, seems to be thinning out in the squeeze; nonetheless, South Africa will not explode. Whites will abandon apartheid and other notions of white supremacy when both objective and subjective conditions have sufficiently matured.

I say this having lived through a similar struggle in Rhodesia.   10
As a member of the Zimbabwe African National Union, I watched whites move right—and then change. Now when I look south, I see two ways of looking at apartheid. One way is to view it as the work of irrational men; the other is to see it as the work of rational men. Each perception leads to a different and opposite   15
scenario.

A picture has been circulated by politicians, journalists and, regrettably, by learned circles that the architects and perpetrators of South Africa's racist policies were united by some sort of "covenant," that they were an ideologically blinded but "tough"   20
people determined to pursue their philosophy of racial supremacy at all costs. And as such, the Afrikaner should be seen as a pathological person, as an irrational racist, who will kill every black man and himself in order to avoid being ruled by blacks. This view of the Afrikaner is incorrect, I believe; in fact, it's nonsense.   25

The other way to perceive Afrikaners is as normal human beings, susceptible to pain in the usual manner, as people who created the myth of a "covenant" because they needed it in the circumstances of the time. Defeated by the British in the Anglo-Boer War, they created a system of apartheid because dominance looked like a better way to ensure for themselves both individual and group survival. There is nothing special or pathological in all this. These are perfectly rational conclusions arrived at by normal human beings who, in the final analysis, do what they do to survive.

Rational behavior, of course, does not always lead to correct or intended outcomes. Throughout history, the rational mind has miscalculated conditions in many parts of the world. This, however, is a result of the limitations of mortal man from which the Afrikaner, as a human species, is not excluded. Rationally conceived, apartheid turned out to be a miscalculation. It has not brought security to the white South African; instead, it now threatens his very survival. And dying for it cannot be compared to a holy war, an Islamic jihad in which paradise is assured; in fact, for white South African Christians, it is likely to limit such prospects.

In Ian Smith's Rhodesia, black rule was also anathema: "Not in a thousand years," not "in my lifetime," Smith used to boast. A seven-year guerrilla war, intensely fought only for 2½ of those years, brought with it the millennium and an accommodation up to and including total black rule. Commitment to racism may only be a measure of one's security under it. As black resistance in South Africa increases and stiffens, whites will be denied the use of black stooges in black communities and, as such, they will themselves have to go into Soweto, move into the Bantustans, go into the bush and die. As the white body count multiplies, the average Afrikaner will ask the usual combatant's question: "Is this a cause worth dying for?" Is apartheid an ideology of such moral quality that these "tough" men and women must die for it rather than come to an accommodation with the African majority?

Even now, whites are trying to wash their hands of apartheid. In an interview with ABC's Ted Koppel a year ago, South Africa's President P. W. Botha denied responsibility for the apartheid monster, placing all of its sins on the British. "If you mean by apartheid," he said, "the deprivement of fundamental rights to people, I say I'm all against it. But you must remember that this system was not originated by Afrikaners. . . . Most of the domination that existed in this country was instituted under British imperialism."

Increasingly, then, more and more white South Africans are likely to blame the "Brits" for apartheid—a scapegoat all the more convenient because they no longer rule. Sweet reasonableness has already begun. And further delays will actually improve the quality of the outcome for blacks in an eventual accommodation. This, in fact, is what happened in Zimbabwe after Ian Smith 75 tried to work through tribal chiefs and so-called moderate leaders.

The Afrikaner is likely to hold on, trying this and that and many other meaningless stratagems, until nobody is willing to share anything but mercy. But even at that late stage, the Afrikaner will 80 more likely choose to surrender to the mercy of a black government than commit suicide in an explosion. The mental energies and material resources that went into the nervous construction and upkeep of apartheid over the years should convince us that we are dealing with a people who have a pretty well-developed 85 sense of survival. They meant to look after themselves; they are not suicidal. And they likely will change when the price is right.

Until now whites in South Africa have not been quite called upon to defend their moribund ideology with their lives, to actually bleed and die for this untenable ideology of race. When they 90 do, they will reason it's not worth the price. And, as usual, blacks in South Africa will be forgiving. After all, they were in Zimbabwe.

1. Where does the writer use comparison to explain his thinking?

2. Where does he use exemplification?

3. What does the writer see as the reasons behind the Afrikaners' creation of apartheid?

4. Check the etymology, denotation, and connotation of *militancy, covenant, pathological, anathema, millennium, stooges, scapegoat, moribund, untenable.*

12-F   Two Imperatives in Conflict

Richard Shoglow *(student)*

There is some evidence in the world that the phenomenon called the "territorial imperative," or something very like it, exists, and this can lead to pessimistic conclusions about the future of the human race. Ardrey, in his essay called "Of Men and Mockingbirds," points out some evidence to support the idea of 5 "territoriality." For instance, he reports on twenty-four different primitive tribes in various separate areas around the world. Although they were unable to learn from each other, they all formed similar social bands occupying specific permanent territories. This showed the unlearned, perhaps genetic, need of human beings for their own territory.

A second example of these territorial instincts is, I think, in the Middle East today. The situation there is a struggle for possession of an area. Both the Israelis and the Palestinians are in battle over this territory—one to keep it and the other to obtain it. Both regard this land as necessary for their existence and as belonging to them.

Among my neighbors and even in my own family, I have seen further evidence of a territorial imperative. My father, for instance, was very worried when a neighbor decided to build a boathouse near the property boundary of our house. Although we had plenty of land to spare, my father was worried about losing a little part of it. I have seen arguments between neighbors about trees that cross property boundaries and even disputes over whether a boundary marker had been moved a foot or so. If this phenomenon is instinctive, innate, it is therefore inevitable that people must clash for living space. The increasing pressure of a growing population and a severely limited world space may lead to a catastrophic battle, such as a nuclear war, that could mean the end of the world.

But while the potential for disaster may exist in our territorial imperative, there is some evidence that a "social imperative" may also exist. This "social imperative" is our ability to share and to cooperate with our fellow human beings. If this exists, then there is hope for our future. Maybe many of our problems will be solved eventually. Ardrey's article mentions that there are some animals, such as the elephant, the antelope, and the gorilla, who have no territorial bond. These animals wander constantly, moving where food can be found. They have no wars. There is no competition over a particular territory. They move together, sharing the space and the food. The Middle East dispute is in an uneasy equilibrium as both sides, with the help of negotiators, search for a compromise solution that can bring peace. If their "territorial imperative" gets the better of either of them, a terrible conflict may erupt, but as long as both sides are willing to cooperate, they can avoid war. If traditional enemies can really join and share for the betterment of mankind, perhaps there can be a more optimistic view of man's future.

We are born with a genetic structure that helps to determine the adjustment we make in this world. But we are also subject to

the influences of our social environment. We can learn new behavior and we can modify our predispositions. If this were not
true, all constructive influences such as education would be
worthless. I believe—or at least hope—that we will learn to modify our genetic need for territory by accepting the modern reality.   55
We all inhabit the same rapidly shrinking earth populated by a
rapidly rising number of people. We must share and cooperate,
because there is no other way.

1. This essay was written in response to one of the readings assigned in the
course. What use does the writer make of analogy, narration, and comparison in his
analysis of the "territorial imperative"?

2. By what methods does he analyze the "social imperative"?

3. The writer refers to his own individual experience and also to a major
international problem. What is the effect of this use of both small-scale and large-scale
examples?

12-G   Why They Mourned for Elvis
                            Presley

Molly Ivins

This example, a complete news article, first appeared in the *New York Times*
(1977).

Why did 25,000 people stand for hours in an almost unbearable heat, in a truly unbearable crush, trying to get a glimpse of
a rock-and-roll singer? Why did so many drive all night, take
plane trips they couldn't afford, set out from half a continent away
without money or comforts or plans, solely to attend the funeral   5
of Elvis Presley?

The people who came to mourn offered only one reason: "Because," they said over and over, "we love him."

Those who make it their business to explain such phenomena
offered a multitude of reasons. Mass hysteria, they said. Ghoulish-   10
ness. Suppressed sexual yearnings. An acting out of class antago-
nisms. Nostalgia for lost innocence and youth. They attributed it
to generational identification, to Freudian repression, to a mad
media overkill.

But if some observers seemed condescending or embarrassed 15
by the open displays of sentimentality, mawkishness and love, Mr.
Presley's fans saw nothing to be ashamed of in glorying in their
sorrow. They were not offended by an instant commercialization
of their grief, by the T-shirts reading "Elvis Presley, In Memory,
1935–1977" that were on sale for $5 in front of Mr. Presley's 20
mansion.

The Memphis police, whose courtesy was remarkable, carefully
carried water out to the waiting fans, gently carried away the
fainters, and played with the children. When fans emerged dis-
traught after viewing Mr. Presley's body, the police walked up to 25
them, put an arm around their shoulders and walked away with
them, talking soothingly until the fans were calmer.

The police became unpopular at one point, when they shut out
at least 10,000 waiting fans on Wednesday evening. "Why are
you treating us like this?" shouted a man as he was pushed away 30
from the gate. "Why do you have all those helicopters and cops
here?"

"We're afraid of a riot," replied a sheriff's deputy.

The fan was outraged, "You don't understand," he said.
"We're not troublemakers, we didn't come here to . . . we're, 35
we're *family*. We came because we love him."

One seldom expects the country's President to adequately note
the passing of a rocker, but Jimmy Carter's assessment of Elvis
Presley's appeal—"energy, rebelliousness and good humor"—is
remarkably close to the mark. When he started out in the 1950's 40
he looked like a hood, he sang sensually. Part of his appeal in the
1970's was our remembering what we thought was "sexy" back
then. Underneath that greaser hairdo, he had the profile of a
Greek god. Besides, our parents didn't like him, so what could
be better? And the music? Well, the music can be left to the music 45
critics, who by and large seem to think it's pretty good. A teenage
foot that never tapped to "Heartbreak Hotel" in the 50's probably belonged to a hopeless grind.

A large proportion of the mourners in Memphis were the girls
who once screamed and cried and fainted at Elvis Presley concerts 50
in the 1950's. They grew up, but they never got over Elvis.

The idols of one's adolescence tend to endure—you never
forget how you worshipped them. There is never anyone quite
so wonderful as the people who were seniors when you were a
freshman. And the intense crushes of adolescent girls helped 55
create the phenomenon of Elvis Presley.

The fans who came to Memphis, especially the women, tended
to have been Elvis fans "from the beginning." Many of them said

they had married right out of high school and that their last
memories of girlhood are of passionate feelings about Elvis Pres-   60
ley—"My first love."

"I told my husband he'd always be second to Elvis." "I loved
him then and I love him now." They never stopped being Elvis
fans. They kept up their Elvis Presley scrapbooks. They went to
his concerts and grabbed the scarves he used to give away, and   65
had them framed. Some of them seemed to realize that it was,
perhaps, a little silly, but he seemed to represent the only rebellion they ever knew, the dreams of their youth.

Oh, there were some who came to Memphis because "it's
what's happening, man." Just to be there, to be seen, to see,   70
without caring. But for the most part, Memphis was awash with
genuine emotion for three days. It is too easy to dismiss it as
tasteless. It is not required that love be in impeccable taste.

1. According to the author, what reasons did some observers give for the arrival
of 25,000 people from all over the country in Memphis to pay their last respects to
Elvis Presley?

2. What additional reasons does the author find for the large number of
mourners?

3. What descriptive and narrative touches does the author use to bring out her
main point and to make the scene vivid?

12-H   Splitting the Word

Anthony Burgess

These paragraphs begin the chapter on words in *Language Made Plain* (1964),
a book explaining the basic principles and terminology of linguistics to the general
reader. A phoneme is any one of the smallest units of sound of which words are
composed and which distinguish one word from another. In English these are often
not indicated by spelling. For instance, the only phonemic difference between *though*
and *those* is the z sound in *those*.

For the moment—but only for the moment—it will be safe to
assume that we all know what is meant by the word "word." I may
even consider that my typing fingers know it, defining a word (in
a whimsical conceit) as what comes between two spaces. The
Greeks saw the word as the minimal unit of speech; to them, too,   5

the atom was the minimal unit of matter. Our own age has learnt to split the atom and also the word. If atoms are divisible into protons, electrons, and neutrons, what are words divisible into?

Words as things uttered split up, as we have already seen, into phonemes, but phonemes do not take *meaning* into account. We do not play on the phonemes of a word as we play on the keys of a piano, content with mere sound; when we utter a word we are concerned with the transmission of meaning. We need an appropriate kind of fission, then—one that is *semantic,* not *pho-nemic.* Will division into syllables do? Obviously not, for syllables are mechanical and metrical, mere equal ticks of a clock or beats in a bar. If I divide (as for a children's reading primer) the word "metrical" into "met-ri-cal," I have learned nothing new about the word: these three syllables are not functional as neutrons, protons, electrons are functional. But if I divide the word as "metr-; -ic; -al" I have done something rather different. I have indicated that it is made of the root "metr-," which refers to measurement and is found in "metronome" and, in a different phonemic disguise, in "metre," "kilometre," and the rest; "-ic," which is an adjectival ending found also in "toxic," "psychic," etc., but can sometimes indicate a noun, so that "metric" itself can be used in a phrase like "Milton's metric" with full noun status; "-al," which is an unambiguous adjectival ending, as in "festal," "vernal," "partial." I have split "metrical" into three contribu-tory forms which (remembering that Greek *morph-* means "form") I can call *morphemes.*

1. How does the author use analogy? metaphor?

2. Why does he use "fission" in the third sentence of the second paragraph instead of "division" or "splitting"?

3. Why does the author mention dividing words into syllables since he immedi-ately says that doing so gives him no new information about the words?

12-I   Christmas Eve

Christine Conza *(student)*

This essay was written after a class discussion of holiday traditions. Notice how Conza uses the organization of a process description to make a critical analysis of a traditional family gathering.

Christmas Eve arrives at my house each year accompanied by the same heraldry. The center of the celebration is dinner. My mother spends the five preceding days preparing an exotic assortment of sea creatures, including eels, squid, and dried codfish. The guest list is fairly consistent. It is composed of my Aunt Marcy   5 and her husband, my oldest brother, Sal, his wife, and their four children, my sister, Joann, her husband, and their two children, and my second brother, Richard, his wife, and their two children.

My aunt and uncle always come laden with enough pastries and wine for George Washington's troops at Valley Forge. My   10 brother Sal and gang invariably show up an hour early and empty handed. Joann's group is usually late and apologetic. Richie and clan generally arrive on time, bearing gifts for everyone. I have the responsibility of getting the Christmas tree. Remaining in my usual character of the great procrastinator, I emerge through the   15 door, struggling with my half-priced, over-sized evergreen just as the spaghetti is being served.

In keeping with the tradition of over-indulgence, there are two varieties of pasta from which to choose. For the daring, there is the garlic and oil sauce, with anchovies thrown in for good mea-   20 sure. For the more conservative, like me, there is crab sauce. After the spaghetti, the seafood is brought out. All the hours of preparation are wolfed down in a matter of minutes. It is an Italian tradition to have fish on Christmas Eve. Along with the yearly repetition of menu comes the yearly repetition of conversation.   25

My father always dwells on how difficult his childhood was for him. Everyone comments on how good the food tastes and on how "Mom" is the only one who can cook a meal such as this one. My mother then gives a thorough rundown on all the supermarkets from which the fish was purchased. This begins our period   30 of comparison shopping. For at least thirty minutes, we try to outdo each other mentioning the bargains we have found. For example, Joann will mention that Waldbaum's had a sale on cof-

fee, only $2.50 a pound. Then Sal will mention that his wife
bought coffee for $1.99 at King Kullen, and Richie will top that   35
by saying that his wife paid only $1.70 at Pathmark using a forty
cent coupon during double-coupon week.

   Meanwhile, the kids are starting to grow restless. It is all down-
hill for them after the spaghetti. Since the dinner conversation
does not interest me anyway, I usually end up playing the role of   40
Miss Louise of Romper Room fame. Mom then brings out a
mound of fruit and nuts, and trays of Aunt Marcy's pastries. These
are met with a chorus of oohs and aahs from the group, who have
already eaten more than their share. The evening dies slowly.

   This annual gathering occurs out of habit. If my mother did not   45
sponsor this event, we would not know what to do with ourselves.
Personally, I do not feel the need to be with a crowd on Christmas
Eve. Christmas Eve, to me, is a quiet time, a time for reflection.
It is the anniversary of a night on which Mary and Joseph were
cold and without a place to stay. It seems ludicrous to remember   50
a night of such poverty and simplicity with such over-indulgence
and revelry. The excessive noise and confusion of this gathering
contradict my feelings about Christmas. The "celebration" stains
the dignity of the holiday—or, better named, the holy day.

ASSIGNMENTS

1. The simplest subjects for analysis by dissection are definite objects such as a ball
   point pen or mechanical pencil, a sailboat, a tennis court, a football team—in all
   of which the parts are easily discoverable. More challenging is the analysis of an
   institution (school, church, government) or a work of art (a poem, a painting, a
   symphony), in which the existing parts are less readily discernible.
2. Use the analytical process to solve some problem, such as a strongly felt but
   perhaps hitherto unexamined like or dislike of your own (for a person, a course,
   a custom), the popularity of something (a sport, a fad, a curriculum), the success
   of something or someone (a program, a campaign, an individual).
3. Approach through a statement of root principle the analysis of a leader, a form
   of government, war, peace, success, the American way of life.
4. Whatever subject you choose or whatever approach you decide on, keep your
   purpose clearly in mind. A textbook, for example, can be analyzed as an object
   by dissecting thephysical parts of which it is composed, or it can be analyzed by
   dissecting the content. But do not confuse two purposes: A red cover is not to be
   mentioned in the same breath with a clear-cut literary style.
5. Analysis is such a common method by which the mind works that you can find it
   illustrated to some extent in every unit in this book. It operates most conspicuously
   in Unit 16, where you will find it essential to support an argument, in Unit 17 for
   critical writing, and in Unit 18 for the research paper. Study its use in the next
   unit in all the examples.

UNIT 13

Cause and Effect

Two cars collide in the morning rush hour. The immediate cause is obvious to everyone who sees the accident. Although the traffic light had been yellow for some time, one driver tried to beat it as it turned red and speeded into the narrow intersection when the driver on his right was already moving briskly forward. But what caused the first driver to try to beat the light? Was he late for an appointment with an important client? What caused him to be late? Did an emergency at home delay him? What caused the emergency? Was his little boy scratched by the family cat? What caused the ordinarily gentle cat to turn suddenly fierce? Was the child teasing it? and if so, why? and so on.

The immediate effect of the accident is also obvious to everyone—a badly dented fender on each car, two drivers exchanging identification in the road, and backed-up traffic in both directions. But what are the later effects the bystanders cannot see?—the first driver's important client growing impatient over the delay, being rude to the secretary, and canceling the appointment; the second driver's embarrassment when he explains to his sister that her car is damaged; the bruised elbow of his passenger who will now not be able to play in a tennis tournament that week; the conversation between two passengers in another car who had just met that morning, which results in their making a dinner date (with subsequent dates eventually resulting in their marriage); the decisions by three drivers to increase their collision insurance and the resolve by four drivers to start for work earlier; and so on.

One of our most common logical problems is to discover the true causes behind the effects or to trace from the causes the effects that have already resulted or that probably will result. They may be single, as when cough medicine brings relief, or numerous, as when an antibiotic produces several side effects. They may be closely related, as a knife is to a cut, or separated by time, as is contact with poison ivy from blisters the next day. We may see the connection of cause and effect clearly, or we may discover it only after careful analysis. In this unit we shall concentrate on this relationship. But first we should look at some of the *fallacies*—the wrong beliefs—involved.

1. **Do not mistake a time relationship for a cause.** This confusion results in the popular *post hoc* fallacy (named from the Latin *post hoc, ergo propter hoc,* meaning "after this, therefore because of this"). This fallacy is responsible for the origin of many of our superstitions. A black cat crosses our path, and bad luck follows; therefore a black cat is believed to have caused the bad luck. Breaking a mirror, walking under a ladder, and so on—these belong to the mythology of our culture and are attempts to explain something whose true cause is unknown or too unpleasant to be faced. Certainly, we might see these as causing bad effects if we were scratched by the cat or cut by the mirror or spattered with paint; but, as intelligent people, we would look for other, plausible causes of any *unrelated* misfortune that follows. Before we can attribute a series of storms to atomic tests, we need much more research. The tests *may* prove to be a contributing cause, but they may not—after all, we had bad storms long before the atom was split. Note the continuing debate among scientists over the links between some foods and cancer.

2. **Do not mistake for a cause something actually unrelated.** Akin to the *post hoc* fallacy is the assumption that two things that usually happen at the same time must have a causal relationship—for instance, popular opinion holds that leaves turn color in the fall because of the first frost of fall, although scientists insist that the change usually precedes the frost. A causal relationship is often attributed to many pure coincidences: someone who seems to be following you down a lonely street may merely be going in the same direction at the same speed.

3. **Do not settle for one cause if there are more.** One effect may have been produced by multiple causation. Television may contribute to juvenile delinquency, but so do many other social forces. If a normally cheerful man appears surly, he may have had an argument with his neighbor about the neighbor's dog, received an unexpectedly large telephone bill, been criticized by his boss, had a flat tire on the way to work, or may be coming down with a cold. More probably, a combination of these causes has affected him—the proverbial last straw did not break the camel's back all by itself.

4. **Do not mistake cause for effect or effect for cause.** Some medieval philosophers believed that the great European rivers sprang up where the great cities were built: The modern historian sees the process in reverse. The old farmer who said, "If I'd known I was going to have such nice children, I'd have picked a better mother for 'em," might also stand correction.

5. **Distinguish between immediate and remote causes.** Asked why you are here in college, you could truthfully answer, "Because my father and mother married," but the inquirer is probably concerned with more recent causes directly connected with the effect in question.

6. **Be sure the cause could produce the result.** If a large dog is left unwatched in the kitchen and three pounds of hamburger disappear, the dog is a likely suspect—particularly if, as with the disappearance of the teapot and spoons in Huxley's essay (Example H in this unit), there is other circumstantial evidence as well, such as distended ribs and a greasy muzzle and paws. On the other hand, a small puppy may be exonerated, not from lack of motive but of capacity.

7. **Allow for causes that may nullify predicted effects.** Corn needs rain, but a heavy rainfall does not assure farmers of a good crop; it may instead prevent them from planting in time or, if heavy enough, may drown the corn they have already planted. Wage increases do not necessarily result in more buying power; they may instead contribute to an increase in the cost of living.

8. **Avoid predicting contradictory effects.** The campaign promises of politicians to lower taxes and also expand the public works program are not taken seriously by experienced voters.

9. **Avoid the pitfall of rationalization.** In the search for causes and effects, especially the causes of your own opinions or the effects of your own actions, you may be tempted to use false or superficial explanations that let you avoid facing the truth. For instance, drivers involved in car accidents often blame road conditions or mechanical failure, denying their own carelessness; and students may excuse their failure to study adequately by pleading that the assignment was too long or that they needed sleep, rather than admit their laziness.

EXAMPLES

The relationship between cause and effect is particularly evident in the selections in this unit, but it can be found, in varying degrees, in every other selection in this book, notably in Welty's "Listening to Words" (3-A), Jackson's "Challenge" (3-E), Wright's "A Loaf of Bread and the Stars" (5-B), Rodriguez's "Your Parents Must Be Proud" (5-D), Wong's "A Cultural Divorce" (5-E), Mencken's "Le Contrat Social" (6-B), Johmann's "Sex and the Split Brain" (7-B), Collier's "To Deal and Die in L.A." (7-C), all the selections in Unit 9, Kirchoff's "The Downfall of Christmas" (10-C), Lanning's "The Ones Left Behind" (11-B), Brody's "Mental Depression" (11-C), Sithole's "When Blacks Rule in South Africa" (12-E), Ivins's "Why They Mourned for Elvis Presley" (12-G), all the selections in Unit 15, Tudge's "They Breed Horses, Don't They?" (16-B), and Singer's "Parents, Children, and Television" (16-C).

13-A   Living on the Altiplano

Georgie Anne Geyer

These paragraphs are taken from a travel article in the *Atlantic Monthly*.

The Altiplano, that high plain which balances at 14,000 feet like a slate between the two spectacular black ridges of the Andes, has formed and influenced the life of the Incas more than anything else. Its thin stern air has even affected the bodies of the Indians, giving them larger lungs to bear the strain and more red   5
corpuscles to stand the cold.

It is a stunning part of the world, with broad barren valleys and purple mountains dotted by floating clouds that can suddenly erupt in convulsive showers. Historians say that the very barrenness of the land and its prohibitiveness are what prodded the Incas   10
into their astonishing accomplishments. They had to use every piece of land, to terrace and burrow and organize and work together, to be able to live there.

1. The author mentions several possible effects of living on the Altiplano. Which ones can be tested scientifically to determine whether or not there is a genuine cause-and-effect relationship and which can only be a matter of opinion? Why?

2. What difference in wording is there in presenting the provable effects and the ones that are opinion?

13-B   Death of an Island

Pat Conroy

These paragraphs are from *The Water Is Wide,* an autobiographical account of the author's year on a small island off the coast of South Carolina. Unit 4-F is also about the island.

ANALYSIS
Effect
 [Yamacraw] is not a large island, nor an important one, but it represents an era and a segment of history that is rapidly dying in America. The people of the island have changed very little since the Emancipation Proclamation. Indeed, many of them have never heard of this ⁵ proclamation. They love their island with genuine affec-

Cause
tion but have watched the young people move to the city, to the lands far away and far removed from Yamacraw. The island is dying, and the people know it.

Background
 In the parable of Yamacraw there was a time when the ¹⁰ black people supported themselves well, worked hard, and lived up to the sacred tenets laid down in the Protestant ethic. Each morning the strong young men would take to their bateaux and search the shores and inlets for the large clusters of oysters, which the women and old ¹⁵ men in the factory shucked into large jars. Yamacraw oysters were world famous. An island legend claims that a czar of Russia once ordered Yamacraw oysters for an imperial banquet. The white people propagate this rumor. The blacks, for the most part, would not know a ²⁰ czar from a fiddler crab, but the oysters were good, and the oyster factories operating on the island provided a substantial living for all the people. Everyone worked and everyone made money.

Cause
 Then a villain appeared. It was an industrial factory ²⁵ situated on a knoll above the Savannah River many miles away from Yamacraw. The villain spewed its excrement

Effect
into the river, infected the creeks, and as silently as the pull of the tides, the filth crept to the shores of Yamacraw. As every good health inspector knows, the unfortu- ³⁰

Effect
nate consumer who lets an infected oyster slide down his throat is flirting with hepatitis. Someone took samples of

the water around Yamacraw, analyzed them under a microscope, and reported the results to the proper officials. Soon after this, little white signs were placed by the oyster banks forbidding anyone to gather the oysters. **Effect** Ten thousand oysters were now as worthless as grains of sand. No czar would order Yamacraw oysters again. The muddy creatures that had provided the people of the **Effect** island with a way to keep their families alive were placed under permanent quarantine.

Cause Since a factory is soulless and faceless, it could not be moved to understand the destruction its coming had wrought. When the oysters became contaminated, the **Effect** island's only industry folded almost immediately. The great migration began. A steady flow of people faced **Effect** with starvation moved toward the cities. They left in search of jobs. Few cities had any intemperate demand for professional oyster-shuckers, but the people were somehow assimilated. The population of the island diminished considerably. Houses surrendered their ten- **Effect** ants to the city and signs of sudden departure were rife in the interiors of deserted homes. Over 300 people left the island. They left reluctantly, but left permanently and returned only on sporadic visits to pay homage to the relatives too old or too stubborn to leave. As the oysters died, so did the people.

35

40

45

50

55

1. Here the relationship of cause and effect is plainly visible. Where does it start?

2. List the sequence of effects that follow the initial cause of trouble.

3. What words suggest that the writer feels certain that his analysis of the cause-and-effect relationship is correct?

4. Check the etymology, denotation, and connotation of *tenets, intemperate, assimilated, sporadic* (*bateaux,* the French for *boats,* is borrowed from the French settlers of Louisiana).

13-C   Vietnam Memories: The War
Within

Amy Drew Teitler *(student)*

The writer, a student in an advanced composition course, relies mainly on
narrative to present her memory of an important experience. She trusts her readers
to perceive the dramatic importance of her ending without additional comments from
her.

Bombs seemed to explode inches away from my unprotected
skull, while grenades soared like bats all around me, draining the
blood from all who stood in their way. Tanks roared in, grinding
the soft, moist jungle earth. The Vietnam War was always at its
most exciting in Theater No. 3 of the Mid-Plaza Sixplex.   5

Such was my knowledge of Vietnam, cultivated by "Apocalypse Now," right on up to "Full Metal Jacket."

Back in my senior year of high school, an English term-paper
assignment coincided with the release of the film "Platoon."
Inspired by the movie, I decided to do my paper on some aspect   10
of Vietnam. After attempting to write about the history of the
war, using several incredibly boring, encyclopedia-type texts, my
interest in the war began to wane. It was then that I remembered
my cousin Michael.

Michael was someone I had not seen since I was in eighth   15
grade. I remembered him, from one of our boring family functions, as one of the few tall men of my family. He had brave hazel
eyes that seemed just a little sad. He kept mostly to himself,
though he used to take me for walks on Brighton Beach and
sometimes on the rides at Coney Island while our relatives sat   20
around folding poker tables and eating.

When I remembered that Mike had been in Vietnam, I told my
mother that I wanted to talk to him about it. I wanted to pay him
a visit. I asked her where he lived, but oddly enough, she
wouldn't tell me.   25

"He won't appreciate you prying into his personal business,"
she told me. "It's something that I'm sure he won't want to talk
about."

My curiosity grew upon hearing my mother's insistence that I
abandon the topic. I went back to the library with new fervor. I   30

chose books that had been written by the veterans themselves, painful, brutal, hostile interpretations of the war from those who had fought there.

I was shocked, not only by the stories of combat, but by the details of the second war that these men fought: the homecoming. 35 After draining their strength in physical battle, they returned to their homes to fight a psychological one.

The men were attacked, not with shells and grenades, but with silence, shame and bitterness. Heroes wore their medals of honor and bravery much in the same way that Hester Prynne wore her 40 scarlet A. They were ignored. I was horrified by my country and its neglect of these courageous men. And I wanted to know why the vets had not spoken about the war. I had to talk to Mike.

I found out that he worked in Manhattan on the weekends, so I took the train into the city and set about finding my cousin. The 45 directions took me to a dilapidated taxi garage on the West Side. I couldn't believe that this was correct. Mike was a taxi driver?

I recognized Mike at once, but he was not the same man I remembered so vividly. The man with whom I had once walked on the beach had changed. 50

I knew that he was about 40, but his eyes looked older. His handsome brow bent sadly over them, and I realized sadly that the word that entered my mind was "broken."

He looked as if the years had eroded his honor, like a mustang that man had forced to submit to the confinement of a saddle. Sad 55 as they were, his eyes lit up with recognition and elation. We greeted each other with warm hugs and kisses, and he asked his boss if he could take the day off. His boss agreed, so we hopped on the train for Coney Island.

Upon arriving in Brooklyn, we walked the boardwalk for a 60 couple of miles, retracing the steps we took years earlier.

We ate lunch at Nathan's, made fun of our relatives, and eventually ended up on the sand, sitting by the rocks as we always had. The conversation finally took the turn I had been waiting for. He mentioned an old friend from the war, and I took my chance. 65

"Mike, what was Vietnam like?" I asked carefully and confidently. His eyes seemed to grow younger as the stories poured out of him, gruesome, horrific, amusing, tear-jerking.

He talked for what seemed like minutes, though I know it was hours. I laughed until I had to wipe my eyes and held him as he 70 cried out all the horrors he had held in for so long. Sometimes I cried along with him.

I sat and wondered what it must be like to share your life with people, care for them, and have them gone before you could say

goodbye; what it must be like to be sent someplace you never   75
heard of and fight in a war that you didn't comprehend; what it
must be like to have your dreams of college and a career shattered
by a draft that you could not refuse.

I sat and marveled at how my cousin Michael could have lived
through all of this and still want to continue, and my heart swelled   80
with admiration. The term paper was not even in my thoughts.

When the sun began to set, we got up and headed back toward
the platform. My train arrived first, and as we said goodbye I
asked one final question: "Mike, how come you never talked
about all of this before?"   85

He sighed and smiled a tired, relieved but mostly grateful
smile.

"Nobody ever asked," he replied.

1. What narrative devices does the writer use to make her account vivid?

2. Who was Hester Prynne and what did the "A" represent? How is this
reference relevant to the writer's point? (If you do not recognize the name, check
Nathaniel Hawthorne's novel, *The Scarlet Letter,* a classic of nineteenth-century American literature.)

13-D   The Decisive Arrest

Martin Luther King, Jr.

In these paragraphs from his book, *Stride Toward Freedom* (1958), Dr. King
shows a real cause that has been obscured by more obvious but false ones. Note that
here he tries to explain only why Mrs. Parks broke the law; she was not the *cause* of
the great bus strike but rather, as King wrote later, a "precipitating factor." The
immediate effect was her arrest, but this in turn touched off a series of larger effects
that are still operating. Another example of Dr. King's writing is on pages 487–490.

On December 1, 1955, an attractive Negro seamstress, Mrs.
Rosa Parks, boarded the Cleveland Avenue Bus in downtown
Montgomery. She was returning home after her regular day's
work in the Montgomery Fair—a leading department store. Tired
from long hours on her feet, Mrs. Parks sat down in the first seat   5
behind the section reserved for whites. Not long after she took
her seat, the bus operator ordered her, along with three other
Negro passengers, to move back in order to accommodate board-

ing white passengers. By this time every seat in the bus was taken. This meant that if Mrs. Parks followed the driver's command she   10
would have to stand while a white male passenger, who had just boarded the bus, would sit. The other three Negro passengers immediately complied with the driver's request. But Mrs. Parks quietly refused. The result was her arrest.

There was to be much speculation about why Mrs. Parks did   15
not obey the driver. Many people in the white community argued that she had been "planted" by the NAACP in order to lay the groundwork for a test case, and at first glance that explanation seemed plausible, since she was a former secretary of the local branch of the NAACP. So persistent and persuasive was this   20
argument that it convinced many reporters from all over the country. Later on, when I was having press conferences three times a week—in order to accommodate the reporters and journalists who came to Montgomery from all over the world—the invariable first question was: "Did the NAACP start the bus   25
boycott?"

But the accusation was totally unwarranted, as the testimony of both Mrs. Parks and the officials of the NAACP revealed. Actually, no one can understand the action of Mrs. Parks unless he realizes that eventually the cup of endurance runs over, and the   30
human personality cries out, "I can take it no longer." Mrs. Parks's refusal to move back was her intrepid affirmation that she had had enough. It was an individual expression of a timeless longing for human dignity and freedom. She was not "planted" there by the NAACP, or any other organization; she was planted   35
there by her personal sense of dignity and self-respect. She was anchored to that seat by the accumulated indignities of days gone by and the boundless aspirations of generations yet unborn. She was a victim of both the forces of history and the forces of destiny. She had been tracked down by the *Zeitgeist*—the spirit of the time.   40

1. What words show that Dr. King feels certain that his analysis of the cause-and-effect relationship is correct?

2. Check the origin of the word *boycott.*

3. How does the connotation of *plausible* differ from that of its synonym *credible?* How do the etymologies of *intrepid* and *aspiration* help us to understand their meanings?

13-E   Dix Hills: The Grown-Ups'
                                    Toy

Donna Satriale *(student)*

Note the writer's attention to both immediate and long-term effects.

My first glimpse of Dix Hills was from the back seat of my
mother's '62 Falcon as we drove from one model home to another. Dead, brown leaves dangled from the twisted branches of
scrawny trees. The ground was a smear of coagulated mud, rip-
pled in places and strewn with rivulets. It sucked my sneakers   5
from my feet as I walked past the naked skeletons of houses until
we came to the one which Dad said was ours. We went there
often, as if we were visiting a sick relative in the hospital.

We were one of the first families to move in. My sister and I
thrived among the pounding hammers and roaring bulldozers.   10
The unfinished houses invited us to romp in them. Every empty
lot was our playground. We were French explorers discovering
exotic lands, archaeologists digging up the ruins of an ancient
Palestinian city, medieval knights conquering a fortress, and mes-
sengers struggling through the Egyptian desert. Dix Hills was a   15
land of make-believe where a child's creative imagination could
expand.

A shabby cornfield marked the end of our pebbly street. Care-
free, we sprinted between the bristly stalks, playing tag and hide-
and-seek as if the field were ours and it was the only place on   20
earth. We lost shoes, toys, and hair ribbons there. Sometimes we
lost ourselves, dozing between the mounds with the silver sunlight filtering through the corn.

As time went on we found that we had to go farther and farther
away to play in the empty housing lots. More families were con-   25
stantly moving in. Shiny, civilized moving vans replaced the fero-
cious bulldozers, velvety sod carpeted our digging sites, and cars
interrupted our kickball and hop-scotch games. The cornfield was
plowed under, and more houses were built.

Across the street was a dense patch of woods, and we began to   30
play there. Mighty forts were built, traps set, and holes dug. We
climbed trees and swung on vines, scratching our arms and legs.
Afterwards, we were afraid to go home because we were coated
with dirt and were often the victims of "creeping crud" or poison

ivy. But they knocked down our forts, our trees, and our woods   35
to expand the parking lot for the public library.

Because the library was so close, we did a lot of reading. We
read about faraway places where children played in untouched
cornfields and open woods—children who were not trapped in
suburbia.   40

It wasn't long until everything was frosted with an upper-middle-class snobbery. Dix Hills was suddenly ripped from the hands
of the children and given to the grown-ups. There was nothing
left for the children to do except to play the adults' games. Cliques
and clubs formed even among the children. It was no longer "My   45
Pop can lick your Pop," but "My father makes $45,000 a year,
what does your father make?"

Today, there are no children playing kickball in the street.
They are in air-conditioned houses watching "Sesame Street" or
swimming in private, fenced-in pools. The neighbors rarely com-   50
municate, and when they do the falseness of their artificial smiles
shines from their gleaming capped teeth. It is a quiet community,
and the people like it that way. For me, it is too quiet. It is sterile.

1. Compare this presentation of changes in a place with the presentation of
changes in Example B in this unit.

2. Could this writer have made more extensive use of the alternating pattern
of comparison to emphasize the cause-and-effect theme underlying her material?

13-F   Passing on the Legacy of
                          Nature

Linda Claus *(student)*

In her discussion of our civilization's destructive effect on the environment, the
author indicates her father's constructive effect on her and, through her, on her
children. Note the many specific examples with which she illustrates and supports her
opinions and the brief narrative that forms the ending.

One of my father's most nourishing gifts was an appreciation
and deep love of nature. There are few things that fill me with
joy more than the discovery of a fawn pausing to drink from an
icy brook, or the sight of a porpoise swimming off the shore of
a deserted beach. The vibrant cacophony of color that explodes   5

on a hillside as autumn takes possession brings with it an ecstasy that enriches my life and leaves me searching for ever more fulfillment.

When I was a child, Sunday, the day I looked forward to, gave me an opportunity to snuggle up to my father on the couch for an evening of television. Although "Victory at Sea" did not capture my attention, "Mutual of Omaha's Wild Kingdom" always kept me enthralled. My father would comment on the beauty of the landscape, even as a lion crouched for the kill.

Dad also kept a copy of National Geographic around the house and pointed out how nature enhanced our lives. He could identify birds by their calls and often held whistling conversations with them before he left for work. I can also remember times, after winning the battle for the window in the back seat of the car, when my view of the landscape would be disturbed by roadside litter. The importance of preserving the beauty around us began to take form at that early age.

As my intelligence grew, so did my knowledge of the scope of the problem. Litter was not the only material marring our precious heritage. There was the problem of air pollution caused by factories that burned fossil fuel inefficiently. Larger and faster automobiles produced rising amounts of carbon dioxide. Acid rain was found to cause large fish kills up north and was being blamed for the destruction of woodland.

I also became aware that my life-long hometown of Plainview-Old Bethpage was renowned for having one of the most hazardous landfills in the country. I felt hatred for the men who dumped these poisonous substances as well as for the people who were in a position to stop the abuse but who chose instead to accept bribes to turn the other way. I was overwhelmed by a sense of futility because of the magnitude of the situation. My inner feelings of rage could have no impact on the problem, however, and although I had fantasies of capturing someone in the act of illegal dumping I did not see what I could do single-handedly to assuage the destruction.

In the summer of 1987 I read a book that helped crystallize my conviction. Rachel Carson's "Silent Spring" was published in 1962, but her insight into our current ecological problems was astounding. As the title suggests, if we fail in our efforts to stop the widespread annihilation of our natural resources through toxic chemicals, we may find ourselves approaching a day when there will be an absence of nature altogether.

Besides the damage accomplished through industry's lack of concern and unwillingness to sacrifice profits, and government's infatuation with the destruction of life rather than improving the quality of it, each one of us contributes to the devastation of our planet. Miss Carson examines the effect of insecticides and herbicides on our scarce water supply, as well as on the food chain, from the smallest insect up to man.

The toxic chemicals that have been introduced into our environment are cumulative in our bodies, and their deleterious effects have yet to be determined. The poisons we apply to our lawns and shrubberies will eventually wind up on our dinner table and in our breast milk. And as I read this enlightening book written almost 30 years ago, the New Jersey shore was experiencing an onslaught of dead porpoises washing up on shore, due to some "mysterious" illness.

The legacy I hand down to my children is very different from the one I received from my father many years ago. I teach them never to accept nature the way it is, but to work hard to bring it back to its full potential. It frightens me to realize that they are growing up in an era in which toxic dumps, beach closings and smog alerts are taken for granted.

It is important for them to realize that this is not the way it is supposed to be. I stress the importance of knowledge in an area in which deceptions abound, and the price we pay is our precious wildlife. An informed citizen does not place complete trust in an Environmental Protection Agency that allows destructive practices to continue. I teach them never to accept our current circumstances with apathy.

Like my father before me, I have planted the seeds of conservation deep within my children. Our family camping trips provide many fertile opportunities to nourish the love and devotion that are needed to protect the future of our environment so that we may hand it on to future generations.

As we packed our camping equipment to head home after our last vacation, I noticed my 14-year-old daughter, Katie, walking around the campsite picking up paper and debris with unaccustomed cheerfulness. I called her over to thank her and asked why she was performing this task voluntarily. She explained that when she sets up her tent, she cleans the area so she is not sleeping on trash. She realized that when we camp in the woods, we are living with the animals. She is sure that they would not want to sleep on garbage either.

1. To support and illustrate her thesis, the writer uses several brief narratives; where are they and what is the main point of each?

2. Check the etymology, denotation, and connotation of *cacophony, enthralled, enhanced, assuage, crystallize, herbicides, deleterious.*

13-G   Bring Back the Out-Loud
                      Culture

Donald Hall

This essay, here complete, is by a noted poet, short-story writer, and essayist.

As a boy in the 1940s, I stood in the tie-up watching my New Hampshire grandfather milk eight Holsteins while he recited poems for my entertainment. His hands stripped milk to the poem's beat. He threw back his head, rolled his eyes in high drama and pounded out: "But there is no joy in Mudville— 5 mighty Casey has struck out."

Often—for he was a cheerful man—he followed with the ballad set years later when a local team, far behind late in the game, lost a player to injury and called for help from the stands. Of course the portly, gray-headed volunteer hit a home run with two out in 10 the ninth to win the game. Begged to reveal his identity, the old fellow sobbed forth—and my grandfather in his blue cap and worn overalls sobbed also—"I'm mighty *Casey* who struck out just twenty years ago!"

My grandfather's memorized anthology was not the greatest 15 poetry. Its vigorous rhythms featured models of perseverance and satires of vanity and hypocrisy. In his youth he had learned these verses to speak as pieces, in a rural culture that entertained and edified itself by communal showing-off.

His gigs took place in Danbury, N.H. In his old house, where 20 I live, I recently found records of the South Danbury Oratorical and Debating Society, which met biweekly in the 1890s for programs that included piano solos, recitations and debates on foreign policy—"Shall the United States undertake further territorial expansion?" Danbury was not unusual then, for public read- 25 ings and performances lived at the center of American culture— city, town and countryside. Every school scheduled Prize Speaking Day, with its impassioned recitations of Whittier, Longfellow, Lincoln, and William Jennings Bryan.

Before the late 1920s and 1930s, American culture was *out* 30 *loud.* We continually turned print into sound. Mother read or recited to infant. (Memorization allowed entertainment even while both hands made bread.) Grandfather read from Prophet

and Gospel; his grandson performed chapters from Scott and
Dickens. At school we recited in chorus multiplication tables,   35
state capitals and Latin declensions. We studied spelling, Shakespeare and history by committing them to memory.

Technology replaces memory. We invented the alphabet so
that we needed no longer to commit Homer to memory; Gutenberg took us another mile. With radio we stopped singing for   40
each other; Bing Crosby took over. We listened no more to comic
recitations about "Darius Green and His Flying Machine." Jack
Benny and Fred Allen told new jokes every week.

When we put away childish things we tend to despise what we
leave behind. Among educators it has been progressive or for-   45
ward-looking to deplore learning by rote and to oppose it to
thinking. Maybe this is true for mathematics. But when we
stopped memorizing and reciting literature, our ability to read
started its famous decline. It was the loss of recitation—not its
replacements (radio, film, television)—that diminished our liter-   50
acy.

My grandfather who recited poems spent only a few years in
school, but he was a better reader than most college graduates I
meet today. Good readers hear what they read even though they
read in silence: speed reading is barbaric. When we read well, in   55
silence, we imagine how the words would sound if they were said
aloud. Hearing print words in the inward ear, we understand
their tone. If we see the sentence "Mr. Armstrong shook his
head," the inner voice needs to understand whether Mr. Armstrong disapproved or was outraged—before the inner voice   60
knows how to speak the words.

If when we read silently we do not hear a text, we slide past
words passively, without making decisions, without knowing or
caring about Mr. Armstrong's mood. We might as well be watching haircuts or "Conan the Barbarian." In the old Out-Loud   65
Culture, print was always potential speech; even silent readers,
too shy to read aloud, inwardly heard the sound of words. Their
culture identified print and voice. Everyone's ability to read was
enhanced by recitation. Then we read aggressively; then we demanded sense.   70

We have become a nation of passive readers, and passive reading makes for diminished literacy. To solve our problem, it will
not do to blame TV. Blaming serves no purpose except self-
praise, and television for that matter can encourage active reading, itself lending a voice to texts, as "Reading Rainbow," a   75
children's literature program, has done on PBS. Television can do
much more—if we want it to.

Fathers and mothers, teachers, Boy Scout leaders, babysitters, librarians, uncles and aunts, *we must read aloud to children.* But first we must learn again to perform the text, out-ham our ancestors,   80 take pleasure in word and story and hand this pleasure on. We must encourage our children to memorize and recite. As children speak poems and stories aloud, by the pitch and muscle of their voices they will discover drama, humor, passion and intelligence in print. In order to become a nation of readers, we need again   85 to become a nation of reciters.

1. The writer begins by narrating an anecdote that illustrates his thesis, but he does not make a specific statement of the thesis until the concluding paragraph. At what point in the essay did you begin to guess what the thesis would be?

2. Check the etymology, denotation, and connotation of *perseverance, hypocrisy, edified, communal, gigs.*

13-H   Is Anyone Listening?

Isaac Asimov

In the past forty years Asimov has published over 300 books. He is the best-known science fiction writer of this century and one of the most respected. This essay, here complete, first appeared in 1988 in the magazine *Fantasy and Science Fiction.* His warning of imminent disaster has been made by many others, but he gives it special force by supporting his predictions with specific facts and figures.

Everyone who has reached my level of late youth and has spent his time watching people and listening to them is bound to have become cynical. I, too, have become cynical. I have difficulty accepting things according to appearances and have trouble believing promises and assurances.   5

One justification for cynicism is that people don't listen, even when warnings are explicit, and even when the outlook is threatening.

I devoted at least two essays in *Fantasy & Science Fiction* magazine to warning of Earth's growing population. In May 1969,   10 there was "The Power of Progression." At that time, Earth's population was 3.5 billion as compared with about 2 billion at the time of my birth nearly half a century earlier. In that half-century, it had increased 75 percent.

In the May 1980 issue of *Fantasy & Science Fiction* I published   15
"More Crowded!" At that time, Earth's population was 4.2 billion, so that in 11 years the number of human beings had increased by 700 million, which is nearly the present population of
India. In 11 years, in other words, we had added another India
to the world, from the standpoint of numbers.   20

In "More Crowded!" I made the statement: "It is quite likely
that we will end the 1980s with a world population edging toward
5 billion."

As usual, I was conservative. We are not edging toward the 5
billion mark, we have passed it. And we did it not by the end of   25
the 1980s, but some time late in 1986, or early in 1987.

In the seven years after "More Crowded!" then, the Earth
added 800 million people, 100 million more than it had added
in the previous 11 years. In the 18 years between 1969 and '87,
Earth's population grew by 1.5 billion people (as much as it had   30
gained in the previous 50 years), and that is equal to the population of *two* present-day Indias. What's more, since the birthrate
in poor and industrially undeveloped nations is far higher than in
long-industrialized ones, about 90 percent of the new mouths are
born in poor nations. We have therefore added two Indias not   35
only in terms of numbers, but in terms of poverty.

And this has taken place despite the fact that the rate of increase
has dropped from 2 percent a year in 1970 to 1.6 percent a year
now, thanks chiefly to stern measures taken in China to reduce the
birthrate.   40

Are we entitled to be relieved at the drop in birthrate? No, for
the increase in population more than compensates for that. An
increase of 2 percent a year in 1969, when the population was 3.5
billion, meant an increase of 70 million that year. An increase of
1.6 percent a year in 1987, when the population was 5 billion,   45
meant an increase of 80 million that year. So we're growing both
in total numbers and in numbers of increase.

Let's take a closer look. An increase of 80 million people in one
year means an additional Mexico in a year. That is equivalent to
220,000 new people every day, or one new Lima, Ohio, every   50
time you wake up in the morning. It is also equivalent to 150
additional people every minute or five more people every two
seconds. If we had a digital recording on which the Earth's population could be read off at each instant, the units figure would be
flipping up new digits at more than twice the rate that the seconds   55
figure would change on a digital watch.

Is anyone listening? Does anyone care?

In "The Power of Progression" I began with a world popula-

tion of 3.5 billion and a doubling rate of once every 47 years, and
worked out an equation that would give me the world population   60
at any time in the future, provided the doubling rate stayed
constant.

I showed that by 2554 A.D., the world population would be
20,000 billion, so that the average population density over the
entire surface of the earth, land, and sea would be equal to the   65
average density, today, of Manhattan at noon.

I then assumed that every star in the Universe had 10 habitable
planets and that we could transfer people from planet to planet
at will and instantaneously. By 6170 A.D. every planet in the
Universe would be filled to Manhattan density.   70

Since the birthrate has dropped since 1969, we can calculate
the doubling rate right now at once every 50 years. This gives us
a little more time. It won't be till 2585 A.D. that we achieve
Manhattan density over all of Earth's surface. But at that point,
another few years to do it in is not going to help one iota.   75

We *can't* continue multiplying at this rate for very long, no
matter what we do. It won't help us to advance technology by any
conceivable amount. For instance, it won't help us to go out into
space at any conceivable rate. After all, since we're going to have
80 million more people a year, when will we be able to put that   80
many people in space in one year so as to stabilize our population?
Do you want to be optimistic and say we can do that 50 years from
now? Well, by then we'll be gaining 160 million new mouths
every year, and the people in space will be multiplying, too.

Don't get me wrong. I'm not saying that we'll maintain this   85
increase indefinitely, because we won't. We won't for the most
insuperable reason in the world: We *can't*. The only question
about population that we can ask is how to *stop* the population
increase.

And the answer to that is that either a) the birthrate will con-   90
tinue to decrease, or b) the death rate will increase, or c) both.
There are no other alternatives. I've said that before and I'm now
saying it again.

Is anyone listening? Does anyone care?

The feeling on the part of demographers is that by the year   95
2000 the population will begin to level off and that by 2100 it will
stabilize, though by then it will have reached some 10 billion, or
twice what it is now.

Is that a big sigh of relief I hear?

Then think! What kind of a world will it be by the time popula-   100
tion stability is achieved?

The population of Earth is not going up evenly. I said earlier
that 90 percent of the population increase is in the under-

developed nations. Within those nations, the rural areas are
ground ever deeper into poverty as population multiplies. With   105
land less and less available, the peasants drift into cities in search
of jobs, so that the cities of these nations are growing at a cancer-
ous rate.

In "More Crowded!" I expressed my surprise that the second
largest city in the world was Mexico City. Between 1967 and '79   110
its population had gone from 3,193,000 to 8,628,074. In merely
12 years it had increased its population nearly three-fold, going
from the size of Chicago to more than the size of New York.

The latest figure I could find on its population is 13 million, and
that is probably low. I have heard larger figures. In any case, by   115
1988 it had become the world's most populous city.

Before World War II, London was the largest city with 8 million people, and New York City was second with 7 million. New
York has kept its population at that height (with its suburbs
growing rapidly, of course) and London has actually shrunk.   120

New York is now, according to the latest statistics I can find,
only the fourteenth largest city in the world and London is the
sixteenth. Here are the figures, which I imagine err on the low
side:

Mexico City, Mexico	13,000,000	125
São Paolo, Brazil	12,600,000	
Shanghai, China	12,000,000	
Cairo, Egypt	12,000,000	
Seoul, South Korea	9,600,000	
Beijing, China	9,300,000	130
Calcutta, India	9,200,000	
Rio de Janeiro, Brazil	9,000,000	
Tokyo, Japan	8,500,000	
Bombay, India	8,300,000	
Moscow, U.S.S.R.	8,000,000	135
Tianjin, China	7,900,000	
Jakarta, Indonesia	7,700,000	
New York, U.S.A.	7,200,000	
Guangzhou, China	6,800,000	
London, U.K.	6,700,000	140

Statistics vary among sources.

Of the 13 largest cities in the world, one is in Africa, three are
in Latin America, eight are in Asia. Only one is in Europe, and
that is Moscow.

None of this alters the fact that the richest very large city   145

remains New York, and this is significant. Size does not necessarily mean wealth. In fact, the very large cities in the non-industrial countries tend to contain square mile upon square mile of hovels, shacks, and shanties deprived of any of the amenities that an average dweller in a large city in an industrialized nation takes for   150
granted.

And this will only get worse. Fast though the world's population is growing as a whole, and still faster though the world's underdeveloped population is growing, the *fastest* growth rate is in the cities of the underdeveloped nations. By 2000, even   155
though the population will begin to move into its stabilizing period, the cities of the underdeveloped nations may still be expanding and may collapse into rotting nightmares.

Consider, too, that the terrible need for agricultural land forced by the population increase, together with the need for   160
firewood (which is the most important fuel in many underdeveloped areas), is already resulting in the slaughter of the forests, particularly the rain forests, which are being hacked down at a fearful rate. Almost 15 million acres are being cleared each year, and, by the year 2000, half Earth's present forests may be   165
gone.

Remember that forests aren't just pretty trees taking up land that might better be used by human beings. Forests have root systems that conserve the soil and prevent the violent runoff of excess water. The trees give off water into the air, instead, cooling   170
and moistening it. Forests also produce oxygen at a rate higher than will any form of vegetation replacing them.

The soil in which rain forests grow is not very good and will be soon leached of nutrients by crops planted in them, while rain runoff will gully and destroy the soil altogether. Far from supply-   175
ing us with agricultural land, the vanishing rain forests will yield to deserts.

The deserts are indeed expanding as a result of forest destruction, overfarming, and general human mishandling, and, by the year 2000, the area of new desert will be perhaps 1½ times the   180
area of the United States. And the fact that there will be less and less good land to cultivate will send more and more people into the overcrowded, festering, fetid cities.

The forests, too, are the habitat of myriad species of plants and animals, a couple million of which (mostly insects, to be sure)   185
have not yet even been classified. Destroying the forests destroys habitats, and about a fifth of the animal and plant species now living will be extinct by the year 2000.

This is not something to be dismissed lightly. Such extinctions will upset the ecological balance and wreak havoc far beyond the   190

extinctions themselves. There is also the question of what com-
pounds of important medicinal and industrial value might exist in
the plants and animals we have not yet investigated, and which
will vanish forever together with whatever good they might have
done us.   195

Then, too, the more people there are, the greater the rate
at which we must consume the Earth's finite resources. Worse
yet is the fact that the more people there are, the greater the
rate at which we must produce waste products, many of them
toxic.

Usable fresh water supplies will decrease, since larger and
larger portions of them will be polluted to the point where they
will be undrinkable without costly treatment that many regions
will not be able to afford. Nor will life be able to thrive in   200
polluted water. Acid rain will grow worse and kill more lakes and
more fish.

Even the ocean rim, the richest portion of the sea, is being
increasingly polluted (and remember that microscopic forms of
plant life in the uppermost layers of the ocean produce 80 percent   205
of the oxygen that we cannot do without).

The atmosphere, too, is being increasingly polluted, and cities
are becoming more and more smog-bound.

Even carbon dioxide, which is itself a rather benign and relatively non-toxic substance, is a deadly danger. The fuels we burn   210
for energy at an ever-increasing rate are producing carbon dioxide at a rate greater than Earth's vegetation can utilize it and the
ocean dissolve it. The result is that the percentage of carbon
dioxide in the air (quite likely only .035 percent) is slowly but
steadily increasing from year to year.   215

By 2000 A.D., the carbon dioxide content of the air may have
increased by one third beyond today's content. This won't interfere with our breathing noticeably, but it will conserve more of
the heat Earth receives from the sun so that Earth's average temperature will go up somewhat. This will change the weather   220
pattern, probably for the worse, and increase the rate at which the
polar ice-caps melt, raising the sea-level noticeably and causing
coastal areas to suffer more from high tides and storms—in short,
the greenhouse effect.

Other forms of pollution are just as slowly and just as surely   225
destroying the ozone layer in Earth's upper atmosphere. This will
increase the intensity of ultraviolet light from the sun at Earth's
surface. The warning here is that skin cancers will increase, and
so they will, but there may be worse. We don't know what the
additional ultraviolet will do to the microscopic forms of life   230
living in the soil and in the uppermost layers of the ocean. If these

are badly damaged, the very viability of Earth as a planet may be decreased markedly.

To be sure, Earth's resources may be made more efficient use of and wastes may be more rationally disposed of, if we make the   235
social and technological effort, but there is a limit to what can be done if we continue to pour tens of millions of new human beings onto Earth's surface each year.

And as the population increases, as people crowd together more closely, as people find they can only get a smaller and   240
smaller part of a pie that does not increase as the numbers do (but decreases in many ways), there will be increasing alienation, increasing refuge in drugs, increasing crime, increasing chance of war. In short, the world will become ever more violent.

Every one of these changes, which comes about more or less   245
directly because of the ever-increasing population, will serve to raise the death rate. There will be increasing starvation, and bodies weakened by undernourishment will be more prone to disease. There will be more deaths by violence. In short, the Four Horsemen of the Apocalypse (Famine, Pestilence, War, and   250
Death) will ride the Earth.

This might seem a natural way to make overpopulation self-limiting. It will seem an automatic cure—but what a horrible cure it will be. Surely, the alternative of a deliberate effort to lower the birthrate is far preferable.   255

But is anyone listening? Does anyone care?

1. Where does the writer give specific numbers to support his claims and what may be his reasons for doing so at those points in his discussion?

2. Where does he use these stylistic devices to catch the reader's attention: questions, short sentences, exclamations?

3. Where does he compare the unfamiliar with the familiar to help us to understand the population problem?

4. Check the etymology, denotation, and connotation of *leach, habitat, myriad, festering, fetid, ecological, viability, Apocalypse.*

ASSIGNMENTS

With all these assignments, be sure to look beyond the first causes that come to mind. Find the causes behind them and then the causes behind those, and so on.

1. What made you decide to become a college student and why did you choose the college you now attend? Be sure to go beyond easy explanations, such as that an education will prepare you for a career and that the college has a good reputation.

2. Everyone has prejudices—strong feelings on some subject, for or against, which exist without much thought or reason (see Example G in this unit). If you have noticed a prejudice held by one of your friends, ask what your friend believes to be its cause; then examine the answer and decide whether it is reasonable or whether your friend has been guilty of rationalization. Try the same experiment with a prejudice of your own (areas of taste, religion, politics, and race are good hunting grounds).

3. Choose some incident in your own life that at first seems to have been pure "accident," and search for causes. Consider all possibilities, rejecting those that do not bear up under scrutiny and explaining why you believe others to be the true ones. Determine what you believe to be the cause or causes of one of your present strong interests or hobbies. Then test the validity of your conclusions by checking them against the list of warnings on pages 265–266.

4. Examine some local phenomenon—a campus tradition, a dating custom, a strong interest in some kind of activity (from sports to studies), the presence or absence of the honor system—and try to determine the cause or causes behind it.

5. Write an essay with a title such as "I Changed My Mind" or "I Used to Think So" in which you organize your material into three sections: your original attitude toward something (a sport, activity, profession, person); the cause of your change of mind; your present attitude. Devote most of your attention to the cause of the change and its effects.

6. Choosing as your subject some situation, policy, or plan on your campus, write an essay predicting what the outcome will be. For example, what effects can logically be expected to follow an increase in tuition or enrollment? A change in entrance or degree requirements? the relaxation or tightening of rules regarding class attendance, drinking, visiting hours in dormitories?

UNIT 14

Definition

"By *my* definition, he's too drunk to drive." "Why isn't child psychology considered one of the humanities?" "You may call their behavior rude, but I think they're just silly." "What's a metaphor?" "How dare you call me 'crazy'!"

To explain anything or to get credit for knowing something, we usually must define it. It can be surprisingly difficult, however, to make accurate, generally acceptable definitions in our own words, especially if what we are trying to define is thoroughly familiar to us.

A **formal definition** is based on a concise, logical pattern that lets the writer give a maximum of information in a minimum of space. It has three parts: the **term** (word or phrase) to be defined; the **class** of object or concept to which the term belongs; and the **differentiating characteristics** that distinguish what the term defines from all others of that class.

term		class	differentiating characteristics
Water	is	a liquid	made up of molecules of hydrogen and oxygen in the ratio of 2 to 1.
An owl	is	a bird	with large head, strong talons, and nocturnal habits.

Practice in writing such formal definitions is a good mental discipline and an excellent training in conciseness and care in the use of words. Follow these guidelines:

1. **Keep your class small but adequate.** It should be large enough to include everything covered by the term you are defining but no larger. To define the term *lieutenant,* the class *soldier* is too small, because there are lieutenants in the Navy and police as well as in the Army and Marines. On the other hand, the class *officer* is too large because it includes the noncommissioned and commissioned. *Commissioned officer* is a happy compromise.

2. **Do not define a word by mere repetition.** "A baked potato is a potato that has been baked" adds nothing to what the term "baked potato" has already told us.

3. **State the differentiating characteristics precisely.** "A flute is a musical instrument played by blowing" is too general because it covers many musical instruments that are not flutes.

4. **Define a word in simpler and more familiar terms.** The purpose of definition is to clarify, not to confuse. In his eighteenth-century dictionary Samuel Johnson humorously defined "network" as "anything reticulated or decussated at equal distances with interstices between the intersections"—a well-known example of how *not* to define. Compare it with the definition of the same word in your own college dictionary.

5. **Do not define a word with *is* or *are when* or *is* or *are where*.** In "Vacations are when people don't work" and "A grocery is where food is sold," the "when" and "where" clauses modify the verbs "are" and "is" because they follow them, instead of modifying "vacations" and "grocery." In a definition *is, are, was,* and *were* function like equal marks; the word or group of words forming the definition should match the grammatical structure of the word or words it defines. "Vacations are times when people don't work" ("Vacations = times"); "A grocery is a store where food is sold"; "To run is to move quickly"; *"Lambent means softly bright."*

Exercise: In your own words, without help from a dictionary, write formal one-sentence definitions of the following familiar terms: (1) apple; (2) cow; (3) dictionary; (4) eye; (5) typewriter; (6) vinegar; (7)

microscope; (8) foul ball; (9) professor; (10) democracy. Then check the five "warnings" and make any necessary revisions and corrections before handing in your definitions.

∴   ∴   ∴

In the **essay of definition**, unlike the preceding brief definitions, you may write as much as necessary to make your definitions accurate, clear, and useful for your readers. Try to catch and hold your readers' interest. A formal one-sentence definition usually has as little interest for readers as a mathematical equation. The essay of definition, however, can be personal, amusing, vigorous, stimulating, memorable. In it you may use, singly or in combination, any of the expository methods we have examined.

Always remember, however, that your first duty is to define. It is not essential to include a formal definition, but your paper must be an expansion of the basic material that you would use to make such a definition, never an evasion of it. Without this fact in mind, you may find that you have written a charming informal essay on a given subject, but not defined it.

Choose a generic subject, not a specific one. We define a dog, for instance, rather than our Rover; a cathedral, rather than Notre Dame of Paris; supersonic aircraft, rather than the Concorde. (Note the kinds of topics suggested at the end of this unit.) But use specifics of all kinds to illustrate your subject and make it vivid for your readers. To develop your definition, you will find some or all of the following helpful:

1. **Descriptive details are often valuable.** For example, the bare definition of a dog as a "carnivorous domesticated mammal of the family Canidae" will be clearer with descriptive details as to size, build, color, use, and so on.

> The *masonquo* is a six-stringed lyre having a hollow leather-covered sound-chamber much like that of a banjo. It has a bridge and, since it lacks a neck or fingerboard, the strings are stretched to a framework of sticks. The keys are primitive but ingenious and effective. All six strings are struck simultaneously with a small piece of leather or a feather. (Harold Courlander, *Musical Quarterly.*)

2. **Examples and incidents** (narration) can make the definition of a general subject more specific. Protestantism might be clarified by reference to the Lutheran or other denomination. Or incidents may be used to make abstract terms concrete: the old story of Abe Lincoln's walking miles to return a few cents was popular because, by illustrating honesty in action, it made the idea of that virtue much more vivid than could any discussion of honesty in the abstract.

Drop a cricket ball from your hand and it falls to the ground. We say that the cause of its fall is the gravitational pull of the earth. In the same way, a cricket ball thrown into the air does not move on forever in the direction in which it is thrown; if it did, it would leave the earth for good and voyage off into space. It is saved from this fate by the earth's gravitational pull, which drags it gradually down, so that it falls back to earth. The faster we throw it, the farther it travels before this occurs; a similar ball projected from a gun would travel for many miles before being pulled back to earth. (Sir James Jeans, *The Universe Around Us.*)

3. **Comparisons** may define the unfamiliar by showing how it resembles the familiar or differs from it.

Like gliding, ballooning depends for movement on luck with thermals, which are air currents rising off sun-warmed fields and hills; unlike gliding, ballooning gives a pilot no control of direction—except up and down. *(The New Yorker.)*

A strange object may be described through likeness as having "the shape of a hen's egg" or "the color of a tomato."

To the wanderer from temperate zones, the papaya might be a dwarfed Tom Watson or an unripe cantaloupe. This interesting native of the torrid zone assumes a variety of shapes and sizes. It may be elongated like a watermelon, or almost spherical, or even slightly compressed on one end, like our crook-neck squash. Within, it is much like a muskmelon, with a multitude of seeds which cling tenaciously to a firm, thick, salmon-colored lining which is its edible part. (G. W. James, student, the *Green Caldron.*)

On the other hand, a thing may be described through difference as "larger than a tennis ball" or "not so sour as a lemon." The following example is from a definition of the word *tact.*

A great many would-be socialites entertain the illusion that politeness and tact are the same thing. That is why they are only would-be's. Politeness is a negative, and tact a positive, virtue. Politeness is merely avoiding trampling on another person's toes, while tact is placing a Persian carpet under his feet. (Margaret Van Horne, student, the *Green Caldron.*)

4. **Negative comparisons** may be helpful. Explaining what a thing is *not* can clear the ground for explaining what it *is.* This method is particularly useful in eliminating things that might otherwise be confused with the thing to be defined: "Botanically speaking, a tomato is not a vegetable." "A leprechaun is not to be confused with a ghost."

Research is a word that is often used narrowly, but I am using it not in any mean and cramped sense. It is not, for instance, restricted to the uncovering of specific new facts, or the development of new scientific processes, although it is partly this. It is not encompassed by learned papers in scholarly journals, although it is certainly this among other things. By research I mean, as well as all this, the publication of a biography, or a volume of poetry, or the delivery of a lecture that sets off a mental chain reaction among students. (Claude T. Bissell, *What the Colleges Are Doing.*)

5. **Classification** can extend the definition of a term that denotes a group by indicating the classes of which it is composed; a definition of service organizations might include the major kinds of clubs—Rotary, Kiwanis, and so on.

> I found the Negro community the victim of a threefold malady—factionalism among the leaders, indifference in the educated group, and passivity in the uneducated. All of these conditions had almost persuaded me that no lasting social reform could ever be achieved in Montgomery. (Martin Luther King, Jr., *Stride Toward Freedom.*)

6. **Analysis** is another logical means of expanding a basic definition. You may break down the object to be defined into the parts composing it: "A good composition has a beginning, a middle, and an end."

> A power mower, so popular with homeowners today, consists of a source of power, usually a small gasoline engine; a cutting blade, usually rotary, a transmission system by which the power is applied to the blade; and a frame to support the mechanism, a set of wheels to make it movable and a handle by which the operator can guide it.

7. **The origins and causes** are essential for definitions of some subjects. The meaning of a word like *radar* is implicit in its origin (it is composed of "ra" for *radio,* "d" for *detection,* "a" for *and,* and "r" for *ranging*); and a phenomenon like a geyser or a volcano can best be explained through its cause.

> The meter was originally intended to be one ten-millionth of the distance from the equator to the pole of the earth, measured on the surface. The measurements by means of which the first meter was prepared were inaccurate, however, and the real meter is the distance, measured at the freezing point of water, between two marks on a bar of platinum-iridium kept at the International Bureau of Weights and Measures at Sèvres, France. (W. A. Noyes, *Textbook of Chemistry.*)

8. **The results, effects, and uses** are also essential for some subjects. *Christianity* and *communism,* for example, should be explained in terms of their results as well as of their origins, and *war* and *depression* in terms of their effects. Definitions of mechanisms and processes (radar is again an example) are equally likely to involve a discussion of the uses to which they are put.

In adjusting to his new way of life the hunting ape developed a power-ful *pair-bond,* tying the male and female parents together during the breeding season. In this way, the females were sure of their males' support and were able to devote themselves to their maternal duties. The males were sure of their females' loyalty, were prepared to leave them for hunting, and avoided fighting over them. And the offspring were provided with the maximum of care and attention. (Desmond Morris, *The Naked Ape.*)

∴   ∴   ∴

For the **organization** of your essay of definition you have a wide choice of patterns. No one simple pattern or plan can be laid out for it. You may successfully combine any or all of the patterns mentioned in the list. Your plan will depend entirely on the demands of your subject, the needs of your readers, and your own preference as a writer. A definition of Americanism, for instance, might involve a detailed breakdown of the term into the quali-ties that you believe it covers; it might include examples of true Americanism in action, a comparison of real Americanism with false varieties or with other "isms," and a discussion of its origins and effects on a people and the world. How best to arrange and combine this ample and varied material would depend on your intended readers and your particular purpose.

EXAMPLES

In the following selections, the main purpose of each writer is to arrive at a definition, but you will find definitions are important in many other selections, most notably in Jackson's "Challenge" (3-E), the Encyclopedia Americana's *"The Hellbender" (4-D), Mencken's "Le Contrat Social" (6-B), McBee's "Gob-bledygook" (6-G), Berendt's "The Button" (11-E), Wylie's "The Structure of a Comet" (12-A), Peeples' 'Branch Libraries" (12-B), Shulman's "Love Is a Fallacy" (15-K), in all the examples of critical writing in Unit 17, and in Woolf's "The Patron and the Crocus" ("Essays for Further Reading"-C).*

These selections vary in subject matter from the tangible to the abstract, in style from expanded formal definitions to informal essays, and in length from a single paragraph to several pages. Determine for each, as has been done for Example A, what methods have been used in development.

14-A   Cyclones

Walter Sullivan

This report from the *New York Times* (November 1977), here complete, is by
a writer whose special field is science. It was published shortly after a cyclone caused
severe damage in Bangladesh and parts of India.

ANALYSIS
Introduction

Comparison

Historical
example

Historical
example

Causes and
effect in
example

in general

in example

Details

November is the month dreaded by coastal residents
in India and Bangladesh, for it is then that the most
devastating cyclones occur.

These storms are essentially the same in the way they
form and behave as the hurricanes of the western Atlantic   5
and western Mexico and the typhoons of the western
Pacific.

In the Indian Ocean they are known as cyclones, al-
thoguh they have no relationship to the "cyclone" that
transported Dorothy to the Land of Oz. That was a Mid-   10
dle-Western usage referring to a tornado—a localized,
funnel-shaped cloud.

Indian Ocean cyclones have caused some of the greatest disasters in history. In November 1970, such a storm
swept across the Ganges delta in what was then East   15
Pakistan, and is now Bangladesh. It drove the sea far
inland over the flat landscape, flooding countless villages.
The death toll may have reached a half million.

At the start of November 1971, a similar storm struck
the east coast of India and many more thousands died.   20
When a cyclone hit Darwin, on the north coast of Australia, in 1974 two-thirds of the city's homes were destroyed, but only 49 people were killed.

The explanation for the disparity in the death tolls
appears to be that because of flimsy construction, dense   25
population and flat landscape in the deltas of India and
Bangladesh, those living there are highly vulnerable. Air
pressure drops so radically during such storms that high
tides rise far above normal. The 1970 disaster occurred
at a time in the lunar cycle when tides would have been   30
very high in any case.

Torrential rains add further to the flooding and high
waves are driven inland by the violent winds.

Cause and
effect in
general

Such storms are typically born in the intertropical con-
vergence zone. This is the region where converging   35
trade winds of the Northern and Southern Hemispheres
meet and form an updraft. When that zone is far enough
north or south of the Equator for the earth's rotation to
impart circular motion to the converging winds a storm
may be born. The motion is counterclockwise when the   40
process occurs north of the equator and clockwise when
it occurs in the Southern Hemisphere.

Cause and
effect in
general

Small at first, the storm feeds on the hot, moist air that
it sucks in from surrounding areas. As the air rises inside
the storm, the moisture condenses into heavy rains. The   45
latent heat that evaporated that moisture in the first place
is released to drive the rotating winds even faster, and
more air is drawn in.

Effect

Thus the storm swells to cover an area several hundred
miles in diameter. Like an upside-down whirlpool, it ro-   50
tates about an open funnel in the center—the "eye"—in
which skies are clear and winds minimal. Once over land
the storm loses energy for lack of moist oceanic air and
fades away.

Details

The ideal time for Indian Ocean cyclones is Novem-   55
ber. In the Atlantic, the Caribbean Sea and Gulf of Mexico the hurricane season extends from June to October.

Cause and
effect

Modest efforts have been made to tame such storms by
seeding clouds in front of them, thus dumping their rain
before the clouds are drawn into the storm and feed it   60
energy. Until the effects of such action can be more
accurately predicted than at present, it is feared that,
following such treatment, a storm might change its path
and head for a populated center instead of remaining
harmlessly at sea.   65

1. To define cyclones in the region of Bangladesh and India for American
readers, what information must Sullivan give besides that directly describing the
cyclones themselves?

2. What use does he make of comparison, both literal and figurative?

3. Check the etymology, denotation, and connotation of *typhoons, tornado, disparity, latent, seeding.*

14-B   Parentage and Parenthood

Ashley Montagu

This paragraph is from *The American Way* (1967), an anthropological and sociological study. Note how Montagu defines the two terms by drawing distinctions between them.

It is apparently very necessary to distinguish between parenthood and parentage. Parenthood is an art; parentage is the consequence of a mere biological act. The biological ability to produce conception and to give birth to a child has nothing whatever to do with the ability to care for that child as it requires to be cared for.   5
That ability, like every other, must be learned. It is highly desirable that parentage be not undertaken until the art of parenthood has been learned. Is this a counsel of perfection? As things stand now, perhaps it is, but it need not always be so. Parentage is often irresponsible. Parenthood is responsible. Parentage at best is irre-   10
sponsibly responsible for the *birth* of a child. Parenthood is responsible for the development of a human being—not simply a child, but a human being. I do not think it is an overstatement to say that parenthood is the most important occupation in the world.

1. How are parentage and parenthood defined in an unabridged dictionary?

2. To what extent do the dictionary definitions show—or fail to show—the distinctions Montagu draws?

14-C   No Easy Job

Thomas Bean *(student)*

It has been just in the last year that I have been given the opportunity to experience the most difficult, time-consuming, and exhausting job I have ever had. It is a profession that has been taken lightly by many working men for a countless number of years. Some of us males even thought of this domestic profession as   5
an easy job, although not many of us volunteer to do it. Yes, I am

talking about the job of the Beaver's mother, of Harriet Nelson, and of Father Knows Best's better half, the job of homemaker.

In the past I thought the basic domestic functions of the woman at home were just cooking, laundry and cleaning. Little did I realize the amount of effort and organization these simple tasks involve. The one duty I am familiar with is cooking, from my experience as a restaurant manager, but it never dawned on me that doing the dishes went with the job until the night I ran out of dishes before dinner. That wasn't the only time I was blessed with sudden insight. I let the laundry ride about ten days, till mounds of dirty clothing engulfed our living space. My wife and children read me the riot act for two days, until I swore on my life to organize a laundry schedule and to dissect the dryer to see if it was really getting its nourishment from the numerous missing socks. The last and least pleasurable of the household chores is the cleaning. Keeping floors, carpet, windows, bathroom, and kids free of dirt and clutter is a never-ending task. Children are great, except that they leave trails of toys, dolls, dishes, books, clothes, rocks, frogs, mud, even an occasional playmate, everywhere they go. Is there no end to the homemaker's nightmare?

Oddly enough, getting outside is not an escape; the homemaker's job doesn't stop at the front door. I used to enjoy my time while driving the car—it was man against the elements, the challenge of defensive driving, and the reassuring hum of a fine-tuned engine. Then I became a full-time chauffeur for a carload of kids going to countless extra-curricular activities. Volunteering was not a good idea: it tripled the number of kids in my life for at least an hour a day, often for six days a week. Wow! Some escape! I now understand carpools very clearly; they were invented to give the poor houseperson some time in the week to rest.

Somewhere between the housework and chauffeuring the kids, come the one-on-one times with our own two children, eleven-year-old Jeremiah and eight-year-old Sarah. Time with them means that the happy homemaker has to be a scholar, psychologist, Cabbage Patch Kids' grandpa, and commander-in-chief of the GI Joes.

Although the first few months of the job were helter-skelter, they were also educational. Housewives have won my respect. I have learned that homemaking is a full-time job and several part-time jobs all rolled into one.

1. Which of the kinds of writing listed on pages 290–293 does the writer use to enliven his definition?

2. Where has the writer used humor and exaggeration to assist his definition?

14-D   Lagniappe

Mark Twain

These paragraphs are from Twain's *Life on the Mississippi* (1875). Note how the student writer of Example E makes use of Twain's definition.

We picked up one excellent word—a word worth traveling to New Orleans to get; a nice, limber, expressive, handy word—"Lagniappe." They pronounce it *lanny-yap.* It is Spanish—so they said. We discovered it at the head of a column of odds and ends in the *Picayune* the first day; heard twenty people use it the sec- 5 ond; inquired what it meant the third; adopted it and got facility in swinging it the fourth. It has a restricted meaning, but I think the people spread it out a little when they choose. It is the equiva- lent of the thirteenth roll in a "baker's dozen." It is something thrown in, gratis, for good measure. The custom originated in the 10 Spanish quarter of the city. When a child or a servant buys some- thing in a shop—or even the mayor or the governor, for aught I know—he finishes the operation by saying:

"Give me something for lagniappe."

The shopman always responds; gives the child a bit of licorice 15 root, gives the servant a cheap cigar or a spool of thread, gives the governor—I don't know what he gives the governor; support, likely.

When you are invited to drink—and this does occur now and then in New Orleans—and you say, "What, again?—no, I've had 20 enough," the other party says, "But just this one time more—this is for lagniappe." When the beau perceives that he is stacking his compliments a trifle too high, and sees by the young lady's coun- tenance that the edifice would have been better with the top compliment left off, he puts his "I beg pardon, no harm in- 25 tended," into the briefer form of "Oh, that's for lagniappe." If the waiter in the restaurant stumbles and spills a gill of coffee down the back of your neck, he says, "F'r lagniappe, sah," and gets you another cup without extra charge.

1. What words and phrases indicate Twain's humorous intention?

2. Classify the different kinds of situations in which Twain says *lagniappe* could be useful.

3. Which of the kinds of writing listed on pages 290–293 does Twain use here to enliven his definition?

14-E   "No Sweat"

John D. Myers *(student)*

"No sweat" is one of the most descriptive slang terms that I have ever encountered. I first heard the term used in Korea, where it appeared in almost every conversation among the American soldiers stationed there. It is admittedly a somewhat vulgar expression for formal use, but for saying much in a few words, it is hard to beat.   5

Strangely enough, "no sweat" does not refer to the amount of work involved in doing something, nor yet to the temperature. It refers to the absence of worry and apprehension involved in a certain action. Used properly, it carries a note of reassurance; it is a short way of saying, "Don't work yourself up over this matter, as it is all taken care of."   10

For example, let us suppose that a lovely young lady, in backing her car out of a parking lot, accidentally scrapes a young man's fender. The young man gallantly releases her from all responsibility by saying cheerfully, "No sweat," and the situation probably terminates in a date instead of a lawsuit.   15

But the expression means more than a release from obligation, as can be seen from the following example: a production engineer calls in his foreman and explains that he will need four thousand brake units by the end of the week. The foreman replies, "No sweat," and the production engineer knows he is safe in telling the company's sales representative to confirm delivery.   20

If "no sweat" had been current in New Orleans at the time Mark Twain wrote "Lagniappe," the restaurant scene in which the waiter spilled coffee down the customer's neck would have had a different outcome. Before the careless fellow had had time to make any kind of apology, the injured patron would have looked up with a smile and said, "No sweat," and the incident would have been closed.   25

                                                        30

Which of the kinds of writing listed on pages 290–293 does the writer use here to enliven his definition?

14-F   On Maturity

Carlos Moras *(student)*

This essay and the one following it were written for the same assignment—a definition of maturity. Moras draws on his readings in social psychology, his major, to give a traditional kind of definition.

Maturation involves two processes: internalizing the constraints society puts on us and shifting away from self-centeredness toward an awareness that we are not the only ones on the face of the earth.

When we're children we have to be told what to do. Our   5
parents, teachers, and other authority figures act as mediators between us and that complicated world where "right" and "wrong" don't exist as easily discernible extremes. In our world there are too many shades of "right" and "wrong." Our childish minds are incapable of making a choice from among so many   10
alternatives, and so we have rules. We spend a large part of our childhood obeying or disobeying these rules. As we grow older we begin to see the reasons behind some of them, and we start doubting the validity of others. At this point the internalizing process begins. Our adolescence is a period of rebellion against   15
constraints imposed by others. We want to rule ourselves. But soon many of us come to realize that rules are important in a society as complicated as ours. We then become our own arbitrators between "right" and "wrong," our own rule-makers and enforcers.   20

Maturity is also a shift away from self-centeredness toward a more realistic image of ourselves. A baby's actions are all directed toward itself. The self-centered infant can't be blamed for its selfish attitude, because its world doesn't extend beyond itself. As the baby grows older, its world's boundaries extend, and it then   25
notes that others exist as well. First the baby notes that it has a mother on whom it depends for food. The selfish baby exploits this relationship. It cries until it is fed. It also cries until it receives attention. Quite early in life, the baby learns to see the rewards it can get from this relationship. Later on, the child learns from   30
interactions with the family what a "give and take" relationship is and then starts to shift away from self-centeredness.

As we mature we should become aware of our position in relation to others in our world, a position no greater and no less than that of any other person. Not everyone succeeds in develop- 35 ing a realistic concept of self, and not everyone is able to internalize the constraints society puts on each of us. Thus, mental maturity, unlike physical maturity, does not come automatically to all.

1. Are there any specific details to enliven this generalized definition?

2. How has the writer used classification as an organizing principle?

14-G   **Learning Has No End**

Irma Cruz *(student)*

This essay was written for the same assignment as the preceding essay. The writer, a middle-aged student who had just begun her college career, draws on personal experience to enliven her remarks.

Mature people have a growing understanding of themselves, of others, and of social, moral, and ethical problems. They have the ability to translate words into meanings, to grasp the ideas presented, and to sense the mood suggested. They have curiosity and enthusiasm for a wide variety of experiences, directly and also 5 indirectly through reading, and they relate new ideas to previous experiences. Thus, they acquire new and deeper understandings, broadened interests, rational attitudes, and richer and more stable personalities.

I have few memories of my early childhood. My parents were 10 poor and so involved in the struggle to survive that they could offer me little or no personal enrichment. No books were given or read to me, there were no trips to museums, zoos, theaters, or movies, there was no money to buy the kinds of toys that would have stimulated my imagination. My early days in kindergarten 15 were bright days. I remember looking forward to the mornings that I would spend in school, but another memory like a rainfall, bitter in taste, is of being labeled by the system as a remedial child. I was made to feel that I was not going far in life. A year later when my younger sister joined me in school, my parents and 20 teachers gave me the message that she was bright and I wasn't.

From that moment on I imprisoned my soul with the ridiculous
challenge of proving that I too had abilities.

In my early twenties I fell in love and married. I can truly say,
as I look back many years later, that on the day of my marriage   25
I was born again; I wish that I could change my entire name to
suit my second birth. I entered marriage with no identity, no
sense of myself, no experience of life whatever. Through my
husband's patience, through my struggles with everyday life,
through bearing children, caring for them and trying to meet   30
their needs in a more conscious way than mine were met, through
reading more and reading with a more critical view, and through
developing my love for art, I began to grow and continue to
grow.

I have chosen a career in education and have worked as a   35
paraprofessional teaching "target" children, children who need
to catch up. I am in college, an activity which my relatives and I
had thought I would never be capable of but which I had always
wanted. I look forward with great hope to continuing to experience and to grow more mature in life, for learning has no end.   40

14-H   In the "Lite" Decade, Less
Has Become More

William R. Greer

This essay, here almost complete, appeared in the *New York Times* in 1986.

It used to take so much time—days, sometimes weeks—to read
a classic. "Moby Dick," alone, runs 710 pages. Today, thanks to
a small publishing house called Workman, it takes a minute.
Through abridging, reabridging and editing out "rambling
soliloquies," Workman boasts that it has "cut down the literary   5
canon to a lean pistol," producing an audio-cassette tape that
offers listeners "Ten Classics in Ten Minutes."

The result is light literature, the latest demonstration that in the
1980's light beer is not the only thing that is less filling. What
started out as a way to justify drinking three beers instead of   10
two—the creation of a light beer with a third fewer calories—has
become part of a broader phenomenon in which less is valued
above more. This is the Light Decade, or as some would have it,
Lite.

"Light is a way of thinking that we've come to in the 80's," says   15
Dr. Robert T. London, a psychiatrist at New York University
Medical Center. "It's an umbrella phenomenon where lightness
transforms itself into the cars we drive, the lightness in a room,
our diet, as well as lightness in the relationships we have."

Sociologists say that "lite," which started as a marketing term   20
used to denote dietetic products, has become a metaphor for what
Americans are seeking in disparate parts of their lives. In their
relationships, for example, they have turned away from soul-
searching and the stress of emotional commitment; at the movies,
they would rather watch an invincible hero, like Rambo or the   25
Karate Kid, who never lets the audience down.

"The notion of the word 'lite' tends to follow what seems to
be a trend in American culture," said Ray B. Brown, chairman
of the department of popular culture at Bowling Green State
University in Ohio. "That is for everybody to be utterly selfish   30
about themselves, for people to want easy cures, easy riches, easy
jobs and easy wealth."

The Light Decade is a time when men and women can "fall in
love without paying the price," as a Honda Civic advertisement
promises. They can undergo psychoanalysis in one sitting, be-   35
cause today's psychotherapy skips the formative years, namely
childhood. For health care, busy executives can turn to a so-called
Doc in a Box, a storefront medical clinic with extended hours,
higher prices and no appointment, no referral—no medical history necessary.   40

There is light culture (books on tape), light shopping (buying
clothes by video), light politics (candidates who run on image,
not issues), light responsibility (the lowest voter participation
rates of any democracy) and light music (Lite FM, where the
heavy bass line has been removed so that the sound does not jar   45
or stir listeners). And, of course, there is light food, with which
people can cut calories without changing their diets by using
products like Jell-O Light, Cornitos Light Corn Chips, Heinz Lite
Ketchup and Glacé Lite, which, its manufacturer, Sweet Victory,
says "gives you all the rich, delicious pleasures of 300-calorie   50
premium ice cream" at 100 calories a scoop.

Food, notably dietetic food, is where the Light Decade started.
It is also the clearest example of how the philosophy has caught
on. "Lite," or "light," foods are now "one of the fastest growing
segments of the American food industry," according to a recent   55
Federal Food and Drug Administration report.

By the count of one market research company, Marketing Intelligence, 352 "lite" or "light" products have been added to the
shelves of the nation's supermarkets and liquor stores since 1982.

Seven years ago the Miller Brewing Company tried to claim   60
"Lite" as its own, part of its trademark for its low-calorie beer,
and went to court to keep other brewers from using it. The courts
ruled that "lite" was just an alternative spelling of "light."

Before the 16th century, the word "lite" meant "little, not
much, few" in English and was pronounced differently from   65
"light," according to Traugott Lawler, a medievalist at Yale University. But the word fell out of use.

Today's "lite" is used to indicate fewer calories or less salt, and
essentially refers to weight in the same way that light is a reference to weight, Mr. Lawler said. "Its spelling has been simplified   70
in the 20th century by advertisers who use it to suggest ease and
simplicity," he said. "It's a light spelling."

The effect of light foods on weight loss has been, well, light.
"We know that the number of people who are obese has increased in the past 10 years," said Thomas A. Wadden, a psychol-   75
ogist at the Obesity Research Group of the University of Pennsylvania. "And the percentage of children who are obese is increasing."

Bernard Phillips, a sociologist at Boston University, calls the
Light Decade a "smorgasbord" approach to life, where people   80
convince themselves that they can have the best of all worlds,
immediately, by having a lightened version of everything.

"What happens is the light things become a gloss to fool ourselves into thinking that we are getting what we want," he said.
"When you go to the supermarket and buy light beer, this is   85
getting you away from the notion that there are serious problems
with your not being able to lose weight. You don't face the
weight problem. You go for the quick fix."

1. What specific examples does Greer use to explain the generalization in his
second paragraph?

2. How does he use classification to extend his definition of "Lite"?

3. What does the first paragraph contribute to Greer's definition?

4. Check the etymology, denotation, and connotation of *abridging, canon, disparate, smorgasbord.*

ASSIGNMENTS

1. There are many types of terms from which you may draw subjects for essays of
definition:

a. words like *ruana, sukiyaki, goober, pedicab,* which may be in common use in some areas but which are so limited in locale that they are unfamiliar to many readers;

b. technical terms like *azimuth, ombudsman, recidivism, onomatopoeia,* which are so specialized as to be either unknown to most readers or not well understood by them;

c. slang terms like *gam, smokey, pad, spiv, skedaddle,* which are either too dated or too limited in use to be generally understood in all their implications;

d. abstract terms like *culture, sportsmanship, education, freedom,* which continually require specific definition because of the variety of interpretations possible;

e. familiar terms like *freshman, spring fever, conscience, homesickness,* which are known to all but which may have a special personal meaning for you that you would like to express.

2. Many words may be usefully defined in pairs to overcome frequent confusion of the two: courtesy and etiquette, job and profession, art and science, knowledge and intelligence, house and home, infer and imply, naturalist and biologist, religion and theology, possibility and probability.

3. When you have chosen a subject,

a. Write a formal one-sentence definition.

b. Expand that definition into a paragraph by increasing the differentiating details, but keep it formally informative.

c. Expand it into a longer essay of definition by using devices and adding information that will make it enjoyable as well.

4. The importance of definition can be seen by the number of times that it is used in the examples of other units. See Unit 4-D, 8-A, 11-A and C, and 12-H. In which is it needed more? In Unit 5-A the failure to accept each other's choice of words brings a waitress and customer into conflict.

UNIT 15

Induction and Deduction

If a new restaurant opens in your neighborhood, how do you decide whether to try it? Probably, you first check its general appearance from the street. If that seems attractive, you look for a menu posted on the door or a window. If you find one, you glance over it rapidly to determine the general type of food served and the range of choices. If these are satisfactory, you read the menu more closely and check the prices. If you are still attracted to the restaurant, you try to peek through the window to see the interior. If several tables are occupied by people who look pleasant and who seem to be enjoying their food, if the tables are comfortably large with plenty of space between them, if each table looks clean and has sparkling glasses and shining silverware, if the lighting is at a level you like, and if the general decoration is pleasing, you now feel safe in drawing the conclusion that the restaurant is worth trying.

You have used inductive reasoning to reach this conclusion, and you based each step in the process on earlier experiences in reaching conclusions about restaurants—for instance, you had learned from many experiences which types of cooking and which special dishes you like most and what prices are reasonable, what seating arrangements you prefer, how people behave when they are enjoying a good restaurant meal, and so on.

With inductive reasoning we add one piece of information to another until we have enough evidence to draw a conclusion. Usually, we know in advance what question we are trying to answer ("Is that new restaurant worth trying?") and search for relevant information, like the members of a jury who listen to evidence in a criminal case to prepare themselves to answer the question "Guilty or not guilty?" (Sometimes, of course, we may unexpectedly happen on the answer to a question we have not asked, like Sir Alexander Fleming, who was conducting research on the influenza virus when he chanced to notice the antibacterial effect of penicillin on staphylococcus germs.)

With deductive reasoning we use earlier conclusions, reached inductively by ourselves or others, to answer new questions about material. For example, suppose that, after eating several good meals at the restaurant, you learn that the owner has two other restaurants not far away. Curious to see if they are as good as the one you visited, you try both, examine them closely, and conclude that they equal the first in every way. When several of your friends, who also like the first restaurant, try the others and agree with you, your conclusion has further support. If you then hear that the owner plans to open a fourth restaurant and you are so convinced that it will meet the standard set by the others that you recommend it warmly, you have used deductive reasoning to reach a conclusion: you have relied entirely on a previous conclusion to form your opinion about a new case instead of testing it as you did the others.

This kind of thinking can be expressed as a **syllogism,** the classic pattern of deductive reasoning. A syllogism is composed of two statements, called premises, and a conclusion that derives from them. The classic example is this:

> *Major premise*—All men are mortal.
> *Minor premise*—Socrates is a man.
> *Conclusion*—Therefore Socrates is mortal.

In making your recommendation about the fourth restaurant, you derived your conclusion by the same process:

> *Major premise*—All of X's restaurants are good.
> *Minor premise*—Y is one of X's restaurants.
> *Conclusion*—Y is a good restaurant.

The conclusion reached through syllogistic reasoning is logically valid only if the terms are accurate and correctly related to each other. Three kinds of errors are common in trying to draw logical conclusions. Consider this faulty syllogism: "All fish can swim; John can swim; therefore John is a fish." Here, "swimming" includes "fish" and "John," but fish are not the only creatures who swim, and so John's ability to swim does not make him a fish. Also consider this: "All men drown in deep water; John is a man; therefore John will drown in deep water." Here, the major premise is an inaccurate generalization; "drowning" does not include "all men," only those who cannot swim, and if John can swim, he will not automatically drown in deep water. Finally, consider this: "All mammals nurse their young; turtles are mammals; therefore turtles nurse their young." Here, the minor premise is inaccurate. Although all mammals nurse their young, turtles are not mammals, and therefore the major premise does not apply to them. Remember that the truth of a valid conclusion depends entirely on the reliability of the premises and of their relationship to each other.

Syllogistic reasoning may seem only a kind of game, but its importance becomes clear when we examine the logic behind some of our own hasty conclusions. "Bob shouldn't apply to law school; he's one of the stupid Joneses." What is the reasoning here? Part of it looks like the following when we supply the unexpressed but implied major premise:

> Stupid people should not apply to law school.
> Bob is a stupid person.
> Therefore he should not apply to law school.

The generalization in the major premise seems reasonable, but what of the minor premise—what evidence have we that Bob is stupid? For this we must go back to an earlier *implied* deduction:

> All the Joneses are stupid.
> Bob is a Jones.
> Therefore Bob is stupid.

Here the major premise is harder to accept. It may prove on closer examination to be based only on gossip, or at least to be an overstatement; perhaps some of the Joneses are stupid but Bob is one of the exceptions. Or if we are able to accept the generalization, the minor premise may not hold; perhaps Bob is adopted. In any event, by examining our reasoning we may become less satisfied with our first casual conclusion and concede that we should let Bob's fitness for law school be determined by his performance on entrance examinations.

A football player once wrote in a theme that the trouble with his college was that "Writing is taught to too great an extent, thus causing players to be ineligible, games to be lost, and the college to lose its standing among institutions of higher learning." One suspects that even a devoted football fan, faced with the "general truth" lurking behind this remark, would not attempt to defend it, for arranged syllogistically, the major deduction runs something like this:

Major premise: All reputable colleges should have as their primary purpose the winning of football games.
Minor premise: This is a reputable college.
Conclusion: Therefore this college should have as its primary purpose the winning of football games.

Many of our conclusions rest, as do these examples, on general assumptions—often unstated, sometimes not clear even to ourselves, and sometimes found on analysis to be false. An excellent way to learn to analyze the thinking of others and to think more accurately ourselves is to uncover underlying assumptions and check their validity. To do this, we should examine the sources of every generalization; they will probably be one or more of these:

a. an unquestionable assumption like "All men are mortal"—we need not test it because it has been reaffirmed by experience from the beginning of time;
b. an inductive conclusion not yet firmly established—we may need to examine the evidence on which it rests;
c. a conclusion reached through a previous syllogistic deduction, as in the example of Bob's stupidity—we may need to examine the validity of the deductive reasoning that produced it;
d. a statement by a person whose expertise is not known—we need to establish his or her authority adequately;
e. an assumption that we fix arbitrarily by definition—we could, for example, deduce whether or not to classify a certain type of music as good if we accept the assumption that "good music is music that we dance to easily."

∴ ∴ ∴

For a paper in which you practice using inductive and deductive reasoning to reach a conclusion of some kind, choose a topic about which you are really curious because investigating it may take some time. But choose a fairly limited topic so that you will be able to explore it thoroughly in the time allowed. There are several specific suggestions in "Assignments" at the end of this unit.

To convince yourself and others that you have drawn a logical conclusion, follow these guidelines:

1. **Keep an open mind as you work toward a conclusion.** Do not decide in advance what it will be; a preconceived opinion will prejudice you. Your object is to arrive at whatever truth emerges from the evidence, not to select evidence to support your previous idea of the truth. Certainly, an inkling of what you hope to determine can help you to start your investigation, just as scientists begin experiments with a hypothesis—a tentative formulation of the truth they are working to establish. However, like scientists, you must be willing to abandon your hypothesis if the facts fail to uphold it. For example, you might start to investigate the effect of extracurricular activities on student grades because you suspect that the activities interfere with study. But you may find that students study more effectively after relaxing with those activities. Your final generalization must be whatever the evidence supports—not what you would like it to support.

2. **Do not lose sight of the problem you are investigating.** To determine the effect of extracurricular activities on grades, for instance, you must not be distracted by the question of whether such activities help in developing a well-rounded personality, which is quite another matter.

3. **Consider a reasonable number of instances.** Drawing conclusions does not mean jumping to them. A *hasty generalization,* the most common fallacy in inductive reasoning, is one made on insufficient evidence. Your conclusion about the effect of extracurricular activities will have little validity if you based it on observations of only three or four students. What constitutes a "reasonable" number of instances will depend partly on the subject. For example, an investigation of which background, city or rural, has produced more presidents of the United States could easily include all the presidents, but a similar study of American doctors could be reasonably done only through a sampling. The number of instances necessary will also depend on your intention. For practical purposes, you will not need nearly so many as scientists do; their studies may require hundreds, even thousands, of instances, but you may need only a few well-chosen ones. Moreover, you do not have to give the details of all the instances but only the evidence you draw from them.

4. **Use fair instances.** Get a representative sampling. Do not let your preconceptions or haste to finish influence you. Public opinion researchers use elaborate techniques to get fair samples. If you are studying the effects of activities on the grades of students in general, do not limit your examples to those with high or low grades; make a cross section.

5. **Consider carefully any contrary evidence you may find.** Charles Darwin, the nineteenth-century naturalist, kept special records of any evi-

dence that tended to disprove his hypothesis concerning evolution, on the grounds that he could easily remember the data that supported his theory but needed reminders of contrary evidence.

6. **Be cautious in drawing conclusions and generalizing.** Do not conclude, because you know two drama club members who are on probation, that drama club members in general have low academic averages.

The more carefully you guard against any suggestion of prejudice, any loading of the dice, in your choice and analysis of instances, the more reliable and convincing your conclusions will be.

∴ ∴ ∴

In organizing your paper, you may choose between the inductive and deductive rhetorical patterns or use them in combination. These are named after the two patterns of thinking just examined, but each can be used to describe an investigation by either method.

1. **To use the inductive pattern,** start with little or no indication of the conclusions you finally reached in your investigation. Make your readers imagine that they are accompanying you in your examination of material and your search for meaning in it. The conclusions you draw will therefore form a climax at the end of the paper. For example, to write a paper organized inductively on whether to try a particular restaurant, you would begin with whatever first brought the restaurant to your attention and give all the information in precisely the order in which it came to you, including any false leads you followed. You would also give your interpretations and conclusions on the material in exactly the sequence in which you made them, and your final decision, that the restaurant was worth visiting, would form the end of the paper, much as the solution to the crime forms the end of a detective story.

> *Advantages in using the inductive pattern:* Readers have a sense of sharing the investigation with you, and their curiosity will be aroused as to the outcome.
> *Disadvantages in using the inductive pattern:* If the material is at all complex or unfamiliar to your readers, they may have difficulty in following the steps and may not accept your interpretation of the evidence.

2. **To use the deductive pattern,** begin by briefly stating your conclusion. Then describe the steps by which you reached it.

> *Advantages in using the deductive pattern:* Your readers will know from the start precisely where you are leading them and will therefore know

what to look for in the evidence you present. You can describe false
leads very briefly and thus emphasize your conclusions more firmly.
Disadvantage in using the deductive pattern: The ending will be an anti-
climax unless you can present it in particularly forceful words that
catch your readers' imaginations.

3. **To combine the two patterns,** start with a hint about the conclusions you reached and then present your investigation chronologically, ending with a full explanation of your conclusions. In writing on the restaurants
mentioned earlier, you could, for example, start by presenting your conclusion as a question: "Is X's fourth restaurant good?" You would then give the
evidence on the other restaurants, starting with your first view of the first one
and ending with your answer to the question—your conclusion that you are
sure that it is good. You might, instead, start by presenting your conclusion
in the form of a general opinion that can be seen as open to discussion or,
at the very least, in need of explanation and support—for example, "The
quality never varies in any of the restaurants of a careful owner." The third
sentence of Example A in this unit and the first sentences of Examples C, E,
and F present such opinions.

∴   ∴   ∴

In planning, writing, and revising your paper, keep the following
points in mind:

1. **Assemble an adequate quantity of evidence**—if you fear you
have too much, use phrases such as "A minor example of this point is
. . ." or "Some additional support is . . ." to let readers know that they can
read those parts rapidly.

2. **Examine all your assumptions** to be sure that they are based on
good sources (the checklist given earlier about Bob Jones will help you), and
explain them fully to your readers.

3. **Define your terms.**

4. **Test the validity of your evidence at every step** and show your
readers that you have done so.

5. **Remember that analogies are never evidence,** merely rhetorical
devices that clarify what they describe (see page 210). Make sure that any
analogies you use are well chosen. The fact that swimming, being a skill,
requires not only an understanding of technique but also much practice may
well illustrate the point that writing, although a very different sort of skill,
also requires a study of technique and much practice. But a country doctor's
need for a car is too far removed from the international scene to make a good

analogy with a nation's need for a merchant marine, even though both situations involve transportation.

6. **Emphasize the logic of your deductions** by presenting the steps clearly.

7. **Be cautious in wording generalizations.** Never overstate your claims. You may not be able to arrive at an absolutely certain conclusion, but there is value in suggesting significant trends. In writing your paper, limit the scope of your conclusions by giving percentages or by using carefully chosen words such as *nearly all, probably, usually, likely, possibly, sometimes, few, seldom, rarely.* (See Example C in this unit.)

8. **Sharpen your thinking throughout** by imagining a very skeptical, "show me!" kind of reader who doubts and questions you at every step.

EXAMPLES

In the selections in this unit, reasoning by inductive and deductive methods is essential, but reasoning plays such an important part in all thinking that you will find it present, at least to some extent, in every other selection in this book. Notable examples on topics related to the social sciences are Tysoe's "Do You Inherit Your Personality?" (6-E), Johmann's "Sex and the Split Brain" (7-B), Seymour St. John's "The Fifth Freedom" (8-A), Sithole's "When Blacks Rule in South Africa" (12-E), all the selections in Unit 13, Tudge's "They Breed Horses Don't They" (16-B), and Douglass's "A Plea for Free Speech in Boston" ("Essays for Further Reading"-D).

15-A   Three Incidents

The New Yorker

This unsigned essay, here complete, appeared in *The New Yorker* in 1980. The writer is surprised by a conclusion reached inductively.

I am fully aware that anecdotal evidence is no longer, if it ever was, in good scientific repute. Nevertheless, in the course of the past few months I have been witness to three aberrations of nature that seem to me to be worth noting. They suggest, if nothing else, that, contrary to much received understanding, man is not the only form of life that is capable of making a fool of itself.   5

The first of these incidents occurred in the spring, just under the eaves on our front veranda. There is a fixture up there, a galvanized-iron box about the size and shape of a thick paperback book (it has something to do with the outdoor lights), that forms a kind of shelf. I came out on the veranda one morning in time to see a bird—a little red-breasted house finch—make a landing there on the top of the box and deposit a beakful of grass. I stood on tiptoe and craned my neck, and saw the beginnings of a nest. It was in many ways an excellent nesting site—dry, airy, nicely sheltered. But it was also as slippery as glass. And, as I watched, a gust of breeze came along and the nest slid off and blew away in pieces. Well, that, I thought, is that. The bird, however, thought differently. It went to work again, retrieving the scattered grasses, and started another nest. Another doomed nest, I should say. Because another little breeze came along and scattered that nest, too. But the finch was undismayed. I watched it start still another nest, and I watched that nest blow away. That was enough for me. I went on with my own affairs. But every now and then through the rest of the day I went over to the door or the window and looked out. The finch was always there—sitting on the box, fluttering away, swooping back with a wisp of grass. And there was still nothing more than the pathetic beginnings of a nest.

The second incident occurred in the house, in the attic. I went up there a couple of weeks ago to look for something or other. I was feeling my way toward an old chest of drawers when something odd caught my eye. It was a strand of ivy espaliered on the wall above the little end window. It was two or three feet long, its leaves were a sickly yellowy green, and it had forced itself, at God knows what exertion, through a tiny crack in the window frame from the life-giving sunlight into the deadly dusk of the attic.

And then, just the other day, I was out weeding the garden and sat down on the bench to rest and noticed an anthill at my feet. There was much coming and going around the hole—a stream of foraging workers. I leaned down and watched a worker emerge from the hole, race away through the grass, pounce on a tiny something—a seed, maybe, or an egg or a minuscule creature—and head quickly back toward the hole. Only, it headed in the wrong direction. It raced this way and that, back and forth, farther and farther away from home. I had to get up from the bench to follow it. I finally lost it, in a weedy jungle, a good eight feet (the equivalent, perhaps, of a couple of miles) from where it wanted to be. I went back to the bench and sat down again and wondered.

It might be possible, I thought, to somehow see the strivings of the finch as an example of determination, an iron procreative perseverance. And the ivy: its suicidal floundering, too, might be explained—as an evolutionary thrust, an urge (like that of some aquatic organism feeling its way up a beach) to try a new environ-   55
ment. But the ant! There was no way of rationalizing that: the phenomenon of a worker ant—an ant bred exclusively to forage for its queen—unable to find its way home. It shook and shattered the concept of a knowing and nurturing instinct, of a computer-ized infallibility, in nature. I felt a tug of something like sympathy   60
for that errant ant. And also for the finch and the ivy. They gave me a new vision of nature: a nature unmechanized, a nature vulnerable, a nature appealingly natural.

1. The writer gives the three incidents chronologically—in the order in which they occurred. Do you find any additional reason for this sequence?

2. Where does the writer use specific, concrete details? specific, concrete words?

3. Check the etymology, denotation, and connotation of *aberrations, received understanding, espaliered, foraging, minuscule.*

15-B   The Importance of Not Being Smith

Bob Bagnall

The writer, a Scottish scientist, teaches at the University of Edinburgh. Here, in a humorous speculation, he uses inductive reasoning to formulate his hypothesis: The more unusual a scientist's surname is, the more likely he or she is to become famous. In your own experience, how logical does Bagnall's hypothesis seem? The essay was first published in *New Scientist* in 1989.

Science is a system for ordering knowledge, built on a foundation of laws, hypotheses and principles which usually carry the name of the person most closely associated with them. Like all trained scientists, I have learnt many of these names, partly to pass examinations and partly for my own interest. Boyle's law,   5
Charles' law, Le Chatelier's principle, Avogadro's hypothesis, Einstein's law of relativity, Hess's law, are but a few of them.

Chemistry, for example, has a whole gamut of reactions bearing the names of their discoverers, names which sometimes trip not so lightly from the tongue. 10

Musing on this one day, it occurred to me how confusing it would be if several scientists with a very common surname all had laws named after them. Now, in Britain at least, Smith is one of the most common names, and I began to imagine a plethora of Smith's laws appearing in the textbooks. How would we know 15 which was which? Life could get tedious if Smith's law of thermodynamics could be confused with Smith's law of conservation of energy, or Smith's law of genetics. The marking of examination answers beginning "Using Smith's law; we can show . . ." could be a nightmare. Thankfully, no such surfeit of Smith's laws exists, 20 and we are indeed fortunate in having such a diverse range of names at our disposal.

While this idea was still bouncing around in my head, a stunning fact revealed itself to me. Not only was science spared a glut of Smith's laws; in fact I didn't know a single one! Nor could I 25 recall a Jones's law, or a White's law or any other law associated with one of the very common surnames in Britain.

This struck me as odd. Assuming the brains to be spread equally among the population, the number of Smith's laws should simply reflect the proportion of Smiths. Pick up a telephone direc- 30 tory, however, and a different picture emerges. Take, for example, my own telephone directory, for Fife, and consider the case of Boyle. There are about 25 times as many Smiths as Boyles listed, so perhaps there should be about 25 Smith's laws to counterbalance the one Boyle's law. But there aren't. Want another 35 example? Try the name Newton. According to my directory, there are more than 50 Smiths to every Newton, yet it was Newton who made a name for himself. Similarly, there are 25 Smiths for every Rutherford, more than 400 Smiths to every Dalton, about 13 Smiths to every Maxwell; and Faradays and Darwins are 40 so thin on the ground that they don't even have an entry.

Now, I haven't yet fully formulated Bagnall's hypothesis of scientific eminence, but I am beginning to suspect that the likelihood of eminence is inversely related to the frequency of surname. Whether or not there is an exact mathematical form to the 45 relationship, or whether it is merely a trend, is unclear at this stage, and would require not only a thorough investigation of scientists from Britain but also of those from other countries.

How common are the surnames of all the Nobel prizewinners, for example? How many people have the name Mendeleev in 50 Russia? How many Avogadros are there in the world? (The answer is not 6.022137×10^{23}.) Is Dirac a common surname? How many Turings are there? Is the world teeming with van der Waals, and is the connection between them weak? The list is endless, but the results may share a common thread.   55

I must admit that I am at a loss as to how to explain these observations. However, I cannot imagine that the Smiths or the Joneses of this world are any less capable than anyone else. Perhaps, and I offer this only as the merest suggestion, rarity of surname acts as a subliminal flag when a scientific paper is read,   60
marking it out as memorable for reasons other than mere excellence. Then again, perhaps those with the rare surnames feel that they have to try harder to stop themselves being swamped by the rest.

The relationship may also hold good for other fields of human   65
endeavour. Perhaps a close investigation of the worlds of politics or business would reveal a similar trend in relating success with scarcity of surname, though once again I offer the thought as mere speculation.

I could of course be mistaken in all this. However, if my chance   70
observation has any substance, then the advice to any Smith, Jones or White aspiring to the dizzy heights of science is simple. Forget it! The odds are stacked against you from the start. Your only hope of becoming a scientific superstar is to change your name by deed poll to the rarest name you can think of.   75

And what about my own name? In my local telephone directory at least, it's even rarer than Newton. By my reckoning, therefore, Bagnall's hypothesis stands a reasonable chance of acceptance. Whoever hands out the fame, please note that I'm sitting here waiting. . . .   80

Check the etymology, denotation, and connotation of *gamut, plethora, surfeit, glut, inversely, subliminal;* a *deed poll* (1.75) is a legal document involving a single individual or group.

15-C   The Language of Uncertainty

John Cohen

In these paragraphs from an essay in *Scientific American,* Cohen reports the results reached **inductively** through experiments and suggests applying them **deductively** in intelligence testing.

ANALYSIS
General
conclusion
Examples

Analysis of
example

Analysis of
conclusion

General
purpose of
experiments

Classification
of data

Specific
purpose of
experiments

Method for
analyzing
data

Uncertainty pervades our lives so thoroughly that it dominates our language. Our everyday speech is made up in large part of words like *probably, many, soon, great, little.* What do these words mean? "Atomic war," declared a recent editorial in the London *Times,* "is likely   5
to ruin forever the nation that even victoriously wages it." How exactly are we to understand the word *likely?* Lacking any standard for estimating the odds, we are left with the private probability of the editorial writer.

Such verbal imprecision is not necessarily to be con-   10
demned. Indeed, it has a value just because it allows us to express judgments when a precise quantitative statement is out of the question. All the same, we should not and need not hide behind a screen of complete indefiniteness. Often it is possible to indicate the bounds or   15
limits of the quantitative value we have in mind.

The language of uncertainty has three main categories: (1) words such as *probably, possibly, surely,* which denote a single subjective probability and are potentially quantifiable; (2) words like *many, often, soon,* which are also   20
quantifiable but denote not so much a condition of uncertainty as a quantity imprecisely known; (3) words like *fat, rich, drunk,* which are not reducible to any accepted number because they are given values by different people.

We have been trying to pin down, by experimental   25
studies, what people mean by these expressions in specific contexts, and how the meanings change with age. For instance, a subject is told "There are many trees in the park" and is asked to say what number the word *many* means to him. Or a child is invited to take "some" sweets   30
from a bowl and we then count how many he has taken. We compare the number he takes when alone with the

number when one or more other children are present and are to take some sweets after him, or with the number he takes when instructed to give "some" sweets to 35 another child.

Category #1:
Results of
analysis
Examples

First, we find that the number depends, of course, on the items involved. To most people *some friends* means about five, while *some trees* means about twenty. However, unrelated areas sometimes show parallel values. 40 For instance, the language of probability seems to mean about the same thing in predictions about the weather and about politics: the expression *is certain to (rain,* or *be elected)* signifies to the average person about a 70 per cent chance; *is likely to,* about a 60 per cent chance; *probably* 45 *will,* about 55 per cent.

Category #2:
Results of
analysis
Examples

Secondly, the size of the population of items influences the value assigned to an expression. Thus, if we tell a subject to take "a few" or "a lot of" beads from a tray, he will take more if the tray contains a large number of 50 beads than if it has a small number. But not proportionately more: if we increase the number of beads eightfold, the subject takes only half as large a percentage of the total.

Category #3:
Results of
analysis
Deductive
application
of results
Examples

Thirdly, there is a marked change with age. Among 55 children between six and fourteen years old, the older the child, the fewer beads he will take. But the difference between *a lot* and *a few* widens with age. This age effect is so consistent that it might be used as a test of intelligence. In place of a long test we could merely ask the 60 subject to give numerical values to expressions such as *nearly always* and *very rarely* in a given context, and then measure his intelligence by the ratio of the number of *nearly always* to the one for *very rarely.* We have found that this ratio increases systematically from about 2 to 1 65 for a child of seven to about 20 to 1 for a person twenty-five years old.

1. The writer gives the results of the experiment, not all the data on which they were based (presumably these are available on request). Are the results convincing without the data?

2. What is the principle of classification of the general subject in ¶3? What is the principle of the classification of the results of the analysis in ¶5–7?

3. Check the etymology, denotation, and connotation of *quantitative, subjective, quantifiable, denote, contexts.*

15-D   Monday—Again?

Denise Goudreau *(student)*

The writer's logic is unassailable, but how many of us have the willpower to
follow her advice?

Bzzz, bzzz, bzzz. ". . . And this is the Grease Man with you this
dismal, gross and disgusting Monday morning. Don't just roll
over, you lazy bum, get in gear, out of bed and rock on into the
shower with DC/101. . . ." It can't be 7:00 already. Just five more
minutes, then John would get up. ". . . Yeah, the one, the only   5
Grease Man with ya here, and if you gotta be somewhere by 7:30,
honey, you're late! It's 7:31. . . ." With an 8:00 class, he knew
he would never have enough time to take a shower, brush his
teeth, dry his hair, get dressed and eat his breakfast. Late again.
John knew he'd never make it to English class on time.   10
    Waking up on Monday mornings is a difficult task because the
body's schedule is thrown off during the weekend. The general
public tends to overexert itself during the weekend. In addition,
people have not prepared themselves for the return of routines.
    Just as a three-year-old child cannot resist the temptation of   15
carelessly caressing various glimmering goods in a crystal shop
with his inquisitive hands, so most people cannot resist the temptation to sleep late on a Saturday or Sunday morning. Of course,
the reason they need to sleep late on weekends is as clear as a
shining star on a coal-black night. Primarily, people need to com-   20
pensate for all of the partying that they missed from Monday
through Thursday by hobnobbing, mixing and mingling on Friday and Saturday nights until the cock's crow sends them home.
The body's schedule is further confused by cat-naps taken during
the course of the day. It is no small wonder that the body protests   25
violently when the alarm's siren sounds to start a new week.
    Of course, people do not prepare themselves for the return of
a routine schedule. First, they neglect to make provision for the
upcoming week. For example, they make no plans for breakfast,
lunch or dinner. Furthermore, the thought of wardrobe prepara-   30
tion never walks across the paths of their mind. Inability to face
these minor problems, in addition to physical fatigue, causes
many a person to roll over rather than rise. Second, goals for the

upcoming week have not been set. Establishing goals often acts
as a motivating factor. The inner drive to grab a challenge by the   35
hand inspires people to leap from their beds like pole vaulters at
the height of competition. Finally, people leave unfinished those
goals which were set for that weekend. For example, the student
has not finished his term paper, and the executive has not completed his presentation.   40

Overexertion is another factor to consider. Primarily, people
schedule too many events in the two days, which leaves them
bouncing like a tennis ball from one event to another. In addition,
almost everyone becomes obsessed with the intense desire to
exercise over the weekend. Exercise performed two out of seven   45
days on a limp, sluggish body unquestionably results in fatigue.

Unfortunately, the fingers of pain delicately dance over the
body a day or so after the exercising is done. Feeling no pain,
people exercise more vigorously than they should. Finally, demanding domestic projects arise. Out of necessity, these menial   50
tasks must be performed. Nonetheless, both house and yard work
consume a great deal of energy and often deplete a person's zeal.

People do have a choice; they can make a change. Determined
never again to face the terror of waking up exhausted on Monday
morning, those who want to change have a chance. People *can*   55
keep to a regular sleeping schedule on the weekend. They *can*
prepare themselves both mentally and physically for the upcoming week. Most important, they *can* limit their weekend activities,
preventing overexertion. Those people who choose not to heed
this advice will find themselves doomed to saying, "Monday—   60
again!"

1. On what premises does Goudreau base her conclusions?

2. What evidence does she give to support her deductions?

3. What pattern does she use to organize her argument?

15-E   Letter from Home

William Zinsser

Zinsser was a member of the Yale faculty when this essay, here complete, appeared in the *New York Times*. His most recent books are *On Writing Well* and *Writing with a Word Processor*. Here, in his analysis of the problems he found students facing, Zinsser applies deductions he had made much earlier on the importance of freedom. What opinions does he share with Hiatt (15-F) and St. John (8-A)? Do the students you know have similar problems? For a student's reply to Zinsser, read Cooper's essay (15-G).

Now is the edgy time for Yale seniors. In three weeks they will graduate and join the rest of us out here in the real world. It is a place that they are inordinately afraid of.

Not all of them, of course, will take the icy plunge. Quite a few will stay on the academic assembly-line—in law school or medical   5
school or graduate school—to study for three or four years more. This doesn't mean that they necessarily want to be lawyers or doctors or scholars. Some are continuing their education because their parents want them to. Some are doing it just to postpone the day of decision. Some are doing it because lawyers and doctors   10
make a good living. Some are doing it to acquire still another degree to impress a society in which they think credentials are the only currency. Some—the lucky ones—really do want to be lawyers, doctors, scholars or specialists in a field that requires further skill.   15

But they all are driven—those who are leaving Academia and those who are staying—by one message: Do Not Fail. It is a message that has been echoing in their heads since they were admitted to the pre-kindergarten of their choice, beating less competitive toddlers. Score high, test well, play it safe. Next   20
month's graduates have been so obsessively bent for four years on measurable achievement (grades) and a secure future (jobs) that they have hardly had time to savor the present and to grow as well-rounded people. They know that the outside world is wary of experimenters, of late starters and temporary losers.   25

I'm talking about Yale students because I live in their midst and know them well. (I am Master of Branford College, one of Yale's twelve residential colleges. In our house I can lie awake and listen

to some of the loudest stereo sets in the East. That, in fact, is why
I lie awake.) And I'm talking about seniors because they are the   30
ones who are most on my mind right now: panicky that they won't
have enough A's to persuade an employer to hire them, though
they are men and women I'd like to have working for me, if I
were an employer, for qualities of intelligence and humor and
humanity that don't show up on any chart.   35

But I could just as well be talking about Yale's juniors,
sophomores and freshmen—or, I suspect, about the students at
most colleges today. They are studying more and enjoying it less.
At Yale, they play in fewer plays and musical groups, join fewer
campus organizations, take part in fewer sports, carve out fewer   40
moments just to linger and talk and put a margin around their
lives. They are under pressure to do too much work in too little
time.

If all their friends are studying in the library until it closes at
midnight (and they are), they feel guilty if they want to go to a   45
Woody Allen movie, though there is as much to be learned
from a Woody Allen movie as from a book—much, in fact, that
they will never learn from a book. Not surprisingly, their emotional health is often far from healthy. I see a lot of psychic
disarray.   50

It is not that I don't wish them fame and fortune, especially the
seniors as they lurch toward graduation, more stuffed with learning and shorn of money than they probably ever will be again.
Obviously I do. But I also wish them a release from fear of the
future. They should know that fame and fortune are not end   55
products that they will automatically win if they follow a straight
and safe route, but by-products that will accrue to them if they
dare to poke down the unmarked side roads that lead to life's
richest surprises.

Risk and change, art and music, joy and affection, the unex-   60
pected friendship of strangers—these are some of the essential
tonics. "To affect the quality of the day, that is the highest of the
arts," said Thoreau. I wish it could be chiseled over the door of
every school, college, corporation and home.

Home is where the words "Do not fail" are first instilled and   65
constantly repeated. One of next month's Yale graduates came to
me on her first day as a freshman in 1973 and said: "I want to be
a great journalist—what courses should I take for the next four
years?" She wanted a blueprint at seventeen. Many students come
to me in the middle of their sophomore year, afraid of changing   70
the curriculum that they mapped but no longer think is the one

that they want to pursue. "If I don't make all the right choices now," one of them said, "It will be too late."

Too late at eighteen? Sad words. They are growing up old and set in their ways. They have been told to prepare for one career— preferably one that will reflect well on their parents—and to stick to it and succeed. They are not told that they have a right to try many paths, to stumble and try something else, and to learn by stumbling. The right to fail is one of the few freedoms not granted in our Bill of Rights. Today it is more acceptable to change marriage partners than to change careers.

"Victory has very narrow meanings and can become a destructive force," writes Bill Bradley, now a senator for New Jersey, in his book, *Life on the Run.* Bradley was an Ivy Leaguer himself and a Rhodes Scholar—an earlier member of the same elite that is now so preoccupied with success—before starting his ten-year career of professional basketball, which had just come to an end. "The taste of defeat," he writes, "has a richness of experience all its own. To me, every day is a struggle to stay in touch with life's subtleties. No one grows without failing."

The fault is not with our children, but with the narrowness of the flowerbed in which we expect them to germinate. We are stunting their growth if we tell them that there is only one "right" way to get through their education or to get through life. America has always been nourished by mavericks and individuals—men and women not afraid to go against the grain.

1. What, if anything, does Zinsser gain by delaying the statement of his major premise almost to the end?

2. The only analogy in the essay is at the very end, but many examples of figurative language are scattered throughout, beginning with "icy plunge" and "assembly-line" in the second paragraph. What others can you find and what do they contribute to the effectiveness of the essay?

3. Check the etymology, denotation, and connotation of *inordinately, credentials, currency, wary, lurch, accrue, tonics, elite, mavericks;* check the origin of *against the grain.*

15-F   After Graduation, What Next?

Fred Hiatt *(student)*

Hiatt was a Harvard senior when he wrote this essay, here almost complete. It appeared in the *Boston Globe* in May 1977. He began by quoting a classmate who claimed that many seniors were as concerned with correcting social injustices as the students in the '60s had been.

One of my goals this year has been to teach the mechanics of typing to a cat I know, a cat who has always been fascinated by manual typewriters, pawing at the letter rods as they jumped out and watching with frustration when they lie quietly beyond his reach. I have spent hours pushing his paws on the keys and   5
encouraging him to see the causal connection, to see that the letters have no life of their own. But the cat, as fascinated as ever, still vainly hopes to catch one alive.

Similarly, many seniors are concerned, even fascinated, by their society and by its injustices, but baffled by the causal links, uncer-   10
tain where the injustice comes from or what they could do about it. And so, though they are concerned—"quiescent, but not acqui-escent," as Harvard sociology professor David Riesman said—within a few years even many who are not yet pre-business will have lost interest in "working towards change."   15

Most of us, then, will pursue lucrative careers in business, law, or medicine. A survey of 1971 Harvard graduates showed more than 50 per cent choosing one of the three within five years, and while the number of 1977 graduates going to law school may drop a bit, more will probably end up in business school.   20

Many will go not because they've wanted to be executives or attorneys, nor just to make money, but because they don't know what else to do. Part of the appeal of the professional career is the desire, or need, for individual recognition. In school we learned to judge the quality of our work by the grade somebody   25
else assigned it. In college we scrabbled for the prominent byline or the leading role on stage.

Now the reputation of the law school seems to matter more than what we will do as lawyers, the prestige of the newspaper more than what we'd like to say in print. Only power and fame   30
can bring "success" and happiness.

To opt for the cooperative, to work in legal aid without head-

ing the office, to write without a byline, would be to reject everything we've been trained to be. And that rejection would be
doubly hard for women, who, instead of receiving praise for   35
spurning ego-gratification, would be blamed by many for regress-
ing to old passive roles.

Then, many seniors just don't see other options. Up to now,
we've always been most rewarded for performing the expected.
To depart from the expected now—to choose a career that   40
doesn't guarantee power and $35,000 a year five years from
now—takes courage. Many Harvard graduates, though certainly
not all, can afford more easily than other college graduates to pass
up the best-paying job; their family background and their degree
render future starvation unlikely.   45

Yet, most of us won't dare pass up that job. In a few years, we
will persuade ourselves that we "need" a car, a sunnier apart-
ment, a winter vacation—and that we "need" more money than
we can imagine needing now. And as we grow discouraged by the
potential for real social change, working "within the system" will   50
seem more and more sensible—until one day we suddenly find
ourselves not infiltrators, but bulwarks, of that system.

Going to professional school is not the same as selling out, of
course, and for many women and minority graduates the struggle
is just beginning. But many of us seem to be headed past quies-   55
cence into acquiescence itself. Maybe the only thing that can
bring about a profound change is sex, the search for new structures of romance. . . . At least some feminist values have seeped
into the undergraduate consciousness and, together with the seri-
ousness with which most women face their careers, have   60
prompted new problems, new ground rules, new questionings of
old assumptions. Whose job should take priority—until now a
problem for only a few middle-class career couples—is an issue,
real or potential, for almost every graduate. If he follows her, will
the relationship suddenly seem more permanent than they want   65
it to be? If she follows him, is she giving in to sexist pressures?

Where political principles and the quest for adventure once
stood in the way of pure ambition, now only love interferes. He
may work in a dead-end job to help her through law school; she
may settle for a second-rate medical school to stay by his side.   70

It will be interesting to see, when we gather for our five-year
reunion, whether we have settled into our law firms with housewives and househusbands at our sides, whether we have forsaken
coupledom entirely—or whether the compromises forced on us
by relationships have derailed us from the straight, ambitious   75
track in a way that, for most of us, the search for adventure and
the commitment of political activism no longer can.

1. On what premises does Hiatt base his conclusions?

2. What specific, concrete details does he use?

3. What relationship can you see between Hiatt's opinions and those of Zinsser in the preceding example?

4. How appropriate is the analogy of the inability of the cat to understand cause and effect?

5. Check the etymology, denotation, and connotation of *camaraderie, quiescent, acquiescent, bulwarks.*

15-G   A Reply to Zinsser and Hiatt

Chris Cooper *(student)*

Today's college students face a multitude of decisions. With rising tuition costs, most students graduate not only with a diploma but with a pile of debts. Can we attend college for personal fulfillment alone and place no monetary value on the degree? I think not, but I do feel that learning to apprecite art, acquiring social skills, and interacting with others are vital parts of a college education. Students must not relinquish their right to question, to disagree, and to be wrong.

According to Zinsser in "Letter from Home," most students are so intent on success, on "making it" in the "real world," that they want to follow a formula instead of experimenting. As a result, he says, they are missing a lot. Some of the true treasures of life are on the "unmarked side roads"—the rewards of human interaction, of art, of individualism, and even of occasional failure, which Zinsser claims can be one of life's best educators.

Fred Hiatt makes some of the same points in "After Graduation, What Next?" He believes that most students are not in college or professional school for an education but to get a high-paying job afterwards, and he wishes that they cared more about correcting social wrongs and were more willing to risk being unconventional. Zinsser, on the other hand, does not put down the students' desire for success but instead argues that a lasting success can be better achieved by suffering from a few pitfalls along the route.

Both authors have valid arguments, but only within the limits of the kinds of colleges they know. I have been a student on three different campuses—a state college, a city college, and a private college. I agree with Zinsser that students are afraid of failure, but

I think their fears are valid. Students today are seeing their middle-aged parents suddenly out of work. The American dream of   30
following the right routes and being sure of success does not
always come true. I cannot sympathize readily with Hiatt's argument. Since he was a Harvard senior when he wrote the essay, it
was fairly easy for him to advocate working for social change
instead of personal success. He admits himself that Harvard grad-   35
uates can usually afford to pass up a job opportunity without
risking starvation, unlike graduates of other colleges. Both authors are writing about Ivy League students but are trying to apply
their deductions to *all* college students. I do not think that these
deductions are general truths. For many students at city and state   40
universities, it is a struggle just to attend class—their parents
would rather that they work to help support the family. I do
belive, however, that students should not be afraid to take risks
or change their minds—a little experimentation is good, even
when we have to pay for our mistakes. But many of the students   45
that I know are expressing their individuality by attending college
in the first place.

1. In your opinion, does the writer present Zinsser's and Hiatt's arguments
accurately?

2. The writer relies on personal experience to make a reply. Is this an adequate
basis? Do you agree or disagree with this writer?

15-H   An Open Letter to Black
                 Parents: Send Your Children
                 to the Libraries

Arthur Ashe

This essay, here complete, is from the *New York Times* (1977). Ashe, an international tennis champion, retired from professional sports in 1980 because of heart
trouble but has since served as captain of the U.S. Davis cup team and is a sports
commentator. He has compiled a reference book, *The History of the Black Athlete in
America* (1984).

Since my sophomore year at University of California, Los Angeles, I have become convinced that we blacks spend too much
time on the playing fields and too little time in the libraries.

Please don't think of this attitude as being pretentious just because I am a black, single, professional athlete. I don't have children, but I can make observations. I strongly believe the black culture expends too much time, energy and effort raising, praising and teasing our black children as to the dubious glories of professional sport.

All children need models to emulate—parents, relatives or friends. But when the child starts school, the influence of the parent is shared by teachers and classmates, by the lure of books, movies, ministers and newspapers, but most of all by television. Which televised events have the greatest number of viewers? Sports—the Olympics, Super Bowl, Masters, World Series, pro basketball playoffs, Forest Hills. ABC-TV even has sports on Monday night prime time from April to December. So your child gets a massive dose of O. J. Simpson, Kareem Abdul-Jabbar, Muhammad Ali, Reggie Jackson, Dr. J and Lee Elder and other pro athletes. And it is only natural that your child will dream of being a pro athlete himself.

But consider these facts: For the major professional sports of hockey, football, basketball, baseball, golf, tennis and boxing, there are roughly only 3,170 major league positions available (attributing 200 positions to golf, 200 to tennis and 100 to boxing). And the annual turnover is small. We blacks are a subculture of about 28 million. Of the 13 ½ million men, 5 to 6 million are under twenty years of age, so your son has less than one chance in 1,000 of becoming a pro. Less than one in a thousand. Would you bet your son's future on something with odds of 999 to 1 against you? I wouldn't.

Unless a child is exceptionally gifted, you should know by the time he enters high school whether he has a future as an athlete. But what is more important is what happens if he doesn't graduate or doesn't land a college scholarship and doesn't have a viable alternative job career. Our high school dropout rate is several times the national average, which contributes to our unemployment rate of roughly twice the national average.

And how do you fight the figures in the newspapers every day? Ali has earned more than $30 million boxing, O. J. just signed for $2 ½ million, Dr. J. for almost $3 million, Reggie Jackson for $2.8 million, Nate Archibald for $400,000 a year. All that money, recognition, attention, free cars, girls, jobs in the offseason—no wonder there is Pop Warner football, Little League baseball, National Junior Tennis League tennis, hockey practice at 5 A.M. and pickup basketball games in any center city at any hour.

There must be some way to assure that the 999 who try but don't make it to pro sports don't wind up on the street corners

or in the unemployment lines. Unfortunately, our most widely
recognized role models are athletes and entertainers—"runnin'" 　　　50
and "jumpin'" and "singin'" and "dancin.'" While we are 60
percent of the National Basketball Association, we are less than
4 percent of the doctors and lawyers. While we are about 35
percent of major league baseball, we are less than 2 percent of the
engineers. While we are about 40 percent of the National Foot- 　　　55
ball League, we are less than 11 percent of construction workers
such as carpenters and bricklayers.

Our greatest heroes of the century have been athletes—Jack
Johnson, Joe Louis and Muhammad Ali. Racial and economic
discrimination forced us to channel our energies into athletics and 　　　60
entertainment. These were the ways out of the ghetto, the ways
to get that Cadillac, those alligator shoes, that cashmere sport
coat.

Somehow, parents must instill a desire for learning alongside
the desire to be Walt Frazier. Why not start by sending black 　　　65
professional athletes into high schools to explain the facts of life?
I have often addressed high school audiences, and my message is
always the same. For every hour you spend on the athletic field,
spend two in the library. Even if you make it as a pro athlete, your
career will be over by the time you are thirty-five. So you will 　　　70
need that diploma.

Have these pro athletes explain what happens if you break a
leg, get a sore arm, have one bad year or don't make the cut for
five or six tournaments. Explain to them the star system, wherein
for every O.J. earning millions there are six or seven others 　　　75
making $15,000 or $20,000 or $30,000 a year.

But don't just have Walt Frazier or O. J. or Abdul-Jabbar
address your class. Invite a benchwarmer or a guy who didn't
make it. Ask him if he sleeps every night. Ask him whether he
was graduated. Ask him what he would do if he became disabled 　　　80
tomorrow. Ask him where his old high school athletic buddies are
now.

We have been on the same roads—sports and entertainment—
too long. We need to pull over, fill up at the library and speed
away to Congress and the Supreme Court, the unions and the 　　　85
business world. We need more Barbara Jordans, Andrew
Youngs, union cardholders, Nikki Giovannis and Earl Graveses.
Don't worry: we will still be able to sing and dance and run and
jump better than anybody else.

I'll never forget how proud my grandmother was when I gradu- 　　　90
ated from U.C.L.A. in 1966. Never mind the Davis Cup in 1968,
1969, and 1970. Never mind the Wimbledon title, Forest Hills,

etc. To this day, she still doesn't know what those names mean. What matters to her was that of her more than thirty children and grandchildren, I was the first to be graduated from college, and   95 a famous college at that. Somehow, that made up for all those floors she scrubbed all those years.

1. As the title indicates, Ashe has written a letter, not a formal argument, but his advice is based on the deduction that there are very few chances for success in professional athletics. What follows from this deduction?

2. What support does he give the deduction?

3. What use does he make of narrative, analogy, and analysis to support his argument?

15-I   "Your Mother Did It to You" Is an Excuse We Overuse

Jerome Kagan and Alvin P. Sanoff

This essay, here complete, was first published in *U.S. News & World Report.* The basis for it was a conversation between Dr. Kagan, a professor of human development at Harvard University, and Alvin P. Sarnoff, who interviewed him for the magazine. Dr. Kagan's most recent book is *The Nature of the Child.*

Americans have many significant misunderstandings about the way children develop. We don't appreciate the impact of historical events on youngsters, and at the same time we exaggerate the importance of what takes place between parent and child. We overemphasize what's happening within the home and underemphasize what's happening in the larger culture.   5

This comes about because Americans dislike causes we can't change and are attracted to explanations that focus on circumstances we can alter. We can't change the Vietnam War, but we can change what parents do. So parents are given advice which   10 implies that if they played more games with their children, then the lives of the youngsters would necessarily be much better. Parents whose nineteen-year-old is in trouble feel that if they had not gone on that holiday or had been a little more strict, then everything would have turned out differently.   15

Mothers, in particular, feel guilty because society has pointed

the finger at them. In that sense, we have victimized the mother.
I'm not minimizing the importance of her role; she is significant.
But we have attributed all the influence to her as if she were a
sorceress. She's a good witch if the child turns out fine and a bad   20
witch if he doesn't.

Non-Western societies do not attribute as much power to the
mother. But once the West generated a large middle class, many
mothers did not have much work to do. They had to have an
assignment—and we gave them one. Also, as strict class divisions   25
began to break down in 18th-century Europe, we had to find a
way to explain why some people became upwardly mobile.
Again, society turned to the mother and said, "It must be what
she does through the teaching of good habits."

Today we live in a complex society in which twenty-five-year-   30
olds try to explain why they didn't get into law school or why they
got divorced. And we have a simple answer: "Your mother did
it to you."

Another misunderstanding about child development is rooted
in our reluctance to acknowledge that biological differences exist   35
among children. America is an egalitarian nation whose citizens
want to believe—and I share this belief—that all of us can attain
equal dignity, equal economic security, equal self-actualization if
we're treated right as children. Because that belief is so strong,
we think that if infants begin life as differentially irritable or   40
active, how will we ever be able to make them politically equal?
Anytime there's talk about biological differences among infants,
people become nervous.

One of the main messages in my new book is that children do
differ in some ways that influence their development. That   45
doesn't mean that their families, peers and teachers can't change
those initial qualities, but we have to acknowledge that children
are born differentially fearful, irritable and alert. In popular
terms, this is the ancient nature-vs.-nurture debate.

One of the unfortunate consequences of an emphasis only on   50
nurture is the conviction that everything is learned. We think that
we have to teach a child a conscience, even though research shows
that in the second year all children develop a moral sense.

Of course, the specific acts they regard as right or wrong have
to be taught. But the child is prepared by biology to be sensitive   55
to right and wrong, as a bird is prepared to sing and a fish
prepared to swim.

We minimize this fact, leading us to say of an eighteen-year-old
delinquent: "His parents didn't teach him a conscience." That is

not correct. He had a conscience, but experiences after age two 60
caused him to lose his ability to experience guilt and shame for
committing an asocial act. When children are two, they experience special emotion when they contemplate doing something
wrong or when they actually do it. This emotion is not exactly
what adults describe as guilt or shame, but it's akin to it. It's an 65
unpleasant feeling, and that feeling prevents antisocial acts. Some
children, as a function of the neighborhoods in which they live,
the homes in which they survive, the television and movies that
they watch, gradually lose this feeling. It's then that they act
antisocially. 70

Despite what I have said about society's overemphasis of the
parents' role, it is still true that the home is the most important
factor in the development of children. It's the place where they
are told what to care about, whether it is grades, athletics or being
kind to people. 75

The family is also vital because it shapes children's beliefs about
themselves. Are they basically good or bad? Are they kind or not?
Whether they respond in the affirmative or negative to such questions will depend on both their actual success in life—if they are
good in school, they gradually learn that they are talented—and 80
on identification with their parents. In the first six years, children
believe that some of the qualities of their parents belong to them.
A girl with a kind, just, nurturing mother will conclude that she
has the same qualities. That belief is going to help her. If her
mother has the opposite qualities, she may think that she is bad. 85
It's harder for a woman at age twenty to conclude that she is good,
despite real-life successes, if she started with a negative identification.

Unfortunatley, many parents do not realize their importance as
role models. They believe that it's what they do to their child— 90
what they punish, praise and reward—and not their own behavior
that matters.

Sibling position also counts in shaping children. Whether you
were first, second or thirdborn, whether you are the middle boy
of three boys or the middle boy with two sisters can have a 95
profound influence. In general, firstborns in the average middle-
class family are somewhat reluctant to disagree with authority
because they admire their parents. The world looks less just to
later-borns because they see the firstborn as having privileges they
do not have. They hold a more skeptical, pessimistic and slightly 100
more rebellious attitude. It is a fact that in middle-class homes,
firstborns generally get better grades than later-borns and go to

better colleges. They pick more-conservative vocations—law and
medicine—rather than less traditional interests like visual studies
and sociology.   105

I'm not saying that ordinal position is more important than
the values the parents promote or their function as role models.
But it's a family factor—and one that parents have no control
over.

There is evidence on the consequences of ordinal position,   110
including a study done by a colleague—Frank Sulloway—who
examined several intellectual revolutions in science. He found
that the majority of firstborn scientists opposed the revolutions;
they accepted the views of existing authority. A majority of scientists who were later-born supported the new ideas; they were the 115
skeptics of tradition.

Moving beyond the family, peers and the school are important.
Peers teach you your position in the rank order because their
attributes, relative to your own, let you know how smart, brave
and physically attractive you are.   120

If you go to a small, one-room school in rural Ohio and have
a 120 IQ, odds are that you are the smartest child in town and
you are going to feel very competent. If the same child lives in
an urban area and goes to school with many talented youths, he
may feel much less competent because there will be so many who 125
are smarter than he. For this reason, there are higher-than-aver-
age number of eminent people who grew up in small towns. Over
three quarters of the initial astronaut candidates grew up in such
environments.

Looking at child development across the life span, I would say 130
that the role of biology is most important in the first five years of
life. The importance of the family overlaps it for a few years, for
family is most important from years two to ten. The influence of
culture, in the form of teachers, peers and historical events, overlaps the family and looms largest between the ages of six and 135
sixteen.

Whenever there's a major change in society, such as the Depression or the Vietnam War, those between 6 and 16 are most
influenced. We need only look at the 1960s, when perfectly
reasonable students from good families suddenly marched on the 140
offices of university presidents and threw bombs at police. This
wasn't, as many people believe, the result of permissive child
rearing. After all, youngsters were marching in Japan and in
France as well as in the U.S. And there was more permissiveness
at the end of the 19th century than in the '50s and '60s.   145

What this phenomenon shows is that some developments can be discontinuous: there can be radical changes in behavior that have little to do with the experiences of early childhood.

1. Does Kagan use an inductive pattern, a deductive pattern, or a combination of the two?

2. Why does Kagan use the terms "good witch" and "bad witch" in paragraph 3? What does his word choice suggest, and is this suggestion appropriate to his argument?

3. Is Kagan's comparison of children with birds and fish logical?

4. Check the etymology, denotation, and connotation of *egalitarian, differentially, nature versus nurture, affirmative, ordinal, discontinuous.*

15-J   The Passing of Little Gibbs Road

Connie Keremes *(student)*

My neighborhood is dying. The houses know it. They creak and groan at the slightest breeze. The trees know it. Their bare limbs rasp dryly together in the wind. The people know it. They gaze out of dusty windows and sigh at the falling leaves.

The houses in my neighborhood are ancient and dilapidated.   5
Many years ago, they were fine, well-cared for buildings with fresh paint and neat lawns. Now, however, the houses, more than fifty years old, have become quite tumbledown. They are simply too old and weathered to endure another fierce winter. The houses are sagging structures. They never seem to stand straight   10
but, rather, they lean heavily to one side as if they might topple over at any moment. The rotting beams and frames groan under the weight of roofs which look like patchwork quilts of mending slate. The shingled fronts are discolored from many winters of snow and ice. Several shingles have come loose from many of the   15
houses and, left unrepaired, creak back and forth in the wind. Every stoop and walk is crumbling and cracked. A few homeowners have placed potted plants on the stoops in an attempt to hide the many cracks—but the plants make the deep fissures all the

more apparent. The houses appear more pathetic than ugly in   20
their dilapidation, for their squeaking paint-chipped doors and
groaning frames seem to say these once fine homes will soon
crumble to dust.

The houses are not alone in their deterioration, for the trees
are also decaying. At one time, the trees along my street were tall   25
and leafy, but now they are bent and twisted with age. The tops
of many trees have been sawed off because their branches had
been tangling the telephone wires. Such trees have now become
rotting stumps overrun with burrowing insects. Those trees which
are standing are gnarled and diseased. Vandals have carved ob-   30
scenities in the trunks of several trees, boldly leaving their names
and dates beside the deed. A few leaves cling to the twisted
branches, but for the most part the trees are barren. They bend
low as the wind whines through their bare limbs. These wasted
old trees will easily be uprooted by the first strong blast that blows   35
this year. They undoubtedly will not survive the winter.

The people themselves seem to be wasting away. Only very old
people live in the neighborhood, for the children who once lived
there have all grown up and moved away. No one ever moves
into the neighborhood—only out. The old people who live here   40
are very frail. They walk slowly along the cracking sidewalks,
their kerchiefed heads bent against the gusty winds. In passing
each other along the street, the old people no longer smile or stop
to talk, but merely nod grimly and continue along their way. They
lack the strength to climb up on their roofs to patch a hole or   45
fasten a loose shingle, and as a result their houses become
progressively more dilapidated. Aware of their failing strength
and inability to make repairs on the decaying neighborhood, the
old people resign themselves to staying indoors and staring dully
out at the leaves that swirl across the cracking sidewalks and past   50
the gnarled trees. There is nothing left for them to do but to
watch the neighborhood die.

1. The subject and main point here are similar to those of Examples 6-C and
13-B and E. What differences and similarities do you find in the four authors' methods
of presentation?

2. Why does the author save her discussion of the people until the last paragraph?

15-K   Love Is a Fallacy

Max Shulman

The writer is noted for his many humorous plays and films, notably *Barefoot Boy with Cheek* (1943), *The Tender Trap* (1954), *Rally Round the Flag, Boys!* (1957), *I Was a Teen-Age Dwarf* (1959), *How Now, Dow Jones* (1967). *The Many Loves of Dobie Gillis* (1951), from which this selection is taken, was filmed as *The Affairs of Dobie Gillis* and formed the basis for a popular television series.

Starting with the first sentence in this selection, Shulman combines humor, self-mockery, and formal logic in a way that illustrates and clarifies the basic propositions of logic, while at the same time producing an amusing story.

Cool was I and logical. Keen, calculating, perspicacious, acute and astute—I was all of these. My brain was as powerful as a dynamo, as precise as a chemist's scales, as penetrating as a scalpel. And—think of it!—I was only eighteen.

It is not often that one so young has such a giant intellect. Take, 5
for example, Petey Burch, my roommate at the University of Minnesota. Same age, same background, but dumb as an ox. A nice enough fellow, you understand, but nothing upstairs. Emotional type. Unstable. Impressionable. Worst of all, a faddist. Fads, I submit, are the very negation of reason. To be swept up 10
in every new craze that comes along, to surrender yourself to idiocy just because everybody else is doing it—this, to me, is the acme of mindlessness. Not, however, to Petey.

One afternoon I found Petey lying on his bed with an expression of such distress on his face that I immediately diagnosed 15
appendicitis. "Don't move," I said. "Don't take a laxative. I'll get a doctor."

"Raccoon," he mumbled thickly.

"Raccoon?" I said, pausing in my flight.

"I want a raccoon coat," he wailed. 20

I perceived that his trouble was not physical, but mental. "Why do you want a raccoon coat?"

"I should have known it," he cried, pounding his temples. "I should have known they'd come back when the Charleston came back. Like a fool I spent all my money for textbooks, and now I 25
can't get a raccoon coat."

"Can you mean," I said incredulously, "that people are actually wearing raccoon coats again?"

"All the Big Men on Campus are wearing them. Where've you been?"   30

"In the library," I said, naming a place not frequented by Big Men on Campus.

He leaped from the bed and paced the room. "I've got to have a raccoon coat," he said passionately. "I've got to!"

"Petey, why? Look at it rationally. Raccoon coats are unsani-   35
tary. They shed. They smell bad. They weigh too much. They're unsightly. They—"

"You don't understand," he interrupted impatiently. "It's the thing to do. Don't you want to be in the swim?"

"No," I said truthfully.   40

"Well, I do," he declared. "I'd give anything for a raccoon coat. Anything!"

My brain, that precision instrument, slipped into high gear. "Anything?" I asked, looking at him narrowly.

"Anything," he affirmed in ringing tones.   45

I stroked my chin thoughtfully. It so happened that I knew where to get my hands on a raccoon coat. My father had had one in his undergraduate days; it lay now in a trunk in the attic back home. It also happened that Petey had something I wanted. He didn't *have* it exactly, but at least he had first rights on it. I refer   50
to his girl, Polly Espy.

I had long coveted Polly Espy. Let me emphasize that my desire for this young woman was not emotional in nature. She was, to be sure, a girl who excited the emotions, but I was not one to let my heart rule my head. I wanted Polly for a shrewdly calculated,   55
entirely cerebral reason.

I was a freshman in law school. In a few years I would be out in practice. I was well aware of the importance of the right kind of wife in furthering a lawyer's career. The successful lawyers I had observed were, almost without exception, married to beauti-   60
ful, gracious, intelligent women. With one omission, Polly fitted these specifications perfectly.

Beautiful she was. She was not yet of pin-up proportions, but I felt sure that time would supply the lack. She already had the makings.   65

Gracious she was. By gracious I mean full of graces. She had an erectness of carriage, an ease of bearing, a poise that clearly indicated the best of breeding. At table her manners were exquis-ite. I had seen her at the Kozy Kampus Korner eating the spe-cialty of the house—a sandwich that contained scraps of pot roast,   70
gravy, chopped nuts, and a dipper of sauerkraut—without even getting her fingers moist.

Intelligent she was not. In fact, she veered in the opposite direction. But I believed that under my guidance she would smarten up. At any rate, it was worth a try. It is, after all, easier to make a beautiful dumb girl smart than to make an ugly smart girl beautiful.

"Petey," I said, "are you in love with Polly Espy?"

"I think she's a keen kid," he replied, "but I don't know if you'd call it love. Why?"

"Do you," I asked, "have any kind of formal arrangement with her? I mean are you going steady or anything like that?"

"No. We see each other quite a bit, but we both have other dates. Why?"

"Is there," I asked, "any other man for whom she has a particular fondness?"

"Not that I know of. Why?"

I nodded with satisfaction. "In other words, if you were out of the picture, the field would be open. Is that right?"

"I guess so. What are you getting at?"

"Nothing, nothing," I said innocently, and took my suitcase out of the closet.

"Where are you going?" asked Petey.

"Home for the weekend." I threw a few things into the bag.

"Listen," he said, clutching my arm eagerly, "while you're home, you couldn't get some money from your old man, could you, and lend it to me so I can buy a raccoon coat?"

"I may do better than that," I said with a mysterious wink and closed my bag and left.

"Look," I said to Petey when I got back Monday morning. I threw open the suitcase and revealed the huge, hairy, gamy object that my father had worn in his Stutz Bearcat in 1925.

"Holy Toledo!" said Petey reverently. He plunged his hands into the raccoon coat and then his face. "Holy Toledo!" he repeated fifteen or twenty times.

"Would you like it?" I asked.

"Oh yes!" he cried, clutching the greasy pelt to him. Then a canny look came into his eyes. "What do you want for it?"

"Your girl," I said, mincing no words.

"Polly?" he said in a horrified whisper. "You want Polly?"

"That's right."

He flung the coat from him. "Never," he said stoutly.

I shrugged. "Okay. If you don't want to be in the swim, I guess it's your business."

I sat down in a chair and pretended to read a book, but out of the corner of my eye I kept watching Petey. He was a torn man.

First he looked at the coat with the expression of a waif at a bakery
window. Then he turned away and set his jaw resolutely. Then
he looked back at the coat, with even more longing in his face.
Then he turned away, but with not so much resolution this time.   120
Back and forth his head swiveled, desire waxing, resolution waning. Finally he didn't turn away at all; he just stood and stared with
mad lust at the coat.

"It isn't as though I was in love with Polly," he said thickly.
"Or going steady or anything like that."   125

"That's right," I murmured.

"What's Polly to me, or me to Polly?"

"Not a thing," said I.

"It's just been a casual kick—just a few laughs, that's all."

"Try on the coat," said I.   130

He complied. The coat bunched high over his ears and
dropped all the way down to his shoe tops. He looked like a
mound of dead raccoons. "Fits fine," he said happily.

I rose from my chair. "Is it a deal?" I asked, extending my
hand.   135

He swallowed. "It's a deal," he said and shook my hand.

I had my first date with Polly the following evening. This was
in the nature of a survey; I wanted to find out just how much work
I had to do to get her mind up to the standard I required. I took
her first to dinner. "Gee, that was a delish dinner," she said as we   140
left the restaurant. Then I took her to a movie. "Gee, that was
a marvy movie," she said as we left the theater. And then I took
her home. "Gee, I had a sensaysh time," she said as she bade me
good night.

I went back to my room with a heavy heart. I had gravely   145
underestimated the size of my task. This girl's lack of information
was terrifying. Nor would it be enough merely to supply her with
information. First she had to be taught to *think.* This loomed as
a project of no small dimensions, and at first I was tempted to give
her back to Petey. But then I got to thinking about her abundant   150
physical charms and about the way she entered a room and the
way she handled a knife and fork, and I decided to make an effort.

I went about it, as in all things, systematically. I gave her a
course in logic. It happened that I, as a law student, was taking
a course in logic myself, so I had all the facts at my finger tips.   155
"Polly," I said to her when I picked her up on our next date,
"tonight we are going over to the Knoll and talk."

"Oo, terrif," she replied. One thing I will say for this girl: you
would go far to find another so agreeable.

We went to the Knoll, the campus trysting place, and we sat   160 down under an old oak, and she looked at me expectantly. "What are we going to talk about?" she asked.

"Logic."

She thought this over for a minute and decided she liked it. "Magnif," she said.

"Logic," I said, clearing my throat, "is the science of thinking. Before we can think correctly, we must first learn to recognize the common fallacies of logic. These we will take up tonight."

"Wow-dow!" she cried, clapping her hands delightedly.

I winced, but went bravely on. "First let us examine the fallacy called Dicto Simpliciter."

"By all means," she urged, batting her lashes eagerly.

"Dicto Simpliciter means an argument based on an unqualified generalization. For example: Exercise is good. Therefore everybody should exercise."

"I agree," said Polly earnestly. "I mean exercise is wonderful, I mean it builds the body and everything."

"Polly," I said gently, "the argument is a fallacy. *Exercise is good* is an unqualified generalization. For instance, if you have heart disease, exercise is bad, not good. Many people are ordered by their doctors *not* to exercise. You must *qualify* the generalization. You must say exercise is *usually* good, or exercise is good *for most people.* Otherwise you have committed a Dicto Simpliciter. Do you see?"

"No," she confessed. "But this is marvy. Do more! Do more!"

"It will be better if you stop tugging at my sleeve," I told her, and when she desisted, I continued. "Next we take up a fallacy called Hasty Generalization. Listen carefully: You can't speak French. I can't speak French. Petey Burch can't speak French. I must therefore conclude that nobody at the University of Minnesota can speak French."

"Really?" said Polly, amazed. *"Nobody?"*

I hid my exasperation. "Polly, it's a fallacy. The generalization is reached too hastily. There are too few instances to support such a conclusion."

"Know any more fallacies?" she asked breathlessly. "This is more fun than dancing even."

I fought off a wave of despair. I was getting nowhere with this girl, absolutely nowhere. Still, I am nothing if not persistent. I continued. "Next comes Post Hoc. Listen to this: Let's not take Bill on our picnic. Every time we take him out with us, it rains."

"I know somebody just like that," she exclaimed. "A girl back home—Eula Becker, her name is. It never fails. Every single time we take her on a picnic—"

"Polly," I said sharply, "it's a fallacy. Eula Becker doesn't *cause*   205
the rain. She has no connection with the rain. You are guilty of
Post Hoc if you blame Eula Becker."

"I'll never do it again," she promised contritely. "Are you mad
at me?"

I sighed deeply. "No, Polly, I'm not mad."   210

"Then tell me some more fallacies."

"All right. Let's try Contradictory Premises."

"Yes, let's," she chirped, blinking her eyes happily.

I frowned, but plunged ahead. "Here's an example of Contradictory Premises: If God can do anything, can He make a stone   215
so heavy that He won't be able to lift it?"

"Of course," she replied promptly.

"But if He can do anything, He can lift the stone," I pointed
out.

"Yeah," she said thoughtfully. "Well, then I guess He can't   220
make the stone."

"But He can do anything," I reminded her.

She scratched her pretty, empty head. "I'm all confused," she
admitted.

"Of course you are. Because when the premises of an argument   225
contradict each other, there can be no argument. If there is an
irresistible force, there can be no immovable object. If there is an
immovable object, there can be no irresistible force. Get it?"

"Tell me some more of this keen stuff," she said eagerly.

I consulted my watch. "I think we'd better call it a night. I'll   230
take you home now, and you go over all the things you've
learned. We'll have another session tomorrow night."

I deposited her at the girls' dormitory, where she assured me
that she had had a perfectly terrif evening, and I went glumly
home to my room. Petey lay snoring in his bed, the raccoon coat   235
huddled like a great hairy beast at his feet. For a moment I
considered waking him and telling him that he could have his girl
back. It seemed clear that my project was doomed to failure. The
girl simply had a logic-proof head.

But then I reconsidered. I had wasted one evening; I might as   240
well waste another. Who knew? Maybe somewhere in the extinct
crater of her mind, a few embers still smoldered. Maybe somehow I could fan them into flame. Admittedly it was not a prospect
fraught with hope, but I decided to give it one more try.

Seated under the oak the next evening I said, "Our first fallacy   245
tonight is called Ad Misericordiam."

She quivered with delight.

"Listen closely," I said. "A man applies for a job. When the boss asks him what his qualifications are, he replies that he has a wife and six children at home, the wife is a helpless cripple, the children have nothing to eat, no clothes to wear, no shoes on their feet, there are no beds in the house, no coal in the cellar, and winter is coming." 250

A tear rolled down each of Polly's pink cheeks. "Oh, this is awful, awful," she sobbed. 255

"Yes, it's awful," I agreed, "but it's no argument. The man never answered the boss's question about his qualifications. Instead he appealed to the boss's sympathy. He committed the fallacy of Ad Misericordiam. Do you understand?"

"Have you got a handkerchief?" she blubbered. 260

I handed her a handkerchief and tried to keep from screaming while she wiped her eyes. "Next," I said in a carefully controlled tone, "we will discuss False Analogy. Here is an example: Students should be allowed to look at their textbooks during examinations. After all, surgeons have X-rays to guide them during an 265 operation, lawyers have briefs to guide them during a trial, carpenters have blueprints to guide them when they are building a house. Why, then, shouldn't students be allowed to look at their textbooks during an examination?"

"There now," she said enthusiastically, "is the most marvy idea 270 I've heard in years."

"Polly," I said testily, "the argument is all wrong. Doctors, lawyers, and carpenters aren't taking a test to see how much they have learned, but students are. The situations are altogether different, and you can't make an analogy between them." 275

"I still think it's a good idea," said Polly.

"Nuts," I muttered. Doggedly I pressed on. "Next we'll try Hypothesis Contrary to Fact."

"Sounds yummy," was Polly's reaction.

"Listen: If Madame Curie had not happened to leave a photo- 280 graphic plate in a drawer with a chunk of pitchblende, the world today would not know about radium."

"True, true," said Polly, nodding her head. "Did you see the movie? Oh, it just knocked me out. That Walter Pidgeon is so dreamy. I mean he fractures me." 285

"If you can forget Mr. Pidgeon for a moment," I said coldly, "I would like to point out that the statement is a fallacy. Maybe Madame Curie would have discovered radium at some later date. Maybe somebody else would have discovered it. Maybe any number of things would have happened. You can't start with a hypoth- 290 esis that is not true and then draw any supportable conclusions from it."

"They ought to put Walter Pidgeon in more pictures," said Polly. "I hardly ever see him any more."

One more chance, I decided. But just one more. There is a limit   295
to what flesh and blood can bear. "The next fallacy is called Poisoning the Well."

"How cute!" she gurgled.

"Two men are having a debate. The first one gets up and says, 'My opponent is a notorious liar. You can't believe a word that   300
he is going to say.' . . . Now, Polly, think. Think hard. What's wrong?"

I watched her closely as she knit her creamy brow in concentration. Suddenly a glimmer of intelligence—the first I had seen—came into her eyes. "It's not fair," she said with indignation. "It's   305
not a bit fair. What chance has the second man got if the first man calls him a liar before he even begins talking?"

"Right!" I cried exultantly. "One hundred percent right. It's not fair. The first man has *poisoned the well* before anybody could drink from it. He has hamstrung his opponent before he could   310
even start. . . . Polly, I'm proud of you."

"Pshaw," she murmured, blushing with pleasure.

"You see, my dear, these things aren't so hard. All you have to do is concentrate. Think—examine—evaluate. Come now, let's review everything we have learned."   315

"Fire away," she said with an airy wave of her hand.

Heartened by the knowledge that Polly was not altogether a cretin, I began a long, patient review of all I had told her. Over and over and over again I cited instances, pointed out flaws, kept hammering away without let up. It was like digging a tunnel. At   320
first everything was work, sweat, and darkness. I had no idea when I would reach the light, or even *if* I would. But I persisted. I pounded and clawed and scraped, and finally I was rewarded. I saw a chink of light. And then the chink got bigger and the sun came pouring in and all was bright.   325

Five grueling nights this took, but it was worth it. I had made a logician out of Polly; I had taught her to think. My job was done. She was worthy of me at last. She was a fit wife for me, a proper hostess for my many mansions, a suitable mother for my well-heeled children.   330

It must not be thought that I was without love for this girl. Quite the contrary. Just as Pygmalion loved the perfect woman he had fashioned, so I loved mine. I determined to acquaint her

with my feelings at our very next meeting. The time had come
to change our relationship from academic to romantic.   335

"Polly," I said when next we sat beneath our oak, "tonight we
will not discuss fallacies."

"Aw, gee," she said, disappointed.

"My dear," I said, favoring her with a smile, "we have now
spent five evenings together. We have gotten along splendidly.   340
It is clear that we are well matched."

"Hasty Generalization," said Polly brightly.

"I beg your pardon," said I.

"Hasty Generalization," she repeated. "How can you say that
we are well matched on the basis of only five dates?"   345

I chuckled with amusement. The dear child had learned her
lessons well. "My dear," I said, patting her hand in a tolerant
manner, "five dates is plenty. After all, you don't have to eat a
whole cake to know that it's good."

"False Analogy," said Polly promptly. "I'm not a cake. I'm a   350
girl."

I chuckled with somewhat less amusement. The dear child had
learned her lessons perhaps too well. I decided to change tactics.
Obviously the best approach was a simple, strong, direct declaration of love. I paused for a moment while my massive brain chose   355
the proper words. Then I began:

"Polly, I love you. You are the whole world to me, and the
moon and the stars and the constellations of outer space. Please,
my darling, say that you will go steady with me, for if you will
not, life will be meaningless. I will languish. I will refuse my   360
meals. I will wander the face of the earth, a shambling, hollow-
eyed hulk."

There, I thought, folding my arms, that ought to do it.

"Ad Misericordiam," said Polly.

I ground my teeth. I was not Pygmalion; I was Frankenstein,   365
and my monster had me by the throat. Frantically I fought back
the tide of panic surging through me. At all costs I had to keep
cool.

"Well, Polly," I said, forcing a smile, "you certainly have
learned your fallacies."   370

"You're darn right," she said [with] a vigorous nod.

"And who taught them to you, Polly?"

"You did."

"That's right. So you do owe me something, don't you, my
dear? If I hadn't come along you never would have learned about   375
fallacies."

"Hypothesis Contrary to Fact," she said instantly.

I dashed perspiration from my brow. "Polly," I croaked, "you mustn't take all these things so literally. I mean this is just class-room stuff. You know that the things you learn in school don't   380
have anything to do with life."

"Dicto Simpliciter," she said, wagging her finger at me play-fully.

That did it. I leaped to my feet, bellowing like a bull. "Will you or will you not go steady with me?"   385

"I will not," she replied.

"Why not?" I demanded.

"Because this afternoon I promised Petey Burch that I would go steady with him."

I reeled back, overcome with the infamy of it. After he prom-   390
ised, after he made a deal, after he shook my hand! "The rat!" I shrieked, kicking up great chunks of turf. "You can't go with him, Polly. He's a liar. He's a cheat. He's a rat."

"Poisoning the Well," said Polly, "and stop shouting. I think shouting must be a fallacy too."   395

With an immense effort of will, I modulated my voice. "All right," I said. "You're a logician. Let's look at this thing logically. How could you choose Petey Burch over me? Look at me—a brilliant student, a tremendous intellectual, a man with an assured future. Look at Petey—a knothead, a jitterbug, a guy who'll never   400
know where his next meal is coming from. Can you give me one logical reason why you should go steady with Petey Burch?"

"I certainly can," declared Polly. "He's got a raccoon coat."

Note: The Stutz Bearcat was an expensive sports car, very popular in the 1920s. For information on Pygmalion, consult any dictionary of classical mythology.

1. In his first sentence the narrator reverses the subject and predicate and in the second sentence uses three exaggerated similes to describe himself. What is Shulman implying about the narrator?

2. In his description of Polly the narrator begins each of three paragraphs with a similar reversal of normal word order. What is the overall effect?

3. Which types of false reasoning does the narrator explain to Polly?

5. Which types of false reasoning does Polly discover in the narrator's pleas to "go steady" with him?

4. Check the etymology, denotation, and connotation of *incredulously* (how does it differ from "*incredibly*"?), *exquisite, gamy, pelt, waif, complied, desisted, cretin, infamy.*

ASSIGNMENTS

1. Discuss the differing kinds of particulars that would be necessary in order to justify the following general statements:
   a. We have a football team.
   b. We have a good football team.
   c. We have the best football team we have had in ten years.
   d. We have the best football team in the state.
   e. We have the best football team in the United States.

2. From one of the biological or physical sciences that you have studied, choose an example of inductive reasoning, preferably one in which you yourself have performed experiments, and write it up, showing the particulars involved and the generalization that can be drawn from them.

3. The first paragraph of Mark Twain's essay (Unit 14-D) recounts particular experiences through which he finally arrived at an understanding of the general meaning of the word *lagniappe*. Write an account either of your own gradual acquaintance with some previously unfamiliar technical word or phrase encountered since you came to college, or of how you arrived, through inquiries and listening, at the meaning of some new slang phrase not yet in the dictionaries.

4. Write an essay in which you discuss what you have found to be the prevailing opinion on your campus or among your classmates on an issue, such as working one's way through college, engaging in extracurricular activities, cheating on examinations, supporting student protesters, joining fraternities or sororities, living in coeducational dormitories. Or if you prefer, write on student opinion on some state, national, or international issue. Be sure that your generalization fits the evidence that you are able to produce and that you make allowances for the size of your sample.

5. After reading "The Language of Uncertainty" (Unit 15-C), decide what percentages you yourself might reasonably imply by, or infer from, each of the following statements. Compare your figures with those of other members of the class.
   a. Everybody voted in the election.
   b. Nearly everybody voted in the election.
   c. Most people voted in the election.
   d. Many people voted in the election.
   e. Some people voted in the election.
   f. A few people voted in the election.
   g. Nobody voted in the election.

6. To test the validity of the following statements, supply the general assumptions that underlie them and arrange them in syllogistic form. Then point out any flaws revealed in the facts or the logic.
   a. I'm glad to find that both my new chemistry professors are fat, because they're sure to be good-natured and easygoing.
   b. Jack must be at least twenty-one because he just got married.
   c. American automobiles are getting better every year: They have more equipment and more different styles and are more expensive.

    d. Maggie must be Irish because she comes from Boston, which has a large Irish population, and her name sounds Irish.

    e. Tom and Jane will never be honor students; they're both Phys Ed majors.

7. Look through a copy of a popular magazine, examining the advertisements in search of examples of deductive reasoning. Do not be discouraged by the absence of an expressed major premise in such appeals as "Use _____, the choice of thousands." Supply the underlying generalization, decide on its source (see page 308), and determine its soundness and the truth and validity of the deductions made from it. (You may have to draw up more than one syllogism in order to express all the implications of the implied reasoning.)

8. In a short story, "The Other Side of the Hedge," E. M. Forster pictures the confusion of a man from the contemporary world who enters a world where athletes run and swim for the joy of the sport, with no one to race against, and singers sing for the joy of singing, even with no one to listen. Being as objective as possible, examine the assumptions underlying some ordinary activities, such as choosing a new pair of slacks, watching a popular TV show, cheering for the home team, participating in student government, joining a fraternity or sorority, playing a musical instrument in private, playing one in public, or refusing (for reasons of time? health? morality? religion?) to enter into some activity that others indulge in and urge on you. Do not be satisfied with the first explanation that comes to mind. Push your thinking as far back into your basic assumptions as you can. When you have found a subject among these possibilities (or among others suggested by them), write an essay that makes clear the deductive logic, or lack of logic, involved.

9. Examine carefully one of your own strongly held and perhaps frequently voiced opinions, or an opinion held by a friend, a relative, a teacher, or a political leader, to determine on what assumption or assumptions it is based. Then write an essay on the subject, using deductive reasoning.

PART IV

Writing for a Larger Purpose

UNIT 16

Argumentation and Persuasion

"What she did was terrible. How can you defend her?" "The critics panned the show, but there's a great scene in it." "You're carrying your right to free speech too far—that's libel." "Despite your objections, I recommend that the committee approve this resolution."

The more a subject is open to different opinions, the more strongly you must try to persuade others to accept your views. The writers of all the examples in this book try to catch our attention and convince us that their interpretations, analyses, and deductions are correct or at least deserve consideration. Notice, for instance, how the general tone of the examples in "Process" (Unit 9) differs from that of the examples in "Induction and Deduction" (Unit 15). The writers in Unit 9 can safely assume that their readers want to learn how to do something or will quickly see the advantages of using the methods described. In Unit 15, however, the writers assume that their readers may have opposing views or that the deductions they present may not be self-explanatory. As a result, most of these writers use the techniques of argument and persuasion.

In composing a persuasive argument, you will find that all the advice and suggestions given in the earlier units are helpful and that the methods of definition, analysis, and inductive and deductive reasoning are essential. These guidelines will also help you:

1. **Define the problem that forms your subject or underlies it.** You may define it by means of description, narration, classification, analogy, analysis, or cause and effect. Most probably, you will need a combination of some of these, perhaps of all.

2. **Analyze the nature of the problem fully.** Be sure to include specific examples. Choose only the best, of course. A few good ones thoroughly explained will be more effective than a superficial description of a large number. For the analysis you will probably need to summarize, compare, contrast, and classify parts of your material. To make your presentation vivid you may need description, narration, and characterization. To make it logical, you will need induction and deduction.

3. **Include a full recognition of the opposing points of view and analyze them to show their strengths and weaknesses.** A one-sided argument convinces no one for long. Moreover, recognizing your opposition will show your fair-mindedness and the thoroughness of your research.

4. **Resist the temptation to oversimplify the problem** or the opinions of the opposition. An oversimplification may make your position seem stronger for the moment, but as soon as your readers have had time to think about it, they will realize that you are slanting the evidence. Do not, for instance, blame voter apathy alone as the cause of a low turnout in a particular election if you know that the candidates ignored local problems or that the weather was stormy on election day.

5. **Give your solution to the problem, if you have a solution, but admit it frankly if you have none.** If your solution is relatively simple and straightforward, you may be able to present it in a single section of your essay. If, however, it is complex or requires making several steps, your reader will probably follow it more easily in a presentation that takes it up point by point and relates each to the appropriate points of the problem. The advice in Unit 10 for organizing comparisons and contrasts will help you here.

6. **End with your most convincing material,** such as a brief restatement of your solution that your readers can remember easily, or a clinching example or analogy, or a quotation from an eminent authority.

7. **Support your argument throughout the main body of your essay.** Remember that your readers may know little or nothing about your subject or that they may hold views very different from yours. A mere

assertion of your opinion, with no support, will tell them only that you hold that opinion and will not change their minds. Give as much factual evidence as you can, such as statistics, historical background, newspaper reports, your own experience, your direct observation of the experience of others, and references to books and articles that present such observations. When you can, support your opinions by briefly quoting or summarizing the views of the experts.

8. **Strengthen your argument by giving your qualifications.** The less your readers are likely to know about you or the more specialized your subject is, the more fully you should describe your qualifications to write on the problem. For example, in writing to your college newspaper to support a candidate in a student election, you would need to say only how long you have been at the college and in what situations you had observed the candidate; but in writing to the editor of a newspaper with a large circulation to give your views on energy conservation, you would need to show that you have special knowledge from your academic training or practical experience. In presenting yourself, be honest about your limitations. If your readers suspect that you are exaggerating your experience or abilities, they will distrust everything you say.

9. **Appeal to your readers' interests and sympathies.** An argument based entirely on logic may convince your readers that your opinion is correct, but it may not move them to action. The most effective argument is also a persuasion. It makes readers want to do or believe what you say by appealing to their emotions. This does not mean that you should rely on a sprinkling of emotionally "loaded" words such as "foul" and "heroic." These may add drama to your essay and show the strength of your convictions, but you must go further. Whenever possible, appeal to your readers' own needs and beliefs. Elderly people in a retirement community may not see why their tax dollars should be spent on improving the playground in a local park, but if you can demonstrate that the rest of the park will be quieter and neater as a result of the playground and that outdoor activity improves children's health and social development, and if you remind them of their own childhood pleasures, you will appeal to their concern for their own comforts, to their sense of duty toward the development of good citizens, and to their sentiments. If you know that other retirement communities elsewhere have supported similar projects, you can also use the "bandwagon" effect—suggesting that your readers join the general trend.

EXAMPLES

The writers of many other selections, besides those in this unit, use the techniques of argument, persuasion, or both, in their efforts to convince their readers, most notably Jackson in "Challenge" (3-E), Ward in "Yumbo" (5-A), Wright in "A Loaf of

*Bread and the Stars" (5-B), Santiago in "Super Bowl Champions" (6-A), St. John
in "The Fifth Freedom" (8-A), Kirchoff in "The Downfall of Christmas" (10-C),
Conza in "Christmas Eve" (12-I), Asimov in "Is Anyone Listening?" (13-H),
Zinsser in "Letter from Home" (15-E), Cooper in "A Reply to Zinsser and Hiatt"
(15-G), Shulman in "Love Is a Fallacy" (15-K), Ashe in "An Open Letter to Black
Parents" (15-H), all the selections in Unit 17, and the selections by Swift, Douglass,
and King in "Essays for Further Reading" (-A, -D, and -G).*

*The following selections differ considerably in emotional intensity because they
differ in purpose and subject matter and therefore in word choice and the degree to
which they emphasize logic. Be sure to take all these features into account in judging
their effectiveness. The first two, however, and parts of the third, take different views
of the same problem—the freedom to express opinions that some may consider hateful
or immoral. In 1986 this problem became acute on a number of college campuses.
Students who protested against apartheid in South Africa and urged their universities
to stop investing in South African industries were sometimes attacked by other students
who wanted the relationship between South Africa and the United States to remain
unchanged. On another issue, students were stopped from displaying banners and
posters attacking the rights of homosexuals on their campus. In each case, freedom of
expression, the cornerstone of the Bill of Rights, was at issue. See also the speech by
Frederick Douglass on this topic ("Essays for Further Reading"-D).*

16-A   Indian Bones

Clara Spotted Elk

The writer is a consultant to the U.S. government in Washington, where she
reprsents Indian affairs. Notice that she *implies* her thesis at the end of her first
paragraph but delays the full explicit statement of it until the end of her sixth
paragraph.

Millions of American Indians lived in this country when Co-
lumbus first landed on our shores. After the western expansion,
only about 250,000 Indians survived. What happened to the
remains of those people who were decimated by the advance of
the white man? Many are gathering dust in American museums.   5
    In 1985, I and some Northern Cheyenne chiefs visited the attic
of the Smithsonian's Natural History Museum in Washington to
review the inventory of their Cheyenne collection. After a chance
inquiry, a curator pulled out a drawer in one of the scores of
cabinets that line the attic. There were the jumbled bones of an   10
Indian. "A Kiowa," he said.

Subsequently, we found that 18,500 Indian remains—some consisting of a handful of bones, but mostly full skeletons—are unceremoniously stored in the Smithsonian's nooks and crannies. Other museums, individuals and Federal agencies such as the National Park Service also collect the bones of Indian warriors, women and children. Some are on display as roadside tourist attractions. It is estimated that another *600,000* Indian remains are secreted away in locations across the country.

The museum community and forensic scientists vigorously defend these grisly collections. With few exceptions, they refuse to return remains to the tribes that wish to rebury them, even when grave robbing has been documented. They want to maintain adequate numbers of "specimens" for analysis and say they are dedicated to "the permanent curation of Indian skeletal remains."

Indian people are tired of being "specimens." The Northern Cheyenne word for ourselves is "tsistsistas"—human beings. Like people the world over, one of our greatest responsibilities is the proper care of the dead.

We are outraged that our religious views are not accepted by the scientific community and that the graves of our ancestors are desecrated. Many tribes are willing to accommodate some degree of study for a limited period of time—provided that it would help Indian people or mankind in general. But how many "specimens" are needed? We will not accept grave robbing and the continued hoarding of our ancestors' remains.

Would this nefarious collecting be tolerated if it were discovered that it affected other ethnic groups? (Incidentally, the Smithsonian also collects skeletons of blacks.) What would happen if the Smithsonian had 18,500 Holocaust victims in the attic? There would be a tremendous outcry in this country. Why is there no outcry about the Indian collections?

Indians are not exotic creatures for study. We are human beings who practice living religions. Our religion should be placed not only on a par with science when it comes to determining the disposition of our ancestors but on a par with every other religion practiced in this country.

To that end, Sen. Daniel K. Inouye will soon reintroduce the "Bones Bill" to aid Indians in retrieving the remains of their ancestors from museums. As in the past, the "Bones Bill" will most likely be staunchly resisted by the collectors of Indian skeletons—armed with slick lobbyists, lots of money and cloaked in the mystique of science.

Scientists have attempted to defuse this issue by characterizing their opponents as radical Indians, out of touch with their culture and with little appreciation of science. Armed only with a moral obligation to our ancestors, the Indians who support the bill have few resources and little money.

But, in my view, the issue should concern all Americans—for it raises very disturbing questions. American Indians want only to   60 reclaim and rebury their dead. Is this too much to ask?

1. What methods does the writer use to support and explain her thesis?

2. What methods does she use to make her pleas dramatic?

3. Read more on this topic in "The Plunder of the Past" in *Newsweek,* June 26, 1989, pp. 58–60.

4. Check the etymology, denotation, and connotations of *decimated, forensic, curation, nefarious, disposition, on a par.*

16-B   **They Breed Horses, Don't They?**

Colin Tudge

The writer combines scientific knowledge, logic, and analysis to reach his conclusion that selective breeding is unlikely to produce race horses that will run notably faster than the horses that established the first records many years ago.

Schoolboy athletes would be ashamed if they could not break virtually all the records that were set at the first modern Olympics, held in Athens in 1896. People now are just so much bigger, better fed, better trained and better equipped than in Victorian times, and are selected from a much wider pool of hopefuls. But   5 the horse that wins next week's Derby will almost certainly return roughly the same time as the winner of a century ago; not much adrift of 2 minutes 35 seconds for the 2.414 kilometres, or one-and-a-half miles as the distance is properly called. Yet modern horses, like modern athletes, are fed and trained with the aid of   10 modern science. And horses have also been subject, as humans have not, to breeding, to improve their performance even more. Why then, doesn't the breeding apparently work?

Obvious point number one is that the ability to run fast is not genetically simple. Fast runners need a hundred different assets,   15 from efficient mobilisation of glycogen, to springiness of tendon.

These characters are not necessarily linked to each other genetically, so that inheriting one does not imply inheriting all the
others. Furthermore, *each* of these characters may involve several
(or many) different genes, and when a single character is genetically complex its "heritability" (as the breeders say) may be low.
As eggs or sperms are created so the chromosomes are scrambled,
and neat little concert parties of genes that produce perfect ten-
dons in the parent may be disassembled, and rearranged to produce mediocrity in the offspring.

In short, it just isn't easy to breed for a character such as the
ability to run well. The chances of two great parents producing
an equally great or even greater offspring are by no means 100
per cent; and as horses are slow-breeding animals, the breeder
does not have too many chances to get it right.

Secondly, breeders of horses deliberately eschew at least some
of the techniques that have enabled the breeders of cattle and pigs
to make prodigious strides during this century. Because cattle
breeders know that many of the characters they are interested in
are not highly heritable (because of their genetic complexity)
those breeders do not assume that a high-performance bull will
necessarily make a good sire. Indeed they test the stud-worthiness
of all candidate bulls by testing the performance of their progeny.
Only if the first few offspring of a potential stud do well do the
breeders let it loose on the rest of the nation's cows—via the
medium of artificial insemination, which enables the most outstanding stud to produce the most offspring.

But horse breeders do not test progeny in this same rigorous
fashion. A male horse that wins races, and has not actually been
gelded, is assumed to be a good sire, and commands fees accordingly. Furthermore, artificial insemination is not allowed in racing
circles, so great combinations of genes are maintained in strictly
limited edition. This is fair enough: horse racing is supposed to
be a sport; and its rules may be as arbitrary as the enthusiasts
choose to make them. But we cannot expect the speed of horses
to improve as prodigiously as the yield of cows has done, unless
they are bred with comparable scientific rigour.

A third point—put to me by a wise vet—is that the ability to
win, among horses, is not just a matter of physique, any more than
it is among humans. Champions have qualities such as "pride"
(they like to be in front); and courage. Arkle, one of the greatest
jumpers of all time, had bad knees, but he didn't let the pain slow
him down. Of course, you could argue that a beautiful physical
specimen who also has courage is more likely to win than a brave
little weed.

But if the weeds get to win (because of their courage), the breeders are liable to breed from them; and the brave weeds' offspring are more likely to inherit their weediness than their courage, because physical weaknesses are likely to be more heritable than special traits of personality. So this psychological factor X is certainly a complication. 65

The fourth point is that the gene pool of the species *Equus caballus* may not be particularly wide: not as wide, for example, as that of the various species of *Canis* which have combined to produce our own staggering variety of domestic pooches. There 70 is variety in horses of course: from Shetland ponies to Shires. But a horse, on the whole, does look very like a horse, whereas dogs can resemble anything from a weasel (Dachshund) to an idealised Chinese lion (Pekinese) to, well, like nothing that's ever lived, such as a pug or a bulldog. 75

If the gene pool is narrow to begin with, and is already specialised to produce a one-toed cursorial quadruped (as Thomas Gradgrind put it), then there isn't too much scope for improvement. It is possible that the perfect combinations of genes have already been found; and that there is nothing to do now but multiply the 80 number of animals that possess that perfect combination. Indeed, although the speed of the best horses has not improved these past 10 decades, the general standard has been raised. The champions are no better than they were but there are many more in the first division. 85

The crux, though, I humbly suggest, is that the relative slowness of modern horses is a non-issue. There is in fact no good reason to suppose that they should run faster now than a hundred years ago. The real reason we expect them to do better is that we have all been badly educated. To be specific, we have been 90 brought up to believe that technical competence is a new phenomenon: that technology is a dead duck without science; that science did not begin until the 17th century; that technology worthy of the name did not therefore get going until the Industrial Revolution, in the late 18th century; and that anyone who 95 aspired to do anything technical before that was groping in the dark—like, as Arthur Koestler said in a slightly different context, a "sleep walker."

In fact, as Joseph Needham has been describing these past few decades (in *Science and Civilisation in China*), the technologies of 100 ancient and mediaeval China (which included inoculation against smallpox, drills for natural gas, and a thousand others) were in some respects *ahead* of anything we have today. The Ancient Greeks were fine technologists, as Richard Gregory records in

Mind in Science. The technology of Europe's Middle Ages was   105
extraordinary (see Jean Gimpel's *The Mediaeval Machine*). It just
isn't true that these ancient technologies were flawed simply because they were not based in science. Indeed, as Colin Russell
points out in *Science and Social Change*, even the technology of the
Industrial Revolution—even the steam engine, indeed—owed   110
remarkably little to science.

The point is, then, that we *assume* that modern horse breeders
are better than ancient horse breeders, simply because they are
modern, and simply because they have knowledge of the laws of
Gregor Mendel. But that is just modernism (in the sense that   115
sexism is sexism). There is in fact no good reason to assume that
the moderns are better—or to assume, indeed, that the ancients
were inferior. Gregor Mendel himself was an excellent plant
breeder *before* he got involved in genetics (and indeed could not
have discovered his laws if this had not been the case). Charles   120
Darwin wrote at length about the wonders of pigeon breeding 30
years before he wrote *On the Origin of Species*. People have been
breeding horses at least since the Hittites of Anatolia, who were
going strong in 1400 B.C. By the mid-19th century, I submit, they
had done all that needed to be done.   125

One last note. At the Berlin Olympics of 1936 Jesse Owens
recorded 9.4 seconds for the 100 yards. Fifty years later, the 100
yards is dead, but the best times for the 100 metres (by Carl Lewis
and others) are just under 10 seconds. This is only a whisker faster
than Owens—virtually the same time. But Owens was so poor as   130
a child that he lived on vegetables, in an age before this was
fashionable; and he wore running spikes, and ran on a cinder
track.

In short, there has been no significant improvement in the
men's 100 metres this past 50 years, despite the coming of science   135
and technology. The reason, we may reasonably assume, is that
10 seconds for that distance is as fast as a human being can run.

So it looks as if horses aren't so different after all.

Note: Thomas Gradgrind is a character in *Hard Times,* a novel by Charles
Dickens. He is excessively practical and believes that logic and statistics can solve
every problem.

1. Throughout the essay, the writer draws deductions based on previous evidence to give his argument a solid foundation. Give three examples.

2. Check the etymology, denotation, and connotation of *glycogen, eschew, stud,
progeny, gelded, pooches, cursorial, crux.*

89   90   91

16-C   Parents, Children, and Television

Jerome L. Singer

The writer, a professor of psychology and child study at Yale, is also codirector of Yale's Family Television Research and Consultation Center.

Just suppose that your 9-year-old child returned from school one afternoon proudly displaying the new class reading primers, somewhat simplified versions of "Fanny Hill" and the exploits of the Marquis de Sade. You and hundreds of other parents would descend the very day in righteous wrath on a beleaguered school   5 board. Why then are parents so inclined to be indifferent to the fact that their children are watching at least three to four hours of television daily, much of which depicts violence and steamy sex?

According to counts done year after year by groups such as the   10 University of Pennsylvania's Annenberg School of Communication, television is a medium on which there are hourly demonstrations of violent behavior and sexual teasing far beyond what most children in our society might encounter in an ordinary life span. Can we safely assume that children, especially younger ones, are   15 quite aware that television is sheer entertainment, a world of make-believe that bears little relation to our family life, values or daily social encounters?

Clearly the television industry does not really believe that television viewing is irrelevant to family life and our expectations of   20 it, because it charges huge sums to business advertisers who are thoroughly convinced that repeated messages about their products will influence the consciousness, values and motives of adult as well as child viewers.

Publicity concerning a recent report prepared for the U.S.   25 Department of Education by Daniel R. Anderson, a professor of psychology at the University of Massachusetts, and Patricia A. Collins, a graduate student there, has appeared to absolve television-viewing of any significant impact on children's reading or homework performance. Careful reading of the actual report,   30 which was issued in April 1988, suggests rather that the data are

in most cases not conclusive enough to provide a "guilty" verdict
against television, but they are certainly provocative enough so
that the issues warrant much more careful exploration. Indeed,
parents ought not simply accept an implication that they can ig-   35
nore their children's television viewing.

The much-quoted statement from the report that "there is no
evidence that homework done during TV viewing is of lower
quality than homework done in silence" really means that no one
has done the necessary research. Pending such studies, are we as   40
parents prepared to try to learn new algebra lessons or to memorize French verb forms while watching "Dallas" or "Wiseguy"?
Why should we expect that children can really master the complex material we want them to learn while at the same time
looking up every minute or so to watch car chases, shoot-outs or   45
MTV?

We need to recognize that children are growing up today in a
new kind of family environment, one in which children, as research indicates, are being talked to, shouted at and distracted by
a medium that provides far more verbal and visual stimulation   50
than parents ordinarily do. Of course, babies, toddlers and pre-
schoolers are not hypnotized by the medium, as the research of
Professor Anderson indicates; they look away when the material
seems difficult and return their gaze when music or sound suggests more familiar content.   55

But Professor Anderson has not measured what sense children make of all of the rapid-fire shifts, cutaways and interruptions that characterize U.S. commercial television. Several studies done at Yale and elsewhere suggest that children who are
heavy viewers of television do not become more sophisticated   60
about the medium. On the contrary. Compared to light viewers,
they seem to have accumulated less general knowledge, they
seem less able to follow the plots of TV dramas, they seem
more prone to accept as possible the train-stopping or building-
high leaps of superheroes and they are less capable of explain-   65
ing the function of commercials. Heavy viewers are also less
likely to show imaginativeness or creativity. The fragmentary
nature of television interferes with reflective thought and the
careful mental repetition of the information presented. Modern
cognitive psychology suggests that such processes are a neces-   70
sary condition for the development of consciously accessible,
voluntarily organized learning.

But do children then learn nothing from their hours of viewing? The sheer repetitiveness of some of the material, the enjoy-

ment of attending to the passing parade and thus not having to   75
notice the sometimes painful unfinished tasks and worries that
characterize our human private stream of consciousness lure us all
to turn to television for surcease and escape.

And yet, the repeated messages on fictional television are full
of violence, car chases and threats. No wonder that heavy-view-   80
ing children, especially those who watch violent action-adventure
programming, are more likely to believe that deceit and danger
surround them in their own neighborhoods, as our Yale studies
show. Repeated follow-up studies by Leonard Eron and Rowell
Huesmann of the University of Illinois in Chicago have indicated   85
that heavy viewing in childhood foreshadows overt aggression 10
and 20 years later.

Studies in other countries support their findings. Research that
my wife Dorothy and I have conducted at Yale during the past
dozen years reveals that child viewers of the more violent car-   90
toons and adult shows are more likely to be aggressive and restless later on in middle childhood.

In some of our research, we have interviewed and observed
parents, and we find that some can be characterized as regularly
using discussion and explanation about the world and about tele-   95
vision with their children. At the other extreme are parents whose
communications with their children consist chiefly of peremptory
commands such as "Stop that!" or "Leave your sister alone" but
who rarely filter the real or TV world for their children with
explanation or commentary. The children of the "mediating"   100
parents turn out to be relatively more immune to the negative
effects of television, and they understand much better what commercials are.

No one who knows the violent history of our country would
attribute all current violence to TV-watching. There is ample   105
evidence that growing up in an aggressive family is the best
predictor of unwarranted aggression in children. But even an
incremental effect upon those millions of children growing up
watching 30 to 40 hours weekly of television is an ongoing phenomenon we cannot treat lightly.   110

There is no argument with Professor Anderson that more research is needed on the cognitive impact of TV-viewing. But,
meanwhile, do you want the purveyors of violence and commer-
cialism on the TV screen to become dominant influences on your
children, or are you prepared by monitoring, controlling and   115
discussing the medium to try to insure that your own family values
will prevail?

Note: *The Memoirs of Fanny Hill* by John Cleland was a pornographic novel published in England in 1748–49. The Marquis de Sade (1740–1814) spent most of his adult life in prison in France and died there in an insane asylum. In his novels *Justine* (1791) and *Juliet* (1798) he describes obtaining sexual pleasure by inflicting physical pain on the beloved; this perversion, now known as sadism, was named for him.

1. What specific examples does the writer give to explain and support his argument?

2. Where and how does he use questions to emphasize his main points?

3. In your opinion, how practical is the solution he recommends in the last paragraph?

4. Check the etymology, denotation, and connotation of *exploits, beleaguered, span, provocative, cognitive, surcease, overt, peremptory, mediating, unwarranted, incremental, purveyors.*

16-D   Socializing Our Children with Television

Sue Lin Peng *(student)*

This essay was written as an in-class exercise in an advanced composition course. The assigned topic was "Should Parents 'Pull the Plug' on Their Television Sets?" Compare the argument and presentation with those in example 16-E, which is by a student in the same class, and 16-C, by a Yale psychologist.

Television is probably the true "opiate of the masses," not religion, as Karl Marx thought. As one of the primary socializing agents, television has two major built-in faults: the one-way nature of the act of watching and the dependence on the sponsors for the choice of programming. These faults make it a dangerous   5
influence on children, many of whom spend an excessive amount of time watching TV, time which would formerly have been spent in other activities.

Television is, by its very nature, a passive medium, inducing a trance-like stare in small children, basking in the light of the   10
cathode ray tube. Although this condition can also be observed in adults, the grown-ups supposedly have a sense of themselves, a life outside of the box. They've been socialized and can better

edit and judge what they view. Children do not have such defenses.   15

The dependence of children on television would be more positive if what is shown were less reprehensible. Most shows for children are violent, mindless cartoons or neo-fascist superman "heroes." Worse yet, such shows subject unformed, receptive minds to an endless flow of commercials. This cynical process   20 gains the sponsors access to parents' money by inculcating in children desires for the worst kinds of zero-nutrition junk food and over-priced toys. To insure that the children are attentive enough to receive these messages, what comes with the hardsell must be loud and kinetic, regardless of the effect such bombard-   25 ment may have on children.

The process of socialization takes place very rapidly in younger children and should give them skills that will carry over into adult life. Learning to interact with others and acquiring the values that most American parents find important for their children to have   30 must be taught; such things are not instinctual. By the sheer amount of time television takes up in some children's lives, other better agents of socialization are relegated to secondary roles. Parents, schools, religious organizations, and peers are much better agents for teaching children about the world and themselves.   35

If parents care about how their children think and what their children think, they had better start caring about how much television their children watch and what kinds of programs their children choose. Television is like a mind-altering drug. Its side effects are bad enough, but its long-range damage may be much   40 worse, creating a generation of zombie-consumers who cannot think for themselves or relate to each other.

1. What use does the writer make of analogy?

2. Where and how does the writer show cause and effect to support her argument?

3. Where and how does the writer use inductive and deductive reasoning?

16-E   Caution: Watching TV May Be Hazardous

Gerry Lightfoot (student)

This essay was written as an in-class exercise on the assigned topic "Should Parents 'Pull the Plug' on Their Television Sets?" Compare it with the preceding essay on the same topic by another student in the class.

Through the years, television has become increasingly important in our lives. It has become our most important and widely shared form of entertainment, especially for children. It has also become a vehicle for influencing children.

Television-watching is on the increase, making its influence   5 continually more dangerous. It is not the watching itself that is dangerous, but the types of programs one watches and the commercials accompanying them. To understand the truth of that remark, one has only to look at what the networks are televising these days. None of the programs is realistic; they are all exagger-   10 ation and fantasy, and they do not show life as it really is. In addition, these programs instill the wrong values in our children by repeatedly showing murder, domestic violence, contempt for society, deceit, and unhealthy competitiveness. Because children are extremely impressionable, they are strongly influenced by   15 what they see on such programs. What our children are learning from TV probably accounts for much of the antisocial behavior that the young exhibit today, and it may also account for the alarming increase in the crime rate among the young.

I do not blame only the television networks or producers. I   20 place a substantial share of the blame on our government and on the major companies that advertise on TV. The government is just as much responsible for offensive programming as are networks and producers because the government is lax in applying restrictions. The government already bans commercials for ciga-   25 rettes and hard liquor; it is time for them to regulate the types of programs allowed on the air and the hours when programs can be shown so as not to expose children to unhealthy, immoral, and unrealistic material.

The companies that advertise, however, are the biggest culprits   30 in exploiting the minds of the young. They use the power of

television to play what I call "the sucker game," and their attempts to sell us "once in a lifetime opportunities" and "swamp-
land" are despicable. Commercials almost never contain realistic
situations; they present fast-paced, colorful lies. The advertisers   35
will go to any lengths to sell, and they deliberately gear their
commercials to the young people who watch television, knowing
full well that they are the most vulnerable viewers. The major
advertisers must be made accountable for what they try to sell and
to whom.   40

     Our children are destroying themselves by watching television
so much. Their actions are shaped by their environment and by
what they think that environment is. TV programming and commercials have helped distort the perception of what is real and
what is not, ultimately shaping our society the way it is now. For   45
the sake of our children and our society, television must be better
regulated and the young must be discouraged from watching
television.

Where and how does the writer use cause and effect? analysis? inductive and
deductive reasoning?

16-F   The Australia-Siberia Solution

Ruth Limmer

     Limmer, formerly director of publications at Hunter College in the City Univer-
sity of New York, now devotes herself full time to writing. This essay, here complete,
first appeared in the *New York Times* in 1989 as part of a series, "Anarchy in the
Streets," on urban problems. Her purpose is serious, but her style is very informal,
with many short questions and contractions. Her use of the pronoun "I" implies her
strong personal concern with the problems she describes.

     Enough statistics, O.K.? Let's just agree that crime, justice, jails,
rehabilitation all present mind-boggling problems. Fine, now let's
move ahead.

     We can define crime as something that offends community
attitudes and sensibilities. (If it didn't offend, we wouldn't want   5
to punish it.) So what offends? Murder? Rape? Insider trading?
Crack? Double parking? Cheating on SAT's? The answer must
surely be that different communities have different sensibilities,

but that some forms of behavior offend all communities—and we all wish the perpetrators gone from us.

That's important. Communities should be able to say: You have passed beyond any behavior we can condone or explain or permit.

Society should be able to say to the "wilding" rapists in Central Park, for example, and to every other criminal who violates another human being in similarly monstrous ways: You terrify us. We fear you and we are right to fear you. We don't want you around.

What we can't agree on is whether, when found guilty, these offenders should be awarded scholarships to graduate schools of criminality and despair or be put to death. I'll not argue for either. I'll merely note that life sentences, including eventual geriatric care, cost more money than I enjoy coughing up.

Moreover, although I'm not philosophically opposed to the death penalty, it seems always to be carried out years after I've forgotten why I thought the perpetrator especially deserved it. Revenge is small beer when you can't remember why you wanted it.

There is, however, a solution we haven't considered: the Australia-Siberia solution. Devil's Island. Exile.

Isn't it time to think about sending the murderously violent away—not to a cell in a shockingly expensive, grimly run hotel for criminals but to a place (island? territory?) where they can apply surplus energy to building shelter, finding and growing food and managing their own lives?

Perhaps we could turn one or more of the Aleutian Islands over to criminal colonies. The location matters not, so long as it is truly unpleasant: cold, distant, uninhabited.

Lawless, violent people are obviously our own product. We reap what we have sown. Having proved we are incapable of establishing a just, humane, crime-free society, we'd do well to step out of the way of a new society in the creation.

The potential colonists have committed crimes so heinous that the stain and shame must necessarily infect those we might ask to live and work in contact with them.

Moreover, if we leave the colonists to their own devices, those who conquer the elements and survive may (or may not, it's up to them) become prideful, coping, independent men and women.

Our job, and perhaps the only one that we can be sure to do well, is to supply items like lumber, nails, tools, copies of "Robinson Crusoe," technical manuals, vegetable seeds and perhaps a couple of pairs of rabbits.

In other words, raw materials but no luxuries: no generators, no TV sets, no branch post offices, and no jailers, no wardens, no doctors, no chaplains.   55

Better we apply their wages to mending ourselves. Better that we turn the money we spend operating death rows and isolation cells over to the innocent needful—to babies who need better nutrition, to toddlers who need day care, to youngsters who need good education.   60

Anyone who thinks I'm not serious deserves to read the feasibility and environmental-impact studies that would be required before the plan was put into effect.

You can guess the contents: complaints that the Aleutians are "strategic" (so, in a far more meaningful way, is Central Park);   65 that the climate is too fierce (American soldiers served there during World War II); that prisoners would escape because friends could get them out via plane, helicopter, boat (possibly, but few prisoners would); that without jailers, they might kill each other (better each other than us), and, that as a punishment, exile   70 is cruel and unusual (what is more cruel than prison or more traditional—think of Adam and Eve—than exile?).

Note: The mention of "the 'wilding' rapists in Central Park" (lines 12–13) refers to a dramatically violent crime committed in New York City in April 1989 that attracted nationwide publicity.

1. Where and how does the writer answer opposing arguments that might be raised against her suggestion?

2. Where are the Aleutian Islands?

3. Where is Devil's Island and which European country used to send prisoners there?

4. Check the etymology, denotation, and connotation of *condone, small beer, heinous, feasibility.*

16-G

The Hands of Anger, Frustration, Humiliation

Editorial from the *Iowa City Press-Citizen*

The anonymous writer uses an emotional appeal to strengthen the argument. The essay, here complete, was first published in December, 1985, the day after Dale Burr, a 63-year-old farmer near Iowa City, faced with the loss of his land and of all his livestock and equipment, killed the president of the bank to which he owed money he could not repay, his wife, and then himself. The tragedy gives a dramatic illustration of the financial difficulties that continue to affect many farm families.

Imagine for a minute that tomorrow, your boss tells you that for the next twelve months, you're going to earn only two-thirds of your salary. You can't quit your job.

What would you do? Quick.

The mortgage payment is already a week overdue. The kids   5
need boots, and it's snowing. Quick.

The last two checks you wrote bounced, and the bank wouldn't pay them. The pediatrician's bill is overdue. The corner grocery store won't let you put anything on your charge account. Quick.

Your spouse is angry; you're not holding up your end of the   10
deal. What are you going to do? Quick.

Your father and grandfather have done the same job as you're doing now. They went through the Depression. They lived on pork and potatoes, and they made it. You are the third generation. You're blowing it. Think fast. You don't have much time.   15
Weeks, maybe months.

The pressure builds, the stress is stronger. You keep going to work, hanging on. It doesn't matter. Nothing you do matters. You are powerless.

This is the kind of thing Dale Burr probably felt. And it is the   20
kind of thing many other Iowa farmers feel every day.

There are accounts of bank transactions and economic explanations and other hypotheses as the murder and suicide story unrav-
els. But that's not what it is really all about. It's about people—
alone, desperate and powerless with nowhere to turn.   25

Once the Burrs were one of the wealthier families in the

county. They were well-thought-of people. Salt of the earth. Churchgoers. A family of farmers carrying on a tradition. That was a year or two ago. That's how fast things crumble.

Target prices, price supports, ceilings, sealing crops. The termi-   30
nology doesn't matter. It's welfare. Farmers know it. And farmers are proud people. Nobody really wants to live that way. But for now, there is no choice.

Many Iowa farmers already have taken deep pay cuts. They've scaled down operations. They've swallowed their pride—gone to   35
stress clinics, sought therapy, stood in line at the market with food stamps in their pockets.

Some of it was bad judgment. Some of it was bad luck. The mid-1970's was a boom time for Iowa agriculture, but everyone else caught on. Physicians' fees rose, hospital costs rose, the cost   40
of cars and homes and tractors and loans and mortgages and a college education rose. Then the bottom fell out—for farmers. Now things are so out of kilter that people who once were pillars of their communities are falling into poverty, depression and disrepute.   45

This is the farm crisis—the people who are alive and hanging on, and those who have died at the hands of anger, frustration, humiliation. And they are here.

Politicians tell us it is only a matter of balancing the books, that if we can reduce the deficit, deflate the value of the dollar, in-   50
crease exports and give the free market rein—then, everything will be all right.

But if there's one thing that is clear from Monday's tragic series of murders and suicide, it is that the farm crisis is *not* numbers and deficits and bushels of corn. It is people and pride and tears and   55
blood.

The time has come for the state and the county to reach out to farmers who are suffering—not because they are failed business-men and women, but because they are human beings whose lives are falling apart—fast.   60

1. What specific details in this editorial are probably intended to appeal to the interests and sympathies of the newspaper's readers?

2. What kind of ending has the writer chosen?

3. Compare this editorial as argumentative and persuasive writing with McCarthy's "The Death Penalty for a Teenage Killer?" (16-I) or with Douglass's "A Plea for Free Speech in Boston" ("Essays for Further Reading"-D). Which essay do you find more persuasive and why?

16-H   Do Workers Have a Right to
                        a Job?

Elias Weatherly *(student)*

This essay was written in class. The assigned topic was the question that forms
the title and that had been part of a general discussion at the preceding class meeting.
Most of the other students had argued that the government has the responsibility of
providing jobs for all who need them. This writer takes an opposing view.

Workers do not have a right to a job. Rights are decided by
members of a political entity and are contained within a written
or understood and accepted constitution. Rights are not decided
by individuals; individuals can assert rights that each would wish
to be allowed, but if these rights are not ratified by the actual or   5
implied consent of their fellow citizens, then they are illusory.
The thirteen colonies contained people who felt that laws should
be made with the consent of the governed, yet the English king
and parliament did not recognize that right. Therefore, it did not
exist as far as they were concerned. Force of arms had to be used   10
to persuade them; it was more than simple persuasion; it was war,
separation, and the formation of a new political entity in which
this was a central right.
    Rights must exist within a political, economic, social, and reli-
gious matrix; the mother of rights is the consent of the governed.   15
In the case of American workers, within an established matrix, the
right to work does not uniformly exist—if at all. The state of
Alabama, for example, still has right-to-work laws. The nomenclature is inaccurate, for it clearly means that business owners and
managers do not recognize the right of a person to have a job,   20
to organize a constituency to lobby for that right, and to use the
political process to have the right to a job legislated.
    Even in states without right-to-work laws, the right to a job is
not clear; there are property rights which limit or negate such a
right. Under capitalism, a system based on the understood owner-   25
ship of one's self, which means that one can therefore reap the
profits from one's ideas, labor, and capital, these property rights
have a strong hold over the capitalists and the workers. It is an
ideology which says that "I own this job" and that "I can hire
whom I please." This is in conflict with the assertion of a non-   30

propertied person who may wish to have that job. But there are
limits to the capitalist ideal. Unions are recognized by the federal
government; the National Labor Relations Board has rules and
guidelines that govern the relations between management and
labor; the federal judiciary has rulings, based on the fourteenth   35
and nineteenth amendments, that affect who can be hired, fired,
or retired, and how and when. With these limitations on the
actions of employers though, it still cannot be clearly shown that
there is a *right* to a job.

Rights are not opinions (unless of a federal court); rights are   40
not the sectarian beliefs of a particular group; rights allow a
person in a society to perform acts that have been agreed upon
by the citizens of that society.

1. Where does the writer recognize opposing views?

2. Where does the writer use the following to develop and support his argument: analysis, definition, historical background?

3. Check the etymology, denotation, and connotation of *ratified, illusory, matrix,
nomenclature, sectarian.*

16-I   The Death Penalty for a
                    Teenage Killer?

Colman McCarthy

This essay, here complete, was first published in the *Chicago Sun-Times* on
December 27, 1985. In November 1986 an essay in *Newsweek* on teenage murderers
reported that 1,311 murderers under eighteen were arrested in 1985, slightly less
than the average for the last eight years, and that 37 of them were awaiting execution.
The article also reported that 26 states now permit the execution of criminals under
eighteen and that a Justice Department study commission has recommended that
murderers under fifteen be treated as adults, a view that the writer of this essay
opposes. (**Note:** The essay is split into many short paragraphs because it was first
printed in unusually narrow newspaper columns that made the paragraphs seem
longer.)

On January 10, James Terry Roach is scheduled to be executed
by the state of South Carolina.

Roach was convicted of homicide in late 1977. He was sen-
tenced to die and has been a Death Row inmate in a Columbia,
S.C., prison since.   5

Roach's case would be slipping by as one more muffled note in the executioner's song except for his age at the time he is said to have murdered: he was seventeen.

Until now, killing adult criminals has been the American way, but not the killing of people who committed crimes as children.   10

Roach's case is being noticed for another reason. He has appealed to the Inter-American Commission on Human Rights, a group within the Organization of American States.

By going to the OAS commission, Roach is making an appeal to international law with a hope of success that he has not won   15
from domestic law. Both the judicial system of South Carolina and the federal courts system, including the Supreme Court, have refused to overturn his death sentence.

Roach's petitioning lawyers—Professor David Weissbrodt of the University of Minnesota and Mary McClymont of the   20
ACLU Prison Project—agree that appealing to the OAS commission is not the standard approach. But it is firmly grounded in the law.

The United States is a member of the OAS. It is subject to the jurisdiction of the Inter-American Commission on Human   25
Rights.

Among the nations of the world, including those in the OAS, the execution of child criminals is rare. Forty-one nations, including the Soviet Union and Poland, forbid it. Executing criminals of any age does not occur in any of the Western industrial nations,   30
except for the United States.

In South Carolina, only clemency from the governor can save Roach.

Another reason exists for extending mercy to Roach. He is anything but the maniacal killer that is the public image of the   35
condemned.

At the time of his involvement in the killing of two juveniles— fourteen and fifteen—his worst previous offense was stealing his father's car to visit a brother in Florida.

Roach was borderline mentally retarded. At his trial, his IQ was   40
reported to be between 68 and 76. He is genetically at risk to Huntington's Chorea, an incurable neurological disease.

Michael Farrell, a Philadelphia attorney who is helping Roach without charge and was involved in the case before the appeal to the OAS, reports that it was never established that Roach pulled   45
the trigger that killed the two teenagers.

He was one of three involved in the crime. The oldest of the trio, who was twenty-four, already has been executed. The youngest, a fifteen-year-old at the time of the murders, testified for the state and is serving a life sentence.   50

No purpose is served in killing any criminal, least of all of a
retarded juvenile.

In a new book, *Who Is the Prisoner,* George Lundy, S.J., the
director of the Institute of Human Relations at Loyola University
in New Orleans, writes that punishment should accomplish four   55
ends: restore what was lost to the victim, provide rehabilitation,
apply equally to all classes of people, and be no harsher than
necessary. As a punishment, death fails on each.

For James Roach, as well as the thirty-five others facing execution for crimes committed under age eighteen, there is a fifth   60
failure: the state seeking vengeance on criminals who were children, the weakest of all.

1. In what different ways does McCarthy support his argument?

2. Where does McCarthy place the first statement of his position?

3. What kind of beginning has McCarthy chosen? Why?

16-J   Literacy Be Damned

Sir Edmund Leach

The writer of this essay, here complete, makes a deliberately provocative attack
on the traditional importance of being able to read and write. He is a member of the
faculty of King's College, Cambridge University, England. Compare his views with
those presented by Donald Hall in "Bring Back the Out-Loud Culture" (13-G).

So after all, despite increased national expenditure on education, academic standards are falling; half the school-leaving
population is illiterate; and so on and so forth. This old-fashioned chorus certainly provides food for thought, but I am
sceptical.   5

I hold it as self-evident that the content of education changes
with fashion and that such changes reflect a positive adaptation to
shifts in the structure of society. As the young Marx put it: "In
every epoch the ruling ideology *(Gedanken)* is the ideology of the
ruling class." For more than a century it has been accepted as   10
dogma that proficiency in the basic skills of reading, writing and
arithmetic is the necessary foundation for any form of universal
school education, but this antiquated fetish was linked historically

with the rise of industrial capitalism and the epoch of European colonial expansion, so perhaps it may be on the way out.

Let me throw a few stray facts into the cauldron.

(a) It seems very likely that Homer could neither read nor write.

(b) There have been many wide-ranging and highly sophisticated political regimes which got along very nicely without reading, writing or arithmetic—the Peruvian Empire of the Incas for example.

(c) Educated human beings of one sort or another must have been around for 50,000 years or more but most of the languages which are today recognized as suitable vehicles for primary school education were only committed to writing less than a century ago. This operation was the work of Christian missionaries who believed that in order to achieve personal salvation it is necessary to read the Bible. The practical effect of such education was to destroy the existing indigenous arts and crafts, which the school children concerned might otherwise have learned, and to produce a superfluity of cheap clerical labor for the white colonialists.

(d) Electronic calculators which can perform all the operations that the average school-leaver is expected to understand can be bought for less than the price of half a dozen visits to the cinema or a dozen pints of beer.

(e) Tape recorders and typewriters provide a much more efficient means of recording speech than any form of calligraphy (either shorthand or longhand).

(f) Signatures can be forged; thumbprints cannot.

(g) The skills of shorthand and typewriting are palpably more useful than the ability to write longhand. But what proportion of school-leavers have been encouraged to learn either?

(h) Written texts, whether in books or in documents, tend to be valued because they can be made unambiguous. But this specious clarity is achieved only at great cost. Since the real world of experience is not one-dimensional and linear, it follows that by gearing our whole educational system to the written word we automatically teach our young to misinterpret their environment.

(i) Laboratory monkeys quickly learn to recognize the scenes that they are shown on a TV screen and the judgments they make about such scenes seem to be very like human judgments.

This surely has implications for human education. Why be complicated when you can be simple? When we listen to speech we decode directly the message received through the ears; when we observe the world we decode directly the message received through the eyes. But if I write a letter I first have to think in words and then transform those words into sensitive movements of my fingers. Conversely, when I read a letter I must first transform a visual message into an aural message "in the mind." No doubt it is very remarkable that we are able to do this, but the acquisition of such skills is in itself very much a circus trick which has no special merit except perhaps that it gives us a comfortable feeling that we are superior to monkeys.

Today, when tape recorders, TV screens, radios, electronic calculators and computers are so readily available, a great deal of this effort is quite unnecessary. A few centuries from now the study of twentieth-century alphabetical texts will have become the quaint specialism of a few learned academics, the equivalent of the tiny coterie of present-day scholars who can read ancient Egyptian in its cursive hieratic form.

Let me be more positive. If it is true (which I rather doubt) that among the school-leaving populatin a general competence in the three R's is on the decline, this may be because the young have a clearer understanding than their elders both about what is available and what is worthwhile in their cultural environment. Reading, writing, and arithmetic are still basic skills if you want to end up as a synthetic member of the nineteenth-century liberal middle class or as a still more synthetic member of the nineteenth-century Whig aristocracy, but these categories no longer represent "the ruling class," and the associated cultural values (despite their continued gross overrepresentation in the school curricula) are no longer the dominant cultural ideology.

On a world scale, *all* information which is conveyed in normal linguistic form, either in speech or in writing, is socially divisive; it favors those who speak that particular language as their mother tongue and excludes all the rest. By contrast, information which is conveyed in nonverbal form—e.g., as traffic signs, silent cinema, silent TV, or in special "international" symbolic languages such as that employed in mathematics—is socially cohesive; it draws African, Asian, European and American into one world.

The art of writing started out as a secret code through which a literary elite exercised bureaucratic control over the illiterate masses. Later, when literature became internationalized as a channel of communication, the medieval literati, both in Europe and in Asia, had the good sense to operate with a very limited number of much simplified languages. But then came the Fall. Gutenberg gave us the fruit of the Tree of the Knowledge of Good and Evil. As the printed word proliferated we became more and more aware of how different we are; today there are the literate Saved and the illiterate Damned, but even among the Saved we go out of our way to be mutually incomprehensible.

Literacy, in the form in which we at present know it, does not deserve its status as the sacred cow of basic education.   105

1. In what specific ways does Leach appeal to the reader's interests and sympathies?

2. What kind of conclusion has he chosen for his essay?

3. Check the etymology, denotation, and connotation of *dogma, fetish, palpably, specious, cursive, hieratic, literati.*

ASSIGNMENTS

1. Reread the examples in this unit. Is there an author with whom you disagree, wholly or in part? If so, write an argumentative essay of about 500 words replying to the author.

2. Choose a recent editorial from your college or local newspaper and write a 500-word argumentative essay, directed to the paper's readers, explaining why you agree or disagree with it. If you agree, be sure to support your argument in ways and with material not used in the original.

3. What improvement do you think is most needed in the neighborhood in which you live? Write an argumentative essay urging the residents and the appropriate officials to make the improvement. Be sure to choose something specific such as a traffic light at a dangerous intersection, better parking facilities in a particular area, a summer recreation program for children, a stricter enforcement of regulations about unleashed dogs, or a bigger selection of books and magazines in the public library.

4. What change do you think is most needed at the college or university you are attending? Choose something specific and write an argumentative essay urging the other students or the appropriate members of the faculty or administration to make the change.

5. What annoying or dangerous habit does one of your friends or a member of your family have that you think can be corrected? Write a tactful argument persuading him or her to break the habit.

UNIT 17

Critical Writing

When you criticize something, do you look only for faults? or do you also look for good points?

Criticism, in the larger sense, is not mere fault-finding but an analysis of strengths as well as weaknesses. It is a dissection and evaluation of all the characteristics of a particular subject. Most of your college instructors will ask you to write critically about assigned readings, such as scholarly articles, chapters of a book, whole books, and works of literature. They will expect you to go beyond what you may have written for high school "book reports," which were probably only summaries of your reading. Instead, you will be expected to compare, contrast, evaluate, and reach conclusions on what an author has to say.

In choosing a subject, you may, depending on the assignment, criticize a complete work, covering all its main points and the methods of presentation, or concentrate on a particular aspect or section. Professional book reviewers, drama and music critics, and so on, cover a whole work or performance because they are writing about new ones and therefore must give their readers an overall view. But critics writing on an established work usually concentrate on a section or an aspect of it that they think has been neglected by the critics or inaccurately evaluated or interpreted.

You are unlikely, for example, to have anything new to say about the whole of Shakespeare's *Hamlet,* at least until you have become an authority on Shakespeare, but you may have some interesting thoughts on a small element of the play, such as one of the minor characters, or two or three lines in an important speech. You may also find that a comparison and contrast between a minor character in *Hamlet* and one in another of Shakespeare's plays sheds light on one or both characters.

A specific critical approach may help you to form a new interpretation. In writing about a minor character in *Hamlet,* for example, you might consider primarily that character's psychology as revealed in words and actions, explaining to your readers the exact psychological theory you are applying and why you chose it. You might examine the same character from a historical point of view to determine Shakespeare's degree of accuracy in portraying the attitudes and customs of a historical period, his own or an earlier one. You might apply linguistic analysis to the words in several lines, determining both their etymology and use by Shakespeare's contemporaries, to arrive at a fuller understanding of his use of language.

When writing on something that others have already criticized, you should take their criticism into account and tell your readers why there is room for another view—yours. The professional criticism can itself be a subject for a critical paper. Instead of giving a new interpretation of a minor character in *Hamlet,* you could show why the interpretation by critic X is better than the interpretations by critics W, Y, and Z—assuming, of course, that X made little or no reference to W, Y, and Z, because if X attacked them effectively you will probably have nothing significant to add.

To find a subject for a critical paper, apply the same principles you used to find subjects for the other kinds of writing discussed in this book. The broader your topic is and the more familiar it is to others, the less likely you are to have something new and forceful to say. Just as you were advised in Unit 1, you should narrow your topic so that you can handle it thoroughly and have something fresh to say.

In writing any criticism, you will find helpful all the skills discussed earlier, particularly analysis, classification, comparison, and definition. Whatever methods you use, be sure to include the four points in this guideline:

1. **Classify the work with which you are dealing.** For example, if it is a written work, you must tell your readers whether it is a biography, a novel, a report on an economic survey, a political analysis, and so on. You must also tell them what areas it covers and to which readers it seems directed. A dictionary, as Mark Twain remarked humorously, can scarcely be blamed for having little plot. Similarly, we apply one set of critical standards

to an article on a particular problem in foreign policy if the article appears in a scholarly journal and a rather different set of standards to another article on the same problem that appears in a general circulation magazine.

2. **Indicate the scope and nature of your critical approach.** If you are going to limit your discussion to a minor character in *Hamlet,* tell your readers exactly that and explain your interest in that character. If you are going to base your criticism on a psychological theory, define that theory and say why you are using it.

3. **Summarize the content of the work.** An adequate summary gives your criticism a firm foundation; however, be brief—include only the essential features of the work, and remember that your main purpose is to criticize it, not to save your readers the effort of reading it for themselves. It is customary to use the present tense to summarize the main actions of any narrative, whatever the literary form, because you then have the past and future tenses to refer to events before and after the part of the narrative under immediate consideration. With paintings, musical compositions, and other works in nonverbal media, give a brief description. If the work is very well known, *Hamlet,* for example, or Beethoven's Fifth Symphony, a summary or description is not necessary, but be sure to let your readers know which section you are discussing so that they can recognize it quickly and easily. (**Note:** for a discussion of summary writing, read the introductory section of Unit 7.)

4. **Interpret and evaluate the work by using as many of the skills discussed earlier as are appropriate.** Make your remarks convincing by using the argumentative methods discussed in Unit 16. Have the courage of your convictions and do not feel intimidated by the fame of the writer or artist whose work you are criticizing or of the critics with whom you disagree. As in argumentative writing, use objective analysis and logic as the basis of your criticism and rely on emotional words and phrases only to add vitality and color to it. Be sure to explain how your interpretation and evaluation resembles or differs from those of major critics. Support your remarks with specific illustrations from the work and with any relevant information, such as the historical background, and explain how the illustrations and information support them.

Satire is a special kind of criticism. Writers use it to attack something they think is wrong. Instead of stating their beliefs and objections directly, they take the risk of being indirect. They try to make their readers think for themselves and look through the literal meaning on the surface to the deeper meaning. By their doing this, successful satire can often be more effective than straightforward critical writing. Only a few specialists are now familiar with Jonathan Swift's direct attack on the causes of poverty in eighteenth-century Ireland but his satiric attack, "A Modest Proposal," has become such a classic that any piece now using that title immediately announces to every educated reader that it is satiric.

To be made fun of is always more painful than simply to be scolded, and satire makes what it attacks ridiculous. It may grossly **exaggerate,** as Orwell does in his novel *1984* by taking totalitarian control far beyond what it had reached when the book was published in 1949. It may **reverse** the facts, as Swift does in the fourth book of *Gulliver's Travels,* with human beings (the Yahoos) as savage beasts and with horses (the Houyhnhnms) as intelligent, virtuous creatures. Or it may **transfer** the situation to a different area where its ridiculousness will be apparent, as a writer annoyed by the excesses of time-and-motion studies in a government bureau once did when he applied the efficiency experts' principles to conducting a symphony orchestra.

When you write satire, whatever your method, make sure that your readers will know that it is satire. If you choose exaggeration, you must exaggerate grossly; if you choose to reverse or transfer the facts, you must give clues to your satiric purpose early in your essay.

EXAMPLES

Criticism is the primary purpose of the writers in the selections in this unit, but it has an important part in many other selections in this book, beginning with Dawn Gorlitsky's second essay on Billy Joel in Unit 1, and appearing notably in Jackson's "Challenge" (3-E), Michaels' "Out, Out Foul Phrases" (3-G), Santiago's "Super Bowl Champions" (6-A), Davenport's " 'Trees' " (7-A), Zinsser's "Clutter" (8-D), Kirchoff's "The Downfall of Christmas" (10-C), Quindlen's It's Not That I Don't Like Men" (10-E), Uesugi's "Greed" (12-D), Conza's "Christmas Eve" (12-I), Satriale's "Dix Hills: The Grown-Ups' Toy" (13-E), Hall's "Bring Back the Out-Loud Culture" (13-G), Zinsser's "Letter from Home" (15-E), Cooper's "A Reply to Zinsser and Hiatt" (15-G), Ashe's "An Open Letter to Black Parents" (15-H), Kagan's " 'Your Mother Did It to You' " (15-I), and all the selections in Unit 16.

The critical methods in the following examples can be applied to any subject. Since most of your critical writing in college will be on what you read, six of the examples are criticisms of written works. The first five show some of the many critical approaches possible even when the work—in this case Shakespeare's Romeo and Juliet*—has been criticized many times before. Because all the writers include enough information on the play to make their points clear,* **you do not need to have read the play to follow their criticism.**

Of the remaining examples, notice particularly Manuela's "Robert Coles' Privileged Ones" (17-F), a good example of the kind of essay often required in courses in the social sciences.

17-A   Misadventures in Verona

Brendan Gill

These paragraphs begin a review of a 1977 production of Romeo and Juliet. *The writer, the chief drama critic for* The New Yorker, *first states his general opinion of the production—it was "an honorable failure"—and then, to show the basis for his judgment, gives his interpretation of the play. In the rest of the review, omitted here, he explains how the production failed to fulfill his expectations.*

The new production of *Romeo and Juliet* at the Circle in the Square is an honorable failure. The director of the play, Theodore Mann, has evidently worked hard with a large and motley cast, but he is not known for having a light touch, and, oddly enough, it is a light touch that the play requires. For *Romeo and Juliet* is a   5
tragedy that must be played as if it were a comedy, or it won't succeed; tether it to solemnity and it becomes an earthbound recounting of a series of preposterous misadventures. Because its tone is continually at odds with its content, it is a play far more difficult to perform than one would expect from a mere reading   10
acquaintance with it. From first to last, bodies pile up on the stage at a fearful rate, and the emotions aroused in us by a carnage almost as ample as that in *Hamlet* ought surely to be pity and terror, but no such thing: the language of the play is so lyrical, so springlike, so charged with the energetic hopefulness of first   15
love that we scarcely take in the grim evidence of our senses. After an ideal performance, we leave the theatre elated rather than deeply moved, remembering Romeo and Juliet not as corpses in a tomb but as dear, harmless, amorous children. Though Romeo takes two men's lives and is a suicide, these   20
formidable offenses against God and the state strike us, in their romantic context, as only mildly reprehensible. Moreover, if *Romeo and Juliet* were an authentic tragedy instead of a nominal one, the protagonists would be, of course, Capulet and Montague, who by their senile pride and other flaws of character bring   25
ruin to those presumably dearest to them.
    That Shakespeare himself intended the play to be taken lightly is hinted at in its last words, spoken by Escalus, Prince of Verona: "For never was a story of more woe / Than this of Juliet and her Romeo." The couplet reduces the play to a pretty toy, which one   30
may be grateful for but need not take too seriously; the effect is

startlingly like that evoked by the ending of *A Midsummer Night's Dream,* which Shakespeare is thought to have written a year or so earlier. Both plays are washed in the same blue moonlight, and the celebrated "aria" describing Queen Mab could have been   35
given as readily to Theseus as to Mercutio. The passage has, at the very least, the look of being a delectable leftover, too precious to discard.

1. To support his claim that the play "is a tragedy that must be played as if it were a comedy," what use does the writer make of specific examples? of quotation? of comparison with other plays?

2. Check the etymology, denotation, and connotation of *motley, tether, preposterous, formidable, reprehensible, nominal, protagonists, senile, aria, delectable.*

17-B	Clues to Meaning

John Hankins

These paragraphs are from a 3000-word essay introducing a widely used paperback edition of *Romeo and Juliet.* The essay is intended to give the general reader an overall view of the play and the chief critical interpretations.

ANALYSIS
Classification
#1
analysis

In recent years numerous attempts have been made to state a central theme for the play. One critic views it as a tragedy of unawareness. Capulet and Montague are unaware of the fateful issues which may hang upon their quarrel. Romeo and Juliet fall in love while unaware that   5
they are hereditary enemies. Mercutio and Tybalt are both unaware of the true state of affairs when they fight their duel. In the chain of events leading to the final tragedy, even the servants play a part and are unaware of the results of their actions. The final scene, with Friar   10
Laurence's long explanation, is dramatically justified because it brings Montague, Capulet, Lady Capulet, and the Prince to at least a partial awareness of their responsibility for what has happened. Supplementing this view of

Classification
#2
analysis

the play is one which finds it to be a study of the whole-   15
ness and complexity of things in human affairs. The issues of the feud may appear to be simple and clear, but in

reality they are highly complex, giving rise to results
which are completely unforeseen. The goodness or bad-
ness of human actions is relative, not absolute, an idea   20
symbolically set forth in Friar Laurence's opening speech
on herbs which are medicinal or poisonous according to
the manner of their use.

Classification   Other clues to the meaning of the play may be found
#3   in the repetitive imagery employed by Shakespeare. The   25
                  images of haste, of events rushing to a conclusion, are
analysis   found throughout. When Romeo says, "I stand on sud-
                  den haste," Friar Laurence answers, "They stumble that
                  run fast," and thus expresses one moral to be drawn from
                  the play. Romeo and Mercutio symbolize their wit-com-   30
                  bat by the wild-goose chase, a reckless cross-country
                  horse race. "Swits and spurts," cries Romeo, using the
                  imagery of speed. Numerous other instances may be
                  found.

Classification   Closely allied to the imagery of haste is the violence   35
#4   expressed in the gunpowder image. The Friar warns that
analysis   too impetuous love is like fire and powder, "which, as
                  they kiss, consume." Romeo desires a poison that will
                  expel life from his body like powder fired from a cannon.
                  This may identify the Apothecary's poison as aconite,   40
                  since elsewhere Shakespeare compares the action of aco-
                  nite with that of "rash gunpowder" (2 Henry IV, IV, iv,
                  48). Violence is also expressed in the image of shipwreck
                  which may end the voyage of life. Capulet compares
                  Juliet weeping to a bark in danger from tempests. Romeo   45
                  describes his death as the shipwreck of his "seasick weary
                  bark." Earlier, after expressing a premonition that at-
                  tendance at Capulet's party will cause his death, he re-
                  signs himself to Him "that hath the steerage of my
                  course," anticipating his later images of the ship and the 50
                  voyage of life.

Classification   Also repeated in the play is the image of Death as the
#5   lover of Juliet. She herself uses it, her father uses it beside
analysis   her bier, and Romeo uses it most effectively in the final
                  scene. The effect of this repeated image is to suggest that   55
                  Juliet is foredoomed to die, that Death, personified, has
evaluation   claimed her for his own. It thus strengthens the ominous
                  note of fate which is felt throughout the play.

Classification   That Romeo and Juliet is a tragedy of fate can hardly be
#6   doubted. Shakespeare says as much in the Prologue. The   60
analysis   lovers are marked for death; their fortunes are "crossed"

by the stars. The reason for their doom is likewise given:
only the shock of their deaths can force their parents to
end the senseless feud. At the end of the play Capulet
calls the lovers "poor sacrifices of our enmity," and the   65
Prince describes their deaths as Heaven's punishment of
their parents' hate. Romeo's premonition of death before
going to the party attributes it to "some consequence yet
hanging in the stars." The note of fate is struck repeatedly during the play. "A greater power than we can   70
contradict / Hath thwarted our intents," says Friar Laurence to Juliet in the tomb. The numerous mischances
experienced by the lovers are not fortuitous bad luck but
represent the working out of some hidden design. Critics
who attack the play for lacking inevitability have misun-   75
derstood Shakespeare's dramatic technique. Like Ham-
let's adventure with the pirates, the sequence of mishaps
here is deliberately made so improbable that chance
alone cannot explain it. Only fate, or the will of Heaven,
affords a sufficient explanation.   80

1. What transitional devices does the writer use to lead the reader from one
"central theme" to another?

2. What kinds of support does the writer give for the various interpretations
of the central theme?

3. Check the etymology, denotation, and connotation of *hereditary, supplementing, imagery, apothecary, bark* (as used here), *steerage, bier, thwarted, fortuitous.*

17-C   Puns and Other Wordplay in
Romeo and Juliet

M. M. Mahood

These paragraphs conclude the chapter on *Romeo and Juliet* in *Shakespeare's
Wordplay* (1957), a scholarly book devoted to a close analysis of a specific aspect of
Shakespeare's writing to determine what light it may shed on interpreting the plays.

Some of the most notorious puns in Shakespeare occur in this
scene between Juliet and her Nurse, when the Nurse's confusion
misleads Juliet into thinking Romeo has killed himself:

Hath Romeo slaine himselfe? say thou but *I*.
And that bare vowell *I* shall poyson more   5
Then the death darting *eye* of Cockatrice,
I am not *I,* if there be such an *I*.
Or those *eyes* shut, that makes thee answer *I:*
If he be slaine say *I,* or if not, no.
                                    (III.ii.45–50)   10

Excuses might be made for this. It does achieve a remarkable
sound-effect by setting Juliet's high-pitched keening of "I"
against the Nurse's moans of "O Romeo. Romeo." It also sustains
the eye imagery of Juliet's great speech at the opening of this
scene: the runaways' eyes, the blindness of love, Juliet hooded   15
like a hawk, Romeo as the eye of heaven. But excuses are scarcely
needed since this is one of Shakespeare's first attempts to reveal
a profound disturbance of mind by the use of quibbles. Romeo's
puns in the next scene at Friar Laurence's cell are of the same
kind: flies may kiss Juliet, but he must fly from her; the Friar,   20
though a friend *professed,* will offer him no sudden means of death,
though ne'er so mean; he longs to know what his concealed lady
says to their cancelled love. This is technically crude, and perhaps
we do well to omit it in modern productions; but it represents a
psychological discovery that Shakespeare was to put to masterly   25
use in later plays. Against this feverish language of Romeo's,
Shakespeare sets the Friar's sober knowledge that lovers have
suffered and survived these calamities since the beginning of
time. For the Friar, "the world is broad and wide," for Romeo,
"there is no world without Verona wall." When the Friar tries to   30
dispute with him of his "estate," the generalised, prayer-bookish
word suggests that Romeo's distress is the common human lot,
and we believe as much even while we join with Romeo in his
protest: "Thou canst not speak of that thou dost not feele." Tragedy continually restates the paradox that "all cases are unique and 35
very similar to others."
   The lovers' parting at dawn sustains this contradiction. Lovers'
hours may be full eternity, but the sun must still rise. Their
happiness has placed them out of the reach of fate; but from now
on, an accelerating series of misfortunes is to confound their   40
triumph in disaster without making it any less of a triumph. With
Lady Capulet's arrival to announce the match with Paris, love's
enemies begin to close in. Juliet meets her mother with equivocations which suggest that Romeo's "snowie Dove" has grown wise
as serpents since the story began, and which prepare us for her   45
resolution in feigning death to remain loyal to Romeo:

Indeed I neuer shall be satisfied
With Romeo till I behold him. Dead
Is my poore heart so for a kinsman vext.
                    (III.v.94–96)   50

This is a triple ambiguity, with one meaning for Juliet, another
for her mother and a third for us, the audience: Juliet will never
in fact see Romeo again until she wakes and finds him dead beside
her.

A pun which has escaped most editors is made by Paris at the   55
beginning of Act IV. He tells the Friar he has talked little of love
with Juliet because "Venus smiles not in a house of teares." Here
house of tears means, beside the bereaved Capulet household, an
inauspicious section of the heavens—perhaps the eighth house or
"house of death." Spenser's line "When oblique Saturne sate in   60
the house of agonyes" shows that the image was familiar to the
Elizabethans, and here it adds its weight to the lovers' yoke of
inauspicious stars. But this is one of very few quibbles in the last
two acts. The wordplay which, in the first part of the play, served
to point up the meaning of the action is no longer required. What 65
quibbles there are in the final scenes have, however, extraordinary force. Those spoken by Romeo after he has drunk the poison
reaffirm the paradox of the play's experience at its most dramatic
moment:

O *true* Appothecary: 70
Thy drugs are *quicke*. Thus with a kisse I die.
                    (V.iii.119–20)

Like the Friar's herbs, the apothecary's poison both heals and
destroys. He is *true* not only because he has spoken the truth to
Romeo in describing the poison's potency, but because he has   75
been true to his calling in finding the salve for Romeo's ills. His
drugs are not only speedy, but also *quick* in the sense of "life-
giving." Romeo and Juliet "cease to die, by dying."

It is the prerogative of poetry to give effect and value to incom-
patible meanings. In *Romeo and Juliet,* several poetic means con- 80
tribute to this end: the paradox, the recurrent image, the juxtaposition of old and young in such a way that we are both absorbed
by and aloof from the lovers' feelings, and the sparkling wordplay. By such means Shakespeare ensures that our final emotion
is neither the satisfaction we should feel in the lovers' death if the 85
play were a simple expression of the *Liebestod* theme, nor the
dismay of seeing two lives thwarted and destroyed by vicious

fates, but a tragic equilibrium which includes and transcends both these feelings.

1. What generalizations does the writer give to guide us among the many specific examples he cites?

2. Check the etymology, denotation, and connotation of *notorious, keening, sustains, imagery, quibbles, confound, equivocations, feigning, inauspicious, yoke, paradox, apothecary, potency, salve, prerogative, juxtaposition, Liebestod, equilibrium, transcend.*

17-D · Juliet's Nurse

Susan Ross *(student)*

This essay was written for an open-book essay test. The assignment was to show how one of the minor characters in the play helps us to understand one or more of the major characters. Countless critics have written on Shakespeare's use of minor characters, and students are unlikely to find anything fresh to say. This student, by concentrating firmly on the nurse, makes a vigorous statement that avoids clichés and sweeping generalizations and that shows a close reading of the play.

The most important minor character in *Romeo and Juliet* is the nurse. Her enthusiasm for sex and her lack of inhibitions are shown in her constant joking references to sexual intercourse. She makes it easy for us to understand Juliet's capacity for love and making love even though she is so young—only fourteen. In one   5
sense, Juliet has led a sheltered life, but because she has been brought up by the nurse she is not an ignorant little girl who knows nothing of the facts of life. When she falls in love with Romeo she acts like a passionate woman, not a teenager with a crush.   10

The nurse also shows us how young Juliet is in many ways in most of the play. She gives Juliet advice on all sorts of things, and Juliet turns to her constantly. She even trusts the nurse to keep the secret of her marriage to Romeo.

All of this makes us realize how much Juliet grows up in the   15
few days covered by the action of the play. In her last scene with the nurse Juliet is desperate because her father is insisting that she marry Paris or be thrown out of the house. Juliet again turns to the nurse for advice. The nurse knows all about Juliet's secret marriage to Romeo and up to this point has been full of praise   20

for Romeo's good looks and charm, but now she tells Juliet to go ahead and marry Paris because Paris is rich and handsome, Romeo is in exile, and a bird in the hand is worth two in the bush. The fact that this would be bigamy doesn't bother the nurse at all. Horrified by this treacherous immorality and insensitivity, Juliet   25
calls the nurse "Ancient damnation! O most wicked fiend!" and swears never to trust her again. From there on, Juliet realizes that she must solve her problems alone.

By using contrasting characters Shakespeare helps us to understand Romeo and Juliet and the picture of a beautiful young love.   30
An essential contrast is the nurse. Her crude earthiness and materialism make her a perfect foil for Juliet's passionate idealism.

17-E   For Love or Money

John Porter *(student)*

This essay was written as homework on the assigned question: How important is money in *Romeo and Juliet?* Note how the writer examines carefully all the relevant lines to find their significance to the larger elements of the play and uses quotations and specific references to support his interpretations. In the last paragraph he shows how the quotation illustrates both his particular point about money and also the main theme of the play, the doom of the young lovers.

When most people think of *Romeo and Juliet* they think of the beauty of the balcony scene or the tragedy of the lovers' deaths in the tomb, but in the background there is a busy city where money talks. We notice this particularly with Juliet's father, Capulet.   5

In the first act one of his servants describes him as "the great rich Capulet," and Juliet's nurse tells Romeo that the man who marries Juliet "shall have the chinks," meaning that he will get a wife with a big dowry. In the third act Capulet tells Juliet that she must marry Paris. When she refuses, he is furious and threatens her. He tells her to "beg, starve, die in the streets" if she   10
won't obey him and says he will cut her off without a penny: "What is mine shall never do thee good." In the next act Juliet takes the potion and goes into a coma. Capulet thinks she is dead and is overcome with grief, but even in his grief he thinks about   15
his money:

Death is my heir:
My daughter he hath wedded. I will die
And leave him all. Life, living, all is Death's.

At the end of the play he is still thinking of money. He meets   20
Romeo's father when the dead bodies of Romeo and Juliet are
discovered in the tomb and asks to shake hands with him, saying,

This is my daughter's jointure, for no more
Can I demand   25

When Romeo's father answers that he will have a pure gold statue
of Juliet made in her honor, Capulet meets the bid and says that
he will have a statue that is just "as rich" made of Romeo. In
Capulet, Shakespeare shows us a very realistic picture of a rich
businessman who is used to bossing people around. All these   30
references to money, particularly to Juliet's dowry and inheri-
tance, help us to understand the pressures on Juliet to obey her
father and make us appreciate all the more her courage in defying
him.
      There are other examples of the importance of money to some   35
of the characters. For instance, the nurse is pleased to take a tip
from Romeo when she gives him a message from Juliet, and at
the beginning of the last act Romeo gets some illegal poison by
giving forty ducats to an apothecary who says he is too poor to
refuse the bribe.   40
      Throughout the play, Shakespeare combines realism and ideal-
ism, and all these mentions of money make an ironic contrast to
the attitudes of the lovers. It is very appropriate that when Romeo
first sees Juliet he says that she

hangs upon the cheek of night   45
Like a rich jewel in an Ethiop's ear—
Beauty too rich for use, for earth too dear!

The lovers' feelings are far above the world of money and business, and that is why they are such perfect symbols of young love.

17-F   Robert Coles' *Privileged Ones*

Antonia Manuela *(student)*

This essay was written for a course on current social problems. From the instructor's list of important, recently published books in the field, each student chose one to examine in detail—a typical assignment for courses in the social sciences.

"Talk with the big important rich white people" was a repeated directive given by black and white Southerners to psychiatrist and social scientist Robert Coles. He later came to know the significance of that advice which he heeded by writing *Privileged Ones,* the fifth volume of his *Children of Crisis* series.   5

The writing of *Privileged Ones,* a work twenty years in the making, began in the late 1950s during his encounter with blacks and whites in the New Orleans school desegregation crisis. While being interviewed, they expressed interest in what he was doing. Their interest, however, ultimately turned into anger as they   10 strongly urged him to talk to the rich and powerful people whose decisions actually determined the way the poor and working class lived. Coles' reason for writing the book is as important as the book itself; it is the acknowledgment that the problems of racism, poverty, and class must be analyzed from all sides in order to   15 understand their causes and their processes, if not their solutions.

Privileged Ones is not only an analysis of the way the rich and well-to-do live, their power, interests, and fears. Nor, ironically, is it only about rich children growing up, although on almost every page the book provides representative accounts of their   20 curiosity and concern about racism and poverty. It is rather a psychological and sociological analysis of the attitudes by which the well-to-do and the rich have justified their lives and the processes by which these attitudes are passed on to their children.

Coles initially responded with doubt and professional igno-   25 rance to the request that he talk to the rich people. His awareness that even he is not exempt from having stereotyped attitudes is exemplified in his amazement that the sophisticated and insightful request to talk with the rich came directly from the "not very well-educated people."   30

Coles' cross-cultural research took him to southern states. Ap-

palachia, the Midwest, and the North. He interviewed eighty-five
children between the ages of five and fourteen from black and
white poor, working-class, and rich families, visiting them twice
a week for a period of no less than one year each and some for   35
up to four years. He is making these visits, he tells the children,
because he is interested in their ideas. They oblige by speaking
freely, and he obtains from them drawings of their homes,
schools, family members, pets, servants, friends, and teachers.
Forty-nine of these drawings are reproduced in the book. Coles'   40
method of interviewing is to listen to these children as a friend.
Since he has altered the children's names and places of residence
in order to protect their identity and only sometimes wrote or
used a tape during his interviews, the accounts are not verbatim.
Rather they are condensed and representative composite ideas   45
based on dialogue and events that, trusting his memory, he wrote
down shortly after the interview.

He talked as well with the children's parents, friends, and
teachers, and began to realize the importance of studying the
privileged ones, the well-to-do, the top five percent who hold   50
forty percent of this country's wealth. These people, whose
money can buy privacy, protection and power, backed by lawyers,
accountants, and advisers, are preferentially treated by the law,
the police, school authorities, and city officials.

The privileged ones, however, are troubled—a problem ex-   55
pressed by a wealthy Florida grower as he urged Coles to "find
out about the suffering children in our homes, find out the cost
of success." The cost of success is indeed evident in the way these
children have been taught to regard themselves. Moreover, it is
evident in their contradictions and confusion, prompted by the   60
inquiries on race, class and poverty, that are "logically" explained
by their parents, and, often, by their private school teachers.
Coles' depiction of the privileged is carefully devoid of generalizations about their similarities or differences as he acknowledges
that the rich and well-to-do, although having the commonality of   65
being privileged, are varied and have distinctions according to
region, profession, origins of acquired wealth, lifestyles, and patterns of socializing their children. The most common similarity
among the privileged in the South, Appalachia, Southwest, and
Alaska is that their residences are usually close to their source of   70
wealth, whether it is plantations, ranches, land-developing, or
mines. In the North, however, the privileged urban and suburban
residents are usually separated from their source of wealth, which
is often derived from real estate or stock market investments, and

they are high-salaried professionals such as lawyers, doctors,   75
bankers, corporate executives, or owners of businesses.

What Coles has done with *Privileged Ones* has more than allowed
us to exmaine the process of socialization of the privileged young.
He has enabled us to come into these households and see the
process of maintaining a class and the psychological and sociologi-   80
cal complexities involved. Coles has not written the book with the
intention or promise of a solution; that would be unrealistic. What
he has done is to point in the direction which some of the solution
may come from. The key can be taken from his dedication, in
which he states his hopes that *"all* [emphasis added] boys and   85
girls . . . [will] affirm themselves as human beings." "There must
be more meeting grounds between the rich and the poor, more
mutual exposure to the way they are living and more sharing of
the individual pain and trouble that the creation of classes has
prevented for so long." The key can also be taken from a Louisi-   90
ana black woman Cole interviewed who asks the Biblical question, "What profits are there under the sun?" Indeed the cost of
inequality and inhumanity is not worth all the wealth in the world.
And lastly, the key can be taken from James Agee's words in *Let
Us Now Praise Famous Men:*   95

All that each person is, and experiences, and shall never experience, in
body and mind, all these things are differing expressions of himself and
of one root, and are identical; and not one of these things nor one of
these persons is ever quite to be duplicated, nor replaced, nor has it ever
quite had precedent; but each is a new and incommunicably tender life,   100
wounded in every breath and almost as hardly killed as easily wounded:
sustaining for a while, without defense, the enormous assaults of the
universe.

1. Where does the writer use chronological patterns of organization?

2. Where and how does she use summary? direct quotation?

3. Why does she devote a relatively long paragraph, the fifth, to describing
Coles's methods in conducting interviews?

17-G   Virtuous Sin

The New York Times

This short satire, here complete, makes its point by a transfer of the real object of the criticism—the use of gambling and pornography—to other areas.

By sponsoring weekly bingo games, churches and synagogues across the land have long enjoyed the tribute that vice can be made to pay to virtue. Their example has led to "Las Vegas Nights," on which such pastimes as blackjack, roulette and even craps are turned to worthy purposes. And now we learn from   5 *Variety* of senior citizens in Bemidji, Minn., who arranged for showings of an X-rated film, "Erotic Adventures of Zorro," to raise money for a new senior citizens center. It brought $825. Clearly, the vistas of vice are vast: pot parties for the benefit of the American Cancer Society perhaps; after-hours clubs run by   10 Alcoholics Anonymous; massage parlors to finance Planned Parenthood. Since the goods would no doubt be exemplary, the prices fair and the advertising honest, the cause of moral uplift would be well served.

1. How appropriate are the other areas to which the satire is transferred?
2. Check the full dictionary entry for *exemplary.*

ASSIGNMENTS

In each of these assignments, try to persuade your readers to accept your point of view. Remember to support your criticism with specific details about your subject and to make use of the aids to exposition, organizing, and reasoning discussed in earlier units.
1. Write a critical review of a movie, TV drama, book, or play that you saw or read recently.
2. Which one of the essays you have read so far in this book has interested you most? Write a critical analysis of its good points—and of its bad points, if you find any—and explain why you think other readers might like it.
3. Which TV commercials do you think are the best? the worst? Write a critical analysis, contrasting one or two commercials that you like with one or two you dislike.

4. Who is your favorite singer, composer, music group? Write a critical analysis of the qualities you admire. Include discussion of any weaknesses.
5. What recent record album do you think shows decided talent or lack of talent? Write a critical analysis explaining exactly what you think is right or wrong in it.
6. Write a critical analysis of the performance of the best and poorest players on the athletic team you watch most often.
7. Rewrite one of your essays as a satire.

UNIT 18

The Research Paper

The label "research paper" is applied to a considerable range of writing and is frequently used interchangeably with "report," but the further you go in scholarly work the more you will see the difference between a report and a true research paper. Both are based on information the writers have gathered from various sources, and for both this process of gathering information from assorted facts and opinions is "research." There the similarity ends.

Report writers do not try to find facts unknown before or to make new interpretations of known facts. Although they may include many of their own opinions, they make no claim that these opinions have never been expressed before. Many magazine and newspaper writers perform this kind of research. The information they present may be new to their readers, but it is already available in books or other publications and was not first discovered by the writers. Writing such a paper can be a very rewarding activity for you: You learn something new to you, and your paper will inform others. However, you are not adding anything new to the existing body of facts and opinions.

The writer of the true research paper, on the other hand, has as a primary purpose casting a wholly new light on a subject, either by finding new facts and forming new opinions or by reevaluating known facts and opinions, or by using both methods. The writer of a true research paper not only gives a clear, orderly report on information gathered from various sources but also uses that information to say something original. As you go on in scholarly work, you will be increasingly expected to perform research of this kind.

As an undergraduate you are unlikely to have a chance to discover something that is both new and important, such as a cure for cancer or evidence proving absolutely that Egyptians visited Mexico 4,000 years ago. But this does not mean that you cannot do original research that will be interesting and valuable. Two general approaches are open to you.

1. **You can gather information on a relatively small subject that no one has examined before or that no one has examined thoroughly.** For example, you can collect all the available facts on a local political situation or environmental problem, or use newspaper files to put together the story of an unsolved crime and work out your own suggestions for the solution, or interview an elderly person and, with the help of background reading in appropriate historical material, write a chapter in a projected biography of that person. There are thousands of such subjects, full of facts that have not yet been sorted out and interpreted.

2. **You can examine a well-known subject in a new light.** For example, new theories continue to appear on the assassination of President Kennedy, and a good researcher will examine each new theory, comparing and contrasting it with earlier ones and also reexamining the earlier ones in the light of the new one, so that with each new theory a reevaluation must be made of all previous theories, if only to conclude, with supporting evidence, that the new one does not change anything.

Whichever general approach you choose, expect to gather information from printed sources of all kinds, from laboratory experiments, from opinion surveys, or from a combination of these. The more you can learn about your subject, the more authoritative you will be on it, and the more likely to say something significant.

Writing a research paper is hard and exacting work, and most of that work takes place before the actual writing of the paper. You will spend many hours searching for and selecting source materials. You will go down blind alleys and will have to try to reconcile conflicting opinions or contradictory evidence. The process is often like detective work. Sometimes an answer you are seeking will escape you, but the search itself can be exciting, and each new piece of evidence that you discover will make you feel triumphant.

To write a research paper you must complete five major overlapping actions: (1) choose a subject; (2) build a bibliography; (3) gather information from reading and whatever other sources are appropriate, such as opinion surveys, interviews, and laboratory experiments; (4) sort out and organize the information until you can define your specific topic and determine your main point; (5) write and document the paper.

∴   ∴   ∴

Choosing a general subject

Choosing a general subject, narrowing it to a specific topic that you can handle in a paper of the assigned length, and forming an opinion—a thesis—on that topic will be a long procedure. The more you learn about your subject in general, and your topic in particular, the more precisely you will be able to define what you wish to cover and the main point that you wish your readers to see. Also, you will probably find, as you gather material, that at least some of the opinions you held at first have changed. Be sure to keep your mind open for such changes. They are at the heart of the research process.

The more your subject interests you, the better your research paper is likely to be. Compared to most of your other writing assignments, a research paper is a long, drawn-out affair, and you will have to live with your subject for several weeks. What are you interested in? What would you like to know more about? If you are a business major, you might examine the economic forecasts published in newspapers and business magazines in a particular month in the recent past and then determine their accuracy by finding out about the present state of the economy. If you are a science major, you might examine the published opinions on the value of a new drug or on a new health threat, find out its history and that of others similar to it, ask several physicians for their opinions, and arrive at your own conclusions. If you are a sports fan, you might analyze your favorite team's performance in the last year, the opinions of sports writers and of the coach and players themselves. If you are interested in history, you have an irreplaceable resource in any elderly person you know, and you can write a biographical study by setting the facts on an interesting part of his or her life in the appropriate historical context. If you are curious about human behavior you can devise a questionnaire on a controversial topic, make an opinion survey of the students on your campus, and use the results along with your reading on the subject as the basis for an analysis of the psychological, political, or social significance of the students' answers. And so on—the opportunities are as wide as your interests.

Whatever subject you choose, plan to *limit* it so that you can cover it thoroughly. The broader the subject is, the harder it will be to find anything new to say. For example, if you are writing a biography of one of your grandparents, concentrate on a few years or even on a few months or weeks and give those in full detail, with only a brief summary of the rest of his or her life as a frame for the part you have chosen.

Using the reference collections

The reference collections in your college and local libraries will almost certainly be essential to your research. They will be your chief means of finding material on any subject. Familiarize yourself with what they contain. Walk beside the shelves, reading titles and leafing through any work that seems promising. Knowing how to take full advantage of a reference collection is as necessary for a researcher as knowing how to use the telephone is for most Americans.

Begin by obtaining a bird's-eye view of what is known on your subject. Look it up in several sources of general information. Encyclopedias are most likely to be helpful. These include not only the *Britannica, Americana,* and *New International,* but others specializing in a single field, such as religion, education, or sociology; collections of brief biographies, such as the international *Who's Who,* the *Dictionary of National Biography* for the British, and *Who's Who in America* for Americans; and collections of facts and statistics, such as the *World Almanac* and other yearbooks. *Winchell's Guide to Reference Books,* kept up to date by occasional supplements, classifies by type and subject matter all kinds of reference works besides the famous ones just mentioned.

Browse through the whole reference collection to form an overall picture of what is available. As you do, make notes on index cards (the most convenient sizes are $3'' \times 5''$ or $4'' \times 6''$). Record the names and facts they emphasize. Write only one note on each card so that you will be able to arrange and rearrange them later as you explore relationships in the material you have gathered. On each card, write the title, page number, and library call number of the work from which you made the note. These notes will help you to keep the main outlines of your subject clear so that you will see the significance and relationships of the parts. If an encyclopedia article mentions important books on your subject, make notes of these by author and title on separate cards so that you can check later on their availability in your library.

The library catalog and the appropriate periodical indexes will be the two big sources of information on the material printed on your subject.

The catalog, whether it is in card or book form or computerized, lists every book in the library alphabetically by both author and title and usually also under several headings for the subjects with which the book deals. For example, you will probably find *The Uses of Enchantment* by Bruno Bettelheim listed not only under *B* by the author's name and under *U* by its title, but also in several subject categories, such as "Fairy Tales—History and Criticism," "Psychoanalysis," "Folk-lore and Children," and "Child Psychology."

The periodical indexes, probably shelved in the reference room of the library, will help you find articles in periodicals—newspapers, magazines, and journals of all kinds.

The *Reader's Guide to Periodical Literature* is issued monthly in magazine form and at intervals cumulated into volumes covering several years. It indexes, under both author and subject headings, the contents of the better-known American (and a few British) periodicals on general subjects since 1900.

Poole's Index covers British and American periodicals from 1802 to 1906.

The International Index covers a selected list of American and European periodicals in the humanities, social sciences, and sciences, from 1916 to 1965. The *Social Science and Humanities Index* covers about 175 American and British periodicals from 1965 to 1974. Two separate publications continue the listings, the *Social Sciences Index* and the *Humanities Index.*

There are many specialized indexes for particular fields, such as agriculture, engineering, psychology, industrial art, literature, dentistry, medicine, and law. Some of these list books and bulletins as well as articles and periodicals.

The *New York Times Index,* published annually, covers all that newspaper's stories and articles. Since most major news is handled on the same or the following day by all the principal newspapers, this index can help you locate material in other papers as well.

Check the catalog to determine which periodicals related to your subject are in your library; ask a reference librarian what others are available at nearby libraries and how to arrange for photocopies of articles in periodicals held by libraries you cannot visit—the reference librarians will be your most valuable source for information in the library. They are specially trained in information retrieval. Turn to them whenever you find yourself in a blind alley, but always first try to solve problems yourself—the more practice you have, the more efficient a researcher you will be.

Important: In your preliminary survey of resources, do not try to make a thorough search or you may be overwhelmed by the quantity available. Instead, make sure that there is plenty of material on your general subject and that it includes up-to-date items—check publication dates. Also, all the time you are looking over the catalog and the indexes, be alert for clues that will help you to narrow your subject to a manageable topic. The titles of books and articles will give you an overall impression of what others have written and may suggest a topic that will be appropriate for you. Keep your mind open for such possibilities, and be sure to jot them down as they occur to you.

Narrowing your subject to a specific topic

When you have a clear idea of what resources are available to you—books and periodicals, laboratory facilities, knowledgeable people—you are ready to decide on a specific topic. First, make a quick review of the available material. Then, think over what you now know of your subject. Keep in mind the constraints of the project: the **length** of the paper, the **deadline**, and the importance of giving your readers **something fresh** on your subject—facts, or opinions, or both—that they will not find elsewhere. Choose a specific topic that will fit your needs and theirs, but remember that you may revise it more than once as you continue your research and think it over.

This topic will be the basis for your next step, building a bibliography.

Building a working bibliography

Keep a list of every printed item you find mentioned that seems worth at least a glance. Eventually, this will be the basis for the list of your sources that must appear at the end of your paper.

With a supply of $3'' \times 5''$ index cards in hand, go back to the library catalog and the periodical indexes. For every work listed that looks at all promising, take down the information you need to find it in the library, using one card for each book or article. The general information that you have already gathered from reading the encyclopedias and surveying the library resources will help you to recognize what may prove useful, as may the titles of the works. If you are in doubt about the value of something, fill out a card on it anyway. It is better to have to discard items later than to miss a good one.

For each book, record the library call number for your later convenience in locating it in the stacks, the full name of the author (last name first for convenience in alphabetizing your cards), and the title (underlined to indicate that it is a book). Also record the place of publication, the name of the publisher, the date of publication, and any special information that the library catalog gives as to an editor, translator, or edition other than the first. All this will be required for your final bibliography. A typical card will look like this:

PR
13. B8
no. 191

Crutwell, Patrick
The English Sonnet
London : Longmans, 1966

The information needed for periodical articles is slightly different. For each, give the author, with last name first, as before (if the article is anonymous, leave blank the line where the author's name would regularly go and alphabetize the cards by the article title instead); the title (in quotation marks to indicate that it is only part of something); the title of the periodical (underlined); the volume and issue numbers (if it is not a weekly or monthly periodical) and full date of the issue that contains the article; and the first and last page numbers of the entire article.

There are two kinds of source material: primary and secondary. For example, if your topic is a particular company's chance for future success, then any information issued by the company and any statements made by its officials, either oral or written, are primary sources. Information and opinions of writers discussing the company in books and periodical articles are secondary. But if your topic is an evaluation of the accuracy of the forecasts about the company made by financial analysts, then their opinions become primary sources, and secondary sources for such a study would be other analysts' opinions of their opinions.

Base your opinions on primary sources whenever possible—information "straight from the horse's mouth." Use secondary sources to show the extent to which you agree or disagree with others who have written on the subject and to give general background information. For example, if your topic is a biographical study of your grandfather and his struggles as a farmer in the Depression of the 1930s, your chief source of information will be what he and any of his contemporaries can tell you (primary) and economic and agricultural reports published at that time (primary). For background material you should rely on facts and opinions about the period given in books and articles by respected authorities (secondary), especially the more recent ones, since those writers will have the benefit of greater perspective.

Examine all your sources with a sharply critical eye. When you begin your project you may not know which writers are respected, well-known authorities, which are respectable though little known, and which are questionable. Your ability to judge will grow as your familiarity with the subject grows. But even at the start, watch out in your secondary sources for any signs of biased opinions, illogical deductions, unsupported claims, and sweeping generalizations. What sources do the writers use? What other writers on the subject do they refer to as authoritative? If you are in doubt about the value of a book, find out what reviewers have written about it by checking the *Book Review Digest* and reviews in appropriate scholarly journals, and, of course, ask your instructor for advice.

Note: Remember that articles in newspapers and popular magazines are intended as introductions to a subject. They are very useful for up-to-the-minute information, but for a more thorough analysis you must go to specialized magazines, scholarly journals, and books. Always check the most recent publications as well as the famous and basic ones.

Researching your topic

Begin serious reading and note-taking when you have listed on your index cards all the promising materials on your subject that are available in the library.

1. **Skim through all the available material** to select what you will look at carefully later. Remember that the preface of a book may often indicate whether it is likely to include anything for your purpose. The table of contents is even more useful; a glance at chapter headings may save you from going further or direct you quickly to the one section that may be all that will be useful. Learn to "skim"—to glance rapidly through material in search of the significant. By these means, eliminate items that now seem unsuitable. Then you can settle down to a thorough reading of what seems really worthwhile.

2. **Take accurate notes,** while reading, of any facts and opinions that you may later wish to quote or refer to in your paper. Good notes will not only form the basis of your paper but will also help you to organize it. As you form a general picture of your subject, decide on its main divisions and subdivisions and use these as headings for the note cards, always remembering that you can at any time make further subdivisions or change a note from one subdivision to another as your knowledge of the subject grows. For example, for a biographical study of your grandfather, you may want to subdivide a preliminary heading "education" into "education—elementary

school" and "education—high school" or into "education—formal" and
"education—practical."

3. **Write your reading notes on cards.** (Convenient sizes are $4'' \times$
$6''$ and $5'' \times 8''$; be sure to stick to one size for convenience in handling and
filing.) Limit each card to a single note on a single topic taken from a single
source and give each a classifying heading. Then, instead of a hodgepodge,
you will eventually have a mass of material that you can arrange easily under
common headings and will be able to rearrange and discard items without
disturbing the rest. The flexibility of such notes makes selecting and organizing the material relatively simple.

Note: Make your work easier for yourself by writing on only one side of each
card so that you can see the whole note at a glance. If a note is too long for one card,
continue it on a second card, marking it at the top with the source and "cont.—p.
2" so that if it is ever separated from the first you will know instantly where it
belongs.)

4. **Record the exact source** of the borrowed material on each note
card. Your finished work must show not only the book or article from which
the words or idea came but also the page number. After each note you take,
jot down the page number or numbers on which you found the information.
In the upper right-hand corner identify the source by giving the author's last
name or a short form of the title of the work or both, as briefly as possible
but with enough information to avoid any chance of confusion with another
author or work with a similar name.

5. **Copy accurately any material you may wish to quote** in your
paper. Most of your notes will be summaries; they will give in your words
the gist of the material you read. But in your paper you may often wish to
support important points with the exact words of your source. Be sure to copy
these precisely as they appear in the original, with all the grammar and
punctuation intact and even with any errors in facts or writing that they may
contain. Set each one off with a pair of double quotation marks so that later
you will be able to see at a glance that they are quotations. Make a photocopy
of any material more than four or five lines long so that you can be sure of
the accuracy of your copy. You may eventually use only a few of these
quotations, but remember that although you can easily summarize a direct
quotation when writing your paper, you cannot turn your summary back into
a quotation unless you have the exact words before you.

6. **Learn to combine reading and note-taking.** If you read a long
article without jotting down notes on it, you will almost certainly have to
reread parts, perhpas many times; but if you pause to make notes at frequent
intervals, many of your notes will repeat each other. How much to read

before taking notes depends on the nature of the material and the strength of your memory.

Important: Be prepared to add to your bibliography as you go along. You may discover some of your best material through references made in your reading and the bibliographies that most scholarly works include.

Composing and revising your paper

Begin composing your paper when you have gathered most of what you think will be your important material—by reading, interviewing, conducting a survey, performing an experiment, and doing whatever else is necessary for your project. For detailed advice on composing, review Units 1 and 2, especially the log kept by the student writer (pages 34–39). Remember that at this point your insights and plans are still tentative. In any research project there is always the possibility of turning up some fact or having some new insight that will make you recast part of your work, perhaps all of it. Keep your mind open for new ideas and for reseeing earlier ideas.

1. **Glance over all your material,** jotting down any new ideas that occur to you and looking for other ways to divide and subdivide it that may show new relationships. Then, with your specific topic in mind, draft a tentative statement of your main point and make an informal outline for your own use. These steps will help you to determine how much more research is needed and in exactly what areas. If your instructor requires a formal outline of your paper, these steps will be the basis for it.

2. **Make your outline definite** when you have finished whatever additional research you find necessary. Imagine that your readers know something about your subject but that their opinions differ from yours, and compose a rough draft for a tentative ending of your paper—what you want those readers to have in mind when they finish reading. Glance rapidly over your outline and your ending, looking for ways to make them stronger and clearer. Next, with the same imagined readers in mind, compose a rough draft of your beginning—what your readers will need so that they can easily follow what you say in the main body of the paper.

3. **Now begin to write your rough draft**—perhaps the first of several—of the whole paper. Remember that all the basic principles of clear logical writing discussed in earlier units apply to writing a research paper. Review the advice in Units 9 through 16 on the chief ways to develop and support the main point and to present evidence coherently and logically. Also review Unit 8 on how to quote, paraphrase, and summarize effectively to support your argument.

4. **Remember that revision is a continuous process** throughout the composition of any paper, particularly longer ones. Each new fact and opinion gathered may make you resee and therefore revise your ideas. Each time you review your work you may see new relationships among the parts. Certainly, when your first rough draft is complete and you can see the paper as a whole, you will want to make changes to unify and strengthen it. You may even want to make drastic changes in the organization and content. Professional writers often find that their final draft bears little resemblance to their first draft.

5. **Make the final copy and proofread it.** As you do, review the directions in Unit 1 and also follow the directions in the next section of this unit on documenting the sources of your material.

Documenting your sources: General advice

You must document all your sources for your research paper. The chief support for your opinions will, of course, be the facts you have gathered and the opinions of others that you quote, paraphrase, or summarize. Whenever you use facts or opinions that can in any way be considered the property of someone else, and whenever you quote the words written or spoken by someone else, you must give full credit to your sources by documenting them. Failure to do so is plagiarism—a form of theft and therefore a legally punishable crime. You do not need to give sources for well-known facts mentioned by many writers, such as the date of the signing of the Declaration of Independence, or for widely held opinions, such as that Rembrandt was a great painter. If, however, you use another writer's exact words to present such facts or opinions, you should acknowledge that writer as your source, no matter how familiar the facts or opinions may be. Notice how Debra Connolly, the student who wrote the sample research paper presented later in this unit, supports her opinions by drawing on other writers and how she documents her sources. Any reader who wishes to check on her accuracy or read more about the topic can quickly learn not only exactly which books and essays she consulted but also the precise numbers of the pages on which she found the material.

Two systems for documenting the printed sources of scholarly writing are widely used: that of the **Modern Language Association, or MLA,** and that of the **American Psychological Association, or APA.** The MLA system was devised primarily for use in scholarly writing on literature, history, and biography but has traditionally been used in works, regardless of subject matter, directed to the general reader. In its latest version, presented in the *MLA Handbook* (1984) and the *MLA Style Manual* (1985), the MLA style is very similar to the APA style, which is used, with minor variations, in scholarly writing in the social sciences and laboratory sciences. In each course in which you are to write a research paper, ask your instructor which style you should use.

Whatever the style, you must make an alphabetized list of all the sources you mention in your paper, whether in quotations, paraphrases, summaries, or direct references. This is variously called a bibliography, a list of works cited, a list of works consulted, a source list, or a reference list. The historic meaning of the word "bibliography" is "a description of books," but the term is usually stretched to cover any printed sources, such as articles in magazines and newspapers. In precise usage, a bibliography does not include unprinted sources, such as lectures, broadcasts, and unpublished letters. "Works cited," in precise usage, includes only works, whether printed or not printed, that writers specifically mention, either in the main body of their books or essays or in notes. "Source List" and "Reference List" can cover printed and unprinted material and can include works that writers read as preparation but do not specifically refer to in their own writing. The MLA recommends that writers use the heading "Works Cited," even for lists including material that contributes ideas but is not directly referred to by the writers. The APA recommends using "Reference List" as the heading. Writers who have a large number of sources—roughly thirty or more—often divide them into groups according to whatever classifications are appropriate to the material.

Documenting in the MLA style: List of works cited

If your instructor asks you to use the MLA style, follow these forms in listing your sources. Notice the kinds of information given in each example and the arrangement, punctuation, and use of abbreviations. Since the sources will be arranged in alphabetical order, the author's last name appears first in each entry in the list, followed by a comma and whatever form of first name or initials the author uses. Alphabetize unsigned works by title, always omitting *A, An,* and *The* from consideration. Use a period after each of the three main divisions of each entry: the author's name, the title of the work, and the publication data, which for books includes the place of publication, the name of the publisher in a short form, and the date of publication. If the place of publication is not well known or might be confused with another of the same name, give the state or country as well in an abbreviated form. Use a period also after any additional information, such as the edition or number of volumes, that comes between the title and the publication data. Use parentheses only around a year that is preceded by a volume number in an entry for a periodical.

Underline the title of each book and periodical—this indicates that it should be printed in italics. Set off the title of each shorter work with a pair of double quotation marks, and end the entry for it with inclusive page numbers to show all the pages it occupies in the larger work. If the book title you are citing contains a title normally enclosed in quotation marks, such as that of a poem or essay, keep the quotation marks and underline the entire title. If a book title contains a title normally underlined, such as the title of another book or a periodical, do not underline the shorter title or set it off in quotation marks.

Use reverse paragraph indentation for each entry to make the alphabetized word stand out clearly. Begin the first word of each entry at the left margin; if the entry requires more than one line, begin all other lines five spaces inside the left margin. In the publication data, the MLA recommends using a short form of the names of publishers, for example, "Harcourt" for "Harcourt Brace Jovanovich, Inc." and "Yale UP" for "Yale University Press." If more than one city of publication is listed, give only the first. If readers might not recognize the city or might confuse it with another, include an abbreviation of the name of the country, for example, "Eng." for "England" and "It." for "Italy."

The following examples, presented in the MLA style, include many types of sources to suggest how wide the field of research can be and to encourage you to explore new areas. The numbers are for your convenience in class discussion. In your own source list, alphabetize the entries; do *not* number them.

In each example, notice what types of information are given, the sequence in which they appear, and the punctuation that sets them off from each other, and the use of abbreviations, if any:

1. **The first edition of a book by one author** This requires only the most basic information—the author's name, reversed for alphabetizing, the title of the book, and the publication data:

Ardrey, Robert. <u>African Genesis</u>. New York: Atheneum, 1961.

2. **Another book by the same author** Instead of repeating his or her name, type three hyphens or draw a line of equivalent length at the beginning of the entry. You may arrange works by the same author either chronologically by publication date or alphabetically by title. Whichever method you choose, use the same one throughout your bibliography:

- - -. <u>The Territorial Imperative</u>. New York: Atheneum, 1966.

3. **A book by two or more authors** Only the first author's name is in reverse order because the book will be alphabetized by that, no matter how many other authors' names are listed:

Bosworth, Joseph, and T. Northcoate Toller. <u>An Anglo-Saxon Dictionary</u>. Oxford: Oxford UP, 1898.

4. A book printed in two or more volumes

Davison, Frank Dalby. <u>The White Thorntree</u>. 2 vols. Sydney: Ure Smith, 1970.

5. A book that has been reprinted Give the year of the first edition immediately after the title:

Durrell, Gerald. <u>My Family and Other Animals</u>. 1956. New York: Viking, 1963.

6. A later edition revised by the author Always try to use the latest edition of any book unless an earlier edition is significant in some way to your research:

Empson, William. <u>Milton's God</u>. Rev. ed. London: Chatto, 1965.

7. A specially edited edition of another author's work

Dickens, Charles. <u>American Notes</u>. Ed. John S. Whitley and Arnold Goldman. <u>Harmondsworth</u>, Eng.: Penguin, 1972.

8. A letter published in a collection

Keats, John. "To John Taylor," 5 Sept. 1819. Letter 149 in <u>The Letters of John Keats</u>. Ed. Maurice Buxton Forman. 2nd <u>ed.</u> London: oxford UP. 1942. 379-82.

9. A work translated from another language

Gadamer, Hans-Georg. <u>Dialogue and Dialectic</u>. Trans. P. Christopher Smith. New Haven: Yale UP, 1980.

10. An essay, poem, or other short work published in a book

Miller, J. Hillis. "Optic and Semiotic in <u>Middlemarch</u>." <u>The Worlds of Victorian Fiction</u>. Ed. Jerome Buckley. Cambridge: Harvard UP, 1975. 125-45.

11. An introduction or preface by an editor or another writer The inclusive page numbers of the introduction are in lowercase Roman numerals because these were used in the original:

Lane, Margaret, Introduction. <u>Shirley</u>. By Charlotte Brontë. London: Dent, 1970. v-x.

12. An article in an encyclopedia Some encyclopedias give only the author's initials at the end of each article, but an index elsewhere in the set lists the authors' full names; with well-known encyclopedias, and also with dictionaries, you may omit the place of publication and the name of the publisher; you may also omit the volume and page numbers since the articles are arranged alphabetically by title; be sure, however, to give the number of the edition or the date of publication because other editions may not contain the same article:

Onati, Oscar. "Migrant Labour." Encyclopaedia Britannica:
    Macropaedia, 1974.

13. **An article in a monthly or weekly periodical in which the
pages are numbered separately for each issue** Give the full date of the
issue, abbreviating the names of all the months except May, June, and July:

Powers, Thomas. "What Is It About?" Atlantic Monthly, Jan.
    1984: 35-55.

14. **An article in a periodical in which the pages are numbered
consecutively through all the issues of each year** Give the volume number after the title of the periodical (like many scholarly journals, the periodical in the following example is known by its initials):

Sudrann, Jean. "Daniel Deronda and the Landscape of Exile."
    ELH 37 (1970): 433-55.

15. **An article in a newspaper** Give the edition, section number,
date, and page number; if the article continues on another page, write a plus
mark after the number of the page on which it begins:

Wiggins, Phillip H. "Dow Passes 2,400 on a 15.20 Advance." New
    York Times 7 Apr. 1987, late ed.: D1+.

16. **An unsigned article of any kind in a periodical**

"Statistical Spotlight: Venturing Abroad," Forbes 20 Apr.
    1987: 112.

17. **A pamphlet** Follow the forms used in examples 1 through 6 for
books. In this example the corporation issuing the pamphlet is both author
and publisher, a common practice with such publications. No publication
date is given, as indicated by *n.d.,* the abbreviation for *no date:*

Fidata Trust Company. Unitholder Reference Handbook. New
    York: Fidata Trust Company, n.d.

18. **A government document** Government publications use many
abbreviations; in this example "Cong." stands for both "Congressional" and
"Congress," "GPO" for "Government Printing Office," and "sess." for
sessions":

United States. Cong. Joint Committee on the Investigation of
    the Pearl Harbor Attack. Hearings. 79th Cong., 1st and 2nd
    sess. 32 vols. Washington: GPO, 1946.

19. **A published abstract of a dissertation** An abstract is a summary,
usually composed by the author of the full-length work and used by readers
as a quick means of locating relevant material; formerly, abstracts of most
Ph.D. dissertations were published in *Dissertation Abstracts,* a serial publication referred to as *DA;* in 1969 it became *Dissertation Abstracts International*

[*DAI*] and now appears in three series, A for the humanities, B for the sciences, and C for European dissertations:

Gatton, John Spalding. "Lord Byron's Historical Tragedies: A Study in Form." DAI 43 (1982): 451-A. U of Kentucky.

20. An unpublished Ph.D. dissertation

Worthington, Mabel Parker. "Don Juan: Theme and Development in the Nineteenth Century." Diss. Columbia U, 1953.

21. An unpublished letter in a collection

Benton, Thomas Hart. Letter to Charles Fremont. 22 June 1847. John Charles Fremont Papers. Southwest Museum Library, Los Angeles.

22. An unpublished letter that you received yourself

Porter, Harriet. Letter to the author. 15 Oct. 1985.

23. An interview on a public broadcast

Atwood, Margaret. Interview by Sherrye Henry. WOR Radio. New York. 10 Feb. 1986.

24. A personal interview that you conducted yourself

Porter, Harriet. Personal interview. 24 Oct. 1985.

25. A lecture, speech, or address that you heard

Heilbrun, Carolyn. Presidential address. General session. MLA Convention. Chicago, 28 Dec. 1985.

26. Unpublished raw data from research

"Parking problems: Should the college enlarge student parking space?" Opinion survey conducted by David Benson at the West Campus lot and Jane Phillips at the South Campus lot, Mayfield College, Smithtown OH, 8:00 to 10:00 a.m., 30 Jan. 1991.

27. A commercially available recording
Begin with the name of the person or group you wish to emphasize—the composer, the conductor, the soloist, or the band or orchestra; include the title, performers, conductor, catalog number, and year of issue; underline record titles, but do not underline or place quotation marks around titles of musical compositions known only by form, number, and key:

a. An LP recording

Beethoven, Ludwig van. Symphony no. 7 in A, op. 92. Cond. Herbert von Karajan. Vienna Philharmonic Orch. London, STS 15107, 1966.

Streisand, Barbra. People. Cond. Peter Matz and Ray Ellis. Co-
    lumbia, CS 9015, n.d.

b. A compact disk recording

Mozart, Wolfgang Amadeus. The Horn Concertos. With Hermann
    Baumann horn soloist. Cond. Pinchas Zukerman. St. Paul
    Chamber Orchestra. Philips, 412 737-2, 1985. Digital com-
    pact disk.

c. An audiocassette

Vaughan, Sarah. Songs of the Beatles. Audiotape. Atlantic CS
    16037, 1981.

d. Radio and television broadcasts

"Goddess of the Earth, The" Narr. and writ. James Lovelock.
    Nova, PBS. WNET, Newark. 4 Feb. 1986.
Porgy and Bess. By George Gershwin. With Grace Bumbry, Gwen-
    dolyn Bradley, Veronica Tyler, Barbara Conrad, Robert
    Mosely, Charles Williams, Gregg Baker, and David Arnold.
    Cond. James Levine. Metropolitan Opera. Texaco-Metro-
    politan Radio Network. WGAU, Athens, GA. 8 Feb. 1986.

28. **Printed material accompanying a recording** Give the author's
name, the title, if any, of the material, and a brief description, for example,
"jacket notes" or "libretto":

Baumann, Hermann. Untitled pamphlet. Trans. Miriam Verhey-
    Lewis. Cond. Pinchas Zukerman. St. Paul Chamber Orches-
    tra. Horn Concertos by Wolfgang Amadeus Mozart. Phillips
    412 737-2, 1985. Digital compact disk.

29. **Films and videotapes** Begin with the name you wish to emphasize—the whole work, a performer, the director or the scriptwriter:

Color Purple, The. Dir. Steven Spielberg. With Whoopi Gold-
    berg. Warner Bros., 1985.
Wilson, Ryall, dir. Creation vs. Evolution: "Battle of the
    Classroom." Videocassette. PBS Video, 1982. 58 min.

30. **Live performances of drama, music, or dance** Begin with the
name you wish to emphasize, as with recordings and films:

Jumpers. By Tom Stoppard. Dir. Peter Wood. With Paul Edding-
    ton, Felicity Kendal, and Simon Cadell. Aldwych Theatre,
    London. 3 Oct. 1985.
Ewing, Maria, soprano. Carmen by Georges Bizet. With Catherine
    Malfitano, Placido Domingo, and Michael Devlin. Metro-
    politan Opera. New York. 10 Mar. 1986.
Atlanta Ballet. Return Trip to Tango. Chor. Joan Finkelstein.
    With Maiqui Manosa, Matthew Wright, and Jill Murphy.
    Score by Michael Sahl based on Argentine tangos. Whitman
    Hall, Brooklyn College, New York. 1 Feb. 1986.

31. **Works of art** Begin with the artist's name and also give the name of the institution where the work may be found:

Cranach, Lucas, the Elder. <u>Portrait of Anna Buchner</u>. Institute
    of the Arts, Minneapolis, Minnesota.

If you are using a printed photograph of the work, also give the complete information on the book or pamphlet in which the photograph appears:

Giotto di Bondone. <u>Esau and Isaac</u>. Church of San Francesco,
    Assisi, It. Plate 54 in <u>Early Italian Painting</u>. By Robert
    Oertel. London: Thames, 1968.

32. **Computer software** In an entry for a commercially produced computer program, give the name of the writer, if known; the title, underlined; the descriptive label "computer software," neither underlined nor set off in quotation marks; the distributor; and the date. Place a period after each of these items except the name of the distributor, which should be followed by a comma. At the end of the entry, give any other significant information, such as the computer for which the program is designed, the number of kilobytes, and the operating system, for example, PC-DOS 2.0. Since almost all software is now on floppy disks, you need not mention the form unless the program you are describing is on a cartridge or cassette.

a. **Compiler for a programming language**

<u>Turbo Pascal</u>. Version 3.01. Computer software. Borland Inter-
    national, 1985. 40K. MS-DOS, CP/M-80.

b. **Program for a word processor**

<u>Word Perfect</u>. Version 4.1. Computer Software. Satellite Soft-
    ware International. 1985. 256K. PC-DOS 2.0 and MS-DOS
    2.0.

c. **Similar programs using different hardware for spreadsheets in accounting**

<u>1-2-3</u>. Version 1A. Computer software. Lotus Development
    Corp., 1983. 192K. PC-DOS $\geq$ 2.0 and MS-DOS $\geq$ 2.0.
<u>Jazz</u>. Version 1.0. Computer software. Lotus Development
    Corp., 1985. Macintosh. 512K.

33. **Legal references** The standard forms for referring to legal documents and court cases are often complicated and include many special terms and abbreviations. The following are examples of several common types. Notice that the names of the cases and statutes are neither underlined nor enclosed in quotation marks. Follow that practice in your list of works cited, but in the text of your paper underline the name of a case but not of a law:

a. A court case at trial level in a state court

Abrams v. Love Canal Area Revitalization Agency, 132 Misc. #2d
    232, 503 N.Y.S. 2d 507 (1986).

This refers to the case of Abrams, the plaintiff, against the Love Canal Area
Revitalization Agency, which is number 132 in the *Miscellaneous Reporter,*
second set, beginning on page 232; it is also in volume 503 of the *New York
Supplement,* second series, page 507; the case was decided in 1986.

b. A federal district court opinion

Washington Federal Sav. & Loan Assoc. v. Federal Home Loan Bank
    Bd., 526 F. Supp. 343 (N.D. Ohio 1981).

This court opinion on the case of the Washington Federal Savings and Loan
Association, plaintiff, against the Federal Home Loan Bank Board is in
volume 526 of the *Federal Supplement,* beginning on page 343, and was tried
in the federal district court for the Northern District of Ohio in the year
1981.

c. A court case at appellate level (a case appealed to a state supreme court)

United Nuclear Corp. v. General Atomic Co., 96 N.M. 155, 629
    P.2d 231 (1980).

This case is in volume 96 of the *New Mexico Reports,* page 155, and also
in volume 629 of the *Pacific Reporter,* second series, page 231, for the year
1980.

d. A court case appealed to a U.S. court of appeals

Apple Computer Inc. v. Franklin Computer Corp., 714 F.2d 1240
    (3d Cir. 1983).

This case is in volume 714 of the *Federal Reporter,* second series, page 1240,
and was decided in the U.S. court of appeals for the 3d circuit in 1983.

e. A case appealed to the U.S. Supreme Court

United States v. Nixon, 418 U.S. 683 (1974).

This case appears in volume 418 of *United States Reports,* page 683, in the year
1974.

f. A statute in a state code

Subway Loitering Act, N.Y. PENAL LAW §240.35(7) (McKinney
    1980).

This statute appears in *New York Penal Law,* subsection 240 of section 35,
part 7, published by McKinney in 1980.

g. **A statute in a federal code**

```
Racketeer Influenced and Corrupt Organization Act §901(a), 18
    U.S.C. 1962 (1970).
```

This statute appears in section 901, subsection *a* in title 18 of the *United States Code,* section 1962, and was codified in 1970. For more detailed information on legal references, consult *A Uniform System of Citation* (Cambridge: Harvard Law Review Association).

Quotations and source notes: MLA style

Follow conventional methods for presenting quotations of prose and poetry and use notes to identify your sources, to show that your opinions and research have a firm basis, and to give your readers the information they will need if they wish to consult your sources further. Since you will identify all your sources fully in your list of works cited, the information you give in the text of your paper should be brief.

Long prose quotations Set a long quotation, one of more than four typed lines, in a block indented ten spaces from your left margin. If you are quoting a single paragraph or less, do not indent the first line. If you are quoting two or more paragraphs, indent the first line of each paragraph an additional three spaces. If, however, the first sentence you quote does not begin a paragraph in the source, do not indent it, but indent the first sentence of any subsequent paragraph in the quotation. Give the author's last name at the end, if you have not given it in your introduction to the quotation, and the page number or numbers where the quoted material can be found in the source. Enclose this information in parentheses, beginning two spaces after the final punctuation mark.

The work quoted in the following example would have this documentation in a list of works cited:

```
Ardrey, Robert. The Territorial Imperative. New York:
    Atheneum, 1966.
```

```
At the mention of African wildlife, most people think of
elephants, lions, and gorillas, but many other animals
are remarkable, for example, the kob:
    The Uganda kob is among the supreme beauties of the
    antelope world, a photographic delicacy for ante-
    lope connoisseurs. Less graceful than the impala,
    less majestic than the kudu with its corkscrew
    horns, the kob has a sturdy elegance unlike either.
    His coat is golden brown, like proper toast. (Ar-
    drey 42)
```

If you identify the author in your introduction to the quotation, give only the appropriate page numbers in your note and place it before the final punctuation mark. The quotation just given would then end

```
His coat is golden brown, like proper toast (42).
```

If you include two or more works by the same author in your list of works cited, give the appropriate title or a shortened form of it each time you make a specific reference to one of the works or quote from it.

If a work has three or more authors, you may shorten the note by giving the surname of only the first, following it with "et al.," an abbreviation of the Latin phrase *et alii,* meaning "and others." If two authors have the same surname, distinguish between them in your notes by giving their first initials as well.

Short prose quotations Enclose a short quotation, one of four typed lines or less, in quotation marks, incorporate it in a sentence or paragraph of your own, and give the identifying information in parentheses after the closing quotation mark:

```
An observer of animal behavior has described the coat of the
Uganda kob as "golden brown, like proper toast" (Ardrey 42).
```

or

```
Ardrey has described the coat of the Uganda kob as "golden
brown, like proper toast" (42).
```

Long quotations from poetry Present a long quotation from a poem—four complete lines or more—in a block indented ten spaces from your left margin. Give the documentation at the end of the last quoted line, two spaces after the final punctuation mark. If the identifying information is too long to fit easily on the final line, place it on the line below, close to the right-hand margin.

If you quote only one line or less, incorporate it in a sentence of your own and give the identifying information after the closing quotation mark, as you would with a short quotation of prose. If you quote more than one line but less than four, you may present them as a block or you may incorporate them in your own sentence or paragraph, indicating the end of each line within the quotation by a slash mark with a space on each side (/). For an example, see Unit 7, page 154.

Quotations from well-known poetry or prose If you are quoting from a work that has been reprinted in many different editions, such as the Bible, a play by Shakespeare, or a novel by Dickens, your list of works cited should include full information on the particular edition you used, but in the text of your paper give not only the page number in the edition you used but also the number of the chapter or of the act, scene, and line so that your readers can find the material easily in any edition they have at hand.

Accuracy in quoting Always take care to quote the original exactly, word for word and comma for comma. You may, however, omit words not relevant to your point, if the omission does not alter the meaning of the original in any way, and you may add a brief explanation to clarify something that might otherwise confuse your readers. For examples, see Unit 7, page 155.

Paraphrases, summaries, and little-known facts Use the same methods to document the sources of any paraphrases, summaries, or mentions of little-known facts that you include in your paper, and also document the sources in full in your list of works cited. Although the words of the paraphrase and summary will be your own, the content is not. Moreover, the notes will show your readers that you have based your research on authoritative sources. The following example is based on the passage quoted earlier in this chapter:

```
Uganda kobs, a kind of antelope, have black-and-white markings
on their faces that vary from individual to individual so much
that finding two who look exactly alike is as rare as finding
human twins (Ardrey 42).
```

Documenting in the APA style: Reference list

In the APA style, the list of sources is called the reference list and includes only sources directly referred to by the writer. The information given on each source and the method of presentation are similar to those of the MLA style, with these differences:

a. Give only the initials of the authors' first names.

b. Give the date of publication in parentheses immediately after the authors' names.

c. Capitalize only the first letter of the first word in the titles and subtitles of articles, books, and chapters of books. With all proper names, however, including those of periodicals, capitalize the first letters of words in conventional fashion.

d. Italicize (underline) not only book and periodical titles but also volume numbers of periodicals.

e. Do not enclose article titles in quotation marks.

f. Omit such terms as "Publishers" and "Co." in publishers' names but give significant words in full, for example, "Yale University Press," not "Yale UP," and "Harcourt Brace Jovanovich," not "Harcourt."

g. Give the names of the months in full, for example, "August," not "Aug."

h. Give inclusive page numbers for essays and articles. Use the abbreviations "p." (page) or "pp." (pages) before page numbers in references to newspaper and magazine articles but not in references to articles in scholarly journals.

i. Begin each entry at your left margin as in the MLA style, but indent subsequent lines only three spaces.

The following examples of the APA style present many of the sources given earlier in the MLA style and are numbered in the same sequence to make discussion and comparison easy. Do *not* number sources in your reference list.

1. **The first edition of a book by a single author**

Ardrey, R. (1961). African genesis. New York: Atheneum.

2. **Another book by the same author** Arrange the books in chronological order and repeat the author's name:

Ardrey, R. (1966). The territorial imperative. New York: Atheneum.

3. **A book by two or more authors** Give the name of each author in reverse order; connect the name of the last with an ampersand:

Bosworth, J. & Toller, T.N. (1898). An Anglo-Saxon dictionary. Oxford: Oxford University Press.

4. **A book printed in two or more volumes**

Davison, F. D. (1970). The white thorntree (Vols. 1-2). Sydney: Ure Smith.

5. **A reprinted book**

Durrell, G. (1963) My family and other animals. New York: Viking Press. (First published 1956).

6. **A revised edition**

Empson, W. Milton's God (rev. ed.). London: Chatto & Windus.

7. **A specially edited edition of another author's work**

Eliot, G. (1967). Daniel Deronda. Ed. B. Hardy. Harmondsworth, England: Penguin. (Original work published 1876).

8. **A letter published in a collection** The APA *Publication Manual* does not include an example of this kind of source.

9. A work translated from another language

Gadamer, H.-G. (1980). Dialogue and dialectic. (P. C. Smith, Trans.). New Haven: Yale University Press.

10. An essay or other short work published in an edited book

Miller, J.H. (1975). Optic and semiotic in Middlemarch. In J. Buckley (Ed.), The worlds of Victorian fiction (pp. 125-145).

11. An introduction or preface by an editor or another writer

Lane, M. (1970). Introduction. In C. Brontë, Shirley (pp. v-x). London: Dent.

12. An article in an encyclopedia The APA *Publications Manual* does not include an example of this kind of source.

13. An article in a monthly or weekly periodical

Powers, T. (1984, January). What is it about? The Atlantic Monthly, pp. 35-55.

14. An article in a periodical in which the pages are numbered consecutively through the year

Sudrann, J. (1970). Daniel Deronda and the landscape of exile. ELH, 37, 433-55.

15. An article in a newspaper Give the numbers of all the pages on which the article appears:

Wiggins, P. H. (1987, April 7). Dow passes 2,400 on a 15.20 advance. The New York Times, pp. D1, 12.

16. An unsigned article in a periodical

Statistical spotlight: Venturing abroad. (1987, April 20). Forbes, p. 112.

17. A pamphlet from a private organization, with the organization acting as both author and publisher

T. Rowe Price New Era Fund. (1986). Annual Report. Baltimore, MD: Author.

18. A government document

National Institute of Mental Health. (1982). Television and behavior: Ten years of scientific progress and implications for the eighties (DHHS Publications No. ADM 82-1195). Washington, DC: U.S. Government Printing Office.

19. A published abstract of a dissertation

Gatton, J. S. (1982). Lord Byron's historical tragedies: A
    study in form (Dissertations Abstracts International, 43,
    451A. University Microfilm No. 82-07, 153.

20. An unpublished dissertation obtained from the university

Worthington, M. P. (1953). Don Juan: Theme and development in
    the nineteenth century. Unpublished doctoral disserta-
    tion, Columbia University, New York.

21. An unpublished letter available to the public

This kind of material is not specifically covered in the APA *Publications Manual.* If you use such material, give the name of the author, the date, the person to whom it was addressed, and the place where the material may be examined:

Benton, T. H. (1847, June 22). Letter to Charles Fremont. John
    Charles Fremont papers. Southwest Museum Library, Los An-
    geles.

22, 23, 24, 25. An unpublished letter that you received; an interview on a public broadcast; a personal interview that you conducted; a lecture, a speech, or address that you heard

These sources of information are not publicly available in recorded form, and they should not be included in a reference list that follows APA guidelines. Cite them only in the text of your paper. Since they will not be part of an alphabetized list, give the names of any persons concerned in natural order—beginning with the initials of their first names:

H. Porter (personal communication, October 15, 1985).

26. Unpublished raw data from research

Do not underline the topic. Give a brief description of the material and enclose the description in brackets to indicate that it is not a title:

Benson, D. & Phillips, J. (1986, January 30). Opinion survey on
    parking problems at Mayfield College, Smithtown, OH. Un-
    published raw data.

27. A commercially available recording

The APA *Publication Manual* gives information only on references to cassettes:

Vaughan, S. (singer), (1981). Songs of the Beatles. (Audiotape
    CS 16037). New York, Atlantic Recording.

28. Printed material accompanying a recording

The APA *Publication Manual* does not cover this source of information.

29. Films and videotapes

Begin with the names of the originators or primary contributors in the order of their importance to your research, and specify the medium in brackets after the title:

Spielberg, S. (Director) & Goldberg, W. (Performer). (1985).
    The color purple (Film). Los Angeles: Warner Brothers.

30, 31. **Live performances of drama, music, or dance; works of art** These sources of material are not included in the APA *Publication Manual.* If you refer to such sources in the text of your paper, identify them as fully as you can, but do not include them in your reference list.

32. **Computer software** Begin with the author's name, if known; in brackets after the name, identify it as a computer program; give the location and name of the organization that produced it; end with any further information needed to identify it, enclosed in parentheses.

```
Watton, D. (1982). Realtime clock interface program [IBM Per-
    sonal Computer program]. Irvine, CA: AST Research, Inc.
```

33. **Legal references** Follow the style of presentation described earlier for documenting references in the MLA style.

Quotations and source notes: APA style

Certain features of the APA style are identical with the MLA style. When quoting, follow the directions for the MLA style for the following features: single or double quotation marks, a capital or lowercase letter to begin the first word, the form and position of punctuation following the last quoted word, ellipsis dots to mark omissions, and brackets to enclose additions.

The APA style differs from the MLA style in a few details, as shown in the following examples. The work quoted in them would have this documentation in a reference list in the APA style:

```
Thomas, L. (1983). The youngest science: Notes of a medicine-
    watcher. New York: Viking.
```

Long quotations Present a quotation of forty or more words as a block. Indent the quotation five spaces from the left margin, beginning with the first quoted line, whether or not it is the first line of a paragraph. Indent the first line of any subsequent paragraphs in the quotation an additional three spaces.

Introduce each long quotation with the author's last name, followed by the publication date in parentheses. After whatever punctuation mark ends the quotation, give the page number or numbers of the original, enclosed in parentheses and followed by a period.

```
    In 1936, doctors who had graduated from the Harvard Medical
School in the classes of 1927, 1917, and 1907 gave some surpris-
ing answers to a questionnaire. Thomas (1983) reports the fol-
lowing statistics:

    The average income of the ten-year graduates was around
    $3500; $7500 for the twenty-year people. One man, a urol-
```

ogist, reported an income of $50,000, but he was an anom-
aly; all the rest made, by the standards of 1937, respectable but very modest sums of money (5-6).

Short quotations Incorporate a quotation under forty words long in
your own paragraph. Identify the source by either of the methods shown in
these examples:

a. In his reminiscences, a doctor mentioned that the answers to a questionnaire sent out by the Harvard Medical School in 1936 showed that
"the average income of the ten-year graduates was around $3500"
(Thomas, 1983, p. 5).
b. In his reminiscences, Thomas (1983) mentions that, according to the
answers to a Harvard Medical School questionnaire sent out in 1936,
"the average income of the ten-year graduates was around $3500" (p.
5).

Content notes

Content notes are different from notes documenting sources. Use a
content note to tell your readers something that would not fit smoothly into
your paper but that you think they may want to know, such as an explanation,
a definition, an illustrative anecdote, or a critical side comment. You may
present content notes as footnotes, placing each at the bottom of the page
on which the material it refers to appears, or you may present them as
endnotes in a list at the end of your paper just before your list of sources.
In either case, number the notes consecutively and place matching numbers
in the text of your paper immediately after the words to which the notes
refer. In your list of sources, give full documentation for any printed sources
for your content notes.

EXAMPLE

*Many of the writers presented in this book draw on research, their own and that
of others, to support their opinions. For relatively informal uses of* **quotation, paraphrase, summary,** *and* **historical reference,** *see particularly Davenport's
"Trees" (7-A) and Greer's "In the 'Lite' Decade, Less Has Become More" (14-H).
For the use of* **statistics,** *see particularly Cohen's "The Language of Uncertainty"
(15-C). For the* **logical investigation of raw material,** *see Asimov's "Is Anyone
Listening?" (13-H). For references to* **literary sources,** *see Mahood's "Puns and
Other Wordplay in* Romeo and Juliet*" (17-C), Ross's "Juliet's Nurse" (17-D),
and Porter's "For Love or Money" (17-E). For* **reporting on the research of**

others, *see Tysoe's "Do You Inherit Your Personality?" (6-E), Johmann's "Sex and the Split Brain" (7-B), Brody's "Mental Depression" (11-C), and Manuela's "Robert Coles'* Privileged Ones*" (17-F).*

The research paper that follows is documented according to the revised MLA system. Notice throughout the student's formal use of her research as evidence to support her thesis. Notice particularly her punctuation and varying ways of fitting material from other writers into her own sentences and paragraphs. The parenthesized notes documenting her sources make examples easy to spot. The following show particularly useful methods for presenting evidence from outside sources:

1. *long quotations presented as blocks—those beginning in lines 50, 112, and so on throughout the essay*

2. *short quotations incorporated in the student's sentences—lines 20–24, 27–31, 45–46, and throughout the essay*

3. *omissions of unnecessary parts of a quotation or the addition of explanatory words—the block quotation that begins "Jesse achieved . . . the perfect legend."*

4. *introductory remarks to lead into a quotation—lines 48–49, 63, and throughout the essay*

5. *paraphrases and summaries—lines 47–48, 64–66*

6. *reference to another writer as the source for a writer's words or ideas—the quotation from Settle's biography given in the next-to-last paragraph. When you cannot determine where a quoted remark was first published, or if the original source is not available for you to check, give the full information for the work in which you found the material so that your readers will have the same information on it that you have.*

Jesse James—Outlaw or Hero?

Debra Connolly *(student)*

The writer clearly focuses her research on Jesse James, but she gives her conclusions a broader significance than that of his single case. Notice how she has designed her two opening paragraphs to catch the attention of her readers and stimulate their curiosity while at the same time stating her thesis: the ways people have responded to Jesse James' crimes may be more important than the crimes themselves.

Jesse James. What does that name bring to mind? Bandit? Robber? Killer? Outlaw? How about "hero"? All the literature about Jesse James indicates that, although he was a thief and killer, he

is commonly thought of as a hero. Biographers have stressed his
heroic rather than his notorious qualities, and movies have glamo-   5
rized his supposed robbing from the rich and giving to the poor.
Children look up to Jesse James in their cops-and-robbers games
because of his ability to avoid getting caught.

Why have people overlooked James' killings and train robberies? Were there noble qualities in Jesse James? Examining James'   10
career as outlaw and studying reactions to his deeds show that the
ways people have responded to his crimes may be more important
than the crimes themselves. After all, these responses have created a legendary heroic figure of Jesse James.

History shows us that Jesse James is not the first outlaw to be   15
treated as a hero. Romanticizing of outlaws has followed a pattern, beginning with the most famous outlaw of all, Robin Hood.
The belief that Robin Hood "robbed from the rich and gave to
the poor" is a myth often cited as reason to praise later outlaws.
This myth sees the bandit as "the fearless, independent outlaw,   20
dedicated to the defense of the helpless, the righting of wrongs,
the humbling of the rich and powerful, and the dauntless display
of extraordinary courage, deemed to be beyond the ken of the
common run of men" (Angiolillo 1). People believed that the
outlaw was not a criminal, but a protector of justice; not a killer,   25
but a servant of the people.

Why do people admire the outlaw? Is he really "dedicated to
the defense of the helpless"? Most outlaw heroes emerge when
"living conditions are such that frustration, anger, fear, in-
security, poverty, discrimination, protest, and lack of hope are   30
widespread among the people" (Angiolillo 2). The masses see
only corruption, the rich getting richer and the poor poorer.
When the government doesn't promote justice, the outlaw steps
in.

Robin Hood was just such an outlaw. Although his deeds in-   35
cluded barbaric acts, like shooting the Sheriff of Nottingham with
arrows and beheading him, the peasants supported him because
they hated the king's hunting laws, which forbade them to hunt
deer for food but allowed the king to hunt deer for sport. They
hated the Sheriff, the king's local agent, and they hated the   40
wealthy landowners. That Robin Hood did treacherous things to
members of the ruling class only made him appear more just in
their eyes; to the oppressed, revenge and justice went hand in
hand.

Part of the myth of the outlaw involves "humbling of the rich   45
and powerful" or "robbing from the rich and giving to the poor."
Robin Hood, according to legend, told his men to rob only

knights and abbots, never good yeomen (Greenway 338). A ballad tells of Robin Hood's generosity:

> Chryst have mercy on his soule,   50
> That died on the rode!
> For he was a good outlawe,
> And dyde pore men much god. (Greenway 338)

People also applaud the outlaw because they believe he kills only in self-defense. According to John Major, a sixteenth-century   55 English historian, Robin Hood never killed unless he was attacked or resisted. Similarly, the nineteenth-century American outlaw Billy the Kid supposedly killed "only to protect himself, and those he did kill deserved what they got" (Greenway 340). People view the outlaw as a hero because they think he is not an   60 aggressor.

In the Robin Hood tradition, the outlaw is usually killed by a traitor. Indeed, as Greenway notes, "If a betrayer did not exist, folklore would invent him" (341). Robin Hood was bled to death by his cousin; Billy the Kid was killed by a friend; and Sam Bass,   65 another outlaw, was "sold out" by Jim Murphy (Greenway 341). When the outlaw is betrayed, people see his death as the death of justice and the death of their hopes for a better world.

The myth of the outlaw takes on special characteristics when it concerns the American Western outlaw. The myth is created by   70 those who witness the outlaw's career and, more particularly, by the journalists and the newspapers that record and publicize the outlaw's activities. Richard K. Fox, editor of the *National Police Gazette* from 1877 to 1922, listed ten characteristics of the Western hero-outlaw: 1) prodigious accuracy with any weapon; 2)   75 unparalleled bravery and courage; 3) unfailing courtesy to all women, regardless of rank, age, or physical charm; 4) inherent gentleness and modesty; 6) notable handsomeness—sometimes almost prettiness (but he is, of course, very masculine, and exceedingly attractive to women); 6) piercing blue eyes which turn   80 gray as steel when he is aroused; 7) undeserved ostracism—his life of outlawry results from his quite properly defending a loved one from an intolerable affront with lethal consequences; 8) commendable honor—he shields widows and orphans, robs only bankers and railroad monopolists; 9) treacherous undoing—he   85 dies by betrayal; and 10) inconclusive death—he keeps on turning up in other places for many years; it is indeed arguable whether he is dead yet (Lyon 35–36). If an outlaw lacks one of these ingredients, journalism and folklorists create it for him.

Jesse James, perhaps the most famous of Western outlaws, be-   90

came a legend in his own time, his career following the pattern
set by Robin Hood. People admired him because they saw him
as a protector of the helpless, a "symbol of revolt and protest
against the forces of tyranny and injustice" (Botkin 71).

Why did Jesse James become a bandit? What happened to the   95
Jesse who grew up "attending church regularly, going to Sunday
school, reading the Bible, and singing hymns"? (Ernst 7). Frank,
Jesse's older brother, was the first of the two to join an outlaw
band. For his support of the South in the Civil War, Frank was
jailed and forced to swear never to fight against the government   100
again. Breaking his promise, Frank joined a guerrilla band.

Frank's activities and his family's sympathy for the South caused
trouble for the Jameses. In June 1863, Union militia tortured
Frank and Jesse's stepfather, abused their pregnant mother, and
whipped Jesse with a rope to show what could happen to Southern   105
sympathizers. Soon afterward Jesse, then seventeen, joined his
brother Frank in "Bloody Bill" Anderson's gang of guerrillas,
and his career as an outlaw began (Castel 12).

During the war, the brothers' activities were confined to fighting and killing Union soldiers. After the war, however, Jesse and 110
his brother found themselves living in a state

> which did not allow former Confederates to practice law, medi-
> cine, or other professions. They were not even allowed to serve
> as officers of a church. Furthermore, although ex-Union soldiers
> were pardoned for all of their wartime activities, Confederate   115
> veterans were not pardoned and could be jailed for crimes com-
> mitted during the war. (Ernst 16)

Southern sympathizers wanted someone to restore law and order
and to stop the lynchings, robbings, and killings. "Jesse symbol-
ized the gallant Rebel, ground down beneath the boot of the   120
victorious Yankee oppressor" (Lyon 39).

James' robberies consisted of bank and train hold-ups. In fifteen
years he held up eleven banks, seven trains, three stages, one
county fair, and one payroll messenger, stole over $200,000—
worth ten times as much today—and killed at least sixteen men   125
(Lyon 39). Since the banks and railroad monopolies were stealing
from the common man and the government was doing nothing
to stop them, many saw Jesse James as their champion, the people's justice and a friend to the poor.

One story tells how the James boys and their gang, while look-   130
ing for something to eat, stopped at an old widow's farmhouse.
The poor woman was crying. When Jesse asked what was wrong,
she said that the mortgage holder was coming to repossess her

farm. "Jesse," so the story goes, "was always tenderhearted and couldn't stand a woman's tears. He laid down $1,400 on the table and told her she wouldn't lose her farm after all" (Botkin 109). When the mortgage was paid, Jesse robbed the mortgage holder, so he not only aided a poor widow, but he got his money back! Here, James fits the myth of the Western outlaw: courteous, gentle, helping the poor, shielding a widow, and, in general, standing up for the rights of the common man. James won many admirers by claiming that he never robbed from women, preachers, or ex-Confederates. Southern sympathizers in particular applauded him because they believed that his crimes were "intended as a way of taking revenge against the North" (Ernst 27).

James helped to make himself a hero. After holding up a train in Rocky Cut, Missouri, he wrote a letter to the Kansas City *Times,* denying the testimony of a man named Hobbs Kerry. He wrote,

> Early on the morning after the train robbery, I saw the Hon. D. Gregg and Thomas Pitcher, both of Jackson County, and talked with them for thirty or forty minutes. Those two men's oaths cannot be impeached, so I refer the grand jury of Cooper County, Mo., and Gov. Hardin to those men before they act so rashly on the oath of a liar, thief, and robber. (Breihan 137)

This was one of many letters that Jesse James published in newspapers. He always had someone to give him an alibi proving that he was nowhere near the site of a hold-up that he was accused of committing. Often the men who covered for him were respectable, so people believed the accusations were corrupt efforts to frame an innocent common man.

One newspaperman was almost a press agent for the James brothers. John N. Edwards

> acted as their apologist from the beginning of their criminal careers. He glorified their exploits, praised their characters, minimized their misdeeds. They were, in his view, "men who might have sat at the Round Table, ridden at tourney with Sir Lancelot or won the colors of Guinevere." (O'Brien 10)

Until his death on April 3, 1882, James continued robbing trains and banks, killing people, and claiming he was committing such crimes for the Southern cause. Robert Ford, who had joined Jesse's band with his brother Charles, made a deal with the sheriff and Kansas police to deliver James dead. Ford's opportunity arose when James was dusting a picture on the wall and had his back to Ford. He shot Jesse, who died instantly. Ford, instead of being considered a hero for killing the outlaw, was branded a traitor.

A popular ballad describes the event and refers to Jesse as "Mr. Howard," an alias he used to protect his family:

> Jesse had a wife to mourn for his life,
> Three children, they were brave,   180
> But that dirty little coward that shot Mr. Howard
> Has laid Jesse James in his grave. (Botkin 108)

In killing Jesse, Ford put the finishing touch on Jesse's life in more than one sense. Castel rightly summarizes Ford's contribution: 185

> . . . Jesse . . . achieved the perfect legend. [. . .] His death and the manner of it wiped away, in the popular mind, the harsh reality of his deeds and transformed him into the classic bandit-hero whose daring and cunning render him invincible until he is brought down by base treachery. In this sense Bob Ford did   190 Jesse a favor: it would not have been the same if he had died in bed, like . . . [his] brother Frank, from old age. (18)

From the time of his death to the present, James' career has been so glamorized in folktales and ballads, books and movies that it is almost impossible to separate fact from fiction. As B. A.   195 Botkin puts it, "The bare outline has been filled in by old-timers, journalists, and dime novelists with some of the most lurid and fantastic traditions and fictions that the popular imagination has ever concocted" (108). From 1901 to 1903 *six million* copies of 121 novels about Jesse James were published by Street and Smith,   200 publishers (Fishwick 150).

Jesse James was a box-office hit as well, and inspiration for a popular television series. The first Jesse James movie, *The Train Robbery,* appeared in 1903. The best remembered film, *Jesse James,* came out in 1939; Tyrone Power starred as Jesse, with Henry   205 Fonda as Frank. Producer Darryl Zanuck spent $1,600,000 making it. James' granddaughter, Jo Frances said, "The only resemblance to fact that I could see is that once there was a man named Jesse James and he rode a horse" ("Movie of the Week" 54). The Jesse James story has been told more than three dozen times in   210 feature-length films (O'Brien 10).

James was so admired that many believed that Ford had not really killed him. As late as 1948, a J. Frank Dalton claimed to be the real Jesse. If Jesse had been alive then, he would have been 101! Instead of ignoring the old man's story, newspapers splashed   215 it on the front page. People flocked from thousands of miles away to see the famed outlaw in the flesh. Time and again historians have had to check out impostors' claims, but the days of men pretending to be the famed outlaw are long gone. Time has abolished this practice. Any man claiming to be Jesse today would have to be 140 years old. [220]

Though the man is long dead, the legend lives. People will go on believing that he murdered only to take revenge on the North, that he robbed from the rich and gave to the poor, and that he killed only in self-defense. They ignore the facts: James committed several cold-blooded murders, and he never asked his victims [225] whether they were preachers or ex-Confederates. He murdered at least two unarmed bank tellers, who, far from resisting or attacking him, were groveling at his feet (Lyon 48).

Maybe James did kill to avenge the South, but justifying his [230] actions by attributing them to vengeance is questionable at best. Many opposed the banks and the railroads, but few used guns to deal with the problem. Many ex-guerrillas returned home to lead normal lives, but not Jesse James. There is no evidence that the money that he stole went to the poor. The widow story is only [235] folklore. The standard biography, William Settle's *Jesse James Was His Name,* calls Jesse and his brother "cold-eyed bandits who gunned down unarmed men and terrorized the countryside" (qtd. in O'Brien 11). His most recent biographer says that Jesse was [240]

> a violent, ruthless marauder who stole what he refused to earn honestly and killed whoever stood in his way. He himself helped create and promote the myths that sought to excuse his lawlessness. . . . Although he possessed likeable qualities, the fact that [245] he was not in all respects a monster leaves him far from being a hero. (Ernst 72)

The times in which James lived and the age-old need for heroes have promoted to legendary status a man who spent his life stealing and killing without mercy. As one writer explains, "We cherish our desperadoes. If the James boys did not steal from the rich [250] and give to the poor in real life, no matter: they will do it forever in the cozy badlands of our dreams. A good outlaw is hard to find" (O'Brien 11). The legend not only pardons but defends a career of armed robbery and murder.

Works cited

Adams, Ramon F., comp. *Six Guns and Saddle Leather: A Bibliography of Books and Pamphlets on Western Outlaws and Gunmen.* Norman: U of Oklahoma P, 1969.

Angiolillo, Paul F. *A Criminal As Hero: Angelo Duca.* Lawrence: Regents Press of Kansas, 1979.

Botkin, B. A., ed. *A Treasury of American Folklore: Stories, Ballads, and Traditions of the People.* New York: Crown, 1944.

Breihan, Carl W. *The Complete and Authentic Life of Jesse James.* New York: Fell, 1953.

Castel, Albert. "Men Behind the Masks: The James Brothers." *American History Illustrated* June 1982: 10–18.

Ernst, John. *Jesse James.* Englewood Cliffs: Prentice, 1976.

Fishwick, Marshall. *The Hero: American Style.* New York: McKay, 1969.

Greenway, John, ed. *Folklore of the Great West.* Palo Alto: American West, [1969].

Lyon, Peter. "The Wild, Wild West." *American Heritage* Aug. 1960: 35–36.

"Movie of the Week: *Jesse James.*" *Life* 30 Jan. 1939: 54–55.

O'Brien, Pat. "Frank and Jesse James: How Two Killers Became National Heroes." *TV Guide* 15 Feb. 1986: 10–11.

Smith, Dwight L., comp. *The American and Canadian West: A Bibliography.* Santa Barbara: ABC-Clio, 1979.

PART V

Writing for
Special Purposes

UNIT 19

Essay
Examinations

"What do you mean—'two questions out of three'? Didn't we have to write on all of them?" "When the bell rang, I was only halfway through the second question." "Ye gods! I just realized that I left out the most important example!" "When I saw everybody else still writing like crazy, I got scared and added a lot of junk the professor won't like." "When I got to the ending I realized I should have started differently, but it was too late to change things." "I thought I had an easy A for that course, but I think I've blown the final."

Some of your most important writing in college will be on examinations. Many good students, who have been conscientious about their work all term, do not get the final grade they expected because they give too little thought to their writing on the final examination and produce essays that are a confusing jumble. You may know a great deal about a subject, but unless you present your knowledge in a clear, well-organized form, your readers will not be able to evaluate it. In composing an effective essay for an examination, apply all the advice and suggestions given earlier in this book, especially those in Units 1 and 2.

Take time to plan. For each question, jot down notes on scrap paper and make a rough outline. Then you will not risk forgetting an important point or losing track of your overall organization. Do not give in to your impatience or let the sight of your classmates writing away feverishly make you begin before you are ready.

First, read all the directions carefully. The student who handed in an unfinished paper late and complained that there was not enough time to answer ten questions got little sympathy from the instructor, who pointed out that the directions called for answering only seven of the ten.

Read through all the questions. Every set of questions represents an instructor's estimate of what most of the students in the class should be able to do in the time allowed. If you spend too much time on the first question, you will be rushed on the last ones. Also, by reading through all the questions before starting to write, you can discover the ones you are best prepared to answer. An exceptionally good and complete discussion of some questions may compensate for a brief treatment of those about which you know less. Moreover, if you find that some questions overlap, you can decide in advance what to include in each answer and save time and effort later.

Pay close attention to directions on the manner in which each question is to be answered. For example, among the questions that call for true essays there may be factual questions that you can answer in a few words. If you are asked to "list six results" or "enumerate eight causes," do not write a long discussion of results and causes. You cannot expect your instructor to take time to dig the vital points out of your discussion. If you are asked to state something in a single sentence, use no more and no less; but when you are told "discuss at length" or "explain fully," you should write at least a paragraph.

Determine the length of your answers on the basis of three factors: the number of questions, the time allowed, and your knowledge of your own speed of thinking and writing. When instructors give a single question as a three-hour final, they naturally expect a wealth of detail that they definitely do not expect when they give five questions to be answered in an hour. The more comprehensive your answer is supposed to be, the more care you should take in planning it.

Remember that there is no special value in mere length. Your instructor, who must read dozens of examination papers every time you write one, is likely to be more favorably impressed by a concise answer that drives straight to the point than by a long and flowery piece of rhetoric. A brief generalization supported by a few well-chosen examples is always worth pages of vague abstraction.

In answering discussion questions, you will find a use for the types of writing analyzed in this book. You may be asked to describe a battle or the characteristics of a political leader (Unit 4); to narrate the chief events in the life of a literary or historical figure (Unit 5); to give specific examples of a general concept (Unit 6); to summarize or outline the main points of an argument, event, or theory (Units 7 and 8); to tell how to make a piece of laboratory equipment or carry on an industrial process (Unit 9); to compare two characters in a book of fiction or the circumstances leading up to two events (Unit 10); to classify people, poems, or natural phenomena (Unit 11); to name and explain the parts of a flower or a piece of machinery, or to analyze a social problem (Unit 12); to discuss causes and effects, such as the reasons for the Depression or the results of Prohibition (Unit 13); to define terms from the new vocabulary that almost every course forces you to learn (Unit 14); to report the results of an experiment, to draw conclusions from evidence, or to apply general laws of science or principles of economics to specific cases (Unit 15); to defend an opinion or theory (Unit 16); to make a critical analysis of your outside reading (Unit 17); or to correlate various reading materials, as in a research paper (Unit 18). In fact, the fields you are studying are so varied and the possibilities for kinds of essay examinations are so numerous that there is no limit to the methods of thinking and writing that you may be called on to use.

Always reserve a few moments at the end to reread your work, to catch errors in spelling, grammar, and punctuation as well as in content. Remember that a single slip of the pen may change the meaning of a whole paragraph. Your instructors may not consciously lower grades for inaccuracies in composition, but they cannot avoid being at least subconsciously put off by careless errors and impressed by careful writing. No one will object to corrections and deletions or to additions placed between the lines on the examination paper, but the more easily your instructors can read your papers, the better. Write legibly in ink—it is wise to take a spare pen with you—and leave reasonable margins. This is not to imply that college instructors place a "grade school" premium on neatness, but they can appreciate the good points of a paper more easily if they can read it easily.

Another mechanical but important aspect of examination writing is the numbering of your answers. Your replies should not only appear in the order of the questions but should be carefully labeled to match them. Questions labeled with Roman numerals may be subdivided into parts labeled with capital letters, and ones with Arabic numerals may have parts marked "a," "b," and so on. Be sure to label your corresponding answers with both designations, clearly and in order, and place them at or in the margin where they can be seen immediately, not buried within a paragraph. If there is a question that you cannot answer, include its number and leave a space so that you can return to it later if something suitable occurs to you. This method will also prevent your instructor from suspecting that you left out the number deliberately.

Much of this advice applies to objective examinations of all kinds— true-false, filling-in-blanks, multiple-choice, matching. Read each question carefully and follow all the directions exactly. If you read hastily through true-false statements and jump to conclusions, if you use plus and minus signs when "T" and "F" were asked for, if you write your answers at the sentence ends instead of in the designated places, or if you use ink when a No. 2 pencil is required, you may fail even though you know all the answers. Correction keys and computers make no allowances for personal idiosyncracies and give no credit for good intentions.

The objective examination is frequently a time test as well as an information test, designed to check your speed as well as your knowledge. Consequently, you should first read through it rapidly, answering only those questions whose answers occur to you immediately. Then you can return and spend the necessary time on the troublesome ones, without worrying that you will be caught at the end of the period with some obvious ones unanswered.

Note: You have probably been told many times that cramming is a vicious habit—and every word you were told is true. Have the good sense and willpower to make reviewing a simple everyday matter instead of cramming all night before an examination. You will be rewarded not only with higher grades, which, after all, are only an immediate, temporary concern, but with a far better and more lasting knowledge of the subject. If you do your reviewing the day before, get a good night's sleep, and go to the examination without further study, you will gain far more from your resulting clear-headed perspective on the whole subject than from frantically cramming your mind with jumbled details up to the last minute.

This may sound like an impossible ideal—but you can achieve it.

EXAMPLES

19-A   Freedom of Speech

Richard Peterson *(student)*

This essay was written for the final examination in an introductory course in American government. The question was "What rights are guaranteed by the First Amendment and what limitations are placed on them in ordinary practice?" The instructor recommended that the students spend one hour on the question. The information in this student's essay is accurate, the examples are appropriate, and the overall organization is firm and clear. The result, although not brilliant, is satisfactory.

The most important "right" defined by the Bill of Rights is freedom of speech. It is essential in a democracy, and all our other rights and freedoms depend on it. That is why it was the first amendment made to the Constitution.

If we want to decide any question intelligently, we should hear the arguments on all sides. An argument may seem very strong and good, but we cannot be sure that it is completely right until we have heard the opposing views. They may show us something that we have overlooked. If we think the opposing views are wrong or foolish or even immoral, we should remember that listening to them doesn't mean accepting them. I think the students should have listened last June instead of shouting down Jeane Kirkpatrick when she tried to give a speech at their college. So what if they didn't like her foreign policy? They didn't have to agree with it, but she had a right to present her ideas.

The only danger in giving everyone freedom of speech is that someone may use that right for the wrong purpose, just to make trouble. The standard example is the maniac who shouts "Fire!" in a crowded theater just to see the panic and the stampede to the exits. Even when there really is a fire, we shouldn't use that way to alert people. It's an abuse of free speech. A more common abuse of free speech occurs when a speaker deliberately stirs people up to make them riot and turn to violence, doing such things as overturning cars, setting fire to buildings, and beating up other people.

Earlier in this century two Supreme Court Justices, Oliver Wendell Holmes and Louis Brandeis, ruled that anyone who used the right to free speech to stir up trouble was wrong and should be punished. This ruling is known as the "clear and present danger test." A related ruling by the Supreme Court says that the government can limit someone's right to free speech if that person's remarks *might* lead others to do illegal things. This ruling is much more difficult to interpret, and it was a key point in the court case that developed over the American Nazi Party's plan to march through Skokie, Illinois, a town where many Jewish people lived who had been refugees from the Nazi Holocaust of World War II. The American Nazis claimed that they just wanted to have a peaceful parade and that they had a right to express their opinions that way, but the Skokie residents claimed that what the Nazis really wanted was to stir up a violent reaction by the Jews so that they could have a fight.

Cases involving freedom of speech are usually very hard to decide and are likely to cause a lot of bad feelings on both sides, but the right involved is well worth the trouble because it is so important to a democratic way of life.

1. Notice the short introductory and concluding paragraphs giving the writer's subject and general opinion and acting as a frame for the essay.

2. Why does the writer give two paragraphs to the dangers of free speech but only one to explaining why he thinks it is important?

19-B The Greenhouse Effect

Lisa Weber *(student)*

This essay was written for the final examination in an introductory course in natural science. The question was "What is the 'greenhouse effect' and why do many scientists think we may be endangered by it?" The instructor recommended that the students spend thirty minutes on it. The student has given accurate information and organized it in a clear, simple pattern.

The "greenhouse effect" is the name that scientists have given to what may result from having more carbon dioxide in the earth's atmosphere than we used to have.

Scientific measurements have shown that the amount of carbon dioxide in the atmosphere of the earth is increasing rapidly. This   5
is happening because coal, oil, natural gas, and wood all give off carbon dioxide when they burn, and we are using more and more fuel for energy. Also, many forests in the world are being destroyed or at least reduced in size because of the expansions in farms and cities as the population of the world increases. Trees   10
convert carbon dioxide into oxygen, and so the more trees we cut down, the fewer converters of carbon dioxide will be here to help us, the more carbon dioxide there will be in the atmosphere, and the less oxygen for us to breathe.

Another result creates a more immediate danger. The visible   15
rays of the sun can go through carbon dioxide and reach the earth, warming it up. The warmth makes the earth give off infrared rays. These rays are absorbed by the carbon dioxide instead of escaping into space, as they would if there were less carbon dioxide. The earth will work like a huge greenhouse, growing warmer and   20
warmer from these combined effects.

If the warming process continues, there will be many major changes in ecology. The polar icecaps would melt, gradually raising the sea level all over the world and flooding low-lying coastal areas. Cities like Boston, New York, Miami, New Orleans, and   25
Los Angeles would disappear. Also, the desert areas all over the world would grow larger because many kinds of plants will not grow in a warmer climate and the heat in the air would dry up

small rivers. These results would mean not only major changes in
the way we live but would also create worldwide hunger.   30

If the scientists are right in their predictions, we should be
taking action now to reduce the greenhouse effect as quickly as
possible.

1. In what ways is the overall organization of this example similar to that of
19-A?

2. How and where does the student use cause-and-effect relationships and
deductive reasoning to arrive at conclusions?

ASSIGNMENTS

1. If you have access to files of old examination questions, look through them to
   discover the type of writing that is required in the answers. If among them are
   questions covering the work of courses you are now taking, try writing answers
   to any with which you are already familiar.
2. Save your own examination questions and compare them with your answers after
   your paper has been returned. If your grade was lower than you expected, try to
   discover whether you were penalized for lack of preparation or poor presentation.
   (If in doubt, ask the instructor to go over the paper with you.) Practice rewriting
   some of your answers, after referring to the suggestions given in the preceding
   units for the types of writing they require.

   One of the most important results of your college training in composition
   should be that through leisurely and painstaking writing, like that in the themes
   you prepare outside of class, you gradually learn to write papers of acceptable
   quality while working rapidly and under pressure, as you are obliged to do in
   writing examinations and themes in class.

UNIT 20

Business Letters
and Résumés

Many books and whole courses are devoted to business English, but here we shall consider only the kinds of letters that you as an individual are likely to write. "Business English" requires as much clearness and correctness as does all your other writing. But, because it has the practical purpose of getting something done rather than only informing or entertaining, it tends to be simpler and more direct. The modern trend is in sharp contrast to the past, when letters were often only collections of elaborate set expressions. A publisher, promoting better business letters, writes:

> If we're not careful, the standard terminology of business letters can be pretty silly. Used thoughtlessly, it can be downright insulting. Here are some common expressions—with the possible reactions of a modern reader:

I have before me your letter . . . . Okay, answer it!
In due course of time . . . . After the usual boondoggling.
I wish to state . . . . Why wish? Just say it!
We are this day in receipt of . . . . By George, they got it!
Kindly advise the undersigned . . Who's writing the letter, anyhow?
Please accept our order . . . . Any time!
Thank you for your patronage . . Patrons went out of style long ago.
And so did these expressions . . . . (Economics Press, Fairfield, NJ)

Such time-wasting patterns are being dropped in favor of a direct, simple reply. Beginnings such as "Replying to your letter of March 6" and endings such as "Hoping to hear from you soon, we remain" now sound old-fashioned. Simplicity may go to an extreme, however. In the telegraphic style, the writer lops off words as if they cost a dollar each:

Received your letter. Adjustment suggested is satisfactory. Will return goods at once and await immediate refund.

Make your business English the language of natural speech, but remember that complete sentences are usually more understandable, even in speaking.

∴ ∴ ∴

The conventional business letter has five parts, besides the message itself. Before the message are the heading, the inside address, and the salutation; after the message are the complimentary close and the signature. See the model letters on pages 446 and 447 for illustrations.

1. The **heading** includes your address and the date on which you are writing. It usually occupies three lines in the upper right corner, far enough to the left to allow the longest line to end at the right-hand margin. Business firms use stationery with letterheads giving their names and addresses; if you have stationery with a letterhead, you need only add the date below it, either near the right margin or centered under the letterhead. (Include the correct zip code numbers in all addresses—heading, inside address, envelope— always after the state and with no punctuation.)

2. The **inside address** contains the name and address of the person or firm to whom you are writing, just as it will appear on the envelope. Although its use is essentially a matter of office procedure for convenience in filing, it has become conventional for all business letters. Begin it at the left margin at least two spaces below the date. (More space is allowable here, if you are arranging a short letter on a large page.)

If your letter is addressed to a firm but you wish it to come to the attention of a particular person or officer, you may include an "attention note" (see page 447) beginning at the margin between the inside address and the salutation, with a space above and below.

3. The **salutation** appears at the left margin, two spaces below the inside address, and consists of the words with which you greet the person to whom you are writing. Whatever the occasion, follow these rules:

a. Choose a salutation that matches the inside address in number and gender disregarding any intervening attention note.

b. Choose one expressing the degree of formality suited to the occasion.

c. Capitalize the first word and all nouns.

d. Punctuate with a colon always—nothing more.

For a formal salutation when you do not know whether you are addressing men or women, or when you know that you are addressing both, use one that includes both sexes.

To more than one recipient:	*To one recipient:*
Dear Sirs and Mesdames:	Dear Sir or Madam:
Ladies and Gentlemen:	Dear Committee Member:
Dear Committee Members:	Dear Classmate:
Dear Classmates:	

If you know the sex but nothing else, use "Gentlemen" or "Sirs" for men and "Mesdames" for women.

When you know the name and sex of the recipient, choose among these conventional phrases:

To a male recipient:	*To a female recipient:*
Dear Sir:	Dear Madam:
My dear Mr. Blank:	My dear Miss (*or* Ms. *or* Mrs., as appropriate) Blank:
Dear Mr. Blank:	Dear Miss (*or* Ms. *or* Mrs., as appropriate) Blank:

Plurals: For "Mr." use "Messrs."; for "Mrs." and "Madam" use "Mmes."; for "Miss" use "Misses"; "Ms." may be either singular or plural.

"My dear Mr. Blank," "My dear Miss Blank," and so on, are generally considered slightly more formal than "Dear Mr. Blank," "Dear Miss Blank," and so on. (This is the reverse of British usage.) "Dear Sir" and "Dear Madam" remain the most formal salutations of all. *Never* write "Dear Gentlemen" or "Dear Ladies." For a less formal salutation that avoids the problem of a title for the recipient, simply use his or her full name: "Dear John Blank" or "Dear Jane Blank."

4. The **complimentary close,** the words by which you take your leave, should begin far enough from the right margin for your name and title, if any, to end before the right margin. Place them at least two spaces below the last line of your letter. (This space, like that between the heading and the inside address, can be increased for arrangement's sake.) Like the salutation, the complimentary close has become conventionalized into a few acceptable phrases, of which these are the most popular:

    a. Very truly yours, Yous very truly, Yours truly,

    b. Sincerely yours, Yours sincerely, Yours very sincerely, Sincerely,

    c. Cordially yours, Yours cordially, Cordially,

The first group is very impersonal, the second friendlier, the third the warmest. Words like "faithfully" and "respectfully" have gone out of general business use in America.

    a. Choose a close that will match the degree of formality expressed in your salutation.

    b. Capitalize the first word only.

    c. Punctuate with a comma.

5. Directly under the complimentary close, **sign your name** as you are in the habit of writing it. Be sure that it can be easily read; do not pride yourself on one of those highly distinctive signatures that look more like a careless drawing than a row of letters (experts say they are more easily forged than are decipherable ones). If you type your letter, type your name also, to make certain of its legibility, but leave room (four lines will do it) between the complimentary close and the typed name for your handwritten signature, to certify the letter as your own. If you are writing in any official capacity, your title should appear below your name:

Jane Blank
President
Pre-Med Society

As for social titles, a man never signs himself "Mr.," since that title is taken for granted. But a woman may wish to indicate her marital status with "Miss," "Ms." or "Mrs." for the convenience of the person replying. Those titles are not part of her legal signature, however, just as "Mr." is not part of a man's, and they should therefore be enclosed in parentheses:

(Miss) Jane Blank	for an unmarried woman
Jane Blank	for a married woman (traditional
(Mrs. John Blank)	style requires both names)
(Mrs.) Jane Blank	for a married woman with a career
	or for a formerly married woman
(Ms.) Jane Blank	for any of the above

Two pairs of initials that usually appear at the left margin of a business letter opposite or slightly below the signature are those of the person sending the letter and of the secretary who typed it, for purposes of record. As an individual writing your own business letters, you do not need to add initials in this spot.

Abbreviations You must use the abbreviations "Mr.," "Mrs.," and "Ms." since these forms are never written out. Other abbreviations in common use include "Dr." and (after names) "Jr.," "D.D.S.," "M.D.," and so on. You may abbreviate first names to initials (especially if the owners do so themselves), terms describing businesses if the business itself does (Sears, Roebuck and Co., Mumford & Jones), and directions (1014 E. Morton Street, 444 Vermont Street N.W.—designating a section of a city). Names of countries are not abbreviated except "U.S.A." and "U.S.S.R.," but those of states usually are when they are part of a written address. Use the two-letter abbreviations of the states authorized by the U.S. Postal Department.

Other abbreviations (of months, street names, etc.) are generally frowned on in business letters; the slight saving of time is not enough to offset the appearance of haste or lack of effort.

·:·   ·:·   ·:·

In the general format for your letter, observe these six conventions.

1. **Type your letter** or write neatly and legibly in blue or black ink— never use pencil or ink of any other color. Make a carbon or photocopy for your own records; it may prevent many problems later.

2. For **stationery,** use a good grade of white paper of standard "typewriter size" ($8\frac{1}{2}" \times 11"$). It should always be unruled (use a ruled guide under a handwritten letter to keep lines reasonably straight). For very brief letters you may use the half-sheet size of paper ($8\frac{1}{2}" \times 5\frac{1}{2}"$). On this size you may write either the long way, producing a short letter of standard width (this is generally preferred, for convenience in handling and filing), or the short way, producing a miniature letter of standard proportions (this is chosen by some for its appearance).

3. **Arrange your whole letter** carefully on the page. Whatever size paper you use, the letter should look like a well-framed picture.

   a. Make the spacing of the parts and the width of the margins appropriate to the length of the letter as a whole.

   b. All four margins should be approximately equal; each should be at least $1\frac{1}{2}"$ wide, with the bottom one slightly wider than the others.

c. Use single-spacing, with double-spacing between paragraphs for typed letters of three or more lines. For a very brief letter, use double-spacing and a half-sheet of paper to avoid the lonely look of a single line or two of message.

d. Hyphenate very long words at the ends of the lines to keep the right-hand margin roughly in line. (Check the dictionary to determine where to divide words.)

e. Be concise; try to keep to one page. If your letter must be longer, keep the margins at least 1½" wide and make sure that you have at least three lines of the message on the last page. Number each page after the first.

f. *Never* write on the back of a sheet.

4. **Arrange the parts** of the letter in **semiblock** or **full-block** style.

a. In semiblock (see the example on page 446), all the lines of the inside address begin at the left margin, as does the salutation; all the lines of the heading begin at one inside margin, and the complimentary close and signature begin at another. In typed letters, the paragraphs may begin at the left margin because double-spacing between them will be enough to show paragraph divisions. In handwritten letters, indented paragraphs are advisable.

b. In full-block (see page 447), all the lines of the heading, salutation, complimentary close, and signature begin at the left margin.

c. The only punctuation *ending* these parts is a colon after the salutation (a comma is conventional in a social letter) and a comma after the complimentary close.

d. The only punctuation *within* these parts is a comma in the traditional style of date, separating the day and year, and in the address, separating the name of the town or city from that of the state.

5. Use a **white envelope** of the same quality and finish as your paper. The standard small size (3¾" × 6½") will take a half-sheet letter or a full-sheet letter of one page. For a longer letter, use the official size (4¼" × 9½").

a. Make the outside address identical with the inside, beginning it at the approximate center of the envelope so that it will occupy roughly the lower right quarter of the envelope face.

b. Put your name and complete address in the extreme upper left corner.

c. Place any special directions such as an attention note, "Personal," or "Please Forward" in the lower left corner.

d. Attach the stamp—right side up—well inside the upper right corner of the envelope. It will look better and be protected from accidental tearing.

6. **Fold the letter** so that the recipient can withdraw it easily.

a. Fold a half-sheet letter in three parts. The two wings should be slightly narrower than the center section.

b. Fold a one-sheet letter into six parts. Bring the bottom up to within half an inch of the top, and crease; then fold it as you would a half-sheet letter.

c. Fold a longer letter into three parts, bringing the bottom up about two-thirds of the way to the top and the top down to about half an inch from the resulting crease.

∴ ∴ ∴

425 Merton Road
Danville, OH 43014
December 2, 1991

Dr. William Macauley
25 Manistee Boulevard
Cleveland, OH 44107

Dear Dr. Macauley:

I regret that I cannot keep my appointment with you on Tuesday, December 15, at 4 p.m. A change in my examination schedule will keep me in Danville on that date.

May I see you at 4 p.m. on Monday, December 21? Please write confirming this time, or suggesting a later one at your convenience.

Sincerely yours,

Robert G. Weston

Robert G. Weston

This is in semi-block style. Note the spacing of the parts:

— 2–4 spaces

— 2 spaces

— 2–4 spaces

Route 3, Box 61
Naylorton, TN 37836
January 19, 1991

The Acme Photo Company
1018 East Moore Street
Detroit, MI 48200

Attention: Mr. H. A. Green, Framing Department

Gentlemen:

The price you quote in your letter of January 11 for
enlarging and framing the photograph of my two sons,
about which I wrote you in December, is entirely
satisfactory.

I am therefore enclosing the negative and the folder
with mat samples on which I have marked my preference. I
look forward to receiving the completed picture in about
ten days, as you have indicated.

Very truly yours,

Linda Williams

Linda Williams
(Mrs. Arthur Williams)

1. Identify the conventional letter parts before and after the messages in the model letters just shown.
2. Name the arrangement used in each.
3. In what respects are the forms of the two letters identical? in what different?
4. Which form is the more commonly used? What are the advantages and disadvantages of each? Which do you prefer?
5. Do the choices of salutation and complimentary close correctly indicate in each letter the degree of formality that seems to be intended?
6. Address an envelope (an appropriately sized rectangle will serve for practice) for the letter in semi–block style, including your return address.
7. Practice folding an $8\frac{1}{2}"\times 11"$ sheet and inserting it properly into a commercial-size envelope; into an official-size envelope. Repeat with a half-sheet and a commercial-size envelope. Practice until you can perform the required operations smoothly and correctly, without pausing to think.
8. How many errors can you discover in the letter form that follows:

```
                                   January 22, 1990
                                   145 Glassell Ave.
                                   Syracuse, New York


   Brandon Brothers
    1818 Dover Street
    Pullman, Washington.
    Dear sir,


   . . . . . . . . . . . . . . . . . . . . . . . . . . . .


                        Yours Truly
                        Kim Saunders.
```

Four types of letters

1. For a **letter making an inquiry**—one asking for prices, catalogs, accommodations, general information—use the basic form already described and also follow these directions:

a. **Be explicit.** Include enough details to make a definite reply possible. A letter asking a hotel if rooms are available is pointless if you omit the date for which you want them, the number of people concerned, and the type of accommodations preferred. Make your inquiry so clear that the reply can be an answer instead of a request for more specific information.

b. **Be brief.** Include all the necessary details but nothing that is beside the point. A request for information about a company's product may appropriately include the use to which you plan to put it, but an inquiry about theater tickets need not include your reasons for seeing the play.

c. **Be courteous.** Even though your inquiry may lead to a sale that the firm will be glad to make, remember that you are asking a favor. "Send me your catalog" will doubtless get results, but "please" and "thank you" are still welcome oil in the gears.

Notice how the two letters that follow meet these requirements.

> Will you please send me a copy of your current "Gardener's Guide" advertised in the May issue of *Flower and Garden.*

(A question like this—really a politely worded command—is usually punctuated with a period instead of a question mark. Mentioning where you learned of the literature requested is an added courtesy; it helps the company to know exactly what you wish and also to check on the effectiveness of its advertising.)

I own a four-quart pressure cooker, model 2K64B, that my parents bought about thirty years ago. The gasket on the cover has begun to leak steam, reducing the pressure inside. Except for this difficulty, the cooker works well, and I would like to continue to use it, but my local hardware store has no gaskets the right size.

Do you still have gaskets for this model in stock? If you do, please let me know the types and prices. If you do not, can you suggest a substitute?

(This gives all the details that the company will need to make a reply. The letter could have been treated as one paragraph because it is brief and all on one subject, but the short final paragraph emphasizes the writer's inquiry. Notice that the first and last sentences in that paragraph are real questions, unlike the polite command in the first letter, and therefore have question marks.)

2. **For a letter making an order** from a catalog or advertisement, use the general form already discussed and also observe the following directions:

a. £Give an exact description of the article desired—quantity, size, color, price, and catalog or order number, if there is one.

b. **Give the method of shipment:** air, parcel post, express, freight; the "fastest" or "cheapest" way; special delivery; prepaid or collect.

c. **Give the arrangement for payment:** C.O.D.; cash, stamps, check, money order; a charge to your account or credit card, with the name and number.

Please send me one (1) pair of your new line of stereo headphones with the SM-700 "Studio Master," using 2¾-inch Mylar diaphragm drivers.

I enclose my check for $65.00, the advertised price, and understand that you will send it postage paid.

(This letter is both brief and explicit. It makes clear the item desired, the method of shipment, and the arrangement for paying.)

3. **In a letter making a complaint,** tact is important. Remember that courtesy is not only pleasing but profitable—as the old saying goes, more flies are caught with honey than vinegar. Any business firm finds it easier to say "The customer is always right" if he or she is also reasonable.

a. **Be sure that you have real cause to complain.** Better to wait a day or two, for instance, than to send a complaint of nonarrival that crosses the shipment in the mail.

b. **Be sure that your complaint is just.** Check your order to make sure that you wrote the size correctly and legibly, before blaming the store because your new boots do not fit.

c. **Write reasonably and courteously.** Be exact and clear in explaining the cause for your dissatisfaction, and suggest what you regard as a suitable adjustment.

Consider the probable effects of the two letters that follow.

> Last week I spent good money to go clear into Centerville to buy a sweater at your Sports Bar. I got one, but your salesclerk was careful not to tell me that it was soiled from lying around too long on your shelves waiting for a sucker like me, and I didn't see the soil marks until I got home. I think that any store that does that kind of trick ought to be ashamed of itself, and I can promise you that you won't get any more trade from me or any of my friends.

(The writer now probably feels much better for the time being, but the store has been given no suggestion for a suitable adjustment and no opening to make one. If the writer is wise, he or she will follow Mark Twain's practice and tear up this caustic masterpiece and start again.)

> When I was in Centerville last week I bought a beige wool pullover sweater at your Sports Bar for $45.98. Not until I got home did I see that there were two badly soiled areas on the back caused by lying folded on the shelf.
> Do you wish me to return it in exchange for another, or would you prefer to pay me for having it cleaned locally? (The cost would be $8.00.) I would prefer to have it cleaned, because I did not see another one in your stock of just this style and color.

(The lack of recrimination is not only courteous but fair, since no one seems particularly at fault. Customers can scarcely blame the salesclerk for not noticing what they themselves overlooked. The psychology of taking for granted that an adjustment will be made is particularly good, far superior to merely asking if the firm will make one. Also, the suggestion of specific adjustment possibilities, with a statement of the customer's preference, simplifies the whole transaction.)

4. **Letters of application** may be the most important letters that you ever write. If you are applying for an award, for admission to a special program, or for a job, your letter may change your life.

a. **Make the letter appealing.** Courtesy and clearness are all you need for inquiries, orders, and complaints, but the application letter is essentially a sales letter.

(1) **Think first of the viewpoint of your prospective readers.** They will be interested in what you may be able to contribute to the field, not in your purely personal considerations. You are "selling" your skills, not yourself. "Because of my long interest in popular music and because I have been taking piano lessons for the past three years, I believe I can be useful in your record store" is more likely to appeal to the store owner than "I want to work for you because I would like a discount on buying records" or "because my best friend works in the coffee shop across the street and can give me a ride."

(2) **Do not be too modest.** The door-to-door salesman who asked "You don't want to buy some magazines, do you?" may have gotten

a few orders out of pity, but he didn't get fat on commissions. Never begin with such expressions as "I don't know whether I can do this work" or "I know nothing about your program." In an application letter, put your best foot foremost and keep the other safely out of sight.

(3) **Do not be boastful.** A statement like "I have always been a super salesman ever since I was a child" or "I have always outranked every other student in my class" may be perfectly true, but it is likely to antagonize. Leave such information for others to supply in the letters of recommendation they write for you.

(4) **Do not sound superior** to whatever you are applying for. No reader was ever won by such remarks as "I am willing to work in your program until I can find one that suits me better," "My experience has been in colleges with more prestige than yours," or "I am looking for a job only because of recent financial problems in my family."

(5) **State honestly the achievements that are relevant** to whatever you are applying for. What may be an important asset for some applications may be irrelevant boasting for others. "All through high school I spent my spare time helping in a sports program for neighborhood children" would be valuable if you were applying for work as a camp counselor or for admission to a child psychology program but not for work in accounting.

(6) **Try to make your letter stand out favorably** from others. Your prospective readers may receive dozens or even hundreds of letters from qualified persons, and you must try to make them notice yours. But do not mistake mere freakishness for individuality. Your letter of application should be serious and dignified, without any of the extra devices often used in other types of sales letters.

b. **The content of your letter of application** will normally fall into five main sections: introduction, personal data, qualifications, list of references, and conclusion.

(1) Your introduction will depend on your particular situation. If you are answering an advertisement or announcement, begin with a reference to it. If you learned indirectly of the award, program, or job opening, mention how you learned of it. If you have no definite knowledge of an opening but are hopeful that one may develop, begin with some mention of your reasons for applying to the particular awards committee, college, or firm to whom you are writing.

(2) Give the personal data relevant to the situation—a list of objective facts about yourself, such as your age, sex, marital status, and any other items, such as health, citizenship, or religion, that may be pertinent.

(3) Give the qualifications that fit you for whatever you are applying for: your education, experience, interest, aptitudes.

(4) List your references—the names, official positions, and addresses of the people best qualified to recommend you, as to both character and

ability. (You will, of course, have already gotten their permission to name them as references, and later you will thank them for recommending you.)

(5) Conclude your letter of application with something to ensure a reply: a request for an interview; a reminder that you have enclosed a stamped, self-addressed envelope for your reader's convenience; an indication that you hope for an early reply.

(Which of these many items to stress and which to omit will depend, of course, on the nature of what you are seeking. Religious education, for instance, may be important in becoming a counselor in a church-supported summer camp but not for admission to an intensive foreign language program. Experience and references from previous employers are always important. Since you are a student, your education, with specific references to relevant courses, and recommendations from faculty members who know you well will probably be your chief assets.)

c. **Compose a résumé** (data sheet) if the material that you wish to include covers half a typed page or more. This is a separate unit listing the objective, or factual, information (personal data, qualifications, references). Here, the information can be neatly and clearly arranged under suitable headings and subheadings that readers can consult easily and quickly. A big advantage of the résumé is that you can photocopy it, thus saving time. The actual letters of application must, of course, be written individually. Another advantage is that you can make the letter itself shorter and more readable, more like a little essay on your interest in the field, your general aptitude and inclination for it, and your hopes for future accomplishment. Remember that the letter of application is essentially a sales letter.

d. **Notice the organization, content, and effort to appeal** to readers in the following examples of letters of application. The heading, inside address, and complimentary close are omitted to save space. The first is an answer to a newspaper advertisement with only a box number to which to reply: "Wanted—college student to read to invalid, afternoons or evenings. Box 41, Sheldon *Post.*"

Dear Sir or Madam:

In answer to your advertisement in today's *Post* for a college student to read to an invalid, I would like to be considered for the position.

I have already had some experience as a reader because my grandmother, who had lost her eyesight, lived in our home while I was in high school. Now I am a sophomore in the university, where I am majoring in speech, and I am particularly interested in interpretive reading.

Professor John Secord of the Speech Department has kindly agreed to write a recommendation about my ability to read aloud, and Mrs. Elizabeth Davis, director of volunteer services at Northside Hospital, where I worked as a candy-striper last summer, may be consulted about my personality and character.

My present schedule leaves me free on Monday, Wednesday, and Friday afternoons and most weekday evenings. I would very much like to have several hours a week of such congenial part-time work. May I have an interview? My telephone number if 586-6774.

The second is an application for a known opening in a program for special study.

Dear Professor Hamilton:

Dr. R. M. Baker, head of the Biology Department here at Sheffield College, has told me that your institute offers an intensive summer program in biology for undergraduates with special abilities. I would like to apply for admission to the program this summer.

I expect to complete my work at Sheffield for the B.A. with a major in biology in June of next year and hope to go on immediately to graduate school. My goals are a Ph.D. and a position in a research laboratory.

At the end of this semester I shall have 36 hours of credit in biology at Sheffield. My average for all my undergraduate work to date is B, and in biology it is A—. My special interest is in enzymes, and last summer I helped in measuring enzymes in the umbilical cord as part of a study at Memorial Hospital of the effects on the newborn of their mothers' having smoked during pregnancy.

Throughout the current year I have worked as an undergraduate laboratory assistant for Dr. Baker in the introductory biology course. He has offered to write to you about me, at your request, and so has Dr. Jane Allen, director of my junior thesis, and Dean John Davis of the Liberal Arts College. If I am considered for admission to your program, I shall be glad to send my complete transcript for your evaluation and to supply any additional information you may need about me, my work, or my plans.

The third letter is written in the hope of an opening in a company for which the student particularly wants to work, as her letter indicates. She addresses it to the chief personnel officer, whose name she learned by telephoning the company's head office, and includes a résumé on a separate sheet of paper.

Dear Mr. Robinson:

My chief ambition has always been to become a flight attendant, and because I also have a special interest in South America, I would particularly like to work for Panagra. Since your main flights are to South American cities, and since I speak fairly good Spanish and some Portuguese, I think I can be particularly useful to your company.

At present I am a senior at Flanham College, where I am majoring in psychology with special emphasis on personnel work. I am also active in a number of campus organizations and so am gaining experience in working with people. My college minor is in Spanish and Portuguese. Also, I have always been much interested in all phases of aviation and

Resumé

Personal
  Name: Linda Katherine Harris
  College address: Sarah Black Residence Hall, Flanham
                   College, Danvers, Iowa 51091
  Home address: 286 Oak Street, Moulton, Ohio 43786

  Age: 22   Nationality: American
  Height: 5'5"   Marital status: single
  Weight: 120 lbs.   Health: excellent

Education
  Moulton High School graduate, February, 1981
  6 months in Wahl Business College, Moulton, 1981
  B.S., Flanham College (expected in June, 1985)
  Major in psychology
  Minor in languages
  General courses: English, history, mathematics,
                   physics, chemistry, psychology,
                   sociology
  Special courses: Meteorology, navigation,
                   engineering, drawing, service and
                   operation of aircraft

Activities
  Airways Club (vice-president)
  Dramatic Society (parts in three major productions)
  Science Club (program chairman, 1 year)

Experience
  Secretary to director of personnel, Ames Aircraft
    Corporation, Benzie, Illinois (1 year)
  Student assistant to head of Sarah Black Residence
    Hall, Flanham College (2 years, part-time)

References
  Dr. Ernest Beers, Head of Psychology Department,
    Flanham College
  Ms. Edna Markham, Director of Personnel, Ames Aircraft
    Corporation, Benzie, Illinois 61572
  Mr. Ted Houston, Manager, Hoadley Airport, Danvers,
    Iowa 51092

am learning to fly at Hoadley Airport nearby. I now have twelve hours of flying time to my credit.

The accompanying résumé will give you more details on my preparation and experience and includes a list of persons to whom you may write for further information about me. I do not know whether you accept beginners for your special training course, but if you do I shall be happy to come to Chicago for an interview any time this spring (preferably on Saturday, when I have no classes). If you have no openings at present but anticipate some in the near future, I hope that you will keep my application on file.

ASSIGNMENTS

The following requirements are stated generally, instead of being given in the form of specific problems, so that you can choose subjects that interest you, real-life situations for which you can write actual letters instead of merely going through the motions of a classroom exercise.

1. Write an inquiry about vacation tours, resort accommodations, services offered, goods for sale, to any actual business firm from whom you would really be interested in getting information. (Look through the current issue of a popular magazine for suggestions.)
2. Write a letter ordering merchandise, repairs, tickets—anything that you would really like to have from a real firm with a real address.
3. Write a letter complaining about any unsatisfactory goods or services (repairs, transportation, and the like) that you have recently had the misfortune to encounter.
4. Write a letter replying to a classified ad in your local paper, in which you apply for a position that you are qualified to fill.
5. Write a letter applying for summer work at some place where you know there is an opening in some line of work for which you are qualified.
6. Write a letter of application, accompanied by a data sheet, applying for the position that you think you would like when you graduate. Direct it to an actual firm, institution, or person by whom you would like to be employed.

PART VI

Essays for
Further Reading

Essays for
Further Reading

The seven essays that follow span three centuries. The writers are as different in style and personality as are the events that inspired them, yet each is recognized as an important influence on contemporary writing and thought.

Four of the essays were first delivered as speeches. A good speech is, by nature, always a good essay. Rhetorical theory began with the orators of ancient Greece, and good writers ever since have used their methods. In all these essays you will find examples of the patterns of organization and the devices for effective writing discussed in the other units of this book.

Notice particularly the description of the early stages of President Kennedy's inaugural address, which includes a comparison of the rough drafts of several sentences. The principles shown there apply to effective writing of all kinds.

A   # A Modest Proposal

Jonathan Swift (1667–1745)

Although Swift had little love for Ireland and felt the years he lived there were an exile, his devotion to justice made him a passionate fighter for Irish rights and humane treatment of the Irish poor. "A Modest Proposal" is the bitterest and most forceful attack in the English language on the exploitation of the weak by the powerful. Swift wrote it in 1729 when, after three years of poor harvests, thousands of homeless people were begging on the roads in Ireland—whole families, unable to pay rent on their farms, had been evicted by callous landlords, most of whom lived abroad to avoid paying taxes.

In this essay, perhaps the most famous in the English language, Swift assumes a "persona": he pretends to be completely unimaginative and concerned only with calculating ways to save the government money. By writing of people as if they were animals to be raised for butchering and by seeming blind to the horror of his suggestion, he satirizes the attitudes of the government and the landlords and shocks the reader into seeing their inhumanity.

Watch especially for the following: (1) satiric word choice—for example, referring to women as "breeders" (1. 45 and thereafter) to emphasize that the government is treating them as mere animals; (2) specific calculations of costs and detailed directions for using babies as meat to imply that the government thinks only of money, not human welfare; (3) the carefully numbered list of the advantages that would result from his proposal (11. 186–235); (4) the contrast of his serious recommendations of humane ways to solve the problem of Irish poverty and homelessness (11. 250–269); (5) his despair at the misery of the Irish poor (11. 289–307); (6) his concluding paragraph, which acts as a kind of footnote to declare his lack of any selfish interest in his proposal and which, incidentally, continues his use of a "persona" because it was well known by Swift's contemporaries that he had never married and had no children.

It is a melancholy object to those who walk through this great town[1] or travel in the country, when they see the streets, the roads, and cabin doors, crowded with beggars of the female sex, followed by three, four, or six children, all in rags and importuning every passenger for an alms. These mothers, instead of being   5 able to work for their honest livelihood, are forced to employ all their time in strolling to beg sustenance for their helpless infants, who, as they grow up, either turn thieves for want of work, or

[1]Dublin.

leave their dear native country to fight for the Pretender in Spain,
or sell themselves to the Barbadoes.[2]   10

I think it is agreed by all parties that this prodigious number
of children in the arms, or on the backs, or at the heels of their
mothers, and frequently of their fathers, is in the present deplor-
able state of the kingdom a very great additional grievance; and
therefore whoever could find out a fair, cheap, and easy method   15
of making these children sound, useful members of the common-
wealth would deserve so well of the public as to have his statue
set up for a preserver of the nation.

But my intention is very far from being confined to provide
only for the children of professed beggars; it is of a much greater   20
extent, and shall take in the whole number of infants at a certain
age who are born of parents in effect as little able to support them
as those who demand our charity in the streets.

As to my own part, having turned my thoughts for many years
upon this important subject, and maturely weighed the several   25
schemes of other projectors, I have always found them grossly
mistaken in their computation. It is true, a child just dropped from
its dam may be supported by her milk for a solar year, with little
other nourishment; at most not above the value of two shillings,[3]
which the mother may certainly get, or the value in scraps, by her   30
lawful occupation of begging; and it is exactly at one year old that
I propose to provide for them in such a manner as instead of being
a charge upon their parents or the parish, or wanting food and
raiment for the rest of their lives, they shall on the contrary
contribute to the feeding, and partly to the clothing, of many   35
thousands.

There is likewise another great advantage in my scheme, that
it will prevent those voluntary abortions, and that horrid practice
of women murdering their bastard children, alas, too frequent
among us, sacrificing the poor innocent babes, I doubt, more to   40
avoid the expense than the shame, which would move tears and
pity in the most savage and inhuman breast.

The number of souls in this kingdom being usually reckoned
one million and a half, of these I calculate there may be about two

[2]The pretender to the throne of England was James Stuart (1688–1766),
son of James II, who was living in exile in Spain. Many Irishmen, sympathetic to his cause, had joined him there; others had gone as indentured
servants to Barbados and other British colonies in the West Indies.

[3]The British pound sterling was subdivided into twenty shillings; a crown
equaled five shillings.

hundred thousand couple whose wives are breeders; from which   45
number I subtract thirty thousand couples who are able to maintain their own children, although I apprehend there cannot be so
many under the present distress of the kingdom; but this being
granted, there will remain an hundred and seventy thousand
breeders. I again subtract fifty thousand for those women who   50
miscarry, or whose children die by accident or disease within the
year. There only remain an hundred and twenty thousand children of poor parents annually born. The question therefore is,
how this number shall be reared and provided for, which, as I
have already said, under the present situation of affairs, is utterly   55
impossible by all the methods hitherto proposed. For we can
neither employ them in handicraft or agriculture; we neither
build houses (I mean in the country) nor cultivate land. They can
very seldom pick up a livelihood by stealing till they arrive at six
years old, except where they are of towardly parts;[4] although I   60
confess they learn the rudiments much earlier, during which time
they can however be looked upon only as probationers, as I have
been informed by a principal gentleman in the county of Cavan,
who protested to me that he never knew above one or two instances under the age of six, even in a part of the kingdom so   65
renowned for the quickest proficiency in that art.

    I am assured by our merchants that a boy or a girl before twelve
years old is no salable commodity; and even when they come to
this age they will not yield above three pounds, or three pounds
and half a crown at most on the Exchange; which cannot turn to   70
account either to the parents or the kingdom, the charge of nutri-
ment and rags having been at least four times that value.

    I shall now therefore humbly propose my own thoughts, which
I hope will not be liable to the least objection.

    I have been assured by a very knowing American of my ac-   75
quaintance in London, that a young healthy child well nursed is
at a year old a most delicious, nourishing, and wholesome food,
whether stewed, roasted, baked, or boiled; and I make no doubt
that it will equally serve in a fricassee or a ragout.

    I do therefore humbly offer it to public consideration that of   80
the hundred and twenty thousand children, already computed,
twenty thousand may be reserved for breed, whereof only one
fourth part to be males, which is more than we allow to sheep,
black cattle, or swine; and my reason is that these children are
seldom the fruits of marriage, a circumstance not much regarded   85

[4]Smart for their age.

by our savages, therefore one male will be sufficient to serve four females. That the remaining hundred thousand may at a year old be offered in sale to the persons of quality and fortune through the kingdom, always advising the mother to let them suck plentifully in the last month, so as to render them plump and fat for a good table. A child will make two dishes at an entertainment for friends; and when the family dines alone, the fore or hind quarter will make a reasonable dish, and seasoned with a little pepper or salt will be very good boiled on the fourth day, especially in winter.

I have reckoned upon a medium that a child just born will weigh twelve pounds, and in a solar year if tolerably nursed increaseth to twenty-eight pounds.

I grant this food will be somewhat dear, and therefore very proper for landlords, who, as they have already devoured most of the parents, seem to have the best title to the children.

Infant's flesh will be in season throughout the year, but more plentiful in March, and a little before and after. For we are told by a grave author, an eminent French physician,[5] that fish being a prolific diet, there are more children born in Roman Catholic countries about nine months after Lent than at any other season; therefore, reckoning a year after Lent, the markets will be more glutted than usual, because the number of popish infants is at least three to one in this kingdom; and therefore it will have one other collateral advantage, by lessening the number of Papists among us.

I have already computed the charge of nursing a beggar's child (in which list I reckon all cottagers, laborers, and four fifths of the farmers) to be about two shillings per annum, rags included; and I believe no gentleman would repine to give ten shillings for the carcass of a good fat child, which, as I have said, will make four dishes of excellent nutritive meat, when he hath only some particular friend or his own family to dine with him. Thus the squire will learn to be a good landlord, and grow popular among the tenants; the mother will have eight shillings net profit, and be fit for work till she produces another child.

Those who are more thrifty (as I must confess the times require) may flay the carcass; the skin of which artificially dressed will make admirable gloves for ladies, and summer boots for fine gentlemen.

[5]François Rabelais, the sixteenth-century French satirist, who suggested as a joke that a diet of fish stimulated human fertility.

As to our city of Dublin, shambles[6] may be appointed for this purpose in the most convenient parts of it, and butchers we may be assured will not be wanting; although I rather recommend buying the children alive, and dressing them hot from the knife as we do roasting pigs.   130

A very worthy person, a true lover of his country, and whose virtues I highly esteem, was lately pleased in discoursing on this matter to offer a refinement upon my scheme. He said that many gentlemen of this kingdom, having of late destroyed their deer, he conceived that the want of venison might be well supplied by   135 the bodies of young lads and maidens, not exceeding fourteen years of age nor under twelve, so great a number of both sexes in every country being now ready to starve for want of work and service; and these to be disposed of by their parents, if alive, or otherwise by their nearest relations. But with due deference to so   140 excellent a friend and so deserving a patriot, I cannot be altogether in his sentiments; for as to the males, my American acquaintance assured me from frequent experience that their flesh was generally tough and lean, like that of our schoolboys, by continual exercise, and their taste disagreeable; and to fatten them   145 would not answer the charge. Then as to the females, it would, I think with humble submission, be a loss to the public, because they soon would become breeders themselves: and besides, it is not improbable that some scrupulous people might be apt to censure such a practice (although indeed very unjustly) as a little   150 bordering upon cruelty; which, I confess, hath always been with me the strongest objection against any project, how well soever intended.

But in order to justify my friend, he confessed that this expedient was put into his head by the famous Psalmanazar,[7] a native   155 of the island Formosa, who came from thence to London above twenty years ago, and in conversation told my friend that in his country when any young person happened to be put to death, the executioner sold the carcass to persons of quality as a prime dainty; and that in his time the body of a plump girl of fifteen,   160 who was crucified for an attempt to poison the emperor, was sold to his Imperial Majesty's prime minister of state, and other great mandarins of the court, in joints from the gibbet, at four hundred crowns. Neither indeed can I deny that if the same use

[6]Slaughterhouses.

[7]A French contemporary of Swift's who became a celebrity in London by passing himself off as a native of Taiwan—or Formosa, as the Portuguese explorers called it.

were made of several plump young girls in this town, who with- 165
out one single groat[8] to their fortunes cannot stir abroad without a chair, and appear at the playhouse and assemblies in foreign fineries which they never will pay for, the kingdom would
not be the worse.

Some persons of a desponding spirit are in great concern about 170
that vast number of poor people who are aged, diseased, or
maimed, and I have been desired to employ my thoughts what
course may be taken to ease the nation of so grievous an encum-
brance. But I am not in the least pain upon that matter, because
it is very well known that they are every day dying and rotting 175
by cold and famine, and filth and vermin, as fast as can be reasonably expected. And as to the younger laborers, they are now in
almost as hopeful a condition. They cannot get work, and consequently pine away for want of nourishment to a degree that if at
any time they are accidentally hired to common labor, they have 180
not strength to perform it; and thus the country and themselves
are happily delivered from the evils to come.

I have too long digressed, and therefore shall return to my
subject. I think the advantages by the proposal which I have made
are obvious and many, as well as of the highest importance. 185

For first, as I have already observed, it would greatly lessen the
number of Papists,[9] with whom we are yearly overrun, being the
principal breeders of the nation as well as our most dangerous
enemies; and who stay at home on purpose to deliver the kingdom to the Pretender, hoping to take their advantage by the 190
absence of so many good Protestants, who have chosen rather to
leave their country than stay at home and pay tithes against their
conscience to an Episcopal curate.

Secondly, the poorer tenants will have something valuable of
their own, which by law may be made liable to distress, and help 195
to pay their landlord's rent, their corn and cattle being already
seized and money a thing unknown.

Thirdly, whereas the maintenance of an hundred thousand children, from two years old and upward, cannot be computed at less
than ten shillings a piece per annum, the nation's stock will be 200
thereby increased fifty thousand pounds per annum, besides the
profit of a new dish introduced to the tables of all gentlemen of
fortune in the kingdom who have any refinement in taste. And
the money will circulate among ourselves, the goods being entirely of our own growth and manufacture. 205

[8]An old British coin worth four pennies.
[9]Roman Catholics.

Fourthly, the constant breeders, besides the gain of eight shillings sterling per annum by the sale of their children, will be rid of the charge of maintaining them after the first year.

Fifthly, this food would likewise bring great custom to taverns, where the vintners will certainly be so prudent as to procure the best receipts for dressing it to perfection, and consequently have their houses frequented by all the fine gentlemen, who justly value themselves upon their knowledge in good eating; and a skillful cook, who understands how to oblige his guests, will contrive to make it as expensive as they please.

Sixthly, this would be a great inducement to marriage, which all wise nations have either encouraged by rewards or enforced by laws and penalties. It would increase the care and tenderness of mothers toward their children, when they were sure of a settlement for life to the poor babes, provided in some sort by the public, to their annual profit instead of expense. We should see an honest emulation among the married women, which of them could bring the fattest child to the market. Men would become as fond of their wives during the time of their pregnancy as they are now of their mares in foal, their cows in calf, or sows when they are ready to farrow; nor offer to beat or kick them (as is too frequent a practice) for fear of a miscarriage.

Many other advantages might be enumerated. For instance, the addition of some thousand carcasses in our exportation of barreled beef, the propagation of swine's flesh, and improvement in the art of making good bacon, so much wanted among us by the great destruction of pigs, too frequent at our tables, which are no way comparable in taste or magnificence to a well-grown, fat, yearling child, which roasted whole will make a considerable figure at a lord mayor's feast or any other public entertainment. But this and many others I omit, being studious of brevity.

Supposing that one thousand families in this city would be constant customers for infants' flesh, besides others who might have it at merry meetings, particularly weddings and christenings, I compute that Dublin would take off annually about twenty thousand carcasses, and the rest of the kingdom (where probably they will be sold somewhat cheaper) the remaining eighty thousand.

I can think of no one objection that will possibly be raised against this proposal, unless it should be urged that the number of people will be thereby much lessened in the kingdom. This I freely own, and it was indeed one principal design in offering it to the world. I desire the reader will observe, that I calculate my remedy for this one individual kingdom of Ireland and for no other that ever was, is, or I think ever can be upon earth. Therefore let no man talk to me of other expedients:[10] of taxing our absentees at five shillings a pound: of using neither clothes nor household furniture except what is of our own growth and manufacture: of utterly rejecting the materials and instruments that promote foreign luxury: of curing the expensiveness of pride, vanity, idleness, and gaming in our women: of introducing a vein of parsimony, prudence, and temperance: of learning to love our country, in the want of which we differ even from Laplanders and the inhabitants of Topinamboo:[11] of quitting our animosities and factions, nor acting any longer like the Jews, who were murdering one another at the very moment their city was taken: of being a little cautious not to sell our country and conscience for nothing: of teaching landlords to have at least one degree of mercy toward their tenants: lastly, of putting a spirit of honesty, industry, and skill into our shopkeepers; who, if a resolution could now be taken to buy only our native goods, would immediately unite to cheat and exact upon us in the price, the measure, and the goodness, nor could ever yet be brought to make one fair proposal of just dealing, though often and earnestly invited to it.

Therefore I repeat, let no man talk to me of these and the like expedients, till he hath at least some glimpse of hope that there will ever be some hearty and sincere attempt to put them in practice.

But as to myself, having been wearied out for many years with offering vain, idle, visionary thoughts, and at length utterly despairing of success, I fortunately fell upon this proposal, which, as it is wholly new, so it hath something solid and real, of no expense and little trouble, full in our own power, and whereby we can incur no danger in disobliging England. For this kind of commodity will not bear exportation, the flesh being of too tender a consistence to admit a long continuance in salt, although perhaps I could name a country[12] which would be glad to eat up our whole nation without it.

After all, I am not so violently bent upon my own opinion as to reject any offer proposed by wise men, which shall be found equally innocent, cheap, easy, and effectual. But before something of that kind shall be advanced in contradiction to my scheme, and offering a better, I desire the author or authors will be pleased maturely to consider two points. First, as things now

[10]What follows are serious suggestions that Swift had made in earlier pamphlets.

[11]A remote part of the Brazilian jungle.

[12]England.

stand, how they will be able to find food and raiment for an   290
hundred thousand useless mouths and backs. And secondly, there
being a round million of creatures in human figure throughout
this kingdom, whose sole subsistence put into a common stock
would leave them in debt two millions of pounds sterling, adding
those who are beggars by profession to the bulk of farmers,   295
cottagers, and laborers, with their wives and children who are
beggars in effect; I desire those politicians who dislike my overture, and may perhaps be so bold to attempt an answer, that they
will first ask the parents of these mortals whether they would not
at this day think it a great happiness to have been sold for food   300
at a year old in the manner I prescribe, and thereby have avoided
such a perpetual scene of misfortunes as they have since gone
through by the oppression of landlords, the impossibility of paying rent without money or trade, the want of common sustenance,
with neither house nor clothes to cover them from the inclemen-   305
cies of the weather, and the most inevitable prospect of entailing
the like or greater miseries upon their breed forever.

  I profess, in the sincerity of my heart, that I have not the least
personal interest in endeavoring to promote this necessary work,
having no other motive than the public good of my country, by   310
advancing our trade, providing for infants, relieving the poor,
and giving some pleasure to the rich. I have no children by which
I can propose to get a single penny; the youngest being nine years
old, and my wife past childbearing.

B   A Hanging

George Orwell (1903–1950)

  Orwell, whose real name was Eric Blair, was born in Bengal, India, attended
school in England, and then, between the ages of nineteen and twenty-four, served
in the British police force in Burma. He returned to England and became an essayist
and fiction writer. His satire *Animal Farm* (1946) and his novel *1984* (1949) have
become modern classics.
  This essay records an intense personal experience that has universal applications. Notice throughout how Orwell's use of concrete details makes the experience
come alive for the reader. Examine particularly the brilliantly compact paragraph
(lines 72–86) summing up the moral dilemma posed by capital punishment and the
brief, objectively presented scene at the end implying a criticism of human
behavior.

It was in Burma, a sodden morning of the rains. A sickly light, like yellow tinfoil, was slanting over the high walls into the jail yard. We were waiting outside the condemned cells, a row of sheds fronted with double bars, like small animal cages. Each cell measured about ten feet by ten and was quite bare within except for a plank bed and a pot for drinking water. In some of them brown, silent men were squatting at the inner bars, with their blankets draped round them. These were the condemned men, due to be hanged within the next week or two.

One prisoner had been brought out of his cell. He was a Hindu, a puny wisp of a man, with a shaven head and vague liquid eyes. He had a thick, sprouting moustache, absurdly too big for his body, rather like the moustache of a comic man on the films. Six tall Indian warders were guarding him and getting him ready for the gallows. Two of them stood by with rifles and fixed bayonets, while the others handcuffed him, passed a chain through his handcuffs and fixed it to their belts, and lashed his arms tight to his sides. They crowded very close about him, with their hands always on him in a careful, caressing grip, as though all the while feeling him to make sure he was there. It was like men handling a fish which is still alive and may jump back into the water. But he stood quite unresisting, yielding his arms limply to the ropes, as though he hardly noticed what was happening.

Eight o'clock struck and a bugle call, desolately thin in the wet air, floated from the distant barracks. The superintendent of the jail, who was standing apart from the rest of us, moodily prodding the gravel with his stick, raised his head at the sound. He was an army doctor, with a grey toothbrush moustache and a gruff voice. "For God's sake hurry up, Francis," he said irritably. "The man ought to have been dead by this time. Aren't you ready yet?"

Francis, the head jailer, a fat Dravidian in a white drill suit and gold spectacles, waved his black hand. "Yes sir, yes sir," he bubbled. "All iss satisfactorily prepared. The hangman iss waiting. We shall proceed."

"Well, quick march, then. The prisoners can't get their breakfast till this job's over."

We set out for the gallows. Two warders marched on either side of the prisoner, with their rifles at the slope; two others marched close against him, gripping him by arm and shoulder, as though at once pushing and supporting him. The rest of us, magistrates and the like, followed behind. Suddenly, when we had gone ten yards, the procession stopped short without any order or warning. A dreadful thing had happened—a dog, come goodness knows whence, had appeared in the yard. It came

bounding among us with a loud volley of barks and leapt round   45
us wagging its whole body, wild with glee at finding so many
human beings together. It was a large woolly dog, half Airedale,
half pariah. For a moment it pranced round us, and then, before
anyone could stop it, it had made a dash for the prisoner, and
jumping up tried to lick his face. Everybody stood aghast, too   50
taken aback even to grab the dog.

"Who let that bloody brute in here?" said the superintendent
angrily. "Catch it, someone!"

A warder detached from the escort, charged clumsily after the
dog, but it danced and gambolled just out of his reach, taking   55
everything as part of the game. A young Eurasian jailer picked up
a handful of gravel and tried to stone the dog away, but it dodged
the stones and came after us again. Its yaps echoed from the jail
walls. The prisoner, in the grasp of the two wardens, looked on
incuriously, as though this was another formality of the hanging.   60
It was several minutes before someone managed to catch the dog.
Then we put my handkerchief through its collar and moved off
once more, with the dog still straining and whimpering.

It was about forty yards to the gallows. I watched the bare
brown back of the prisoner marching in front of me. He walked   65
clumsily with his bound arms, but quite steadily, with that bob-
bing gait of the Indian who never straightens his knees. At each
step his muscles slid neatly into place, the lock of hair on his scalp
danced up and down, his feet printed themselves on the wet
gravel. And once, in spite of the men who gripped him by each   70
shoulder, he stepped lightly aside to avoid a puddle on the path.

It is curious, but till that moment I had never realized what it
means to destroy a healthy, conscious man. When I saw the prisoner step aside to avoid the puddle I saw the mystery, the un-
speakable wrongness, of cutting a life short when it is in full tide.   75
This man was not dying, he was alive just as we are alive. All the
organs of his body were working—bowels digesting food, skin
renewing itself, nails growing, tissues forming—all toiling away
in solemn foolery. His nails would still be growing when he stood
on the drop, when he was falling through the air with a tenth-of-a-   80
second to live. His eyes saw the yellow gravel and the grey walls,
and his brain still remembered, foresaw, reasoned—even about
puddles. He and we were a party of men walking together, seeing, hearing, feeling, understanding the same world; and in two
minutes, with a sudden snap, one of us would be gone—one mind   85
less, one world less.

The gallows stood in a small yard, separate from the main
grounds of the prison, and overgrown with tall prickly weeds. It

was a brick erection like three sides of a shed, with planking on
top, and above that two beams and a crossbar with the rope   90
dangling. The hangman, a grey-haired convict in the white uniform of the prison, was waiting beside his machine. He greeted
us with a servile crouch as we entered. At a word from Francis
the two warders, gripping the prisoner more closely than ever,
half led, half pushed him to the gallows and helped him clumsily   95
up the ladder. Then the hangman climbed up and fixed the rope
round the prisoner's neck.

We stood waiting, five yards away. The warders had formed in
a rough circle round the gallows. And then, when the noose was
fixed, the prisoner began crying to his god. It was a high, reiter-   100
ated cry of "Ram! Ram! Ram! Ram!" not urgent and fearful like
a prayer or cry for help, but steady, rhythmical, almost like the
tolling of a bell. The dog answered the sound with a whine. The
hangman, still standing on the gallows, produced a small cotton
bag like a flour bag and drew it down over the prisoner's face.   105
But the sound, muffled by the cloth, still persisted, over and over
again: "Ram! Ram! Ram! Ram! Ram!"

The hangman climbed down and stood ready, holding the
lever. Minutes seemed to pass. The steady, muffled crying from
the prisoner went on and on, "Ram! Ram! Ram!" never faltering   110
for an instant. The superintendent, his head on his chest, was
slowly poking the ground with his stick; perhaps he was counting
the cries, allowing the prisoner a fixed number—fifty, perhaps, or
a hundred. Everyone had changed colour. The Indians had gone
grey like bad coffee, and one or two of the bayonets were waver-   115
ing. We looked at the lashed, hooded man on the drop, and
listened to his cries—each cry another second of life; the same
thought was in all our minds: oh, kill him quickly, get it over, stop
that abominable noise!

Suddenly the superintendent made up his mind. Throwing up   120
his head he made a swift motion with his stick. "Chalo!" he
shouted almost fiercely.

There was a clanking noise, and then dead silence. The prisoner had vanished, and the rope was twisting on itself. I let go
of the dog, and it galloped immediately to the back of the gallows;   125
but when it got there it stopped short, barked, and then retreated
into a corner of the yard, where it stood among the weeds, looking timorously out at us. We went round the gallows to inspect
the prisoner's body. He was dangling with his toes pointed
straight downwards, very slowly revolving, as dead as a stone.   130

The superintendent reached out with his stick and poked the
bare brown body; it oscillated slightly. *"He's* all right," said the

superintendent. He backed out from under the gallows, and blew out a deep breath. The moody look had gone out of his face quite suddenly. He glanced at his wrist-watch. "Eight minutes past eight. Well, that's all for this morning, thank God." 135

The warders unfixed bayonets and marched away. The dog, sobered and conscious of having misbehaved itself, slipped after them. We walked out of the gallows yard, past the condemned cells with their waiting prisoners, into the big central yard of the 140 prison. The convicts, under the command of warders armed with lathis, were already receiving their breakfast. They squatted in long rows, each man holding a tin pannikin, while two warders with buckets marched round ladling out rice; it seemed quite a homely, jolly scene, after the hanging. An enormous relief had 145 come upon us now that the job was done. One felt an impulse to sing, to break into a run, to snigger. All at once everyone began chattering gaily.

The Eurasian boy walking beside me nodded towards the way we had come, with a knowing smile: "Do you know, sir, our 150 friend (he meant the dead man) when he heard his appeal had been dismissed, he pissed on the floor of his cell. From fright. Kindly take one of my cigarettes, sir. Do you not admire my new silver case, sir? From the boxwallah, two rupees eight annas. Classy European style." 155

Several people laughed—at what, nobody seemed certain.

Francis was walking by the superintendent, talking garrulously: "Well, sir, all has passed off with the utmost satisfactoriness. It was all finished—flick! like that. It iss not always so—oah, no! I have known cases where the doctor wass obliged to go beneath the 160 gallows and pull the prissoner's legs to ensure decease. Most disagreeable!"

"Wriggling about, eh? That's bad," said the superintendent.

"Ach, sir, it iss worse when they become refractory! One man, I recall, clung to the bars of hiss cage when we went to take him 165 out. You will scarcely credit, sir, that it took six warders to dislodge him, three pulling at each leg. We reasoned with him. 'My dear fellow,' we said, 'think of all the pain and trouble you are causing to us!' But no, he would not listen! Ach, he wass very troublesome!" 170

I found that I was laughing quite loudly. Everyone was laughing. Even the superintendent grinned in a tolerant way. "You'd better all come out and have a drink," he said quite genially. "I've got a bottle of whisky in the car. We could do with it."

We went through the big double gates of the prison into the 175 road. "Pulling at his legs!" exclaimed a Burmese magistrate suddenly, and burst into a loud chuckling. We all began laughing again. At the moment Francis' anecdote seemed extraordinarily funny. We all had a drink together, native and European alike, quite amicably. The dead man was a hundred yards away.   180

C The Patron and the Crocus

Virginia Woolf (1882–1941)

Virginia Woolf helped to shape the style of the novel in the twentieth century. Notably in *Mrs. Dalloway* (1925), *To the Lighthouse* (1927), and *The Waves* (1931), she brought a new sensitivity to the analysis of human psychology. Raised in a family active in the intellectual life of London, she became one of the central figures in the "Bloomsbury group" of writers and artists and called special attention to the struggles of creative people, particularly women, to develop their talents.

In this essay she analyzes the complexities of the relationship between writers and the readers, who, by buying the writers' work, are in effect their patrons. She uses a crocus first as the subject of an imagined literary work and then as a symbol of the work itself. Starting in line 89, she describes the qualities essential for a good patron/reader: an interest in reading a literary work rather than in seeing it performed, familiarity with the literature of other periods and cultures, an open mind on what constitutes obscenity or sacrilege, the ability to recognize which contemporary social influences are constructive and which are not, the ability to distinguish between mere sentimentality and real emotion, a love of language for its own sake, and, most important, the willingness not only to accept but to encourage each writer's individuality. The good patron-reader should be both sympathetic and discriminating because the fate of literature depends on a happy alliance between writer and reader. In the course of describing what a good "patron" should do and be, she gives useful advice on writing.

Young men and women beginning to write are generally given the plausible but utterly impracticable advice to write what they have to write as shortly as possible, as clearly as possible, and without other thought in their minds except to say exactly what is in them. Nobody ever adds on these occasions the one thing   5
needful: "And be sure you choose your patron wisely," though that is the gist of the whole matter. For a book is always written for somebody to read, and, since the patron is not merely the paymaster, but also in a very subtle and insidious way the instigator and inspirer of what is written, it is of the utmost importance   10
that he should be a desirable man.

But who, then, is the desirable man—the patron who will cajole

the best out of the writer's brain and bring to birth the most
varied and vigorous progeny of which he is capable? Different
ages have answered the question differently. The Elizabethans, to   15
speak roughly, chose the aristocracy to write for and the playhouse public. The eighteenth-century patron was a combination
of coffee-house wit and Grub Street bookseller. In the nineteenth
century the great writers wrote for the half-crown magazines and
the leisured classes. And looking back and applauding the splen-   20
did results of these different alliances, it all seems enviably simple,
and plain as a pikestaff compared with our own predicament—for
whom should we write? For the present supply of patrons is of
unexampled and bewildering variety. There is the daily Press, the
weekly Press, the monthly Press; the English public and the   25
American public; the best-seller public and the worst-seller public; the high-brow public and the red-blood public; all now organ-
ised self-conscious entities capable through their various mouth-
pieces of making their needs known and their approval or
displeasure felt. Thus the writer who has been moved by the sight   30
of the first crocus in Kensington Gardens has, before he sets pen
to paper, to choose from a crowd of competitors the particular
patron who suits him best. It is futile to say, "Dismiss them all;
think only of your crocus," because writing is a method of communication; and the crocus is an imperfect crocus until it has been   35
shared. The first man or the last may write for himself alone, but
he is an exception and an unenviable one at that, and the gulls are
welcome to his works if the gulls can read them.

   Granted, then, that every writer has some public or other at the
end of his pen, the high-minded will say that it should be a   40
submissive public, accepting obediently whatever he likes to give
it. Plausible as the theory sounds, great risks are attached to it. For
in that case the writer remains conscious of his public, yet is
superior to it—an uncomfortable and unfortunate combination,
as the works of Samuel Butler, George Meredith, and Henry   45
James[1] may be taken to prove. Each despised the public; each
desired a public; each failed to attain a public; and each wreaked
his failure upon the public by a succession, gradually increasing
in intensity, of angularities, obscurities, and affectations which no
writer whose patron was his equal and friend would have thought   50
it necessary to inflict. Their crocuses in consequence are tortured
plants, beautiful and bright, but with something wry-necked
about them, malformed, shrivelled on the one side, overblown on

[1]Three major novelists in the nineteenth and early twentieth centuries.

the other. A touch of the sun would have done them a world of
good. Shall we then rush to the opposite extreme and accept (if   55
in fancy alone) the flattering proposals which the editors of the
Times and the *Daily News* may be supposed to make us—"Twenty
pounds down for your crocus in precisely fifteen hundred words,
which shall blossom upon every breakfast table from John o'
Groats to the Land's End² before nine o'clock to-morrow morn-   60
ing with the writer's name attached"?

But will one crocus be enough, and must it not be a very
brilliant yellow to shine so far, to cost so much, and to have one's
name attached to it? The Press is undoubtedly a great multiplier
of crocuses. But if we look at some of these plants, we shall find   65
that they are only very distantly related to the original little yellow or purple flower which pokes up through the grass in Kensington Gardens about this time of year. The newspaper crocus
is amazing but still a very different plant. It fills precisely the space
allotted to it. It radiates a golden glow. It is genial, affable, warm- 70
hearted. It is beautifully finished, too, for let nobody think that
the art of "our dramatic critic" of the *Times* or of Mr. Lynd of the
Daily News is an easy one. It is no despicable feat to start a million
brains running at nine o'clock in the morning, to give two million
eyes something bright and brisk and amusing to look at. But the   75
night comes and these flowers fade. So little bits of glass lose their
lustre if you take them out of the sea; great prima donnas howl
like hyenas if you shut them up in telephone boxes; and the most
brilliant of articles when removed from its element is dust and
sand and the husks of straw. Journalism embalmed in a book is   80
unreadable.

The patron we want, then, is one who will help us to preserve
our flowers from decay. But as his qualities change from age to
age, and it needs considerable integrity and conviction not to be
dazzled by the pretensions or bamboozled by the persuasions of   85
the competing crowd, this business of patron-finding is one of the
tests and trials of authorship. To know whom to write for is to
know how to write. Some of the modern patron's qualities are,
however, fairly plain. The writer will require at this moment, it
is obvious, a patron with the book-reading habit rather than the   90
play-going habit. Nowadays, too, he must be instructed in the
literature of other times and races. But there are other qualities
which our special weaknesses and tendencies demand in him.

²The northernmost point in the mainland of Scotland and the southern-
most point in England.

There is the question of indecency, for instance, which plagues us
and puzzles us much more than it did the Elizabethans. The   95
twentieth-century patron must be immune from shock. He must
distinguish infallibly between the little clod of manure which
sticks to the crocus of necessity, and that which is plastered to it
out of bravado. He must be a judge, too, of those social influences
which inevitably play so large a part in modern literature, and   100
able to say which matures and fortifies, which inhibits and makes
sterile. Further, there is emotion for him to pronounce on, and
in no department can he do more useful work than in bracing a
writer against sentimentality on the one hand and a craven fear
of expressing his feeling on the other. It is worse, he will say, and   105
perhaps more common, to be afraid of feeling than to feel too
much. He will add, perhaps, something about language, and
point out how many words Shakespeare used and how much
grammar Shakespeare violated, while we, though we keep our
fingers so demurely to the black notes on the piano, have not   110
appreciably improved upon *Antony and Cleopatra.* And if you can
forget your sex altogether, he will say, so much the better; a
writer has none.

   But all this is by the way—elementary and disputable. The
patron's prime quality is something different, only to be ex-   115
pressed perhaps by the use of that convenient word which cloaks
so much—atmosphere. It is necessary that the patron should shed
and envelop the crocus in an atmosphere which makes it appear
a plant of the very highest importance, so that to misrepresent it
is the one outrage not to be forgiven this side of the grave. He   120
must make us feel that a single crocus, if it be a real crocus, is
enough for him; that he does not want to be lectured, elevated,
instructed, or improved; that he is sorry that he bullied Carlyle
into vociferation, Tennyson into idyllics, and Ruskin into insan-
ity;[3] that he is now ready to efface himself or assert himself as his   125
writers require; that he is bound to them by a more than maternal
tie; that they are twins indeed, one dying if the other dies, one
flourishing if the other flourishes; that the fate of literature depends upon their happy alliance—all of which proves, as we
began by saying, that the choice of a patron is of the highest   130
importance. But how to choose rightly? How to write well?
Those are the questions.

---

[3]Three major nineteenth-century writers who, Woolf thinks, were influenced for the worse by their "patrons," the serious reading public.

D

A Plea for Free Speech in Boston

Frederick Douglass (1817–1895)

Born into slavery in Maryland, Douglass escaped to Massachusetts and became a leader in the antislavery movement. He described his early years in *Narrative of the Life of Frederick Douglass* (1845). In late November of 1860 an antislavery meeting in Boston was broken up by a crowd of prominent Bostonians who opposed the antislavery movement. A few days later, Douglass delivered this speech in the Boston Music Hall.

Notice how he appeals to his audience's local pride by reminding them of Boston's traditional respect for individual freedom. Notice also his use of inductive and deductive reasoning, repetition, short sentences, balanced structures, and questions to emphasize important points.

Boston is a great city—and Music Hall has a fame almost as extensive as that of Boston. Nowhere more than here have the principles of human freedom been expounded. But for the circumstances already mentioned, it would seem almost presumption for me to say anything here about those principles. And yet, 5 even here, in Boston, the moral atmosphere is dark and heavy. The principles of human liberty, even if correctly apprehended, find but limited support in this hour of trial. The world moves slowly, and Boston is much like the world. We thought the principle of free speech was an accomplished fact. Here, if nowhere 10 else, we thought the right of the people to assemble and to express their opinion was secure. Dr. Channing had defended the right, Mr. Garrison had practically asserted the right, and Theodore Parker had maintained it with steadiness and fidelity to the last.* 15
But here we are to-day contending for what we thought was gained years ago. The mortifying and disgraceful fact stares us in the face, that though Faneuil Hall and Bunker Hill Monument stand, freedom of speech is struck down. No lengthy detail of facts is needed. They are already notorious; far more so than will 20 be wished ten years hence.

*Three prominent and widely respected New Englanders who had been active in the antislavery movement.

The world knows that last Monday a meeting assembled to discuss the question: "How Shall Slavery Be Abolished?" The world also knows that the meeting was invaded, insulted, captured, by a mob of gentlemen, and thereafter broken up and dispersed by the order of the mayor, who refused to protect it, though called upon to do so. If this had been a mere outbreak of passion and prejudice among the baser sort, maddened by rum and hounded on by some wily politician to serve some immediate purpose—a mere exceptional affair—it might be allowed to rest with what has already been said. But the leaders of the mob were gentlemen. They were men who pride themselves upon their respect for law and order.

These gentlemen brought their respect for the law with them and proclaimed it loudly while in the very act of breaking the law. Theirs was the law of slavery. The law of free speech and the law for the protection of public meetings they trampled under foot, while they greatly magnified the law of slavery.

The scene was an instructive one. Men seldom see such a blending of the gentleman with the rowdy, as was shown on that occasion. It proved that human nature is very much the same, whether in tarpaulin or broadcloth. Nevertheless, when gentlemen approach us in the character of lawless and abandoned loafers,—assuming for the moment their manners and tempers,—they have themselves to blame if they are estimated below their quality.

No right was deemed by the fathers of the Government more sacred than the right of speech. It was in their eyes, as in the eyes of all thoughtful men, the great moral renovator of society and government. Daniel Webster called it a homebred right, a fireside privilege. Liberty is meaningless where the right to utter one's thoughts and opinions has ceased to exist. That, of all rights, is the dread of tyrants. It is the right which they first of all strike down. They know its power. Thrones, dominions, principalities, and powers, founded in injustice and wrong, are sure to tremble, if men are allowed to reason of righteousness, temperance, and of a judgement to come in their presence. Slavery cannot tolerate free speech. Five years of its exercise would banish the auction block and break every chain in the South. They will have none of it there, for they have the power. But shall it be so here?

Even here in Boston, and among the friends of freedom, we hear two voices: one denouncing the mob that broke up our meeting on Monday as a base and cowardly outrage; and another, deprecating and regretting the holding of such a meeting, by such

men, at such a time. We are told that the meeting was ill-timed,   65
and the parties to it unwise.

Why, what is the matter with us? Are we going to palliate and
excuse a palpable and flagrant outrage on the right of speech, by
implying that only a particular description of persons should exercise that right? Are we, at such a time, when a great principle has   70
been struck down, to quench the moral indignation which the
deed excites, by casting reflections upon those on whose persons
the outrage has been committed? After all the arguments for
liberty to which Boston has listened for more than a quarter of
a century, has she yet to learn that the time to assert a right is the   75
time when the right itself is called in question, and that the men
of all others to assert it are the men to whom the right has been
denied?

It would be no vindication of the right of speech to prove that
certain gentlemen of great distinction, eminent for their learning   80
and ability, are allowed to freely express their opinions on all
subjects—including the subject of slavery. Such a vindication
would need, itself, to be vindicated. It would add insult to injury.
Not even an old-fashioned abolition meeting could vindicate that
right in Boston just now. There can be no right of speech where   85
any man, however lifted up, or however humble, however young,
or however old, is overawed by force, and compelled to suppress
his honest sentiments.

Equally clear is the right to hear. To suppress free speech is a
double wrong. It violates the rights of the hearer as well as those   90
of the speaker. It is just as criminal to rob a man of his right to
speak and hear as it would be to rob him of his money. I have no
doubt that Boston will vindicate this right. But in order to do so,
there must be no concessions to the enemy. When a man is
allowed to speak because he is rich and powerful, it aggravates the   95
crime of denying the right to the poor and humble.

The principle must rest upon its own proper basis. And until
the right is accorded to the humblest as freely as to the most
exalted citizen, the government of Boston is but an empty name,
and its freedom a mockery. A man's right to speak does not   100
depend upon where he was born or upon his color. The simple
quality of manhood is the solid basis of the right—and there let
it rest forever.

E   ## The Second Inaugural Address

Abraham Lincoln (1809–1865)

When Lincoln delivered his second inaugural address in March 1865, the Civil War was still dragging on. Although he had reason to hope that it would end soon, he could not be sure. His address shows this mixture of hope and doubt. Notice the organization: one very long paragraph reviewing the events and emotions of the past four years, and one short paragraph, composed of a single sentence, looking forward. Notice also his use of comparison and contrast, inductive and deductive reasoning, balanced sentence structures, questions, varied sentence length, and repetition to make his points clear and to emphasize them.

At this second appearing to take the oath of the presidential office, there is less occasion for an extended address than at the first. Then, a statement somewhat in detail of the course to be pursued seemed very fitting and proper; now, at the expiration of four years, during which public declarations have constantly   5
been called forth concerning every point and place of the great contest which still absorbs attention and engrosses the energies of the nation, little that is new could be presented. The progress of our arms, upon which all else chiefly depends, is as well known to the public as to myself. It is, I trust, reasonably satisfactory and   10
encouraging to all. With a high hope for the future, no prediction in that regard is ventured. On the occasion corresponding to this four years ago, all thoughts were anxiously directed to an impending civil war. All dreaded it. All sought to avoid it. While the Inaugural Address was being delivered from this place, devoted   15
altogether to saving the Union without war, the insurgent agents were in the city seeking to destroy it without war,—seeking to dissolve the Union, and divide the effects by negotiating. Both parties deprecated war, but one of them would make war rather than let it perish, and war came. One-eighth of the whole popula-   20
tion were colored slaves, not distributed generally over the Union, but located in the southern part. These slaves contributed a peculiar and powerful interest. All knew the interest would somehow cause war. To strengthen, perpetuate, and extend this interest was the object for which the insurgents would rend the   25
Union by war, while the Government claimed no right to do more than restrict the territorial enlargement of it. Neither party expected the magnitude or duration which it has already attained;

neither anticipated that the cause of the conflict might cease even
before the conflict itself should cease. Each looked for an easier   30
triumph and a result less fundamental and astonishing. Both read
the same Bible and pray to the same God. Each invokes His aid
against the other. It may seem strange that any man should dare
to ask a just God's assistance in wringing bread from the sweat
of other men's faces; but let us judge not, that we be not judged.   35
The prayer of both should not be answered; that of neither has
been answered fully, for the Almighty has His own purposes.
"Woe unto the world because of offenses, for it must needs be
that offense come; but woe unto that man by whom the offense
cometh." If we shall suppose American slavery one of those of-   40
fenses which, in the providence of God, must needs come, but
which, having continued through his appointed time, he now
wills to remove, and that he gives to both North and South this
terrible war, as was due to those by whom the offense came, shall
we discern that there is any departure from those divine attributes   45
which believers in the living God always ascribe to Him? Fondly
do we hope, fervently do we pray, that this mighty scourge of war
may speedily pass away; yet if it be God's will that it continue until
the wealth piled by bondsmen by two hundred and fifty years'
unrequited toil shall be sunk, and until every drop of blood drawn   50
with the lash shall be paid by another drawn with the sword, as
was said three thousand years ago, so still it must be said that the
judgments of the Lord are true and righteous altogether.

    With malice towards none, with charity for all, with firmness
in the right, as God gives us to see the right, let us strive on to   55
finish the work we are in, to bind up the nation's wounds, to care
for him who shall have borne the battle, and for his widow and
orphans; to do all which may achieve and cherish a just and a
lasting peace among ourselves and with all nations.

F   Inaugural Address

John F. Kennedy (1917–1963)

A clear, simple writing style is usually the result of much hard work and many
revisions. Study the samples of Kennedy's rough drafts and, in his final version, notice
his use of short sentences and balanced structures to emphasize important points. His
biographer, Theodore Sorensen, tells us that Kennedy first mentioned the inaugural
address soon after his election in November:

He wanted suggestions from everyone. He wanted it short. He wanted it focused on foreign policy. He did not want to sound partisan, pessimistic, or critical of his predecessor. He wanted neither the customary cold war rhetoric about the Communist menace nor any weasel words that Khrushchev might misinterpret. And he wanted it to set a tone for the era about to begin.

He asked me to read all the past Inaugural Addresses. . . . He asked me to study the secret of Lincoln's Gettysburg Address (my conclusion, which his Inaugural applied, was that Lincoln never used a two- or three-syllable word where a one-syllable word would do, and never used two or three words where one would do).

Actual drafting did not get under way until the week before it was due. As had been true of his acceptance speech at Los Angeles, pages, paragraphs, and complete drafts had poured in, solicited . . . and unsolicited. . . .

The final text included several phrases, sentences and themes suggested by these sources. . . . Credit should also go to other Kennedy advisers who reviewed the early drafts and offered suggestions or encouragement.

But however numerous the assistant artisans, the principal architect of the Inaugural Address was John Fitzgerald Kennedy. Many of the most memorable passages can be traced to earlier Kennedy speeches and writings. For example:

Inaugural Address	*Other Addresses*
For man holds in his mortal hands the power to abolish all forms of human poverty and all forms of human life.	. . . man . . . has taken into his mortal hands the power to exterminate the entire species some seven times over. —Acceptance speech at Los Angeles
. . . the torch has been passed to a new generation of Americans. . . .	It is time, in short, for a new generation of Americans. —Acceptance speech and several campaign speeches
And so, my fellow Americans, ask not what your country can do for you; ask what you can do for your country.	We do not campaign stressing what our country is going to do for us as a people. We stress what we can do for the country, all of us. —Televised campaign address from Washington, September 20, 1960

No Kennedy speech ever underwent so many drafts. Each paragraph was reworded, reworked and reduced. The following table illustrates the attention paid to detailed changes:

First Draft	*Next-to-Last Draft*	*Final Text*
We celebrate today not a victory of party but the sacrament of democracy.	We celebrate today not a victory of party but a convention of freedom.	We observe today not a victory of party but a celebration of freedom.
Each of us, whether we hold office or not, shares the responsibility for guiding this most difficult of all societies along the path of self-discipline and self-government.	In your hands, my fellow citizens, more than in mine, will be determined the success or failure of our course.	In your hands, my fellow citizens, more than in mine, will rest the final success or failure of our course.
Nor can two great and powerful nations forever continue on this reckless course, both overburdened by the staggering cost of modern weapons. . . .	. . . neither can two great and powerful nations long endure their present reckless course, both overburdened by the staggering cost of modern weapons . . .	. . . neither can two great and powerful groups of nations take comfort from our present course—both sides overburdened by the cost of modern weapons . . .
And if the fruits of cooperation prove sweeter than the dregs of suspicion, let both sides join ultimately in creating a true world order—neither a Pax Americana, nor a Pax Russiana, nor even a balance of power—but a community of power.	And if a beachhead of cooperation can be made in jungles of suspicion, let both sides join some day in creating, not a new balance of power but a new world of law . . .	And if a beachhead of cooperation can push back the jungle of suspicion, let both sides join in creating a new endeavor, not a new balance of power, but a new world of law . . .

He [Kennedy] wanted it to be the shortest in the twentieth century, he said. "It's more effective that way and I don't want people to think I'm a windbag." He couldn't beat FDR's abbreviated wartime remarks in 1944, I said—and he settled for the [second] shortest (less than nineteen hundred words) since 1905. . . . He reworked it further. "Let's eliminate all the 'I's,'" he said. "Just say what 'we' will do. You'll have to leave it in about the oath and the responsibility, but let's cut it every-where else." The ending, he said, "sounds an awful lot like the ending of the Massachusetts legislature speech, but I guess it's OK." He worked and reworked the "ask not" sentence, with the three campaign speeches containing a similar phrase (Anchorage, Detroit, Washington) spread out on a low glass coffee table beside him.

Later that day—January 17—as we flew back to Washington from Palm Beach, working in his cabin on the *Caroline,* the final phrasing was emerging. A Biblical quotation that was later used in his American University speech was deleted. The opening paragraphs were redictated.

. . .

Arriving back in Washington, the work went on at his house and in our Senate offices. Kenneth Galbraith suggested "cooperative ventures" with our allies in places of "joint ventures," which sounded like a mining partnership. Dean Rusk suggested that the other peoples of the world be challenged to ask "what together we can do for freedom" instead of "what you can do for freedom." Walter Lippmann suggested that references to the Communist bloc be changed from "enemy" to "adversary." The President-elect inserted a phrase he had used in a campaign speech on Latin America—"a new alliance for progress." At the last moment, concerned that his emphasis on foreign affairs would be interpreted as an evasion on civil rights, he added to his commitment on human rights the words "at home and around the world."

On January 19, one day before inauguration, it was finished.

We observe today not a victory of party but a celebration of freedom, symbolizing an end as well as a beginning, signifying renewal as well as change. For I have sworn before you and Almighty God the same solemn oath our forebears prescribed nearly a century and three-quarters ago. 5

The world is very different now. For man holds in his mortal hands the power to abolish all forms of human poverty and all forms of human life. And yet the same revolutionary belief for which our forebears fought is still at issue around the globe, the belief that the rights of man come not from the generosity of the 10 state but from the hand of God.

We dare not forget today that we are the heirs of that first revolution. Let the word go forth from this time and place, to friend and foe alike, that the torch has been passed to a new generation of Americans, born in this century, tempered by war, 15 disciplined by a hard and bitter peace, proud of our ancient heritage, and unwilling to witness or permit the slow undoing of those human rights to which this nation has always been committed, and to which we are committed today at home and around the world. 20

Let every nation know, whether it wishes us well or ill, that we shall pay any price, bear any burden, meet any hardship, support any friend, oppose any foe to assure the survival and the success of liberty.

This much we pledge—and more.   25

To those old allies whose cultural and spiritual origins we share, we pledge the loyalty of faithful friends. United, there is little we cannot do in a host of cooperative ventures. Divided, there is little we can do, for we dare not meet a powerful challenge at odds and split asunder.   30

To those new states whom we welcome to the ranks of the free, we pledge our word that one form of colonial control shall not have passed away merely to be replaced by a far more iron tyranny. We shall not always expect to find them supporting our view. But we shall always hope to find them strongly supporting   35 their own freedom, and to remember that, in the past, those who foolishly sought power by riding the back of the tiger ended up inside.

To those peoples in the huts and villages of half the globe struggling to break the bonds of mass misery, we pledge our best   40 efforts to help them help themselves, for whatever period is required, not because the Communists may be doing it, not because we seek their votes, but because it is right. If a free society cannot help the many who are poor, it cannot save the few who are rich.

To our sister republics south of our border, we offer a special   45 pledge: to convert our good words into good deeds, in a new alliance for progress, to assist free men and free governments in casting off the chains of poverty. But this peaceful revolution of hope cannot become the prey of hostile powers. Let all our neighbors know that we shall join with them to oppose aggression or   50 subversion anywhere in the Americas. And let every other power know that this hemisphere intends to remain the master of its own house.

To that world assembly of sovereign states, the United Nations, our last best hope in an age where the instruments of war have   55 far outpaced the instruments of peace, we renew our pledge of support: to prevent it from becoming merely a forum for invective, to strengthen its shield of the new and the weak, and to enlarge the area in which its writ may run.

Finally, to those nations who would make themselves our ad-   60 versary, we offer not a pledge but a request: that both sides begin anew the quest for peace, before the dark powers of destruction unleashed by science engulf all humanity in planned or accidental self-destruction.

We dare not tempt them with weakness. For only when our   65 arms are sufficient beyond doubt can we be certain beyond doubt that they will never be employed.

But neither can two great and powerful groups of nations take

comfort from our present course—both sides overburdened by
the cost of modern weapons, both rightly alarmed by the steady   70
spread of the deadly atom, yet both racing to alter that uncertain
balance of terror that stays the hand of mankind's final war.

So let us begin anew, remembering on both sides that civility
is not a sign of weakness, and sincerity is always subject to proof.
Let us never negotiate out of fear, but let us never fear to negoti-   75
ate.

Let both sides explore what problems unite us instead of bela-
boring those problems which divide us.

Let both sides, for the first time, formulate serious and precise
proposals for the inspection and control of arms, and bring the   80
absolute power to destroy other nations under the absolute control of all nations.

Let both sides seek to invoke the wonders of science instead of
its terrors. Together let us explore the stars, conquer the deserts,
eradicate disease, tap the ocean depths and encourage the arts and   85
commerce.

Let boths sides unite to heed in all corners of the earth the
command of Isaiah to "undo the heavy burdens . . . [and] let the
oppressed go free."

And if a beachhead of cooperation may push back the jungle   90
of suspicion, let both sides join in creating a new endeavor, not
a new balance of power, but a new world of law, where the strong
are just and the weak secure and the peace preserved.

All this will not be finished in the first one hundred days. Nor
will it be finished in the first one thousand days, nor in the life   95
of this Administration, nor even perhaps in our lifetime on this
planet. But let us begin.

In your hands, my fellow citizens, more than mine, will rest the
final success or failure of our course. Since this country was
founded, each generation of Americans has been summoned to   100
give testimony to its national loyalty. The graves of young Americans who answered the call to service surround the globe.

Now the trumpet summons us again—not as a call to bear arms,
though arms we need; not as a call to battle, though embattled we
are; but a call to bear the burden of a long twilight struggle, year   105
in and year out, "rejoicing in hope, patient in tribulation," a
struggle against the common enemies of man: tyranny, poverty,
disease and war itself.

Can we forge against these enemies a grand and global alliance,
North and South, East and West, that can assure a more fruitful   110
life for all mankind? Will you join in that historic effort?

In the long history of the world, only a few generations have

been granted the role of defending freedom in its hour of maximum danger. I do not shrink from this responsibility; I welcome
it. I do not believe that any of us would exchange places with any   115
other people or any other generation. The energy, the faith, the
devotion which we bring to this endeavor will light our country
and all who serve it, and the glow from that fire can truly light
the world.

And so, my fellow Americans, ask not what your country can   120
do for you; ask what you can do for your country.

My fellow citizens of the world, ask not what America will do
for you, but what together we can do for the freedom of man.

Finally, whether you are citizens of America or citizens of the
world, ask of us here the same high standards of strength and   125
sacrifice which we ask of you. With a good conscience our only
sure reward, with history the final judge of our deeds, let us go
forth to lead the land we love, asking His blessing and His help,
but knowing that here on earth God's work must truly be our
own.

G
The Nobel Peace Prize
Acceptance Speech

Martin Luther King, Jr. (1929–
1968)

In 1964 Dr. King was awarded the Nobel peace prize. At the ceremonies in
Oslo he made the following speech. Notice his use of inductive and deductive
reasoning, exemplification, figurative language, and analogy to make his thoughts
clear. Notice also his use of repetition and balanced sentence structures to emphasize
important points.

Your Majesty, your Royal Highness, Mr. President, excellen-
cies, ladies and gentlemen:

I accept the Nobel prize for peace at a moment when twenty-
two million Negroes of the United States of America are engaged
in a creative battle to end the long night of racial injustice. I accept   5
this award in behalf of a civil rights movement which is moving
with determination and a majestic scorn for risk and danger to
establish a reign of freedom and a rule of justice.

I am mindful that only yesterday in Birmingham, Alabama, our

children, crying out for brotherhood, were answered with fire   10
hoses, snarling dogs, and even death. I am mindful that only
yesterday in Philadelphia, Mississippi, young people seeking to
secure the right to vote were brutalized and murdered.

I am mindful that debilitating and grinding poverty afflicts my
people and chains them to the lowest rung of the economic lad-   15
der.

Therefore, I must ask why this prize is awarded to a movement
which is beleaguered and committed to unrelenting struggle, to
a movement which has not won the very peace and brotherhood
which is the essence of the Nobel prize.   20

After contemplation, I conclude that this award which I received on behalf of that movement is profound recognition that
nonviolence is the answer to the crucial political and moral questions of our time—the need for man to overcome oppression and
violence without resorting to violence and oppression.   25

Civilization and violence are antithetical concepts. Negroes of
the United States, following the people of India, have demonstrated that nonviolence is not sterile passivity, but a powerful
moral force which makes for social transformation. Sooner or
later, all the people of the world will have to discover a way to   30
live together in peace, and thereby transform this pending cosmic
energy into a creative psalm of brotherhood.

If this is to be achieved, man must evolve for all human conflict
a method which rejects revenge, aggression and retaliation. The
foundation of such a method is love.   35

The tortuous road which has led from Montgomery, Alabama,
to Oslo bears witness to this truth. This is a road over which
millions of Negroes are travelling to find a new sense of dignity.
This same road has opened for all Americans a new era of progress and hope. It has led to a new civil rights bill, and it will, I   40
am convinced, be widened and lengthened into a superhighway
of justice as Negro and white men in increasing numbers create
alliances to overcome their common problems.

I accept this award today with an abiding faith in the future of
mankind. I refuse to accept the idea that the "isness" of man's   45
present nature makes him morally incapable of reaching up for
the eternal "oughtness" that forever confronts him.

I refuse to accept the idea that man is mere flotsam and jetsam
in the river of life which surrounds him. I refuse to accept the
view that mankind is so tragically bound to the starless midnight   50
of racism and war that the bright daybreak of peace and brotherhood can never become a reality.

I refuse to accept the cynical notion that nation after nation

must spiral down a militaristic stairway into the hell of thermonu-
clear destruction. I believe that unarmed truth and unconditional
love will have the final word in reality. This is why right temporarily defeated is stronger than evil triumphant.

I believe that even amid today's mortar bursts and whining
bullets, there is still hope for a brighter tomorrow. I believe that
wounded justice, lying prostrate on the blood-flowing streets of
our nations, can be lifted from this dust of shame to reign supreme
among the children of men.

I have the audacity to believe that people everywhere can have
three meals a day for their bodies, education and culture for their
minds, and dignity, equality and freedom for their spirits. I believe that what self-centered men have torn down men other-
centered can build up. I still believe that one day mankind will
bow before the altars of God and be crowned triumphant over
war and bloodshed, and nonviolent redemptive goodwill will
proclaim the rule of the land, "And the lion and the lamb shall
lie down together and every man shall sit under his own vine and
fig tree and none shall be afraid." I still believe that we shall
overcome.

This faith can give us courage to face the uncertainties of the
future. It will give our tired feet new strength as we continue our
forward stride toward the city of freedom. When our days
become dreary low-hovering clouds and our nights become
darker than a thousand midnights, we will know that we are living
in the creative turmoil of a genuine civilization struggling to be
born.

Today I come to Oslo as a trustee, inspired with renewed
dedication to humanity. I accept this prize on behalf of all men
who love peace and brotherhood. I say I come as a trustee, for
in the depths of my heart I am aware that this prize is much more
than an honor to me personally.

Every time I take a flight I am always mindful of the many
people who make a successful journey possible, the known pilots
and the unknown ground crew.

So you honor the dedicated pilots of our struggle, who have sat
at the controls as the freedom movement soared into orbit. You
honor, once again, Chief Albert Lithuli of South Africa, whose
struggles with and for his people are still met with the most brutal
expression of man's inhumanity to man.

You honor the ground crew without whose labor and sacrifices
the jetflights to freedom could never have left the earth. Most of
these people will never make the headlines and their names will
not appear in *Who's Who.* Yet the years have rolled past and when

the blazing light of truth is focused on this marvelous age in which
we live—men and women will know and children will be taught
that we have a finer land, a better people, a more noble civiliza-   100
tion—because these humble children of God were willing to
suffer for righteousness' sake.

I think Alfred Nobel would know what I mean when I say that
I accept this award in the spirit of a curator of some precious
heirloom which he holds in trust for its true owners—all those to   105
whom beauty is truth and truth beauty—and in whose eyes the
beauty of genuine brotherhood and peace is more precious than
diamonds or silver or gold.

Thematic
Table of
Contents

This list gives some of the possibilities for grouping selections to compare and contrast views on particular topics. Throughout the book, cross-references suggest other groupings and specific points for comparison and contrast.

Individuals versus the law or convention

Inner conflicts

What should our educational goals be?

Can humor make a serious point?

Note: Brief humorous touches, such as a little mild self-mockery or a special turn of phrase, lighten many other selections, for example, Thomas's "On Societies as Organisms" (3-C). Be on the lookout for them when you read.

How independent are our opinions?

Reading Across the Curriculum— An Interdisciplinary Table of Contents

The essays in this book are on a wide variety of topics, with material drawn not only from the humanities but also from the laboratory sciences and especially from the social sciences. Moreover, many of the writers are, themselves, active in those fields. Their essays provide examples of the methods for presenting such material to a general audience, whether as part of the main thesis or as support, and can provide a foundation for learning the more specialized methods of presentation required in courses devoted to those fields.

The following lists group the most clear-cut examples according to the disciplines on which they are based:

The laboratory sciences

Engineering and mechanics

The social sciences

The humanities—language and literature

Acknowledgments

Mortimer J. Adler, "Book Owners"—from "How to Mark a Book," first published in *Saturday Review,* July 6, 1940. Reprinted by permission of Saturday Review-World.

Arthur Ashe, "An Open Letter to Black Parents"—copyright © 1977 by The New York Times Company. Reprinted by permission.

Isaac Asimov, "Is Anyone Listening?"—copyright © 1983 by *Fantasy and Science Fiction.*

Bob Bagnall, "The Importance of Not Being Smith"—copyright © 1989 by *The New Scientist.*

Mary Catherine Bateson, "The Aquarium and the Globe"—pp. 13–16 from *With a Daughter's Eye* by Mary Catherine Bateson. Copyright © 1984 Mary Catherine Bateson. By permission of William Morrow & Company.

John Berendt, "The Button"—copyright © 1989 by *Esquire.*

Sue Birchmore, "If in Doubt, Clout It"—copyright © 1989 by *The New Scientist.*

Jane Brody, "Mental Depression"—Copyright © 1977 The New York Times Company. Reprinted by permission.

Anthony Burgess, "Splitting the Word"—from Anthony Burgess, *Language Made Plain,* The English Universities Press. 1964. Copyright by Anthony Burgess.

Linda Claus, "Passing on the Legacy of Nature"—Copyright © 1989 The New York Times Company. Reprinted by permission.

John Cohen "The Language of Uncertainty"—from John Cohen, "Subjective Probability," copyright © 1957 by Scientific American, Inc. All rights reserved.

Aldore Collier, "To Deal and Die in L.A."—copyright © 1989 by *Ebony.*

Pat Conroy, "Death of an Island" and "Yamacraw"—from *The Water Is Wide* by Pat Conroy. Copyright © 1972 by Pat Conroy. Reprinted by permission of Houghton Mifflin Company.

Doug Cumming, "Dottle and the Bottle with a Punt"—Copyright © 1986 by Newsweek, Inc. All rights reserved.

Guy Davenport, "Trees"—Excerpted from: *The Geography of the Imagination,* Forty Essays by Guy Davenport, © 1981 by Guy Davenport. Published by North Point Press. All rights reserved. Reprinted by permission.

Encyclopedia Americana, "Hellbender"—from the *Encyclopedia Americana,* 1969 edition.

Georgie Anne Geyer, "Living on the Altiplano"—from Georgie Anne Geyer, "Peru's Inca Renaissance," in "Reports: Washington, Hong Kong, Peru," *The Atlantic Monthly,* November 1967. Copyright © 1967 by the Atlantic Monthly Company, Boston, Mass. Reprinted with permission.

Brendan Gill, "Misadventures in Verona"—from Brendan Gill, "Misadventures in Verona." Reprinted by permission. Copyright © 1977 The New Yorker Magazine, Inc.

William R. Greer, "In the 'Lite' Decade, Less Has Become More"—Copyright © 1987 by The New York Times Company. Reprinted by permission.

Donald Hall, "Bring Back the Out-Loud Culture" Copyright © 1985 by Newsweek, Inc. All rights reserved.

John E. Hankins, "Clues to Meaning"—from John E. Hankins, "Introduction" to William Shakespeare, *Romeo and Juliet,* edited by John E. Hankins, in "The Pelican Shakespeare," General Editor: Alfred Harbage (rev. ed.: New York: Penguin Books, 1970). Copyright © Penguin Books, Inc., 1960, 1970. Reprinted by permission of Penguin Books.

S. I. Hayakawa, "How Dictionaries Are Made"—from *Language in Thought and Action.* Fourth Edition by S. I. Hayakawa; copyright © 1978 by Harcourt Brace Jovanovich, Inc. Reprinted by permission of the publisher.

Ernest Hemingway, "The Flight of Refugees"—from Ernest Hemingway, *By-Line: Ernest Hemingway,* edited by William White. Copyright 1937, 1938 New York Times and North American Newspaper Alliance Inc.; copyright renewed. Reprinted by permission of Charles Scribner's Sons.

Fred Hiatt, "After Graduation, What Next?"—from Fred Hiatt, "Valediction to Complacency," first published in the *Boston Globe,* 1977. Reprinted by permission of the author.

Iowa City Press-Citizen, "The Hands of Anger, Frustration, Humiliation" (editorial) Copyright © 1985 by the *Iowa City Press-Citizen.*

Molly Ivins, "Why They Mourned for Elvis Presley"—copyright © 1977 by The New York Times Company. Reprinted by permission.

Jesse Jackson, "Challenge"—from Jesse Jackson, "Make a Decision," an address to the Eighth Annual Convention of Operation PUSH, July 12, 1979, Cleveland, Ohio. Reprinted by permission of the author.

Carol Johmann, "Sex and the Split Brain"—OMNI, August 1983. Reprinted by permission.

Jerome Kagan and Alvin P. Sanoff, " 'Your Mother Did It to You' Is an Excuse Americans Overuse"— Copyright © 1985, *U.S. News & World Report.* Reprinted from the issue of March 25, 1985.

E. J. Kahn, Jr. "The South Africans"—Selection is reprinted from *The Separated People, A Look at Contemporary South Africa* by E. J. Kahn, Jr., by permission of W. W. Norton & Company, Inc. Copyright © 1966, 1968, by E. J. Kahn, Jr.

Michiko Kakutani, "Dashers and Dawdlers"—Copyright © 1983 by The New York Times Company. Reprinted by permission.

Tracy Kidder, "The Photovoltaic Cell" from Tracy Kidder, *The Soul of a New Machine.* Copyright © 1981 by Little, Brown, Inc.

Jerry Klein, "Small Town Summer"—Copyright © 1986 by The New York Times Company. Reprinted by permission.

John F. Kennedy, "Inaugural Speech"—as quoted in *Kennedy* by Theodore C. Sorensen. Copyright © 1965 by Theodore C. Sorensen. Reprinted by permission of Harper & Row Publishers, Inc.

Richard M. Ketchum, "The Farmer—An Endangered Species." From *Second Cutting* by Richard M. Ketchum. Copyright © 1981 by Richard M. Ketchum. Reprinted by permission of Viking Penguin, Inc.

Martin Luther King, Jr., "The Decisive Arrest"—from pp. 43–44 in *Stride Toward Freedom* by Martin Luther King, Jr. Copyright © 1958 by Martin Luther King, Jr. Reprinted by permission of Harper & Row, Publishers, Inc. "The Nobel Prize Acceptance Speech." Reprinted by permission of Joan Daves. Copyright © 1964 by the Nobel Foundation.

Sir Edmund Leach, "Literacy Be Damned"—Reprinted by permission from The Times of London, copyright © 1978.

Ruth Limmer, "The Australia-Siberia Solution"—Copyright © 1989 The New York Times Company. Reprinted by permission.

Susanna McBee, "Gobbledygook"—Copyright © 1985, *U.S. News & World Report.* Reprinted from the issue of February 18, 1985.

Colman McCarthy, "The Death Penalty for a Teenage Killer?"—Copyright © with permission of the Chicago Sun-Times Inc., 1987.

M. M. Mahood, "Puns and Other Wordplay in Romeo and Juliet"—from M. M. Mahood, *Shakespeare's Wordplay.* Methuen & Co., Ltd., 1957. Reprinted by permission of the publishers.

James Michaels, "Out, Out Foul Phrases"—reprinted by permission from *Forbes,* copyright © 1986.

H. L. Mencken, *"Le Contrat Social"*—from *Prejudices.* Third Series, by H. L. Mencken. Copyright 1922 by Alfred A. Knopf, Inc. and renewed 1954 by H. L. Mencken. Reprinted by permission of Alfred A. Knopf, Inc.

Ashley Montagu, "Parentage and Parenthood"—from Ashley Montagu, *The American Way of Life,* G. P. Putnam's Sons, Copyright © 1952, 1962, 1967 by Ashley Montagu.

Anne Moody, "The House"—from Anne Moody, *Coming of Age in Mississippi,* The Dial Press, Inc., New York, 1968. Copyright © 1968 by Anne Moody.

Enid Nemy, "Business Status—How Do You Rate?"—copyright © 1980 by The New York Times Company.

The New Yorker, "Three Incidents"—from "The Talk of the Town," reprinted by permission; copyright © 1980. The New Yorker Magazine, Inc.

The New York Times, "Virtuous Sin" (Editorial) copyright © 1977 by The New York Times Company. Reprinted by permission.

George Orwell, "A Hanging"—from *Shooting an Elephant and Other Essays* by George Orwell, copyright © 1945, 1946, 1949, 1950, by Sonia Brownell Orwell. Reprinted by permission of Harcourt Brace Jovanovich, Inc.

Edwin A. Peeples, "Branch Libraries"—copyright © 1989 by *Country Journal.*

Anna Quindlen, "It's Not That I Don't Like Men"—Copyright © 1989 The New York Times Company. Reprinted by permission.

Louise Dickinson Rich, "Baking Beans"—from pp. 53, 113–114 in *We Took to the Woods* by Louise Dickinson Rich (J. B. Lippincott Company). Copyright 1942 by Louise Dickinson Rich. Reprinted by permission of Harper & Row, Publishers, Inc.

Jonathan Richardson, "In Praise of the Archenemy"—reprinted by permission from *Audubon,* the magazine of the National Audubon Society, copyright © 1985.

Richard Rodriguez, "Your Parents Must Be Proud" from Richard Rodriguez, *The Hunger of Memory,* © 1982 by David R. Godine.

Seymour St. John, "The Fifth Freedom"—in *Saturday Review,* October 10, 1955. Reprinted by permission of Saturday Review-World.

Index

Note: an asterisk (*) marks an example with marginal notes; a dagger (†) marks a rhetorical or logical term.